Revolutions in Cuba and Venezuela

Revolutions in Cuba and Venezuela

One Hope, Two Realities

Silvia Pedraza and Carlos A. Romero

UNIVERSITY OF FLORIDA PRESS
Gainesville

Publication of this work made possible by a Sustaining the Humanities through the American Rescue Plan grant from the National Endowment for the Humanities as well as the Publication Subvention Award from the University of Michigan's Office of the Vice President for Research, University of Michigan Office of Research.

Copyright 2023 by Silvia Pedraza and Carlos Antonio Romero
All rights reserved
Published in the United States of America.

29 28 27 26 25   6 5 4 3 2

Library of Congress Cataloging-in-Publication Data
Names: Pedraza, Silvia, author. | Romero, Carlos A., author.
Title: Revolutions in Cuba and Venezuela : one hope, two realities / Silvia Pedraza and Carlos A. Romero.
Description: Gainesville : University of Florida Press, [2022]. | Includes bibliographical references and index. | Summary: "This book compares the sociopolitical processes behind two major revolutions-Cuba in 1959, when Fidel Castro came to power, and Venezuela in 1999, when Hugo Chávez won the presidential election"— Provided by publisher.
Identifiers: LCCN 2022031554 (print) | LCCN 2022031555 (ebook) | ISBN 9781683402718 (cloth) | ISBN 9781683403197 (paperback) | ISBN 9781683403470 (pdf) | ISBN 9781683403616 (epub)
Subjects: LCSH: Cuba—History—Revolution, 1959. | Cuba—Politics and government. | Venezuela—History—1999– | Venezuela—Politics and government—1999– | BISAC: HISTORY / Caribbean & West Indies / Cuba | POLITICAL SCIENCE / World / Caribbean & Latin American
Classification: LCC F1788 .P43 2022 (print) | LCC F1788 (ebook) | DDC 972.9106/4—dc23/eng/20220722
LC record available at https://lccn.loc.gov/2022031554
LC ebook record available at https://lccn.loc.gov/2022031555

University of Florida Press
2046 NE Waldo Road
Suite 2100
Gainesville, FL 32609
http://upress.ufl.edu

To the memory of Silvia's cousin
Agustín Gómez-Lubián Urioste (*El Chiqui*)
(June 25, 1937–May 26, 1957)
who lost his life in Santa Clara, Cuba,
while actively involved in the Cuban Revolution
fighting for democracy

To the memory of Carlos's mentor
Cole Blasier
(March 16, 1925–June 6, 2021)
who was a distinguished political scientist
at the University of Pittsburgh,
specialist in Soviet and Eastern European
as well as Latin American and Caribbean affairs,
and diplomat

Raro don, don excelso, es la justicia. Todo hombre tiene un poco de león, y quiere para si en la vida la parte del león. Se queja de la opresión ajena, pero apenas puede oprimir, oprime. Claro contra el monopolio ajeno, pero apenas puede monopolizar, monopoliza. No en balde, cuando el Libro de los Hebreos quería dar nombre a un varón admirable, lo llamaba "un justo."

A rare gift is justice, gift sublime. Every man has a bit of the lion in him and wants the share of life for himself. He complains of oppression by others, but no sooner is he able to oppress than he oppresses. He cries out against another's monopoly, but as soon as he can monopolize, he monopolizes. No wonder when the Old Testament wanted to name an admirable man, it called him "one who was just."

José Martí, *Obras Completas* (1891)

Dignaos conceder a Venezuela un gobierno eminentemente popular, eminentemente justo, eminentemente moral, que encadene la opresión, la anarquía, y la culpa. Un gobierno que haga reinar la inocencia, la humanidad, y la paz. Un gobierno que haga triunfar . . . la igualdad y la libertad.

Let us give Venezuela a government that is eminently popular, eminently just, and eminently moral, that can rein in oppression, anarchy, and blame. A government that can make innocence, humanity, and peace reign. A government that can make equality and liberty triumph.

Simón Bolívar, *Discurso de Angostura* (1819)

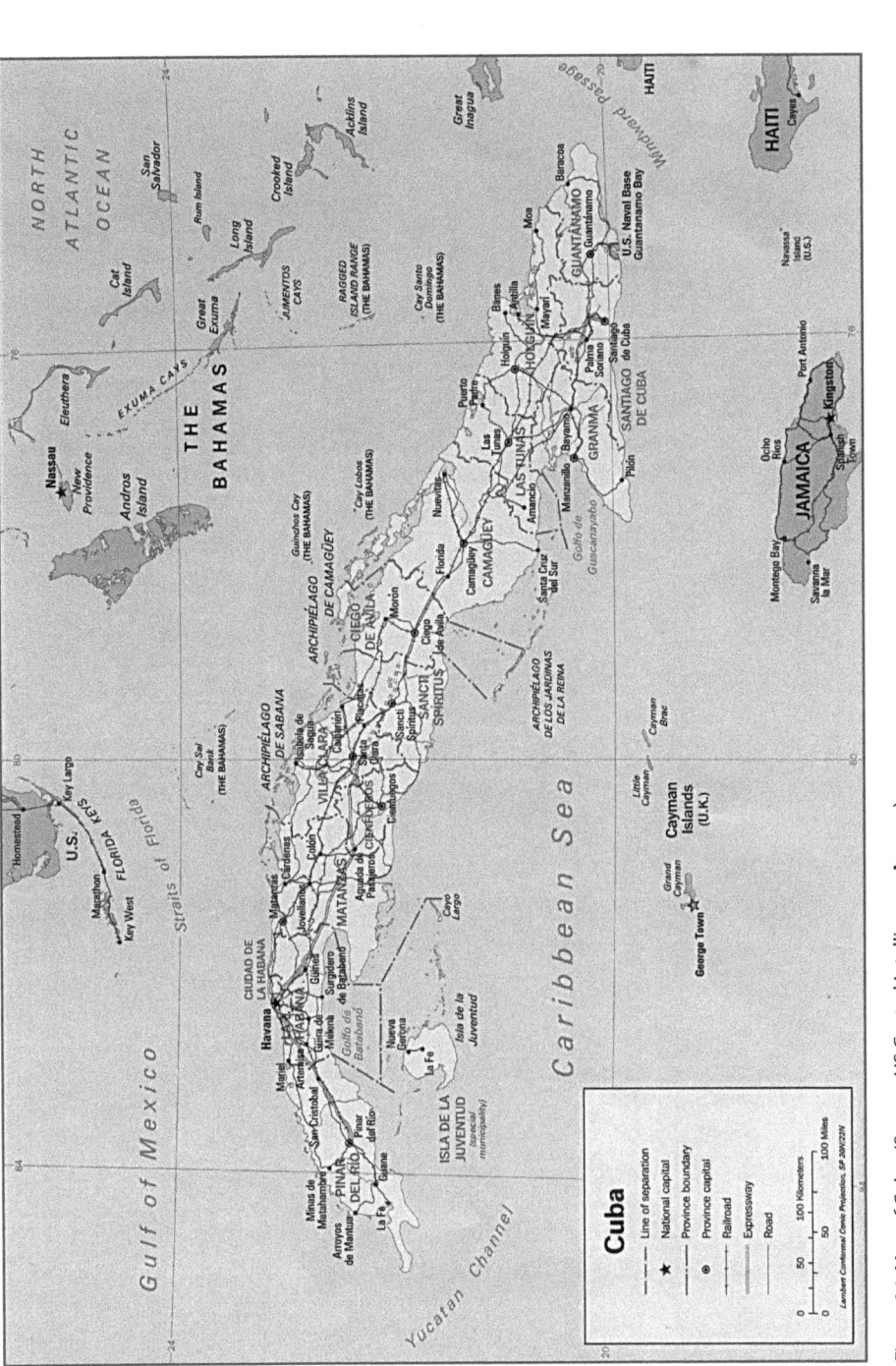

Figure 0.1. Map of Cuba. (Source: US Central Intelligence Agency)

Figure 0.2. Map of Venezuela. (Source: US Central Intelligence Agency)

Contents

List of Figures   xi
Acknowledgments   xiii
List of Abbreviations   xv

PART I. ORIGINS, PROCESSES, AND OUTCOMES OF THE REVOLUTION AND ITS CONSOLIDATION

1. The Study of Revolutions   3
2. The Cuban Revolution: Democracy Betrayed   29
3. The Bolivarian Revolution on Trial   68

PART II. CUBA'S AND VENEZUELA'S INTERNATIONAL RELATIONS

4. Cuba's Foreign Policy: Large Presence, Few Resources   101
5. Venezuela's Foreign Policy: Large Presence, Excessive Resources   128

PART III. CUBA, VENEZUELA, AND THE UNITED STATES: ALLIANCE AND CONFRONTATION

6. The Cuba-Venezuela Alliance   153
7. The Impossible Triangle   184
8. Crisis in Cuba: Revolution and Reform   213
9. Crisis in Venezuela: Revolution and Reform   238
10. One Hope, Two Realities   262

References   297
Index   321

Figures

0.1. Map of Cuba   vii
0.2. Map of Venezuela   viii
1.1. Fidel Castro speaking to the masses, ca. 1961   5
1.2. Raúl Castro and Hugo Chávez as leaders, 2008   7
2.1. Cuba's history and culture collage   30
3.1. World crude oil prices 1946–2020, historical   76
3.2. World crude oil prices 1946–2020, by year   77
3.3. Venezuela's history and culture collage   90
4.1. Cuban refugee family resettled by the International Rescue Committee, ca. 1961   108
4.2. Cuban Americans playing dominoes at a city park in Miami, 2016   114
4.3. Hugo Chávez and Fidel Castro tied together   115
5.1. Venezuelan oil ship arriving to Havana   129
6.1. Cuban doctors taking care of Venezuelan patients   155
7.1. The impossible triangle   198
7.2. Cuban Americans in Miami rally in support of protests in Cuba, July 2021   199
7.3. JetBlue plane, the first to arrive in Santa Clara, Cuba, after the reestablishment of US-Cuba relations, 2016   201
8.1. Cuban *balseros* (rafters) found at sea, 1993   217
9.1. Nicolás Maduro surrounded by the military, 2017   240
9.2. Pro–Juan Guaidó demonstration, 2019   246
10.1. "*Somos Continuidad*" says banner of Cuban leaders of the war of independence as well as the revolution, 2021   267
10.2. Young man waves the Cuban flag, during the July 11, 2021, protests   268

Acknowledgments

We are sincerely grateful to many colleagues and friends for the support they gave during our research. Above all, we thank all the Cubans and Venezuelans who granted us interviews and from whom we learned a great deal.

In addition, we are grateful for all the people who went out of their way to help us procure an interview and to those who gave Silvia a place to stay during her participant observation in Cuba, Miami, and Puerto Rico: Conchita Alvarez-Hirtzel, Liana Blanco-Repilado, Wilfredo Beyra and Zaimar Campins, Annie Betancourt, Raúl Herrero and Beatriz Sánchez-Herrero, José Carlos López-Rosales, José López-Tellez, Lenia Aguila, René Costales, Pedro Ladislao Guerra, Francisco León, Dahily Ricardo-Fernández, and Giraldo Roca-Aquino.

We are particularly grateful to Gloria Anfossi for painstakingly transcribing the interviews. We thank Edras Rodríguez-Torres, librarian at the University of Michigan, for helping us find important sources.

We are also grateful to our editor, Stephanye Hunter, the University of Florida Press, who was relentless in her assistance and always *gentil* (kind).

We regard the visual message that the artwork and photos give to this book as crucial to our intellectual messages. For the beautiful painting that is the cover of our book, we are particularly grateful to the late Aldo Menéndez, who did not get to see the finished product but who had faith in Silvia. All of his life, he struggled with the issues involved in this work. We are grateful to his wife, Ivonne Ferrer, who was responsible for the two collages illustrating Cuban and Venezuelan history and culture. For the photos that also serve to convey the visual message, we are grateful to Getty Images, particularly Angel Simonetti; to Reuters Images, particularly Aaron Dorvinen; to the International Rescue Committee, particularly to Christine Da Cruz; to *Havana Times*, particularly Circles Robinson; and to the *Miami Herald*, particularly Lissette Elquezabal.

A few colleagues went out of their way to offer useful comments, some of which we heeded. All encouraged us to keep going forth. We are particularly grateful for the comments of Carmelo Mesa-Lago (University of Pittsburgh); Javier Corrales (Amherst College); and William H. Sewell Jr. (University of Chicago). Their comments gave us excellent guidance. We also thank Pavel Vidal-Alejandro (Universidad Javeriana de Cali, Colombia); Julieth Stefens Cerón-Ordoñez (Universidad Javeriana de Cali, Colombia); Julie Bunck (University of Louisville); Sergio Angel Baquero (Universidad Sergio Arboleda, Bogotá, Colombia); Mario J. Pentón (*El Nuevo Herald*); Margarita María Rodríguez-Morales (University of Michigan); Julio Cesar Alfonso (*Solidaridad Sin Fronteras*); Tim Gill (University of North Carolina-Wilmington); Carlos de la Torre (University of Florida-Gainesville); Simeon J. Newman (University of Michigan); and Pablo Hernández-Borges (Texas Tech University).

We benefited from presenting our work in several academic venues: in the University of Michigan's Department of Sociology, where faculty colleagues and graduate students participated in the Culture, History, and Politics workshop as well as the Social Movements workshop; in the University of Michigan's American Culture Department, where faculty colleagues and graduate students participated in their workshop; in the Social Science History Association (SSHA) meetings; the Midwest Political Science Association (MPSA) meetings; the Latin American Studies Association (LASA); and the Association for the Study of the Cuban Economy (ASCE) and society, where Carlos and Silvia met.

We are particularly grateful to the University of Michigan's Office of the Vice President for Research, particularly Rebecca Cunningham, and the College of Literature, Science, and the Arts Research Office (LSA), particularly Steve Beach, for granting us their Publication Subvention Award. The award made our incorporating the artwork and many of the photos possible. Without their help, the book would not be the same. They made the visual message we strove for possible.

Abbreviations

ACU	*Agrupación Católica Universitaria*
	University Catholic Group, Cuba
AD	*Acción Democrática*
	Venezuelan Political Party, the Social Democrats
AN	*Asamblea Nacional*
	National Assembly, Venezuela
ANC	*Asamblea Nacional Constituyente*
	National Constituent Assembly, Venezuela
ALBA	*Alianza Bolivariana para los Pueblos de Nuestra América*
	Bolivarian Alliance for Our American Nations
CARICOM	Caribbean Community of States
CELAC	*Comunidad de Estados Latinoamericanos y Caribeños*
CEPAL	*Comisión Económica para América Latina y el Caribe, Naciones Unidas*
ECLAC	Economic Comission for Latin America and the Caribbean, United Nations
CCD	Committee for Cuban Democracy
CDR	*Comités para la Defensa de la Revolución*
	Committees for the Defense of the Revolution
CIA	Central Intelligence Agency
CID	*Cuba Independiente y Democrática*
	Cuba Independent and Democratic
COMECON	Council for Mutual Economic Assistance
COPEI	*Comité de Organización Política Electoral Independiente*
	Venezuelan Political Party, the Christian Democrats
DRE	*Directorio Estudiantil Revolucionario*
	Revolutionary Students' Directorate, Cuba
FEU	*Federación Estudiantil Universitaria*
	University Students' Association, Cuba

FMC	*Federación de Mujeres Cubanas*
	Cuban Women's Association
FRD	*Frente Revolucionario Democrático*
	Democratic Revolutionary Front, Cuban American
FAR	*Fuerzas Armadas Revolutionarias*
	National Revolutionary Armed Forces, Cuba
FANB	*Fuerza Armadas Nacional Bolivariana*
	National Bolivarian Armed Forces, Venezuela
FARC	*Fuerzas Armadas Revolucionarias de Colombia*
	National Revolutionary Armed Forces, Colombia
GAESA	*Grupo de Administración Empresarial, S.A.*
	Group of Business Enterprises controlled by the Military, Cuba
GDP	Gross domestic product
GSP	Global social product, Cuba's measure of GDP
ICC	International Criminal Court
INRA	*Instituto Nacional de Reforma Agraria*
	National Institute for Agrarian Reform, Cuba
IMF	International Monetary Fund
MAR	Mothers Against Repression, Cuban American
MAS	*Movimiento al Socialismo, de Bolivia*
	Movement for Socialism, Bolivian Political Party
MCL	*Movimiento Cristiano Liberación*
	Dissident movement, Christian Movement for Liberation, Cuba
MINTUR	*Ministerio del Turismo*
	Ministry of Tourism, Cuba
MIR	*Movimiento de Izquierda Revolucionaria*
	Movement of the Revolutionary Left, Venezuela
MPLA	*Movimiento Popular por la Liberación de Angola*
	Popular Movement for the Liberation of Angola
MDC	*Movimiento Demócrata Cristiano*
	Christian Democratic Movement, Cuba
MRP	*Movimiento Revolucionario del Pueblo*
	Revolutionary Movement of the People, Cuba
MRR	*Movimiento Revolucionario de Recuperación*
	Revolutionary Movement for Recuperation, Cuban American

MUD	*Mesa de la Unidad Democrática*
	Coalition of the Opposition, Venezuela
	Originally, *La Coordinadora Democrática*; now, *Frente Amplio*
MVR	*Movimiento Quinta República*
	The Fifth Republic Movement, Venezuelan Political Party
OAS	Organization of American States
OEA	*Organización de Estados Americanos*
OECD	Organization for Economic Cooperation and Development
OLAS	*Organización Latinoamericana de Solidaridad*
	Latin American Organization for Solidarity
ONEI	*Oficina Nacional de Estadísticas e Información*
	National Office for Statistics and Information, Cuba
OPEC	Organization of the Petroleum Exporting Countries
ORI	*Organización de Instituciones Revolucionarias Integradas*
	Integrated Revolutionary Organizations, Cuba
PCC	*Partido Comunista de Cuba*
	Cuban Communist Party
PDC	*Partido Demócrata Cristiano*
	Christian Democratic Party, Cuba
PCV	*Partido Comunista de Venezuela*
	Venezuelan Communist Party
PDVSA	*Petróleos de Venezuela, S.A.*
	Venezuela's Oil Corporation
PETROCARIBE	*Acuerdo de Cooperación Energética Petrocaribe*
	Energy Initiative for Cooperation between Venezuela and the Caribbean and Central American Countries
PL	*Partido Liberal*
	Liberal Party, Cuba
PP	*Asambleas del Poder Popular*
	Organs of People's Power, Cuba
PSD	*Partido Social Demócrata*
	Social Democratic Party, Cuba
PSP	*Partido Socialista Popular*
	People's Socialist Party, Cuba

PSUV	*Partido Socialista Unido de Venezuela* Venezuelan United Socialist Party, Venezuelan Political Party
PURS	*Partido Unido de la Revolución Socialista* United Party of the Socialist Revolution, Cuba
SSF	*Solidaridad sin Fronteras* Solidarity without Borders
UJC	*Unión de Jóvenes Comunistas* Young Communists League, Cuba
UMAP	*Unidades Militares de Ayuda a la Producción* Military Units to Aid Production, Cuba
UNDP	United Nations Development Program
UNHCR	United Nations High Commissioner for Refugees
ACNUR	*Alto Comisionado de la Agencia de la Organización de las Naciones Unidas para los Refugiados*
UNITA	*Unión Nacional por la Independencia Total de Angola* National Union for the Total Independence of Angola
UNPACU	*Unión Patriótica de Cuba* Patriotic Union of Cuba, Dissident movement
UNASUR	*Unión de Naciones Suramericanas* Union of South American Nations
UNEAC	*Unión Nacional de Escritores y Artistas de Cuba* Cuban Writers and Artists Union
UNESCO	United Nations Educational, Scientific, and Cultural Organization
USSR	Union of Soviet Socialist Republics, the Soviet Union

I

Origins, Processes, and Outcomes
of the Revolution and Its Consolidation

1

The Study of Revolutions

The Comparative History of Revolutions

While many of Marx's predictions regarding revolution proved inaccurate, as Liebman (1992, 1675) has pointed out, the sociology of revolution "still owes much to Marx's legacy," particularly his focus on actors embedded in concrete institutions and organizations who act within particular historical circumstances. Revolutionary regimes do not just want to break with the past; they also want to impose a new order, including the right to self-determination and independence as a national and global experience. What the classical revolutions of the past (in France, the Soviet Union, and China) as well as the present (in Cuba, Nicaragua, and Iran), had in common was "resistance to a perceived tyranny" (F. Lewis 1984, A72).

Beginning in 1789, France produced the most significant of the eighteenth-century social revolutions. In some ways, the French Revolution resembled the American democratic movement that preceded it. Both the French and the American Revolutions applied the principles of the Enlightenment; both swept away traditional systems; both followed a similar three-stage course, moving from moderate to radical before a final conservative swing; strong nationalism undergirded both; and both helped set in motion modern constitutional government, along with the very notions of freedom, democracy, and social justice. By contrast, the Russian Revolution, the Chinese Revolution, and the Cuban Revolution had their origins in a different ideological paradigm: Marxism-Leninism, which they implemented while producing the demise of the old regime (Chaliand 2008).

Populism has also characterized Latin American politics. In the hemisphere, there have been various revolutionary processes with different forms of development and degrees of radicalization, such as the Mexican Revolution of 1911 and the Bolivian Revolution of 1952. In addition, during the twentieth century, Leftist governments came to power in Mexico, Argentina, Guatemala, Peru, Chile, Bolivia, Nicaragua, Jamaica, Guyana, Suriname, and Grenada. Such were also the historical and recent experiences in Bolivia, Ecuador, and Venezuela. Cuba was considered a unique case (Blasier 1976). In his analysis of populism in Latin America, De la Torre (2019) examines the various recent populist ruptures in the Americas, both Left-wing populism (e.g., Hugo Chávez in Venezuela, Rafael Correa in Ecuador, and Evo Morales in Bolivia) and Right-wing populism (e.g., Donald Trump in the United States, Jair Bolsonaro in Brazil). He focuses on their social construction of "the people" they seek to represent as part of "their mission to redeem their people"—a people who trust and even adore their leader. As De la Torre (2020) stresses, despite their ideological differences, their behavior once they are in power is quite similar, particularly with respect to concentrating power and rendering the opposition ineffective.

Cuba is a Latin American and Caribbean nation, both agrarian and urban. At the time of the revolution, it had a well-developed modern sector and a large middle class. The agricultural sector was intertwined with industry (sugar production, tobacco manufacturing) and also mining (nickel extraction). The industrial sector was developing fast, as was banking, financing, and tourism. At the same time, extreme class inequality existed between that modern sector and the traditional sector of the peasantry surrounding the production of sugar from the cane, its major product and export, as well as—to a lesser extent—tobacco. Thus, at the time of the revolution, modernization had created both beneficiaries and victims, as these deep social cleavages are now conceptualized (see Van Rossem and Roose 2020).

With the success of the Cuban Revolution, Fidel and Raúl Castro and other leaders succeeded in moving Cuba away from the hegemony of the United States and making Cuba part of the Soviet bloc. The government then patterned all social institutions (e.g., the school curriculum, the wage structure) after the Soviet blueprint. Thus, Cuba became a different case: Caribbean and Soviet at once. After the fall of the Berlin Wall and the collapse of the Soviet Union, before Vladimir Putin came to power, Russia's influence in the world declined, and with it the Cuban-Russian partnership. But with Vladimir Putin now in power, Cuba continues to be an ally of post-Soviet Russia, though with much less support from them.

What all the populist and radical movements in the region had in common was their nationalism, expressed in the anti-Americanism of their

Figure 1.1. Fidel Castro-Ruz (1927–2016). Leader of the Cuban Revolution and head of state, Fidel Castro was a formidable orator. Here he is speaking to the masses, ca. 1961 (Photo by Ullstein Bild Dtl. via Getty Images).

foreign policies. Cuba went further than any, as the Castro regime played out its disagreements with the United States within the theater of the Cold War and established a close alliance with the Soviet Union. Others achieved mutual tolerance with Washington, as did Brazil in the new millennium during the presidencies of Luiz Inácio Lula da Silva and Dilma Rousseff. The rest ranged from open conflict to a quiet coexistence with the United States (Domínguez 2013).

The United States responded to Latin American nationalistic aspirations in different ways. With Castro's Cuba, as well as Allende's Chile, there was a head-on political confrontation, while in Mexico and Bolivia both governments sought reconciliation with the United States. In still other cases—Guatemala in 1954, Nicaragua in 1979, Panama in 1989, and Venezuela in 2002, 2014, 2017, and 2019—Washington encouraged internal conspiracies against their radical regimes.

The Comparative Methodology and Research Questions

As Mahoney (2000) points out, comparative historical methods are the right set of tools to explain why specific cases have the outcomes that they do. In this book, we compare and contrast two Latin American revolutions: Cuba under Fidel and Raúl Castro, and Venezuela under Hugo Chávez and Nicolás Maduro. In sociology, the work of Barrington Moore Jr. in *Social Origins of Dictatorship and Democracy* (1966) made the comparative historical method prevalent. From it issued many contemporary analyses of social revolutions, particularly propelled by Skocpol's (1979) comparison of the French, Russian, and Chinese Revolutions. Using a "nonvoluntarist structural perspective," she sought not only to describe those revolutions but also to identify their causes (14). She paid attention to both their "sufficient similarities," which allowed them to be grouped together, rendering the analysis of their common patterns fruitful, and to their differences, which allowed their "particular features" to remain distinctive (42). Although Skocpol's analysis seems to us overly structural, as the focus on state organizations obliterates the actions of particular people and social groups, much can be learned from it, especially her focus on both the sufficient similarities and particular features of the cases compared, as we stress in our analysis of Cuba and Venezuela. We identify closely with the work of Tilly in *From Mobilization to Revolution* (1978) and his focus on collective action (1975): the political conflict generated by organized groups who have access to resources they are able to mobilize, as they contend for power. Even then, governments may successfully repress the will to engage in collective action by making the costs too high to bear.

In part 1 of this book we mainly compare the two revolutions with respect to the origins of their revolutionary processes and consolidation, focusing on what this tells us about the origins and consolidation of their particular revolutions, as well as for what it tells us about revolutions in general. Since the Cuban Revolution is now very old (about sixty-two years) while the Bolivarian Revolution is much younger (about twenty-two years), in this first part we compare them mainly during the first fifteen years or so of their revolutionary processes. We begin by discussing the general conditions that characterize a revolution; then we analyze the causes, process, and outcomes of the Cuban Revolution and the Bolivarian Revolution in turn, taking into account the roles of leadership,

Figure 1.2. Raúl Castro-Ruz (1931–) and Hugo Chávez-Frías (1954–2013), leaders of the Cuban and Venezuelan Revolutions, respectively, and heads of state. Here they are standing in front of the painting of Simón Bolívar, leader of the Venezuelan War of Independence, signifying the historical continuity of their leadership. Caracas, Venezuela, December 13, 2008 (Photo by Harold Escalona via Shutterstock).

ideology and culture, and identities (class, race, religion, and gender). As Tilly and Tarrow (2015, 7) emphasize, we can learn much from looking at these processes through the lens of "contentious politics" when actors make claims on authorities. To do so, they use repertoires they have inherited (and invent new ones), forge alliances with influential political actors, take advantage of existing political regime opportunities, and use both institutional and extrainstitutional routines to advance their claims. Tilly and Tarrow underline that social movements are a historical—and not a universal—category, and they take different forms in various historical settings.

To wit, the speed of social transformation was entirely different in both cases. By 1962, in Cuba, the state had achieved full control of its major social institutions, after the first wave of nationalizations of the American companies, the sugar plantations, the *latifundios*, the large cattle estates, the homes of those who left, and the hospitals and schools in the hands of the Catholic Church. By 1968–69, the state had achieved full control over its people and the economy. The government had crushed the counter-revolution that remained in the Escambray Mountains in Las Villas and implemented the "revolutionary offensive": the nationalization of all the small, private enterprises, such as restaurants, taxis, beauty parlors, dance halls, hotels, shops, and theaters. After this second wave of nationalizations, 70 percent of property passed into the hands of the government—the highest proportion in any socialist country. By contrast, in Venezuela, authoritarianism developed more gradually, and the private sector has never yet disappeared.

In part 2, we discuss the strong alliance that developed between Cuba and Venezuela—economic, political, and military. While both revolutions had a very large presence, influencing other countries, we show that Venezuela had excessive resources, issuing from its oil reserves, while Cuba had few resources, but derived its strength from its alliances—first, with the Soviet Union, and, second, with Venezuela. We underline the implications for both revolutionary processes at present, especially in the distinctive speed of each revolution.

In part 3, we emphasize the various forms the Cuba-Venezuela alliance has taken in recent years, particularly the trade of Cuban doctors and health personnel in exchange for Venezuelan oil, and the positive and negative consequences for both countries. We underscore that a deep revolutionary process over time generates a large diaspora, and that exile community, in turn, may become a political actor. After showing the divisions that exist within the Cuban exile community, we also show how the relationship between Cuba, the United States, and the exile community is an "impossible triangle" that is most unstable, as was the case recently under both Presidents Obama and Trump. We underline that part of the exile community felt betrayed by the United States' rapprochement with Cuba, while another part of the exile community supported the close relations Obama initiated. Trump's strategy of undoing everything Obama accomplished on various fronts (on health care, immigration, Cuba) resulted in a reversal: the United States distanced itself from Cuba. Since Venezuela's revolution is much younger, its exile community is just developing, but it seems to follow in the footsteps of substantial political incorporation of the Cuban

American community. In the concluding chapter, we compare and contrast both revolutions for what it tells us about them, the various possible scenarios for their future, and what we can learn from this comparative exercise more generally.

Throughout this research, we employ several methodologies. First is the historical, comparative method itself. Second is the substantial fieldwork and participant observations in which we engaged in Venezuela, Cuba, and their many immigrant communities in the United States. Third is the analysis of official data from the censuses and surveys of all three countries, as well as international organizations, such as the United Nations and its regional bodies, as well as the UN High Commissioner for Refugees. Fourth is the analysis of survey research on the political attitudes of the immigrants, as well as their voting patterns—important since the state of Florida, where they became concentrated, became a battleground state. Fifth is the in-depth interviews with the Cuban doctors and health personnel in Venezuela. Thus, the work is methodologically rich.

McAdam et al. (2001) and Aminzade et al. (2001) have called for a study of "contentious politics"—revolutions, social movements, and civil wars—not only in terms of their causes and consequences but also as processes, seeking to identify not only the *why* and the *what*, but also the *how*. These are the classic questions of social science research. In this work we address three main questions regarding the origins of the two revolutions, their consolidation and maintenance, and their transformation over time.

Why did the revolution come about? What was its origin? In the first fifteen or so years, how was the Cuban Revolution able to displace the incumbent regime? How did the Bolivarian Revolution achieve state power? What role did populist leadership play in both? What role did the exodus and the international geopolitical setting play?

How did the revolution unfold? How was the Cuban revolutionary state able to gain almost absolute control of the society in the first years of its rule? Why did this not occur in Venezuela? What roles did the geopolitical context and the exodus play?

What were the outcomes of the revolution? What were the historical trajectories that resulted in various social, political, and economic outcomes?

In answering these questions, we also focus on the social dimension of the revolutions, the attention studies of revolution now pay to leadership, ideology, and identities—race, ethnicity, religion, gender, and class.

The Cuban and Bolivarian Revolutions: Similarities and Differences

Two socialist revolutions in Latin America changed the face of this hemisphere and were beacons of hope for many in the Third World (today known as the Global South): Cuba under Fidel and Raúl Castro, and Venezuela under Hugo Chávez and Nicolás Maduro. Several good analyses of both the Cuban and Bolivarian Revolutions exist. For example, on Cuba there is the work of Domínguez (1978a); Domínguez, Pérez-Villanueva, and Barbería (2004); De la Fuente (2001); Guerra (2012); Mesa-Lago (2000); Mesa-Lago and Pérez-López (2013); Pérez Jr. (2015); Pedraza (2007); on Venezuela there is the work of Brewer-Carías (2012), Corrales and Penfold (2015); Corrales and Romero (2013); Romero and Corrales (2010); Cannon (2014; 2010); Fernandes (2010); Smilde and Hellinger (2011); and Levine (2017). However, seldom has either revolution been analyzed in a sustained comparative manner.

A major contribution of our book is that it subjects the two important socialist revolutions in the Western Hemisphere to a systematic comparison. The work of Wickham-Crowley (2018) as well as Foran (2005, 1997) are exceptions, and from them we draw guidance. However, the passage of time has dated their analyses, since they did not incorporate the fall of communism in the Soviet Union and Eastern European countries in the last decade of the twentieth century. In Cuba, this collapse issued a profound economic crisis that Fidel Castro euphemistically called "the special period." Moreover, Foran's excellent comparisons are mostly deductive, while our comparison is both deductive—following Goldstone's (1993) framework—and inductive, building from the social conditions we observed on the ground in three countries and the in-depth interviews with participants.

Some may point out that the Nicaraguan Revolution might be considered a third major revolution; however, the Sandinistas' grip on power has not been constant but intermittent. Thus, we focus on the two revolutions that held on to power for many years (to date, 62 in the Cuban case, 22 in the Venezuelan). We analyze their causes, their processes of consolidation, and their social outcomes, as well as their contemporary crises. This contribution is important, not only because social scientists have long called for comparative analyses of revolutions but also because both the Cuban and Bolivarian Revolutions had deep ties to one another: they relied on each other as faithful allies for their success.

Another contribution of our book lies in our major finding that particularly crucial in both these revolutions are two factors that have not received sufficient attention: first, the influence of the international, geopolitical context; and, second, the crucial role the exodus played in the revolution. Central to Skocpol's (1979) analysis was her emphasis on the importance of international structures. However, she was dealing with large geopolitical powers in competition with other large geopolitical powers, while our comparison is among smaller states in a region dominated by one hegemonic power.

The issue of the geopolitical setting is crucial. It is the stage where each of the revolutions played out, though it differed in its origins and impact. In the 1960s, both the United States and the Soviet Union fundamentally linked geopolitics to the nuclear issue and the so-called balance of terror. This nuclear competition erupted during the Cuban Missile Crisis of October 1962, when a U-2 reconnaissance flight discovered ballistic missiles in Cuba that aimed for the US mainland. For thirteen days, under Soviet leader Nikita Khrushchev and American president John F. Kennedy, the two superpowers nearly arrived at a nuclear confrontation, until Khrushchev agreed at the last minute to remove the atomic arsenal in exchange for the American promise to respect Cuba's territorial sovereignty. Cuba then took advantage of the disagreements between some European governments with the United States regarding the future of the revolution. It also obtained the support of most Asian and African governments who were engaging in the process of decolonization. From then on, a unique and close relationship between Havana and Moscow developed.

By contrast, at the dawn of the twenty-first century, the governments of Chávez and Maduro were able to remain far more independent of both superpowers, in large part thanks to the oil exports that made Venezuela's petrostate a "magical state," as Coronil (1997) has called it. Coronil states that it was during the rule of General Juan Vicente Gómez, widely viewed as a dictatorship since he died in office after ruling for 27 years, that Venezuela truly became an oil nation and a modern nation. To Coronil, the Venezuelan state became "a transcendent and unifying agent of the nation," a "deification of the state" that took place as part of the transformation of Venezuela into an oil nation (4). Then began a democratizing process that was interrupted only by the military dictatorship led by General Marcos Pérez-Jiménez, a member of the ruling Junta in 1948 and president of Venezuala from 1952 to 1958. Thereafter, Coronil emphasizes, a democratic system was consolidated that went on to become one of the longest-lasting in Latin America.

Writing before Hugo Chávez appeared on the national scene, Coronil (1997) nonetheless effectively characterizes the years during which he ruled: "As an oil nation, Venezuela was seen as having two bodies, a political body made up of its citizens and a natural body made up of its rich subsoil. By condensing within itself the multiple powers dispersed throughout the nation's two bodies the state appeared as a single agent endowed with the magical power to remake the nation." Coronil further argues that "the arduous establishment of state authority was achieved in intimate relation with the exploitation of petroleum" (4). So it was during Chávez's years in power, when Venezuela was truly a petrostate. Venezuela shared structural features with other petrostates—not only their financial wealth but also the centrality of the state in their economies (Karl 1997). Coronil underscores the fact that the state became an economic agent with its own base of economic power. Thus, like his predecessors, Chávez was also able to manufacture "dazzling development projects" that engendered "collective fantasies of progress"; the state became like "a magnanimous sorcerer," casting its spell over audience and performers alike—a magical state (5).

Moreover, under Chávez, Venezuela expanded its geopolitical commitments with non-Western countries, particularly China and Russia, key players in the contemporary world. Thus, Venezuela's geopolitical context was far less rigid and confrontational than the one Cuba experienced in the mid-twentieth century. We should add that multilateral organizations and nongovernmental organizations (NGOs) were far less crucial then than they are at present. In addition, the media and other forms of modern communication were far less developed. Today, social media tools have greater weight and at times play a controversial role in the international narrative they spawn, as well as a crucial role in the development of new social movements (e.g., as they did in Tahir Square, downtown Cairo, Egypt). In short, today the game of world power is both more complex and less determined than it was sixty years ago.

The issue of the exodus is also crucial. All major social revolutions spurred sizable exile communities (France, Russia, China). Yet analysts have not regarded the exodus and the exile as central to the process of the revolution, as we do. Here the Cuban case is particularly striking, as over the course of two-thirds of a century fully a quarter of the Cuban population left for other lands, mostly to the United States, but also to Spain, Puerto Rico, and Costa Rica. And the exodus has never ceased. In Venezuela, in the early years of the process the exodus was comparatively small, but a massive exodus has now unfolded and continues to grow rapidly, to the point of a humanitarian crisis. The United Nations' Department of Economic and Social and Affairs, Population Division (2019) global migration data portal gives the official data for both Cuba and Venezuela in mid-year 2019, based on the countries' various censuses over time. At this time, the total population of Cuba was 11.3 million, and the total number of emigrants was 1.7 million—15 percent of the total population. The total population of Venezuela was 28.9 million, and the total number of emigrants was 2.5 million—8.7 percent of the total population. Other data sources give much higher numbers; for example, the UN High Commissioner for Refugees puts the number of Venezuelan emigrants at 5.4 million in 2019. Whatever the actual numbers may be, such a massive exodus means that net migration (immigrants minus emigrants) in the five years prior to 2019 is negative for both countries, as they are experiencing a real population decline and lack of growth. Due to its land proximity to Colombia, Brazil, and Guyana, Venezuela's exodus is more socially diverse than Cuba's originally was. We show the enormous size of the Venezuelan exodus to Colombia, and our research sheds light on the role the exodus played in both social transformations.

We must consider both the Cuban and Venezuelan exodus in the light of the migratory processes that are shaking the world: the large migrant flows that move from the less developed to the more developed world, of people seeking a better economic life, and of people who fear life under their governments and are seeking political asylum. This is particularly evident now along the Mediterranean Sea, at the southern border of the United States, including the Caribbean and the Gulf, as well as at the Colombian-Venezuelan border. If people leave their homelands en masse, originally it is because their countries failed to develop a society that guarantees decent conditions of work, education, health, and freedom. As Amartya Sen (2005) succinctly expresses it, they are driven by "unfreedoms." They emigrate due to the grinding poverty they live with, the deterioration of living conditions; they join the exodus due to the erratic violence they suffer, the systematic violation of human rights; they leave because they cannot see a future that is promising for their family; they flee because they are not free to express their dissenting views; they depart from the erosion of the democratic process. Thus, when people continue to leave the land that raised them and they still love, their exodus testifies to the failure of their nation.

From Amartya Sen's (2005) perspective, development should consist of the removal of various types of unfreedoms that leave people with little choice and opportunity. Thus, freedom is both the means and the end of development. Public policy can expand and enhance people's capabilities "to lead the lives they value—and have reason to value" (18). From this point of view, under their revolutions, Cuba's expansion of public health and education is certainly positive, as is Venezuela's expansion of public participation for the poor. But these should not be used as an excuse to not pay attention to the lack of political and civil freedoms, which Sen sees as central to the process of development itself. As he puts it, "The relevant freedoms include the liberty of acting as citizens who matter and whose voices count, rather than living as well-fed, well-clothed, and well-entertained vassals" (288). During the two major economic crises of 1991–98 and 2017–21 in Cuba, its people could not be said to be well fed, well clothed, or well entertained. Nonetheless, one must acknowledge that while the revolutionary government did expand important forms of freedom—public health and education—it failed to provide its people with economic well-being and consistently silenced the voices of dissent, also forms of freedom.

 A large-scale exodus of the internal opposition did not take place in the Venezuelan case in the early years under Chávez, as it did in the Cuban case, where it was a means to externalize dissent. Recently, under Maduro and the deep-seated economic crisis, a massive exodus of Venezuelans has also taken place. We demonstrate that, particularly when studying revolutions in the developing world, theories of revolution need to take into account the geopolitical and international context as well as the exodus and the development of an exile community that becomes a political actor. We argue that the marriage of the sociology of revolution with the sociology of immigration will issue a greater understanding of what enables revolutions to succeed. The exodus out of Cuba in the early years of the revolution strengthened the revolution as it externalized dissent. Nevertheless, it also undermined the revolution as it robbed it of prized human and social capital that could have helped deliver the island out of poverty. Even more, the United States' invasion of Cuba at the Bay of Pigs garnered enormous international support for Cuba, turning it into a David vs. Goliath story that still endures. A similar process of externalizing dissent is now enfolding with the exodus out of Venezuela. However, this exodus has resulted in a humanitarian crisis that serves as a witness to the excesses of a socialist revolution. Even more, it has robbed Venezuela of international support.

 Our study leads us to highlight the key variables in the success of these revolutions. One was a charismatic, populist leader at the helm of the revolution that articulated the grievances of the masses that the polity had largely ignored. Another was a massive exodus of the opposition that resulted in externalizing dissent, while also creating a large diaspora over time that eventually became a new political actor. Also important was the hegemonic presence of the United States in the hemisphere that aggressively sought to undermine the revolutions through an invasion or a trade embargo—measures that proved counterproductive, as they led to greater internal cohesion in the homeland, where citizens felt under siege.

Studies of political regimes in Latin America and the Caribbean have gone through several stages. In the mid-twentieth century, the optimistic view based on Lipset's (1959) thesis that "economic development equals political development" dominated the academic research agenda. The Cuban Revolution also generated optimism, leading to the important debate regarding modernization and development that dependency theory highlighted—"the development of underdevelopment"—and that both Marxist and liberal intellectuals espoused (Romero 2006). Yet in the 1970s a pessimistic view regarding Latin America politics also rooted: that the deepening of capitalism could only be achieved through authoritarianism. In the 1980s and early 1990s, democratic optimism returned, resting on the critique of a regulatory state and an emphasis on political decentralization and the development of civil society. For that same reason, the Cuban model, showing signs of an autocratic personality in power, was the subject of much criticism. In the 1990s, the pessimistic view reigned again. Stemming from the notion of participatory democracy, that view argued that liberal democracy was impossible in the region (O'Donnell and Schmitter 1986), where even governments ushered in through elections in a transition from authoritarianism were not truly democratic. In such "delegative democracies," as O'Donnell (2004) has called them, a truly representative democracy is absent. Due to its origins in populism, the president becomes the incarnation of the nation, a paternal figure that governs at will, with little accountability to the political parties, judicial institutions, or its citizenry in civil society. As Woldenberg (2020) argues, such democracies need to undergo a second transition to become representative democracies.

The role that populism played in both revolutions is crucial (Müller 2015). At the helm of both were two charismatic leaders with enormous popularity among their own people: Fidel Castro and Hugo Chávez, leaders who had the capacity to attract the masses around their project due to their personalities, ideologies, and policies. In the eyes of some, they were fathers of their nation. Therefore, they were able to deny real democratic representation to their citizens. After their deaths, both were succeeded by new leaders—Raúl Castro and Nicolás Maduro—who lacked the same charismatic draw and leadership abilities.

At the dawn of the twenty-first century, a new wave of leftist governments returned to the region. Their anti-American positions, together with a positive perception of the Cuban Revolution, prompted their domestic and foreign policies (Domínguez 2004). In our view, both the Cuban Revolution and the Bolivarian Revolution belong to the long legacy of revolutionary uprisings in Latin American and the Caribbean. But in comparison to the great revolutions of the Western world (the French, the American, and the Russian), they remain understudied. The study of these issues took a quantum leap as each revolutionary process began to unfold and debates and publications proliferated (e.g., Domínguez 1978a, 2006; Corrales and Penfold 2015; Pérez Jr. 2015; Chilcote 1970).

Similarities

The Cuban and Bolivarian Revolutions share what Skocpol (1979) calls "sufficient similarities." They lead us to some of the classic debates among scholars of revolution. We assess the stages through which revolutions traverse, the roles of the middle classes and other social groups, as well as the Catholic Church and other religious groups. We also assess the roles of international influences and alliances; of a charismatic, populist leader; of ideology and its reinterpretation; of the media and the military; and the structural reorganization of the economy along new principles. Both experiences had in common the attraction of a socialist ideology. We emphasize the important role of ideology, not only as a set of ideas but also as a set of institutions that embedded the ideology. As has been part of the study of the French Revolution, a certain ideology is always necessary to overthrow the *ancien régime*, to create the political conditions for implementing a new revolutionary order, and to promote a new kind of citizen embodying its principles (Sewell Jr. 1985). Such was the function of the socialist ideology that emphasized not only the creation of a new economic order but also the creation of "the new man." While populism of the Right and Left resemble each other in many ways, a major difference lies in that populism of the Right exhibits a strong nostalgia for the past, while populism of the Left is always oriented to the future, as befits the *telos* that underlies Marxism. In both Cuba and Venezuela, the decisive policies of their revolutionary regimes completely polarized their nations. For many, the socialist ideology gave hope that one could create a society with equality, especially of social class and race. For others, those ideas seemed only a smokescreen for a new form of domination.

Our analytical comparison of the Cuban and Bolivarian Revolutions is also justified by the strong alliance that developed between the two, based on their similarities. In the early years, both revolutionary processes established the foundations of the socialist state, went on to propagate their revolutionary ideas abroad, and challenged the regional and international status quo (Carrère d'Encausse 2005). The Cuban Revolution; the leadership of Fidel Castro; and the political, economic, and military alliance between Caracas and Havana all played an important part in the genesis and consolidation of Venezuela's revolution. Venezuela's governing elite did not criticize Cuba's regime, which curtails democracy and human rights and limits the potential of its people to engage in private enterprises. For Venezuela's revolutionary leaders, the Cuban Revolution became a myth to emulate, not only as a model for revolution but also as the basis for their projects and public policies (Romero 2006). Thus, it is hardly surprising that, while visiting Havana in December 1994, long before assuming power, in his speech at the University of Havana, Hugo Chávez made this evident: "In our transformational political project, in the long run, we reach out to experience, to the men and women of Cuba who have spent years thinking about and working on this hemispheric project" (Chávez 2004). In 2005, then-president Chávez noted that "Cuba and Venezuela have joined together. By now, the world must know that our destiny is sealed, that these two nations, in truth only one, will open a new path, whatever it may cost them" (Chávez 2005).

Chávez intended for his revolution to spread to all Latin America. He also underscored that "we are on the path to creating a federation of republics that are Bolivarian, Martian, Caribbean, and South American." And he closed with "We are one sole government" (Chávez 2005). Two years later, he added: "Now we can look even further, Cuba and Venezuela could well configure in the near future a federation of republics" (Chávez 2007b). In their speeches, both leaders emphasized the commitment between Venezuela and Cuba: "Fidel is a father to our people; Cuba is a model for our revolution" (Chávez 2007a; F. Castro 2008). Even after Chávez's loss, when Nicolás Maduro was inaugurated as Venezuela's new president, Maduro also brought Chávez's commitment with Cuba to bear: "We cannot fail to make his dream come true: seeing our two homelands become one united people" (Maduro 2013).

Cuba also derived important benefits from its ties to Venezuela. In the 1990s, Cubans were then experiencing the island's worst political, economic, and social crisis since the Great Depression. The profound economic crisis that Fidel Castro called "the special period" resulted from the demise of the Soviet bloc: the end of the generous Russian subsidy and the loss of its economic lifeline (Domínguez et al. 2004). For Cuba, the new partnership with Venezuela replaced the old partnership with the Soviet Union, making it possible to preserve the revolutionary system after the fall of the Berlin Wall. The Cuba-Venezuela alliance also announced socialism as a positive model for the underdeveloped world, a notion that many people had discarded years before.

Nonetheless, while the similarities are enormous, the differences also loom large. The Cuban Revolution has what Skocpol (1979) calls "particular features": important characteristics that distinguish it from the Bolivarian Revolution. Cuba's revolutionary takeover progressed with great speed due to the general social decomposition that had already taken place under Batista's dictatorship through the armed struggle between the government's military and police versus the Directorio Estudiantil in the Cuban universities, the revolutionary rebels, and the underground resistance. Venezuela's revolution continued to develop within the framework of traditional democratic methods, taking shape through electoral politics. Thus, the revolution was progressing at a slower rate of change, although the question remains open as to whether those democratic methods were replaced step by step by authoritarian ones (McCoy and Myers 2004). Nonetheless, Hugo Chávez's aim was to effect the profound structural changes that we associate with the term revolution (i.e., a complete turn). But it was to be achieved gradually, through the electoral system, where he proved himself remarkably able, as he won several elections. Even so, in 2007 he tried to change the Constitution in a referendum that he lost. In 2008, with the support of the National Assembly, he implemented a constitutional reform that paved the way for him to remain in power indefinitely, demonstrating his true intentions. After Chávez's untimely death, under Nicolás Maduro the Venezuelan government became more authoritarian, and the opposition took to the streets in 2014 and 2017. Occasional violent confrontations occurred between the government and the opposition, with numerous deaths and arrests, while the opposition searched for external political support.

In Cuba, by contrast, immediately after the Cuban dictator Fulgencio Batista left Cuba and Fidel Castro and his followers took power, under the enormous popularity of the revolution, they began to change the major institutions of the state and society. They displaced the old elites with new elites. They vanquished civil society, particularly the electoral system and the independent press. They silenced the Catholic Church as well as all forms of resistance. They squelched the US-supported exile invasion at the Bay of Pigs (Johnson 1964). In less than four years, the Cuban Revolution abandoned its nationalist-populist orientation and declared itself to be, first, socialist, and then Marxist-Leninist (Domínguez 1978a; Pedraza 2007; Pérez Jr. 2015). By contrast, in Venezuela's Bolivarian Revolution the displacement of the elites and the break with the past was less confrontational and proceeded at a slower pace.

Differences

Venezuela deviates from the Cuban model in important ways: there is still some room for electoral democracy; the party's monopoly of domestic policy (the Partido Socialista Unido de Venezuela, or PSUV, formerly called the Movimiento Quinta República), is not total; and the armed forces are not fully under the control of the state. Finally, elections are still ongoing, although the electoral process has many flaws, and the mass participation of citizens has not been achieved, since elections are highly controlled by the state. As of this time, the Venezuelan opposition's main alliance—the Mesa de la Unidad Democrática (MUD) today known as Frente Amplio—massively took to the streets, denouncing the fate of democracy in Venezuela and asking for fair national elections. Moreover, private enterprise is still in place, though part of the private business sector is shrinking. Neither has the middle class left the country in great numbers, though in the wake of the recent economic crisis a significant segment joined the exodus. Nor have diplomatic relations been broken with the Western world (except with the United States, Colombia, Guatemala, Ecuador, and Israel). However, since January 2019, over sixty governments no longer recognize Maduro's government as the legitimate representative of Venezuela. Instead, they recognize the provisional government of Juan Guaidó, the current president of the Venezuelan National Assembly that was inaugurated in 2015 under control of the opposition. Thus, Venezuela lives still under a situation of dual power, a crisis of political legitimacy.

To all of this we must add the historical context in which both revolutions developed. The Cuban Revolution took place squarely within the Cold War, as part of the ongoing confrontation between Washington and Moscow (Domínguez 1978a; Pedraza 2007). The Venezuelan/Bolivarian revolution took place in the context of a growing multipolarity (Romero 2006). Moreover, the Cuban economy declined precipitously from the triumph of the revolution in 1959 onward. Official government data on the average economic growth rates by five-year intervals, using Cuba's measure of GSP (global social product, which excludes the value of nonproductive services), show that the highest rates of economic growth were in 1961–65 (5.2), 1971–77 (7.5), and 1981–85 (7.3). The lowest rates were in 1966–70 (0.4) and 1986–90, plummeting during the special period (-6.7) (in Mesa-Lago 2000, table 3.4). Hernández-Catá (2008) has estimated that the decline was due in part to the American-imposed hemispheric trade embargo, in part due to the massive exodus of the well-educated middle classes, and in part due to the government's mismanagement.

By contrast, the Venezuelan economy has been a mixture of positive results derived from its oil and gold revenues with negative results derived from the government's increasing expenditures due to its reliance on its oil reserves. However, lately, its oil production has fallen, and the external debt has risen, as is often the fate of petrostates (Karl 1997). While Venezuela continues to engage in significant foreign trade and investment, in recent years a profound economic crisis has set in, as the price of oil declined, along with its production, and the State's mismanagement continued.

Revolution Defined and Theories of Revolution

What is a revolution? Skocpol's (1979, 4) definition stresses that "social revolutions are rapid, basic transformations of a society's state and class structures; and they are accompanied and in part carried through by class-based revolts from below." In general, most analysts of revolution agree with the basic definition that a revolution "is a fundamental change in political power or organizational structures that takes place *in a relatively short period of time* when the population rises up in revolt against the current authorities" (Wikipedia 2019, emphasis ours). Interestingly, as Sewell Jr. (1985, 82) points out, the very notion of revolution as we understand it today was one of the products of the French Revolution: "It was the events of 1789 to 1794 that introduced the modern notion of revolution to the world. Revolution came to mean not any sudden change in the affairs of the state, but something much more specific: the overthrow of one government by the people and its replacement by another government. Revolution was henceforth inseparable from the exercise of popular sovereignty."

Goldstone (1982, 2001) argues that theories of revolution have gone through various generations. The third generation pointed to the structural causes of revolutions and to the importance of historicizing sociological explanations (e.g., Paige 1975; Trimberger 1978; Eisenstadt 1977; Skocpol 1979). Skocpol's (1979) structural analysis of the great revolutions has been particularly influential in opening the way for more comparative historical sociology analyses of revolutions. However, as Sewell Jr. (1985) notes, these overly structural analyses obliterate people and the important role that ideology plays in revolutions. Since then, the analysis of revolutions considers both structure and agency, as we do throughout.

While a fourth-generation theory is still in the process of emerging, the critique of the overly structural approach has opened the door for analyses that pay attention to the role of revolutionary leadership, ideology, and identities—ethnic and religious as well as gender and class (e.g., Benford and Snow 2000; Foran 1997; Mahoney and Snyder 1999; Aminzade et al. 2001). In the analysis that follows, we pay attention to the role these played in the origins, processes, and outcomes of both revolutions. Scholars of revolution now see both ideology and culture as shaping revolutionary consciousness and objectives (Goldstone 2001, 2009). In his analysis of the French Revolution, Sewell Jr. (1985, 61) writes that ideology should not be seen just as one more variable but as "anonymous, collective, and as constitutive of the social order." This is a view of ideology that is actually consonant with a structural approach to revolution and that leads us to see ideology not only as a set of ideas a group of people believed in but also as a set of institutions derived therefrom. Thus, in his analysis of the ideology of the French Revolution, Sewell argues that it expressed "a revolutionary ideology that recast the political world in its mold" (68). Sewell expresses it well:

> French revolutionaries of all factions were acutely aware that the whole of social life was infused with ideological significance and were therefore determined to restructure society from top to bottom and across the board. Indeed, I would insist that this totality of revolutionary ambition be included as part of any meaningful definition of "social revolution." (76)

That "totality of revolutionary ambition" is what makes Hugo Chávez's movement also a revolution, though it took place gradually, through elections. Moreover, it is important to realize that events that took place during the revolution also shaped the ideological discourses of the revolution, as was the case with their nationalism. The idea of the nation, *la patrie* (in French), "inspired passionate emotional commitment to the state on the part of its citizens" (Sewell 1985, 82), as it did with Cuban and Bolivarian Revolutionaries. Fidel Castro and Hugo Chávez both insisted they were the very embodiment of *la patria* (in Spanish). In all cases, as Sewell contends, what needs to be demonstrated is "how the ideological dynamic interacted with class struggles, the international system, political alliances, and the exigencies of state building" (74). As we do.

Typologies abound as to the different types of revolutions. Pedraza (2007) distinguishes between political and social revolutions because in its origins the Cuban Revolution was a political revolution that was fought against the tyranny of Fulgencio Batista, to restore the Constitution and the rhythm of elections that his coup d'état had broken. Elected as Cuba's president, Batista served from 1940 to 1944. Wanting to regain the presidency, just a few months before elections took place, he realized he would not win in that fashion. Thus, Batista took over the presidency via a coup. Carlos Prío-Socarrás, of the Partido Auténtico, against whom Batista effected his *golpe* on March 10, 1952, was the first president of Cuba to be born in an independent Cuba and the last to gain the presidency through universal, contested elections among various political parties (Ameringer 2000). He left Cuba immediately for exile, failing to arm the students who expected to engage in the struggle to save the Constitution (Thomas 1971; Martínez-Fernández 2014). Like many Cuban public figures, Prío thought that in exile he would be able to undermine the revolution, only to see his efforts repeatedly frustrated.

In the 1950s, two separate thrusts constituted the opposition to Batista's dictatorship. One was the university students, under the leadership of José Antonio Echeverría, representing the Federación Estudiantil Universitaria (FEU), and the Directorio Revolucionario Estudiantil (DRE); the other was the rebels up in the mountains of the Sierra Maestra, under the leadership of Fidel and Raúl Castro, as well as Ché Guevara. After José Antonio Echeverría lost his life in 1957 in the attack on Batista in the Presidential Palace, the university students lost force to the rebels in the mountains. It was the rebels wearing olive green, hiding there, who became identified with the revolution.

Under the charismatic, populist leadership of Fidel Castro, the political revolution became a social revolution that transformed the society deeply. This distinction is also made in the work of Goodwin (2001). Political revolutions entail the overthrow of a political regime by a popular movement in an extraconstitutional or violent fashion. Social revolutions entail not only mass mobilizations and regime change but also rapid and fundamental social, economic, and cultural change, during or soon after the struggle for state power.

Goldstone (2001) also notes that there are now four major generations of scholars, with different viewpoints and emphasis, who tried to explain revolutions. In the last generation, in which our own work belongs, Tilly (1995, 2001), McAdam, Tarrow, and Tilly (2001), as well as McAdam, McCarthy, and Zald (2008), and others argued that it was more useful to think about social revolutions together with other forms of "contentious politics," especially social movements, with which they overlap, so as to gain insights from the study of both. Most usefully, Tilly (1995) differentiated revolutions from what they are *not*. They are not coups d'état (that do not attempt to transform institutions or the justification for authority). They are not civil wars, a distinction that, to us, is less clear; they are not revolts or rebellions, which can lack a clear aim to be achieved, nor are they abortive revolutions. They are also not peaceful regime transitions through electoral means to democracy (as in Eastern Europe's exit from communism). The great revolutions are certain: the French (1789), the Russian (1917), the Chinese (1949), the Cuban (1959), and the Iranian (1979).

The Cuban Revolution is now over 62 years old—an old revolution. Yvon Grenier (2019) points out that over the course of half a century, too often the Cuban leaders have ascribed thoughts and actions to *la revolución*—an abstract entity. This becomes a way for the government leadership to avoid taking responsibility for their actions and policies, as well as a way for the intellectual leadership to avoid the real analysis of politics: who gets what and why. So Grenier (2019) asked a number of experts the question: When did the Cuban Revolution end? A number of scholars answered it in an essay. Pedraza (2019) argued that here the analysis of Stinchcombe (1999, 50–51) is most helpful, for he conceives "the core of revolution to be uncertainty about who, and what policies, will rule in the near and medium-run future." He emphasizes that "uncertainty about power distribution, then, preserves the condition of rapid changes of relative power—preserves revolution."

Moreover, we think it is possible for a revolution to have more than one ending. There are several major moments in Cuba's history from 1959 on, when the great uncertainty generated by the particular policies of the government (with respect to the relative power of social classes, ethnicities, regions, political parties, legislatures, and military groups) came to an end. Most Cuban specialists would choose either 1960–62 or 1968–76. To some analysts, the revolution first ended in 1960–62, after it swiftly traversed various stages (from Humanism to Marxism-Leninism) and became consolidated when the exile invasion at the Bay of Pigs failed in 1961. Then Fidel Castro stood up triumphantly and owned up to his having been a Marxist-Leninist all of his life, and declared the new government of the revolution to be Marxist-Leninist and communist (Amaro 1981; Pedraza 2007). To other analysts, the revolution ended in 1967–76, after the "revolutionary offensive" confiscated all the small, petit-bourgeois businesses; Ché Guevara died isolated in La Higuera, Bolivia; and the mobilization of all the people in 1970 to cut sugarcane and achieve the ten million tons of sugar ended Fidel Castro's utopian dream. To many Cubans who participated in the initial idealism, the early years felt like a revolutionary effervescence (Pedraza 2007). This period ended just as Stinchcombe specified, with the institutionalization of a new government: the Partido Comunista de Cuba (PCC) in 1975 and the new Constitution of 1976 (Pérez-Stable 2006; Rojas 2012; Martínez-Fernández 2014).

It is also possible to see the period from 2000 to 2014 as the years when the great uncertainty generated by the collapse of Cuba's benefactors—the Soviet Union and the Eastern European communist countries—effectively brought the steep decline and hunger occasioned by *el período especial* (the special period) to an end. This ending resulted from the new alliance that developed with Venezuela under Hugo Chávez from 1999 to date. To Pedraza (2019), this constitutes the third time when the Cuban Revolution came to an end—or, better put, when it survived the social forces that might have caused it to end, building a new government. According to Stinchcombe (1999, 54), "Revolution ends to the degree that governments are built that can slow down rates of change of relative power and decrease uncertainty about who, and what policies, will rule in the near and medium-range future."

In his seminal piece, Stinchcombe went on to establish the various kinds of governments that the uncertainties built into a revolution can give rise to: conservative authoritarianism; independence from colonialism; military defeat and occupation; totalitarianism; *caudillismo*; and political, electoral democracy. His examples were: conservative authoritarianism (Franco in Spain); independence from colonialism (the American Revolution in 1776, and Cuba's independence from Spain); military defeat and occupation governments (Reconstruction in the US South after the American Civil War, and Douglas MacArthur's occupation government in Japan after World War II); totalitarianism (the Nazi, Soviet, and Maoist revolutions, all of which created "special social structures preserving ideological mobilization under regime control," mobilizing assent from below—as was also the case in Cuba, we add); *caudillismo* (common in Latin America, in the former colonies of Spanish America, as with Trujillo's dictatorship in Dominican Republic, Central Africa, and the Sicilian Mafia); and political, electoral democracy.

Przeworski (1986, 64–65) emphasizes that "entrusting one's welfare to the votes of others is the central continuation of the uncertainty of the revolution into a democratic end of revolution." However, for Stinchcombe (1999, 56), electoral democracy was "an unlikely outcome of revolutionary processes alone, without the help of conquest" because electoral democracy requires trust and the creation of the certainty of law, which are hard to generate in a situation of uncertainty.

Moreover, we underscore, in the case of Cuba there are hardly any historical antecedents, since the years of democratic rule were few. This differs greatly from the Venezuelan case, where there were historical antecedents, and democracy was the norm for forty years, since 1958. As Stinchcombe (1999, 71) emphasizes, revolutions "are stopped by building a government" that will render "the distribution of powers more certain than they are during a revolution." To Pedraza (2019), the Cuban government under the years called "the revolution" (1959–today) built and rebuilt itself three times, with the help of an international ally that kept it afloat: first, the Soviet Union, and, most recently, Venezuela. Without these international alliances, the Cuban Revolution could not have survived. Mesa-Lago (2019a) stresses that dependency has always been a major characteristic of the Cuban economy: initially on Spain; then on the United States; then on the Soviet Union; and now on Venezuela. That is the historical record.

At present, the situation in both countries is precarious. In Cuba, the death of its major charismatic father figure, Fidel, was accompanied by the loss of a large part of its economic support from Venezuela in the form of oil and the presence of the Cuban health personnel and military in Venezuela. And the economic reforms initiated under Raúl Castro have not been vigorous enough to provide better economic growth, amid growing social inequalities (Mesa-Lago and Pérez-López 2013). In Venezuela, the loss of its major, charismatic father figure—Chávez—was also accompanied by the decline of a large part of its oil revenues. And the antidemocratic political reforms initiated by Maduro have gone too far and resulted in serious human rights violations.

Goldstone (2001, 148) highlights that the twin pillars of all states can be summed up in two words: effectiveness and justice. States that are perceived as ineffective may still survive if they are seen as just; states that are perceived as unjust may be tolerated if they are perceived as effective; but states that "appear both ineffective and unjust will forfeit the elite and popular support they need to survive"—the dual faults that lead to revolution. In his analysis of the anticommunist revolutions in the Soviet Union and Eastern Europe that took place between 1989 and 1993, Goldstone (1993, 132) argues that we should have been able to predict them and laid out his "conjunctural process-based theory of revolution." His theory focuses not so much on the causes of revolution but on the historical processes and events through which they cumulatively developed from the convergence of three basic conditions:

1) the loss of effectiveness of the state, in its ability to command resources or obedience;
2) the alienation of the elites and the intellectuals from the state; and
3) the mobilization of the population for social protest actions.

Goldstone's theory guides our comparative analysis of the Cuban and Bolivarian Revolutions, past and present. To his three conditions, our own analysis leads us to add three more that seem particularly important in the case of developing countries:

4) the charismatic populist leader that wields an ideology that attracts the masses;
5) the international historical context—the geopolitical theater in which they played out, particularly in its own hemisphere; and
6) the loss of significant sectors of the population through a massive exodus that allowed the revolutionary government to externalize dissent but also entailed the development of a large diaspora community abroad that became a new political actor.

Fidel Castro and Hugo Chávez were both vastly popular leaders at the helm of the revolutions they inspired, leaders who were able to persuade large sectors of the population that their communist, socialist vision was the correct one to usher in a better world—one in which there would be far less inequality and far more justice. In Cuba, under the Castros' leadership, enormous poverty resulted from the mid-twentieth century on, though attenuated by the generous subsidy of the Soviet Union toward the island. In Venezuela, Chávez articulated the vision of a socialism without poverty for the twenty-first century.

The two revolutions played out in vastly different international contexts—the raging Cold War conflict in the Cuban case, and the post–Cold War multipolar world in the Venezuelan case, during the years of Chávez's mandate. Many see the United States' hostility toward Cuba—supporting the exiles' attempts to subvert the revolution as well as intensifying the US embargo that left the island progressively more impoverished and more isolated—as undermining the revolution. However, it is also possible to see it as strengthening the revolution. For anywhere in the world people blame their leaders when they fail to deliver decent economic conditions for them to live and work in. In Cuba, they blame the US embargo instead. Thus, the external hostility expressed in the US trade embargo resulted in greater internal cohesion among Cubans living on the island, and greater loyalty to the Cuban government.

The massive exodus of its citizens originally was also a difference. In Cuba, the organized opposition failed to undo the revolutionary process, so they had no choice but to exit. A massive exodus of its population took place, one that has never ceased. In Venezuela, originally the exodus did not take place to the same extent as in Cuba, as the organized opposition mostly chose to stay and continued to be part of the parliamentary elections. Thus, Venezuela's revolutionary regime initially did not seek to externalize dissent to the same extent as Cuba's. However, after Chávez's death, under Nicolás Maduro, due to his failed economic policies, the Venezuelan economy went into a steep decline, and the exodus of the population also grew tremendously. It has now become a humanitarian crisis. Now it also serves to externalize dissent.

In Cuba, through the exodus, the revolutionary government externalized the dissent of the opposition, serving to make the revolution stronger (see Pedraza-Bailey 1985). That exodus, however, also undermined the revolution, as it robbed it of the talent, education, and social capital the émigrés always took with them.

A couple of examples will serve to make the point. After Cuba defeated the Bay of Pigs invaders, Fidel Castro applauded the exit of the émigrés, derisively calling them *gusanos*. His brother Raúl, then minister of the armed forces, underscored the benefits of externalizing dissent: "It is the normal exodus that takes place when the people take the power in their own hands and liquidate exploitation and the privileged classes. Their departure does not damage the revolution, but fortifies it, as it is a spontaneous purification" (*The New York Times*, July 23, 1961).

Fidel repeatedly expressed the same. When in the middle of the huge, predominantly working-class exodus out of Mariel harbor from April through September 1980, he underlined: "I think that those of them remaining here are people with whom we can work better, much better! . . . So we need not worry if we lose some flab. We are left with the muscle and bone of the people. We are left with the strong parts." At the same time, he assailed the Americans: "In the past, they used to take away our doctors, engineers, teachers, all highly qualified personnel. Now it was their turn to take away our *lumpen*" (F. Castro 1980).

Yet the Cuban government's inability to allow dissent to flourish, to listen to dissenting voices and to incorporate them, also resulted in the significant loss of talented, hard-working people that could have spurred the island's economic and social development. The progressive economic impoverishment of the island over the years is not only the result of the US embargo, as its leaders constantly claim. It is also the result of the government's incapacity to allow people to participate freely—economically and politically. Cuba's economic and social deterioration have been a major cause of the exodus; they have also been its consequence.

Moreover, the massive exodus from Cuba had another important result. Due to the concentration of the exiles in one place (in Miami and throughout south Florida), and the long timespan of the revolution, the exiles were able to become citizens and to exercise power at the ballot box. Thus, they developed a substantial diaspora community that also became a political actor, seeking to influence the course of events (both locally, in Miami and in Florida, and nationally, in Congress). The exodus also externalized their contention, but from abroad they sought to influence the island's domestic activism, developing a transnational activism (Tarrow 2005).

We argue, and show, that particularly when studying revolutions in the developing world, theories of revolution need to take into account the populist leader at the helm and the vision that convinces the masses that together they will build a better world. They also need to take into account the geopolitical international setting within which the revolution takes place, and one of its major products: the massive exodus and the development of an exile community that becomes a political actor.

2

The Cuban Revolution

Democracy Betrayed

Causes of the Cuban Revolution

In the middle of the twentieth century, both Cuba and Venezuela had crossed the threshold of modernity. Neither was a truly underdeveloped nation. In Cuba from 1960 on, and in Venezuela from 2000 on, both countries turned away from capitalism. However, they failed to achieve any other form of economic development, frustrating their citizens' longing for comfort and happiness. In this chapter we analyze the causes and outcomes of the Cuban Revolution in its early years, while paying attention to the costs entailed by Cuba's becoming a socialist society. In the beginning of the process, would it have been possible to take another road?

The Cuban Economic Research Project (1965), organized at the University of Miami, involved numerous economists and social scientists. They bequeathed us an excellent statistical depiction of Cuba's progress and setbacks from the time of Spanish rule until the early years of the revolution, often comparing its outcomes to other Latin American nations. The analysts assembled data from multiple sources: the various Cuban censuses, the Cuban National Bank, the World Health Organization, the statistical yearbooks, as well as data published by Cuba's ministries and professional associations, Cuba's National Economic Council, the Panamerican Union, and the United Nations' regional Economic Commission for Latin America. From these multiple sources, a reliable statistical portrait emerged.

In the 1950s, Havana was one of the most beautiful capitals in the world (Feinberg 2016). At the time when the revolution triumphed, the island

Figure 2.1. Cuba's history and culture, collage by Ivonne Ferrer, Miami, Florida, 2020. Artwork is a map of Cuba overlaid with colorful drawings and photographs of figures and symbols of the country. Among the images are Raúl Castro in uniform, the tocororo (Cuba's national bird), Jose Martí, Carlos Manuel de Céspedes, the *New York Times* front page announcing the blockade, the sugar mill Ingenio Acana, slavery, Uncle Sam, and a man leaving on a raft.

was modern and prosperous. Cuba's population totaled 6.5 million people. According to the census of 1953, racially, it was predominantly White (72.8 percent), with approximately 12.4 percent Black Cubans and 14.5 percent mestizos, and less than 1 percent Asian (mostly Chinese in origin). The White population was not only the result of the Spanish colonization but also of the great waves of migrations from Spain (particularly the Canary Islands, Galicia, Asturias, the Basque Country, Cataluña, and Andalucía) that took place from the end of the nineteenth century until the years of the Great Depression, ceasing around 1940. The Afro-Cuban population was the result of the importation of slaves from West Africa from the 1500s on (particularly the Yoruba, Igbo, and Ashanti peoples). The Asian-origin population was part of the large migration from China in the eighteenth and nineteenth centuries to most Caribbean nations as well as to Panama and Peru in the early twentieth century. As is often the case with racial or ethnic groups everywhere, they settled in different parts of the country. At that time, Cuba had six provinces. The Black and mestizo population was concentrated in Havana (22 percent) and Oriente (47 percent) provinces, with a much smaller proportion in Las Villas (11 percent), while Pinar del Río, Matanzas, and Camaguey were overwhelmingly White (around 94 percent).

The migration from Spain was extremely large, particularly from Galicia—so much so that the term *gallego* became synonymous with Spaniard. At present, the port city of Vigo, in the north of Spain, commemorates this with bronze statues of a *gallego* about to board a vessel, suitcase in hand, leaving his wife and children behind. Cuba's population grew rapidly due to the increase in immigration, from the end of the war of independence, continuing and during the first three decades of the twentieth century. The economic possibilities offered by the new republic, especially with the expansion of the sugar industry, attracted the immigrants, as did the life of the tropics and its radiant culture.

By 1925, Cuba produced 5.2 million tons of sugar a year, about 21 percent of world production thanks to the work of around 170 active sugar mills (Cuban Economic Research Project 1965, table 152). Thereafter, however, sugar production fell. The stagnation of the sugar industry awakened on the island a growing interest in diversification to other products, particularly meat, poultry, fish, and seafood, as well as tobacco and coffee. At the dawn of the revolution, in 1958, the population of Cuba had reached 6.5

million, and the country exported 5.4 million tons of sugar, 3.1 million tons to the United States (table 352).

Cuba considered those born on the island of Spanish parentage to be Cuban citizens. A mostly urban nation then, given the centrality of agriculture in the economy (sugar, tobacco, and coffee), where 42 percent of the economically active population worked, *el campo* was never far away; its customs and music were central to the culture.

Cuba is not a very large country (109,880 km², 42,426 mi²) in comparison to Venezuela (916,445 km², 353,841 mi²). The island had close to one-third the size of Venezuela's population of 28.9 million in a much vaster territory. Yet Cuba was much larger than the rest of the Antilles in the Caribbean, though quite close to the size of several Central American countries (Guatemala, Honduras, and Nicaragua). With 78 percent of the population literate and 22 percent illiterate, its literacy rate compared favorably with other Latin American countries at the time, as only Argentina, Costa Rica, and Chile surpassed it. By contrast, Venezuela in the early 1950s had a literacy rate of only 51 percent.

In addition, Cuba's overall birthrate (28.3 per 1,000 persons) also compared very favorably to other Latin American nations, while Venezuela's birthrate was nearly double (44.7 per 1,000). Likewise, the overall death rate was the lowest in the region (5.8 per 1,000), in comparison to Venezuela's much higher rate (9.4 per 1,000). The infant mortality rate (37.6) was also extremely low, in comparison with Argentina's (61.1), Brazil's (107.5), Chile's (126.8), Mexico's (80.8), and Venezuela's (65.6) (Panamerican Union 1960).

Behind that modernity and prosperity, however, lay another Cuba, another Venezuela. The life of the poor in the cities and in the countryside lacked a great deal. Without decent dwellings, proper nutrition, sanitation, and electricity, they were hardly part of the modern sector of their nation. In Cuba, the survey done by the Agrupación Católica Universitaria (1957) gave evidence of the vast inequality between city and countryside. Thus, most Cubans who lived at the margins of society (peasants, both White and Black, as well as workers on the landed estates) greeted the revolution with enthusiasm, hoping for a real improvement in their lives. A large part of the middle and upper classes also supported the revolution, particularly in its early stages, when it was a political and not yet a social revolution.

The triumph of the Cuban Revolution on January 1, 1959, was one of the most popular political events of the twentieth century. A social movement that most of the Cuban population initially applauded, and for which many risked their lives, it captured the imagination of most citizens. Romantic in its execution, expressing a call for equality and social justice, it had vast international support. Yet the way it unfolded, with its major leader, Fidel Castro, repeatedly denying that it was a communist revolution, gave rise to enormous confusion and opposition within the island as well as a large exodus from it.

The changes—political, social, and economic—that took place in Cuba beginning with the triumph of the revolution in 1959 and throughout the first decade were dramatic, profound, and irreversible: a complete break with the past, with all the traditional elements found in *la Cuba de Ayer* (yesterday's Cuba), for which the early exiles never ceased to long. In an extremely brief time (less than four years, from January 1, 1959, until October 1962), the Cuban Revolution progressed through distinct stages. Yet Fidel Castro repeatedly promised that it was not a communist revolution but an authentically Cuban one—not red, but "green as its palm trees" (F. Castro, 1959a, 1959b). For many Cubans, this was a time of great uncertainty and doubt.

Benford and Snow (2000) argue that the framing of a social movement by its actors is a central dynamic in its development. As in this case, the way the movement is framed needs to have cultural resonance and to issue from an authoritative source for it to be accepted. Castro's insistence that the revolution was not red lasted until 1961, when the failure of the exiles' attempt to restore the democratic republic by a military invasion at the Bay of Pigs in effect consolidated the new revolutionary government. Only then did Castro finally declare that he was a Marxist-Leninist and would remain so until the day he died. Only then did all ambiguity, all doubt regarding its course, cease. This was the moment when rival ideals "were finally swept from the field," as Sewell Jr. (1985, 69) expresses it in his study of the French Revolution. It marked the moment of ideological transformation.

In the history of the revolution, this was the moment of the historic break with the past. This is what Tarrow (2018) refers to as the "synoptic" moment, the significant break where old lines of thought are disrupted, older constellations displaced, and the naming of a new era begins—as Hall (1986) proposes. Tarrow distinguishes these synoptic moments of historical break from the "regrouping" around a different set of premises and themes, the legacy of incremental institutionalization that may follow, triggered by the break but distinct from it, sometimes more long lasting.

As we underlined, two revolutions took place in Cuba. The first was a political revolution that was a response to Fulgencio Batista's military coup in 1952: the revolution that aimed to restore the democratic republic. The second was the social revolution that under Fidel Castro's leadership entailed a radical transformation of society, against the United States and against the middle and upper middle classes, on behalf of *el pueblo*. Carr (1954) has noted that the Russian Revolution also took place in two similar steps in 1917: February and October. Of the first revolution, he judges, the "contribution of Lenin and the Bolsheviks to the overthrow of Tsarism was negligible," as its downfall had "become inevitable; it was waiting only for its successor to appear" (25). So was the overthrow of Batista in Cuba inevitable.

Throughout Latin American history, *caudillos*—political leaders whose mandate to lead is based on their person—rather than political parties have most often spearheaded political change. Two men shaped the history of the Cuban Revolution: Fulgencio Batista, who relied on the support of the army, and Fidel Castro, who relied on the support of the common people. These two men completely polarized the Cuban people. Some fought for or against Batista's government; others fought for or against Fidel's government; still others fought twice—first, against Batista, then against Fidel (Pedraza 2007). In the end, it was the democratic republic that fell, vanquished by both Batista's and Castro's dictatorships.

Process of the Cuban Revolution

The early years of the revolutionary process were marked by five distinct stages, as Amaro (1981) identifies them: democracy, humanism, nationalism, socialism, and Marxism-Leninism. While some of these stages were extremely brief, to the university students who were actively involved in the revolution, such as Nelson Amaro, they were quite distinct. The first stage was that of democracy: the restoration of the republic. Cubans who fought for the revolution at this time—whether in the mountains (the Sierra Maestra, the Escambray) or the cities (Havana, Santa Clara, Santiago)—wanted to restore the rhythm of constitutional elections that Batista's 1952 coup halted. Batista initially rose to power as part of the 1933 Revolt of the Sergeants, which overthrew the provisional government of Carlos Manuel de Céspedes-Quesada. He then appointed himself chief of the armed forces, with the rank of colonel. In 1940, he was elected president of Cuba and served until 1944. In 1952 he ran for president again. When, a few months before the elections, the polls made him realize he would not win, he led a military coup against president Carlos Prío-Socarrás. His coup d'état made him president from 1952 to 1959, but he never had great support or affection among the Cuban people.

At this time, Cuba had a multiparty system: the largest of parties were the Partido de Acción Unitaria (PAU), the Partido Liberal, and two social democratic parties: the Partido del Pueblo Cubano Ortodoxo (los Ortodoxos), and the Partido Revolucionario Cubano Auténtico (los Auténticos). Batista was running as the PAU candidate. During his first presidency, Batista had ruled fairly, engaged in public works, supported organized labor, and promoted the island as a tourist haven. But a national poll conducted in 1952 made clear he would not win office again. Thus, he took power via the illegitimate means of a coup, on March 10. Years later Cubans were to realize that, as José Ignacio Rasco, founder of the Christian Democratic Movement phrased it, "the 10th of March was the father of the 26th of July" (in Pedraza 2007). As De Tocqueville (1955) admonishes, to understand how a new society is born, one needs to visit the grave of the old. With his coup, Batista put an end to the new era of democratic government and to the best aspirations expressed in the Constitution of 1940, the first to be authentically Cuban, in which Cubans took great pride (Mañach 1959). Batista lost the meager backing he had due to his government's corruption and the repression of the police force. Thus, the Cuban people progressively came to perceive him as unjust. They began to refer to him as "the tyrant," as his police force imprisoned, beat, and tortured the opposition, particularly university students in the cities and peasants in the countryside. Sadly, Batista's political takeover destroyed Cuba's economic and social progress. The analysts of the Cuban Economic Research Project (1965, 630) explain it well:

> Cuba's political struggle through most of her republican life had been a struggle *against* something. This negative attitude did not permit Cuba to materialize its best potentialities. In the economic field more harm was done to the country by omission than by any positive actions. Cuba had fought *against* Spain, *against* the United States Intervention, *against* the Platt Amendment, *against* Machado, and

against Batista. It was not until the period 1940–52 that Cuba began to struggle *for* something: a diversified economy, financial institutions, national banking, an improved standard of living, and other socio-economic improvements. This period of political democracy and constitutional continuity was abruptly interrupted by the 1952 coup d'état.

The first stage of the revolution began with the 26th of July Movement that Castro spearheaded, which took its name from the day in 1953 when he and 165 others attacked the Moncada army barracks in Santiago de Cuba. While, militarily, that action was a failure, Fidel Castro emerged victorious, a legendary and romantic public leader (Pedraza 2007). From then on, his enormous charisma led to great popular support. Weber (1978), a founding father of sociology, underscores that charismatic authority is one of the legitimate forms of authority. Initially unknown, the national and international spotlight fell on Castro when Felipe Pazos, head of the National Bank of Cuba, became active in supporting the resistance against Batista's government and arranged for *The New York Times* correspondent Herbert L. Mathews to go to Cuba and meet Castro. Mathews photographed him as a rebel leader in the mountains and presented him as a figure fighting for social justice on behalf of the poor (Mathews 1961). While the 26th of July Movement led the struggle in Oriente, the DRE, the student movement, led it in Havana and other important cities in Cuba. While the opposition mounted, the university students refused to accept Batista's disruption of power and his refusal to call elections as a solution. They roused Cubans to the only option Batista left them: violent, armed struggle.

The Directorio, which was founded to promote the principles of political liberty (democracy), economic independence (nationalism), and social justice (socialism), was responsible for two major revolutionary accomplishments. One was the attack on the Presidential Palace in Havana, in March 1957. The other was the opening up of the second armed struggle front in the Escambray mountains, which Ché Guevara afterward took over, decisively influencing the revolution's outcome (Anderson 2010). The Presidential Palace attack resulted in the death of José Antonio Echeverría, leader of the Directorio and the FEU. His death left a vacuum in the leadership of the Directorio; it also meant the loss of a leader who was fiercely committed to democratic principles and wanted to channel the revolution in a democratic direction. The Directorio and the university students were a constant problem for Batista, as were the public leaders of other groups, such as the Movimiento Demócrata Cristiano (MDC) and the Movimiento Revolucionario del Pueblo (MRP). Many public figures, such as José Ignacio Rasco, Manolo Ray, and Enrique Ros, tried to get Batista to put an end to the situation by holding a fair election. Batista, however, refused to do so, further fueling the revolutionary protest.

A similar situation obtained in Oriente with the death of Frank País, also a committed revolutionary but not a communist (Morán-Arce 1980). Thus, the revolutionary movement fell totally in the hands of Fidel Castro and the 26th of July Movement. Carlos Franqui, a rebel leader who was up in the Sierra Maestra mountains with Fidel and Raúl, identified the different tendencies the movement housed: a Marxist, pro–Soviet Union current; a nationalist revolutionary current; a liberal-reformist current; and a conservative current (Franqui 1983). Franqui was the voice of Radio Rebelde while he was in the mountains fighting together with the other rebel leaders. Later, he was editor of *Revolución*, the revolution's newspaper. To Franqui, Fidel Castro's *caudillismo* and militarism impeded others' efforts to develop civic institutions within the movement and in the labor unions—what we today call "civil society" (in Pedraza 2007, interview). The major thrust thus became the anti-American nationalism and the anti-business and anti–civil society totalitarianism that Fidel and Raúl as well as Ché Guevara espoused. Their commitment was to communism as the solution to all human problems, as the advent of a better world.

The political causes of the Cuban Revolution were, thus, Batista's dictatorship and Castro's charismatic leadership. But the revolution also had social and economic causes. Extreme social inequality drove many Cubans from humble backgrounds to join. As we saw, comparing Cuba in the 1950s to other Latin American countries put it among the top two or three in socioeconomic development, including Venezuela (Mesa-Lago 2000). Thus, inequality was not the sole cause of the revolution, as at that time other Latin American countries experienced greater social inequality. What was distinctive about Cuba was rising modernization in the face of large social inequality. Still, the grievances of the poorest Cubans were seldom heard or heeded.

Moreover, the Constitution of 1940 introduced the notion of social rights and aimed to shape a social welfare state. However, behind the prosperous Cuba of the urban middle classes lay another Cuba: that of the poor in the city slums, docks, ports, and sugar mills; of the immigrants from Spain and

Canary Islands and their children. They lived the rural poverty of *el campo*, the countryside, where they lived in stagnation, misery, and despair. The report of the Agrupación Católica Universitaria (1957), who surveyed the conditions in the rural areas, demonstrated it. The affluence and modernity of the middle class concealed real social tensions and frustrations (Pérez Jr. 2003). Among these were Cuba's economic dependence on the United States, and the vast social inequality, particularly dire for the *campesinos* (peasants), though the sugar workers had developed a well-organized labor movement and achieved impressive gains (Córdoba 1995).

In addition, there was an unacknowledged problem of race. White Cubans socially discriminated against Black Cubans, including the Afro-Cuban middle class, who found refuge in their own social institutions. Even Batista was denied entry to the Havana Yacht and Country Club due to his being mixed-race—and perhaps also his lack of popularity. Social norms subjected women to the double standard then common in Latin America. Among middle-class women, their overall labor force participation was rather low for their level of education, a situation that was to be totally reversed in exile (Prieto 1987). In Cuba in the 1950s they founded the Lyceum, the first institution run by women and for women, as the women at its helm—Rosario Rexach and Himilce Esteve—underscore (in Pedraza 2007, interviews). It enabled many women to develop their leadership abilities and to channel their desire to be of service, not just engaging in charity but reforming society.

As the result of the failed Moncada attack, Fidel Castro and others were imprisoned. A middle-class lawyer, Castro conducted his own defense in 1953 with his first great speech, "History Will Absolve Me" (F. Castro 1973), in which he gave expression to the 26th of July Movement's program of social reform. There Castro promised the Cuban people that "the problems of land, of industrialization, of housing, of unemployment, the problems of education, and of health: these are the six problems we would take immediate steps to resolve, along with the restoration of civil liberties and political democracy." The revolutionary government never made good on his promise of democracy, though it did invest heavily in expanding the educational and public health services, particularly to the rural areas.

The economist Felipe Pazos, head of the National Bank of Cuba, characterized the 26th of July Movement program as typical of all social democratic parties in Latin America (in Domínguez 1986, interview). As Domínguez (1978a) points out, in the *Manifesto* the themes of political corruption and Batista's illegitimacy were far stronger than the theme of nationalism. At this time, the Catholic Church also supported the revolution; for example, the archbishop of Santiago de Cuba, Enrique Pérez-Serantes, interceded with Batista for Castro's life, saving him from death. Other priests joined the rebels. Progressively *el pueblo* came to see Batista as both unjust and ineffective, as his strength became what Mañach (1959, 168) calls "purely physical and rested on bayonets."

Goldstone (2009) highlights that, in the formation of the opposition, elite defection is an important component of a revolution, leading to the overthrow of the old regime when the polarized elites link up with the mobilization of the masses. As Domínguez (1978a, 133) sums it up, "Modernization without modernity, weak political institutions, and an economic depression in a context of political illegitimacy" are the basic ingredients for a classic revolution, as in Cuba. After seven years of tyranny, Batista's departure provoked enormous joy in Cuba. With the advent of the new year on January 1, 1959, Cubans celebrated the triumph of their revolution. They poured out onto the streets, shouting, dancing, and throwing confetti, as if at a carnival. Most of the Cuban people hoped for the return of democracy to Cuba. This first stage lasted into the beginning of 1959.

Fidel Castro defined the second stage as humanism in his visit to the United States on April 22, 1959: "Neither bread without liberty, nor liberty without bread. No dictatorships of man, nor dictatorship of castes, or class oligarchy. Liberty with bread, without terror. That is humanism" (F. Castro 1959c). He also gave assurance that elections would soon be held. Soon after, in Cuba, a crisis began to unfold, as those who had collaborated with Batista, called the *esbirros* (criminals), went before military tribunals, and executions began to take place. Fear took hold. Some who had fought for the revolution in the mountains then joined the opposition. To Rafael Peláez (pseudonym), the executions were like Roman circuses (in Pedraza 2007, interview). In his analysis of the process by which revolutions take place, Goldstone (2009) notes that after the initial overthrow of the regime, further polarization ensues, due to radical regime change and "terror," a cycle that often repeats.

At the same time, the government began a series of social reforms (the rent control law, agrarian reform, tax reform) that incorporated socially marginal groups, such as the peasants. At this time, most Cubans felt genuinely confused regarding the turn the revolution was taking. Yet Castro continued to deny that it was a communist turn (F. Castro 1959a). Explaining the need for the Agrarian Reform Law, he stressed that "this revolution is not red, this revolution is olive green"—green as the palm trees of Cuba (F. Castro 1959b). Cubans hoped this was true.

This second stage of the revolution ended when Huber Matos, one of the *comandantes*, wrote a letter to Fidel Castro in October 1959 denouncing the communist turn the revolution was taking. Imagining Castro was unaware of it, Matos resigned his high position in the Rebel Army. The letter led to his imprisonment for 20 years (Matos 2002). Many who had risked their lives fighting against Batista also changed their political stance when they saw the executions taking place by *el paredón* (execution wall). To them, the revolution they had fought for was betrayed. Members of the First Provisional Government who wanted to restore political democracy also resigned. "The rule of the moderates," as Brinton (1965) calls it, had ended. Amid this crisis, José Ignacio Rasco, Fidel Castro's classmate in Belén Jesuit High School in Havana, founded the Movimiento Demócrata Cristiano as a middle way between capitalism and communism (Rasco 2012; in Pedraza 2007, interview). The Catholic Church began to oppose the revolution and became a site of the opposition. As Eduardo Boza-Masvidal, the auxiliary bishop of the Archdiocese of Havana, expressed it in one of his pastoral letters, the church opposed not the just ends of the reforms—less social inequality—but the unjust means to achieve it: doing away with private property and sullying the good name of many.

The third stage was nationalism, which emphasized the problem of "Yankee imperialism" and lasted until the government completed the nationalization of all the big industries—both Cuban and American—that took place from July to October 1960, deepening the revolution. In 1960, the revolution took its definitive course; the diplomatic and economic war between the United States and Cuba ensued; and the Soviet Union became Cuba's protector and benefactor. At the height of the Cold War, Cuba fell within the Soviet orbit. This opened the door for an endless academic debate on political dependence. The relationship lasted 30 years, until Soviet and Eastern European communism collapsed. Sewell Jr. (1985) emphasizes that one of the products of the revolutionary ideology of the French Revolution was the very ideological discourse. Nationalism—the passionate, emotional attachment to the nation—was one of its products. The French Revolution defined the nation not in terms of the social contract but in terms of land and blood, a definition that holds true for much of Western Europe until today. In Cuba, nationalism was the result of its long struggle for independence from Spain. Now it added other dimensions: the fight against American imperialism, and "the nation under siege." These became major themes, underscored by the Bay of Pigs invasion and the US trade embargo. Today they are the major, and perhaps the only, source of legitimacy.

In 1960, what Havel (1978) has called the independent voice of civil society collapsed. The government took over all the the newspapers and television channels; labor unions retained their names but the government replaced their leaders with committed communists; and the government silenced the Catholic Church. Through his oratory, Fidel Castro was always capable of reaching the hearts and the minds of the people. Crowds listened to him for hours on end, often chanting in delirium "¡Fidel, Fidel, Fidel, Fidel!" On May Day, Castro (1960) gave a major speech in the Plaza of the Revolution in Havana, in which he attacked the democracy of the past, concluding that elections were unnecessary because the people had already chosen:

> *This* is democracy. . . . The Cuban revolution is democracy. . . . This democracy has been expressed directly in the close union and identification of the government and the people, in this direct relationship, in this working and fighting in favor of the majority of the country and in the interests of the majority of the country. . . . Our enemies, our detractors ask about elections. . . . The presence of such a large crowd is the best proof that the revolution has fought for the people.

To Jorge Valls, student leader of the Directorio Estudiantil, the legal order—the notion of political rights as the normative underpinning of society—collapsed with this speech (in Pedraza 2007, interview). That crisis began with Batista's coup in 1952 and reached its climax with Castro in 1960. Importantly, the political culture shifted to being the culture of *la plaza* (the square), the culture of the speech, of direct participation between the leader and the masses, the leader and the led.

In addition, the nationalizations that took place broke the economic backs of the wealthy. Young Cubans from the upper and middle classes, who perceived Castro as a demagogue, increasingly moved into the ranks of the opposition and the underground resistance, *conspirando*, helping the counterrevolution, in movements such as the MRP or the MDC, as well as the Movimiento Revolucionario de Recuperación (MRR). Lacking resources of their own, they accepted help from the US Central Intelligence Agency (CIA), which many later came to regret.

Since the upper classes had deliberately excluded them from their midst, most Black Cubans were enthusiastic about the revolution that opened the pinnacles of society to them. Fagen et al. (1968, 120) note that the race problem was "a boon to Castro." The revolutionary government did away with the old, blatant forms of discrimination on the island—segregated beaches, country clubs, schools, social clubs—thus winning the immediate support of most Afro-Cubans. The revolution also challenged gender inequality by bringing women into the workplace (Casal 1987) and by encouraging their participation in the revolutionary process itself (Shayne 2004), resulting in the creation of the Federación de Mujeres Cubanas (FMC) under the leadership of Vilma Espín. Espín was Raúl Castro's wife and had been his *novia* (girlfriend) when they were both part of the struggle against Batista in Oriente. While Espín always insisted that the Federation of Cuban Women was not a feminist organization, it nonetheless gave women a voice and their own organization to address gender issues in the new society. To many, both efforts, incorporating Afro-Cubans and women to the body politic, spoke of justice.

At the same time, increasingly the revolution became anti-American and pro-Soviet. A diplomatic war ensued between Cuba and the United States, which first cut the sugar quota, then all commerce. "*Cuba Sí! Yanquis No!*" was the slogan of the day. As Pérez Jr. (2003, 243) asserts, the conflict with the United States "necessitated Cuban realignment, both within the internal calculus of power relationships and in the context of international relations. The ensuing realignments further deepened the confrontation. Internal political opposition was at first discredited and subsequently disallowed." At the same time, Cuba and the Soviet Union expanded political and economic ties. Pérez Jr. (2015, 257) highlights that, by the early 1960s, Cuba and the Soviet Union arrived at a number of important trade agreements, as the Soviets agreed to purchase Cuban sugar and pledged financial support in the form of credits, technical assistance, and petroleum. Thus, Cuba continued to export sugar, its major product, but shifted its economic dependence from the United States to the Soviet Union. The Soviet Union and the Eastern European communist countries exerted a profound influence in Cuba for the next 30 years. During that time, Fidel remonstrated against the trade embargo. Although the trade embargo hurt consumption, it also helped Fidel economically and politically. The trade subsidies offered by the Soviet block compensated for the losses due to the break with the United States—in the sugar quota, in arms, in oil, in food, and in technical assistance. At the same time, the government established an internal embargo through their multiple restrictions on the development of private enterprise and capitalism. To this day, revolutionary Cubans blame the embargo as the sole cause for Cuba's economic fiasco.

The political life completely polarized the society, leading to further counterrevolution. In effect, a kind of civil war developed, as present in Goldstone's framework (2009). In his speeches, Fidel Castro led the way, calling those who were against the revolution *contrarrevolucionarios* (counterrevolutionaries) and derisively calling those who left *gusanos* (worms). The exodus became enormous.

Cuba's Exodus

The exodus that began soon after the revolution succeeded has continued for over 62 years, in five major waves. Our analysis of its causes and consolidation focuses mainly on the 15 or so initial years of Castro's revolution in comparison to the same time span of Hugo Chávez's revolution. As in Pedraza's (2007) research, this research is also based on in-depth, semi-structured interviews with hundreds of Cubans who left the island for other lands from 1959 until the present, including Cuban doctors and health personnel that worked in Venezuela helping Chávez's social missions.

The first two waves of the exodus were the result of the profound political disaffection of participants in this major drama. Using the data on the foreign-born from US censuses, we can see the enormous growth in the Cuban population in the United States. The 1990 census provides a better estimate of the early waves of immigration, while the 2000 and 2010 censuses are better for the subsequent waves. In addition, the census's American Community Survey for 2010 and 2018 give us the best contemporary numbers. According to the 1990 census, from 1960 to 1990, fully 677,512 Cubans immigrated to the United States, about 26 percent of them during the first wave (1960–64) and 43 percent during the second wave (1965–74). Data on Cuba's total population come from its censuses of 1957, 1981, 2002, and 2012, as found in the official statistics published by ONEI, their Oficina

Nacional de Estadísticas e Información (Cuba's National Office of Statistics and Information). In 1990, Cuba's total population was 10.6 million. The immigrants in the United States then represented around 6.4 percent of that population. According to the US censuses of 2000 and 2010, from 1959 to 2000, 828,577 Cubans were immigrants in the United States, a number that constituted 7.5 percent of Cuba's population of 11.1 million; by 2010, the number of foreign-born Cubans had risen to over a million (1,104,679); by 2018 it had risen to 1,343,960.

Due to Cuba's low birth rate, large exodus, and aging population, the island experienced a drop in population to a steady 11.2 million in both the 2002 and 2012 censuses. Thus, the percentages the Cuban immigrants in the United States represent of the island population duly increased. In 2010, the number of Cubans born on the island living in the United States represented 9.9 percent of the island's population; in 2018, they represented 12 percent. In the United States, counting not only the foreign-born but also the second-generation Americans who identify as being Cuban, that number rises to 2,381,565 (US Census Bureau, American Community Survey 2019). That constitutes 21.4 percent of the island's population. That number does not include the many Cubans who left for other lands, particularly Spain and the rest of the European continent, Canada, and South America.

The First Wave

In the first wave, those who left were Cuba's elite. These upper and upper middle classes were not tied to Batista's government but were bound to a political and economic structure that, as Amaro and Portes (1972) underline, was completely interpenetrated by the demands and initiative of American capital. They were executives, owners of firms, big merchants, sugar mill owners, manufacturers, cattlemen, representatives of foreign companies, and established professionals who were "most acquainted with the United States' political and economic guardianship of Cuba," and who did not believe that the American government would permit the consolidation of socialism on the island (10). In the first two waves of the exodus, Amaro and Portes distinguished three major types, in their attitudes toward the revolution: "those who wait," "those who escape," and "those who search." "Those who wait," as they labeled the first refugees, came to the United States imagining that exile would be temporary, waiting for the inevitable American reaction and help. The exiles' invasion of the Bay of Pigs in April 1961 was the tragic result.

The 1990 census provides a better estimate for the early waves of migration, while the 2000 and 2010 censuses, as well as the American Community Survey for subsequent years, provide better estimates for the later waves of migration. According to the 1990 census estimates, from 1960 to 1964, around 172,919 Cubans resided in the United States. The first wave ended in October 1962, when, due to the dramatic Cuban Missile Crisis, the Cuban government ended all flights.

In Cuba, a new political culture developed with public ceremonies that attempted to create a new self where the private individual fused with the public citizen (Berezin 1997). To Valls (1991) these years were lived in profound agony, marked by the acme of the public plaza, the concentrations, and collective hysteria. The exodus also brought the Operation Pedro Pan children, over 14,000 unaccompanied minors (Triay 1998; Torres 2003). When the government nationalized the private schools and sent adolescents to the countryside to *alfabetizar* (teach literacy), a rumor spread that the government planned to abolish the parents' *patria potestad* (rights) and send the children to be indoctrinated in the Soviet Union. Frightened parents sent their children out of Cuba, alone. As Kunz (1981, 1973) argues, fear is the defining feature of the refugee experience. Politics deeply divided families. Both sides often insisted that politics needed to be placed above family (see Morello 1998). Casavantes-Bradford (2014) highlights that in a nation profoundly divided by political ideology—between those who remained on the island and rose within the new communism, and those who rejected it and rose within the new exile—both sides insisted they were doing it "for the children."

The Catholic Church then collided against the revolutionary state. Archbishop Pérez-Serantes (1960), known as Fidel Castro's savior, now wrote that the enemy, communism, was within. Yet a large part of *el pueblo* centered their aspiration and hopes in the figure of Fidel Castro, in whom they deposited their trust, thinking he would solve their problems. An ideological combat ensued between the revolutionary government and the churches, especially the Catholic Church. Monsignor Eduardo Boza-Masvidal (1960) often led it. Boza-Masvidal pointed out that the revolution was not Christian—despite its aims of helping the poor, ending racial discrimination, and alleviating extreme social inequality—because the means to achieve this were not just and harmed the rights of others. The revolution, he felt, based itself on hate and the class struggle, rather than charity and love. This ideological combat culminated in the expulsion of the priests and nuns on a ship, the *Covadonga*, which took them away from Cuba in September 1961.

Boza-Masvidal went on to become the priest in the city of Los Teques, Venezuela, until his death some 40 years later. At his funeral, friends threw both Cuban soil and Venezuelan soil onto the casket (Aranguren 2003). For 30 years hence, Cuba defined itself as an atheist society, and few people participated in any religious life. As in the case of the French Revolution, the moment of confrontation with the Church also demonstrated the importance of ideology as a determinant of the course of revolutionary history, as both cause and consequence. Sewell Jr. emphasizes (1985, 84) that the "French Revolution was an ideological event of the first magnitude." So was the Cuban revolution—in this hemisphere and throughout the Third World, caught in the Cold War between the United States and the Soviet Union.

The fourth stage was that of socialism, which began when the large Cuban and American enterprises, *latifundios*, and private property were nationalized in 1960 and lasted until December 1, 1961. Seven months after the failure of the Bay of Pigs invasion, Castro for the first time announced that he was and had always been Marxist-Leninist. As with the French revolutionaries in the eighteenth century, the social order was recast in a new metaphysical mold, down to the smallest details of social life, such as the usual forms of address. In France, the hierarchical, status-laden forms of address of the old regime were substituted by the universal terms *citoyen* and *citoyenne* (citizen; Sewell Jr. 1985, 78–79). In Cuba, the term *ciudadano* and *ciudadana* were replaced by *compañero* and *compañera* (comrade), as befitted the new society.

The Brigade 2506 that invaded Cuba at the Bay of Pigs organized most of the opposition to the revolution's communist turn. The leaders of the major political organizations in prerevolutionary Cuba founded the Frente Revolucionario Democrático by combining all the principal organizations that had opposed Batista: the Auténticos; the Triple A; the Democracia Cristiana; the Montecristi Group; and the Movimiento de Recuperación Revolucionaria. Later the Frente was expanded to include other political factions and it was renamed the Consejo Revolucionario Cubano. Together with the young men who joined the *campamentos*, their goal was to help the underground struggle in Cuba with arms, strategy, and money. They hoped for the return of democracy to Cuba. All collaborated, though reluctantly, with the Americans through the CIA. The invasion force consisted of 1,400 exiles, *invasores* (invaders) accompanied by three Catholic priests who blessed them. Their background was mostly middle- and upper-middle-class and White, though including a sizable number of mixed-race working-class and peasants, as well as Afro-Cubans.

President John F. Kennedy inherited the plan and arrangements for the invasion from President Eisenhower. While committed to the enterprise, Kennedy wanted to hide the American hand in the invasion—a hand that could scarcely be hidden. Thus, Kennedy withdrew the air cover that would have protected the young exiles as they were landing and, in effect, destroyed the operation (Wyden 1979). The government forces killed 114 exiles, a few were executed immediately, and captured 1,189. After being in prison for 20 months, the Cuban government traded the exiles for food and medical supplies from the United States. Cuba's government does not call the event the battle of Bay of Pigs, but the battle of Playa Girón. Today, at the museum there, a sign tells visitors this is where "the first defeat of imperialism in America" took place.

Fidel Castro called the young men *mercenarios* (mercenaries) because they accepted the help of the United States. But those who participated in it did not accept material help. To them, it was as "a struggle between major world powers, and we formed part of that struggle," as Rasco asserted (in Pedraza 2007, interview). Many thought that had it not been for Kennedy's lack of endorsement the invasion would have succeeded. Others felt the Americans turned their back on the Cubans (Wyden 1979; Ros 1994; Kornbluh 1998). The failure of the Bay of Pigs aided the new revolutionary government. Pérez-Stable (1999) also emphasizes that it sealed the identity between Fidel-*patria*-revolution that came to characterize the new order. The international influence was decisive.

As 1961 ended, three years after the revolution's initial triumph, the opposition it generated was largely crushed. As in all social conflicts, people's daily lives bore the suffering. Cuban families became divided between those who supported the revolution and rose within it, and those who rejected it and took the road to exile. For many Cubans, their allegiance to the Church was at the center of that decision. Franqui realized that the revolution, such as it was then—communist, backed by the Soviets, immensely popular—would go on to last a very long time (in Pedraza 2007, interview). The fifth and last period in the consolidation of the revolution was the Marxist-Leninist phase, after Castro publicly declared his ideological allegiance.

As Goldstone (2009) points out, cycles of radical regime change and "terror," followed by revolutionary moderation, often repeat. "Those who escape," as Amaro and Portes (1972) label them, constituted the second phase of the first wave. The exodus then became more middle than upper: middle merchants, middle management and professionals, and skilled, unionized workers, all wanting to escape an intolerable new order. The exodus doubled. "What began as a trickle was, by the middle of 1962, a small flood," as Fagen et al. note (1968, 62).

With the new revolutionary government now at ease, the three major political movements—the 26th of July Movement, the Directorio Revolucionario Estudiantil, and the Partido Socialista Popular (PSP)—all merged into one, the vanguard party. Cuba created the Partido Unido de la Revolución Socialista (PURS) in March 1962. From then on, as Amaro (1981) notes, the Cuban Revolution underwent an essential change: the government placed the emphasis on the enemy within, and criticism was considered a counterrevolutionary activity.

While Cubans left for many lands, the United States welcomed the largest settlement, particularly in Florida and New Jersey. Data from the 1990 US census show that of the 677,512 Cubans who immigrated to the United States from 1960 to 1990, 25.5 percent arrived during the first wave, 1960–64 (US Census Bureau 1993). The Cuban Refugee Program that assisted most of the refugees in Miami began at this time, helping Cubans to translate their Cuban professional credentials into American credentials, and to assimilate (Pedraza-Bailey 1985). The study of Fagen et al. (1968) shows the higher-class origin of these highly educated refugees. The professional, managerial, and middle classes were overrepresented, constituting 31 percent, as well as the clerical and sales workers, at 33 percent.

The Cuban Missile Crisis in October 1962 ended the first wave of the exodus. Nuclear missiles were discovered in Cuba, pointing to the United States. An eye-to-eye confrontation then took place between US president John F. Kennedy and Nikita Khrushchev, first secretary of the Communist Party of the Soviet Union. US secretary of state Dean Rusk expressed it well: "They blinked first." The first Soviet vessels to reach the US blockade turned back, responding to the United Nations' call for peace. Khrushchev gave orders for the missiles to be dismantled and returned. Able to confront the perilous situation, President Kennedy emerged as a hero. Both Khrushchev and Kennedy reached an agreement over Cuba, where Kennedy promised not to invade the island, accepting the Castro regime. For many Cubans in exile, the October Missile Crisis was the second defeat (Ros 1995). Amaro and Portes (1972) call the refugees who left in this second part of the first wave "those who escape."

Outcomes of the Cuban Revolution: The First 15 Years

With the revolution consolidated against its external enemies (the United States and the Cuban exiles) in the early 1960s, in the late 1960s Fidel Castro and Raúl Castro set themselves to the task of consolidating it. They wrestled power away from the old Communist Party; they discredited the counterrevolution that hid in the Escambray Mountains of Las Villas by calling them "bandits"; they imprisoned those who challenged the communist revolution; and they eliminated the market principles of the capitalist economy in part by doing away with the small-business sector and by insisting on the use of moral, rather than material, incentives.

With the revolution consolidated against its internal enemies, in the 1970s they institutionalized it through the First Congress of Cuba's Communist Party in December 1975 and the approval of the first socialist Constitution of 1976. Then the critical juncture of the revolution—the historic break of the early 1960s—gave way to the regrouping around a different set of premises and ideas that the newly created institutions expressed (Hall 1986). In his analysis of the French Revolution, Sewell Jr. (1996) underscores that it was not only the drama of the Bastille that made the revolution of July 1789 so revolutionary. The revolution not only did away with the legitimacy of the monarchy but also brought about the new idea of popular sovereignty expressed in the National Assembly: the natural right of the nation's people to choose its own Constitution. The popular uprising at the Bastille interacted with the new idea of popular sovereignty, consolidating the revolution. Despite its flaws, its moments of real terror, the French Revolution became the model for parliamentary democracy, bequeathing the ideals of liberty, equality, and justice to the rest of the world. Tarrow (2018) argues that this legacy of slow and incremental institutionalization is what transforms society. In the Cuban revolution's first 15 years, the new revolutionary government succeeded in transforming the structure of Cuban society from a capitalist democracy to a communist one-party state.

Next to Fidel Castro, another rebel leader became known worldwide. Ernesto Ché Guevara exerted a major influence on the revolution, seeking to channel it in certain directions. Under Ché's influence, the major ideological thrust became the creation of "the New Man" with an emphasis on moral incentives, rapid industrialization (at the expense of agriculture), and proletarian internationalism. An Argentine doctor (hence the affectionate nickname of "El Ché"), he was given charge of agrarian reform after the triumph of the revolution. The government expropriated the large landowners and distributed small plots of land to thousands of families. As president of the National Bank, he signed the bills that read "*Patria o Muerte*" (Our Homeland or Death) with a rapid "Ché." Together, Fidel and Ché nationalized all the American companies and the large Cuban-owned enterprises, toppling the industrial, capitalist, and landed infrastructure of the economy. Approximately 70 percent of private property passed to the state sector, the highest proportion in any communist country then. Guevara also institutionalized moral incentives to spur work productivity, although it was Fidel Castro (after Ché's departure to Congo and to Bolivia) that implemented this and other ideas from Ché Guevara in 1966–70. *Patria o Muerte* became the slogan of the revolution, uncontested until quite recently.

While the revolution effected radical social changes that benefited *el pueblo*, it also increased the social control over people's lives, generating a great deal of dissent, which the government suppressed. The ideology of humanism coexisted with what the government called revolutionary justice: executing the *Batistianos*, who sided with Batista against the incipient revolution; vilifying those who joined the opposition; arresting people arbitrarily; and sending those who opposed the government to prison. Among the latter were many who had believed in a social and democratic revolution and supported it, but went on to feel betrayed by Fidel Castro. Such was the case of Rafael Peláez (pseudonym), who bore arms twice (in Pedraza 2007, interview). The struggle against Batista included many in the upper and middle classes, like Rafael, who from his childhood had enormous sympathy for the poor in Oriente province. As an adolescent he fought side by side with Fidel Castro when they attacked the Moncada army barracks in Oriente on July 26, 1953, triggering the revolution as an armed struggle. Rafael was among those who chose the colors of the flag for the new revolutionary movement that began calling itself the 26th of July Movement: red and black, to symbolize blood and mourning. He was one of the many anti-*Batistianos* who were pro-democracy. The manifesto of the 26th of July Movement spoke of a social and democratic revolution and expressed a social democratic populism that was long a part of Cuban history. Felipe Pazos, who went on to become head of the National Bank of Cuba, noted that this social democratic populism was typical of Latin American countries then (in Domínguez 1985, interview).

Soon after the revolution triumphed in 1959, however, Rafael was horrified by the massive killings Castro ordered in a stadium, brutality that was reminiscent of a Roman circus, and he also realized, due to his very proximity to the revolutionary center, that Castro was handing the revolution over to the communists. "The hatred," he said, "the killings. . . . That was not the revolution we fought for. The revolution we fought for was not red, but 'green as the palm trees' of Cuba, as Fidel himself said in one of his speeches, and it was to take place through the democratic process." When the armed struggle against Fidel's treason ensued, Rafael joined the organization that was most to the Left, the MRP. He then took to the armed struggle in the hills of the Escambray in Las Villas (Pedraza 2007). For him, joining the new armed struggle was the only option left. Caught working with the underground resistance in Havana, Rafael Peláez became a political prisoner for ten years. The social transformations the Cuban Revolution carried out were so pervasive that they always "pushed" Cubans to leave. The struggle against Batista included many upper-class and middle-income strata. When Fidel turned against both, they had to leave. This first cohort had two characteristics: many were part of the elite, but many were also anti-*Batistianos* and pro-democracy.

Archivo Cuba (Cuba Archive) has carefully documented the deaths and disappearances, due to multiple causes, that took place during all the years of the Cuban revolution. Founded by Armando Lago and María Pino de Cañizares, Maria C. Werlau continues the painstaking work of documenting the death or disappearance of each person named. This includes the date when it happened, during the Batista regime or the Castro regime, and the causes of the death or disappearance—fully 30 causes, such as death in combat, extrajudicial killing, execution by firing squad, hunger strike, or explosion. During the Batista regime (1952–58), there were a total of 1,561 deaths and disappearances. Under the Castro regime, between January 1959 and the end of 1962, there were 2,649 deaths or disappearances. From 1963 to 1969, when the revolutionary forces consolidated the revolution against its internal enemies, the number of deaths and disappearances was 1,861.

In authoritarian and totalitarian societies, both of the Right and the Left, only two alternatives exist for effectively dealing with the dissent they inevitably generate: emigration and imprisonment. Over more than two-thirds of a century, Cuba exercised both.

Internal Conflicts

Conflicts within the government elite took several forms. Internal division in 1968, when a "microfaction" was holding discussions regarding Cuba's serious political and economic problems, shook the Cuban Communist Party. Their effort resulted in arrests, political imprisonments, and forced resignations (*Granma* February 4 and 11, 1968). In the party, a struggle developed between the old communists (Aníbal Escalante and others) and the new communists (Fidel Castro, Raúl Castro, and others). The Soviet Union backed the old guard.

As Domínguez (1978a, 210) points out, of the organizations that made the revolution, only the old communists were well organized. Thus, most of the power of the Integrated Revolutionary Organizations (ORI)—the precursor of the official Communist Party—fell to them, especially since they were in charge of recruitment and promotion. Aníbal Escalante, a founding member of the party in 1925, believed in the communist principle that the party communicated with the masses of the people through its cells, politicizing and educating, and he gave preference to his old communist comrades, challenging the authority of Fidel Castro, then prime minister of Cuba. Escalante's fall was the beginning of a massive restructuring of the party. By 1965, the old communists' share of its Central Committee had fallen from 40 to 23 percent. The road to power in Cuba then ran through close association with the Castro brothers and participation in the military (Domínguez 1978a; Enzensberger 1974). Amaro and Portes (1972) call the second major wave of the Cuban exodus "those who search." However, seeing these migrants as motivated only by better economic opportunities in America misses the political repression they were subject to.

Conflicts also took place between Fidel Castro and Ernesto Ché Guevara, who was the second leader of the revolution and a significant ideological influence in the early 1960s. Castro made him president of the National Bank and put him in charge of agrarian reform at the Instituto Nacional de Reforma Agraria (INRA). The institute created a land redistribution program that expropriated the large landowners and distributed small plots to thousands of families. Together, Fidel and El Ché nationalized the American companies and large enterprises owned by Cubans, which became the property of the state, toppling down the industrial, capitalist, and landed underpinning of the Cuban economy. Guevara's plan was to develop the economy while changing the attitudes of the Cuban people, creating *el hombre nuevo*—a new man who would work to fulfill a social duty through voluntary labor and sacrifice. Thus, material incentives (extra pay) were replaced by moral incentives (recognizing the vanguard worker); rapid industrialization was emphasized, at the expense of agriculture; cost accounting and work-related statistics were eliminated. Policymakers sided either with Fidel (for agriculture) or El Ché (for industry). The economy plummeted, particularly the sugar industry. During those years, El Ché overshadowed Fidel's appeal both domestically and internationally.

Proletarian Internationalism

Ché Guevara also devoted himself to Cuba's proletarian internationalism: the notion, derived from Soviet history, that all communist revolutions were part of a single, global class struggle. Thus, Cuba aimed to trigger or perpetuate revolutions elsewhere. Fidel sent El Ché overseas as a roving ambassador, where he railed against Western colonialism and the socialist countries as accomplices of imperialist exploitation. Since the Soviet Union was keeping Cuba afloat through a generous subsidy as well as thousands of technicians, his criticism of the Soviet Union probably caused him to be sent outside of Cuba, this time to foment revolution elsewhere. Politically marginalized in Cuba, Ché turned his revolutionary fervor elsewhere—first to the Congo, and then to Bolivia, from where he hoped to spread the revolutionary fire to all of Latin America. In the fall of 1967, in the rough terrain of the Bolivian *altiplano*, wounded, asthmatic, and ill, he was also isolated. As expressed in his diary, the Bolivian peasants lacked interest in his efforts (Guevara 1967). Thus, he met his death. Alberto Müller (2014) points out that in Ché's very diary one can see evidence that he felt betrayed by Cuba's leadership.

After Ché's death, Cuba continued its commitment to proletarian internationalism, sending internationalist missions overseas to defend socialist and Cuban interests in Africa and the Caribbean. Although Cuba's foreign policy failed in Latin America, it was a success in Africa. From the mid-1970s on, Africa became the main theater of operations, particularly Angola and Ethiopia, to which Cuba supplied military aid, not only sending troops but also educational services. After the Angolan Civil War, in his speeches Fidel Castro began to stress that Cuba was an Afro-Spanish country (Domínguez

1989). However, to Carlos Moore, an Afro-Cuban in exile, this "Afrocastroism" was politically motivated, as Fidel Castro thought Africa was the weakest link in the chain of world imperialism (1988, 323). Thus, victory in Africa would decide what would rule the world: capitalism or communism.

Beginning in 1975, when Angola became independent from Portugal, and lasting, with interludes, until 2002, Cuba was deeply involved in Angola. The war was a power struggle between two former liberation movements, the communist People's Movement for the Liberation of Angola (MPLA) and the anticommunist National Union for the Total Independence of Angola (UNITA). The war was also a battleground of the Cold War by rival states: the Soviet Union, Cuba, South Africa, and the United States. Those states assisted the opposing factions. Nonetheless, Cuba's assistance with the decisive victory in Angola strengthened its position with African countries (Del Pino 1991; Benemelis 1988; LeoGrande 1980; Domínguez 1978b).

The Trade Embargoes

As Sagás (2003) underscores, what the general public calls "the embargo" and the Cuban government calls "the blockade" is really a collection of presidential orders and laws that restrict or forbid US trade with Cuba during Fidel Castro's government. It began in the retaliation of the early 1960s but acquired a life of its own over six decades of implementation and modification. Worried about Cuba's revolutionary reform, anti–United States stance, and closeness to the Soviet Union, the US embargo began in July 1960 with the cancellation of Cuba's sugar quota. In the fall of 1960, Castro responded by nationalizing—without compensation—all the big companies and enterprises on the island, many of them American. President Dwight D. Eisenhower's administration responded by imposing a complete commercial and economic embargo on the island and a ban on imports from Cuba. Later, in 1962, the Organization of American States (OAS) expelled Cuba; in 1964, the OAS joined the United States by also declaring a hemispheric commercial embargo on the island, which only Mexico and Canada failed to join. The OAS lifted its ban on trading with Cuba in 1975. Thus, Cuba remained economically isolated from nearly all of Latin America as well as the United States and much of the Western world. Cuba developed strong commercial ties with the Soviet Union and the Eastern European countries and was a partner of its common market, COMECON (Council for Mutual Economic Assistance). The Soviet Union and the

Eastern European countries were Cuba's economic lifeline until the collapse of the Soviet Union and Eastern European communism in 1989–90.

We stress that the impact of the US trade embargo has always been twofold. On the one hand, it certainly contributed to making Cuba a poor nation, as Cuba was dependent on the United States for machinery and spare parts, which it could no longer replace, affecting its productivity; even more, Cuba lost the vast market of the United States so close by. On the other hand, the embargo also served to justify the ineffective policies of Cuba's leadership. For over 62 years, Cubans have lived with extreme shortages, particularly in food, clothing, and transportation. In the absence of the trade embargo, such shortages would have led people to conclude that the government was ineffective; instead, the government was always able to blame the dire economic situation on the US embargo. Exhorting Cubans to work harder to overcome Cuba's economic failures, Raúl Castro (1979) plainly acknowledged that the Cuban government blamed the embargo for everything, relying on it as "a convenient crutch. . . . The truly negative consequences of the economic blockade imposed on us, by Yankee imperialism have been used as pretexts to hide our deficiencies and inefficiencies." Rather than undermining the revolution, we believe the embargo strengthened it politically. Economically, since the embargo went on for so many years, Cubans gradually adjusted to a life without many consumer goods, without frills, but often with hunger.

The Second Wave

The second major exodus from Cuba took place in the fall of 1965. A chaotic period ensued when hundreds of boats left from Miami for the Cuban seaport of Camarioca, where they picked up thousands of relatives to come to the United States. "Those who search" characterized this wave of the Cuban migration. In response to president Lyndon Johnson's "open door" policy that welcomed refugees from communism, the Cuban exodus was organized. For eight years, the US administrations and Cuban governments administered an orderly air bridge as the *Vuelos de la Libertad* (Freedom Flights) daily brought around 3,500 Cubans from Varadero to Miami. The Cuban Refugee Program swiftly processed and resettled them, dispersing them throughout the United States. Though for quite different reasons, the US administrations and Cuban governments have often "cooperated with the enemy," as Domínguez (1992) stresses. Jointly, both governments decided who would emigrate, and the migration proceeded through family networks. Cuba barred from exit young men of military service age (15 to 26), as well as professionals and technical and skilled workers whose exit would disturb the delivery of social services, particularly doctors. Together with the economic mismanagement of the leadership, the hemispheric trade embargo imposed by the OAS in 1964 began to be felt. This policy lasted until 1975, when the OAS lifted its sanctions. Cuba failed in her attempts to cease being a sugar monoculture, industrialize, and diversify. Women vastly dominated this wave—58 percent—that also involved many young students and the elderly.

Alfonso (2005) emphasizes that the Camarioca exodus was the first time Fidel Castro used the great emigration of Cubans as a weapon, turning Cuba's internal problems into an American domestic crisis. Years later Castro repeated this model twice: during the Mariel exodus (1980), and during the *balseros* crisis (1994). When the refugee airlift closed in 1974, over 3,000 flights had brought approximately 284,642 persons. The 1990 census showed that 43 percent of Cubans who immigrated came during 1965–74 (US Census Bureau 1993). Cuba had a population of around 6.5 million at the time of the revolution, around 7 percent of which left the island for the United States between 1959 and 1974. Sizable numbers also left for other countries in Latin America, Puerto Rico, and Spain. After 62 years of emigration, today the exodus to many lands is estimated at roughly 25 percent of the population of Cuba.

This wave of immigration was largely working-class and petit bourgeois: employees, independent craftsmen, small merchants, skilled and semi-skilled workers. Amaro and Portes judge (1972, 13) that over time the political exile increasingly became an economic exile as "those who search" were looking for greater economic opportunities. Yet their distinction missed the reality that while life in Cuba grew harsh for all, it turned particularly bitter for those who announced their dissent by declaring their intention to leave. The Unidades Militares de Ayuda a la Producción (UMAP) were established in 1965 under the command of the military. According to Norberto Fuentes (1999), a writer who for many years was very close to Fidel and Raúl Castro, most of the 30,000 to 40,000 young men who were sent to these camps were dissenters. They were Catholic seminarians (among them was Jaime Ortega-Alamino, who went on to become cardinal 30 years later) and Protestant ministers; Jehovah's Witnesses; and other conscientious objectors. They were also homosexuals. In addition, they were persons who engaged in self-employment; university students expelled from the university for "ideological incompatibility"; and peasants who refused to join the cooperatives. The Cuban government spread the rumor that they all were homosexuals, exploiting Cubans' homophobic attitudes in one of the most repressive chapters in Cuban history.

The revolution was consolidated against its external enemies, but, even after the failure at the Bay of Pigs, counterrevolution continued to exist within, as young men went up into the Escambray Mountains to fight the government's forces with their machetes. The civil war was quelled, and the government discredited them by telling the people they were *bandidos* (bandits). Extremely long prison sentences (often more than 20 years) were the lot of the survivors.

Lee's (1966) theory of migration stresses that people move in response to factors that "pull" them and that "push" them, given the intervening obstacles in the way. Once the immigrant communities became established overseas, Cubans were always both "pulled" by their relatives and the lure of a better life and "pushed" by the economic and political circumstances on the island. In 1968–69, the "revolutionary offensive" "pushed" them, when the government confiscated over 55,000 small businesses that were still privately owned (Mesa-Lago 1978), and the little entrepreneur and the employees had to go. These émigrés represented Cuba's "middling service sectors: cooks, gardeners, domestics, street vendors, shoe shiners, barbers, hairdressers, taxi drivers, and small retail merchants (Portes et al. 1977). The Cuban government contemptuously labeled them *parásitos* (parasites).

The United States government, in facilitating the migration, always "pulled" them. Moreover, the Cuban migration is unique in the extent to which both the United States and Cuban governments organized, concerted, and facilitated the exodus. Together, they set in motion a system of political migration that for many years proved beneficial to both. The loss of the educated, professional middle classes indeed proved erosive to the Cuban revolution, but it also served the positive function of externalizing dissent. At the same time, in the United States the arrival of so many refugees who "voted with their feet" also served to provide the legitimacy necessary for foreign policy actions during the tense years of the Cold War (Pedraza-Bailey 1985). Recognizing the need to give over a quarter of a million Cuban refugees already in the United States a legal status, in November 1966 Congress approved the Cuban Adjustment Act, known in Spanish as *la Ley de Ajuste Cubano*, law which allowed Cubans who entered the country legally to adjust their status to permanent residents one year and one day after arrival. Thus, illegality has not been pervasive in the Cuban community in the United States, contrary to other migration flows.

Very soon after the triumph of the revolution, the revolutionary government consolidated the new regime. No doubt remained regarding its nature or its course. The old civil society, independent of government, had died. Now a new socialist Constitution guided the political life. New organizations arose that linked the people with the government, representing them, such as the Asambleas del Poder Popular (Popular Power Assemblies), the Federación de Mujeres Cubanas (the National Federation of Cuban Women) and the UNEAC, or Unión Nacional de Escritores y Artistas de Cuba (National Union of Writers and Artists of Cuba). But the people in them lacked independence from the government and the ability to check its power.

Groups who were socially marginal benefited. Landless peasants received small plots of land. Black Cubans ceased to suffer from institutionalized forms of racial discrimination, such as exclusion from social clubs. The government extended education and health services to serve the poor, particularly those living in remote rural areas. Politics was shaped into a single party, dominated by the new communists. The Soviet Union became the blueprint for all institutions, as well as Cuba's benefactor.

During these early stages of the revolution, the island also became overwhelmingly poor, though the generous Soviet subsidy rescued it. Housing shortages were severe; food was insufficient and controlled by *la libreta* (rationing book); unemployment and underemployment were chronic; and a vast black market developed in which most everyone participated (Roca 1981). After the insurgence against Castro, the government forces crushed the counterrevolution, especially along the mountains of the Escambray, and the underground resistance in cities. The charisma of the leader, Fidel Castro, mobilized the masses. Civil society—the institutions that mediate between the state and the people—disappeared. No independent institutions existed that could limit the absolute power of Fidel Castro and his government. The Marxist-Leninist ideology became the basis of Cuban society, and the influence of the United States was effectively counterbalanced. As a result, the revolution had completely vanquished the democratic republic so many had sought to restore.

Embargo and Exodus Continue

Since we are comparing an old revolution with a much younger revolution, the next part of our story takes place in the 1990s, when Cuba suffered "the special period," as Fidel Castro dubbed it, that resulted from the disappearance of the Soviet Union and Eastern European communism. Thus, in this section we quickly note the changes that took place in Cuba with respect to the embargo and the exodus from roughly 1976 to 1999 (when Chávez became Venezuela's president and our comparison resumes).

Imagining that whoever wanted to leave Cuba had already done so, the Cuban Refugee Program and the second major wave of the exodus ended in 1974. But only a few years later a fresh burst out of Cuba surprised many: the chaotic flotilla exodus that became the third major wave of the Cuban exodus. In November 1978, a dialogue took place between the Cuban government and representatives of the Cuban American community, and as a result the Cuban government agreed to the release of political prisoners, to promote the reunification of families rent by the exodus, and to allow Cubans in the United States to return to visit their families and their homeland. Those return visits were partly responsible for the third major wave, the Mariel exodus.

The Third Wave

With the return visits of the exiles, after many years of separation, families renewed their ties of affection. Moreover, those on the island could see that their relatives in the United States were visibly well and led decent, prosperous lives, contrary to the Cuban government's propaganda about the cruel conditions of life (e.g., unemployment, racism) there. From April to September 1980, through the north coast port of Mariel, close to 125,000 Cubans arrived in Florida (Bach et al. 1981–82). The Cuban government called them *la escoria* (scum). In the Cuban American community, they became known as *los Marielitos*.

In Cuba, these "antisocial elements," as the Cuban government called them, represented a public slap in the face. They were mostly young men, predominantly working-class, though with a large proportion of artists and intellectuals, and a much larger presence of Black and mixed race Cubans than before. No longer were they the immigrants of the transition from capitalism to communism but the children of communism itself. Thus, they constituted different "vintages" of refugees, who could hardly understand or accept one another (Pedraza 2007; Kunz 1973).

In America, they arrived in the midst of an ambivalent government policy that initially welcomed them with "open heart and open arms," as US president Jimmy Carter expressed it (*Miami Herald* 1980), though subsequently he sought to delimit the flow. The media contributed to their damaging portrayal, focusing on the many who had prison records. Indeed, there were many who had been in prison; according to the Immigration and Naturalization Service, of the 124,789 Mariel refugees, around 19 percent had been in prison. However, of those, fully 70 percent were jailed for minor crimes or for acts not considered criminal in the United States, such as dodging military service, refusing to work for the state, participating in the black market, leading an openly gay life, or trying to escape from Cuba. Fully 5,486 were political prisoners—"prisoners of conscience," as Amnesty International calls them—who did not engage in violence and whose political or religious principles were contrary to the Cuban government's (Montgomery 1981). For the many artists and intellectuals that participated in the Mariel exodus, problems of freedom of expression became particularly acute during these years. Given their youth, they clearly constituted a different political generation (Mannheim 1952), one whose coming of age was long after the early revolutionary struggle and sharp social cleavages that demanded enormous sacrifices but also affirmed the loyalty of many. For this wave of young Cubans, comparisons with the years of Batista could no longer serve to promote the consent of a generation that scarcely could remember them. Pedraza (2007) calls this wave "those who hope."

President Ronald Reagan retightened the embargo by curtailing companies operating in foreign countries (e.g., Mexico and Panama, among others) from being a "front" for Cuba—providing American goods and technology to Cuba and thus evading the trade embargo, including televisions, computers, hardware, and the like (Boyd 1986).

During the 1970s and 1980s, Cuba developed strong ties with the Soviet Union and the Eastern European countries. Commercially, Cuba was a partner in its common market, COMECON. The communist bloc countries also trained many Cuban professionals on the island, as well as many young Cubans in their universities in Eastern Europe. Ironically, this happened at a time when *glasnost* and *perestroika* dominated the intellectual discussion there, and these intellectual pro-democracy movements deeply influenced young Cubans, such as the dissident group that became known as Tercera Opción, or "third option"—a different option than those of the Cuban and American governments (Pedraza 2007). Until their collapse in 1989–90, the Soviet Union and Eastern European countries were Cuba's economic lifeline. Their collapse set on "the special period" on the island, when gross domestic product (GDP) contracted by about 35 percent in just a few years, and the vast majority of Cubans suffered enormous want and *hambruna*: a constant hunger.

From the mid-1980s on, the dissident movement began to develop in Cuba. All insisted on the importance of the vote, of electoral democracy for Cuba to determine its political future, and the importance of nonviolent resistance. Progressively it became composed of different organizations with different thrusts. Valdés-Hernández (1997, 2014) stresses the development of civil society from below, from the people in the towns where they lived. Their voices were originally captured in the magazine *Vitral* and can now be heard in the magazine *Convivencia*. The Movimiento Cristiano Liberación (MCL) grew quite popular under the leadership of Oswaldo Payá, expressing the Christian Democratic perspective (2018). Originally articulated as the *Proyecto Varela* (2001), Payá was able to collect far more than the 10,000 signatures the Cuban Constitution then stipulated were necessary to call for change. His sudden death in a suspicious accident (that no one believed was accidental) destroyed his leadership and decimated the organization. UNPACU (Unión Patriótica de Cuba) has since grown quite large and enjoys a great deal of support from people in the poor *barrios* that want to have a real say in their lives. Its leader, José Daniel Ferrer, is still in prison, though adopted by Amnesty International as a prisoner of conscience. While they are minority groups that suffer enormous marginalization from the centers of power, the development of social media has given them a platform and a following they did not previously have. Often this is expressed in a *música contestataria*—anti-establishment music—such as that of Candyman and Los Aldeanos that set their critique of the government's monopoly of power to the rhythms of rap.

The Fourth Wave

In the summer of 1994, yet another dramatic Cuban exodus took place: the fourth major wave. August 1994 marked a historic turn in Cuba, as massive riots broke out on August 5 down the center of Havana, in which thousands of Cubans participated all day long, expressing not only the material want that shaped their lives but also their wish for civil liberties. That summer

Fidel Castro gave the Cuban Coast Guard the order not to detain those wanting to leave. Thousands of Cubans set out to sea on *balsas*—anything that floated. That summer, the US Coast Guard rescued 1,010 Cubans in July; 21,300 in August; and 11,085 in September: a total of 33,395 that were housed in the "safe haven" of Guantanamo. There they lived in tents for months or years, until the US government processed them in an orderly fashion. Many died tragically at sea, during the tumultuous crossing. "Cuba bleeds," headlined Balmaseda (1994), "and the drops are called rafts." Pedraza (1997) calls this fourth wave of the exodus "those who despair."

Attorney general Janet Reno referred to these exiles as "illegal aliens"—quite a contrast to president Lyndon Johnson's welcome of them 30 years earlier as "victims of communism." The change was due, we think, to the end of the Cold War between the United States and the Soviet Union, yet another result of the Soviet collapse. During the Cold War, American policymakers encouraged the exodus, the "flight to freedom," because the émigrés exemplified the rightness of our democratic cause and served to legitimate US foreign policy objectives (Pedraza-Bailey 1985). With the Cold War no longer raging, refugees from communism did not have the same symbolic value. Both in the United States and in Cuba, the media increasingly described them as "economic immigrants." While economic needs clearly were a strong "push" for Cubans to leave the island, most often Cubans who left expressed that the problems they fled from were both political and economic, as they were the economic problems of that political system. As the interviews in Pedraza (2007) demonstrate, in a communist society, then and now, the economic and the political are intertwined, inseparable. The state not only takes political decisions but is also the major employer and investor, it makes all the economic decisions, and it is responsible for distributing food and housing.

In response to the summer of 1994 rafters crisis, in 1994 and 1995 president Bill Clinton signed a new migration agreement and initiated the "wet foot/dry foot" policy toward Cubans hoping to reach the United States by sea. "Wet foot" meant that if the US Coast Guard intercepted Cubans who had put out to sea, they returned them to Cuba, despite the principle of non-refoulement that is supposed to guide refugee policy (Fitzgerald 2019). "Dry foot" meant that if the Cubans managed to reach US soil along the Florida Keys, they were able to remain legally. This policy was in place for 20 years until president Barack Obama did away with it as 2016 opened, only days before leaving office.

The Trade Embargoes Continue

President George H. W. Bush retightened the embargo. Believing that the hardships of "the special period" made the situation ripe for change, in 1992 President Bush signed into law the Cuban Democracy Act (Torricelli bill). These prohibited subsidiaries of US companies located in third countries from trading with Cuba and included other measures to isolate Cuba. However, President Clinton followed with what Sagás (2003, 261) calls "a seesaw policy regarding the embargo; it tightened some aspects of the embargo while relaxing others." The new policy allowed Americans to visit Cuba for study purposes and facilitated telephone communications as well as the émigrés sending remittances.

Under President Clinton, "the zenith of the U.S. trade embargo" was reached when the Helms-Burton Act (the Cuban Liberty and Democratic Solidarity Act) was signed into law in 1996. It marked the "most overarching attempt to bring about political change in Cuba and to prevent a detour in the 'hardline' policy followed by U.S. presidents" until that point (Sagás 2003, 261). The act took away the president's power to modify US policy toward Cuba by requiring the Cuban government to fulfill several conditions before the trade embargo is to be lifted. Those conditions were that a transitional government must be in place; political prisoners must be released; free elections must take place among legalized political parties that include the opposition; and the state security apparatus must be dismantled. The Helms-Burton Act's most controversial piece was Title III, which sought to punish foreign companies in US courts for "trafficking in confiscated property," including properties that were seized by the Cuban government—both American and Cuban American property.

At the same time, the Helms-Burton Act contained an important clause that allowed President Clinton to suspend it for up to six months if necessary to the national interest. Thus, Clinton indefinitely postponed the implementation of Title III, given the intense criticism it received from many important trade partners in the European Union, Mexico, and Canada, who traded with and invested in Cuba. While this provision of the act lay dormant for many years, president Donald Trump sought to reinvigorate it. In 2000, Congress relaxed the embargo, allowing the sale of food and medicines to Cuba, for cash (not credit). This turned the United States into one of Cuba's major trading partners.

The Fifth Wave

Cubans on the island were extremely pleased with the reestablishment of relations between Cuba and the United States under the cooperation of Raúl Castro and Barack Obama. Moreover, they were able to live the improvement in communications and the avalanche of tourists from the United States that arrived in this new period—around 4 million American tourists (not Cuban Americans). But, in truth, not much changed in their lives. Without the wet foot/dry foot policy in place, only Cubans who had immediate family in the United States could hope to emigrate, and the number of people who tried to leave on a *balsa* were few. As a result, a group of Cubans found a new way. Between 2014 and 2016, many Cubans left the island to work in Ecuador, a country that did not require a visa. From there, thousands left on foot, crossing through the Central American countries, hoping to reach the United States to be reunited with their family and friends. The risks were enormous: hunger, death, theft lay in wait for them, especially in the very dangerous forest of the Tapón del Darién between Colombia and Panama. Given how arduous and long the walk was, most were young men alone or with very young families; many were professionals. Though they did not want to stay in any Central American country, after some time Nicaragua blocked the transit of many, despite the insistence of president Luis Guillermo Solís of Costa Rica that they be allowed through so they could reach their families. Many émigrés were forced to end in Mexico. From there, some managed to cross the border, sometimes illegally. Since then, transit via other countries is increasingly rare, though Cubans continue to attempt it. Pedraza (2020) calls this fifth wave "those who walk." Most of the recent émigrés cross through the Southern border.

Within the Cuban American community, the "new Cubans" that have been arriving since the 1990s increasingly have more and more demographic and cultural weight. The new Cubans, as Eckstein (2009) calls them, transformed life on the island through their visits and remittances. Most of the early exiles usually point to the social and economic deterioration that has taken place on the island; they also stress the scarcity of food and the lack of civil liberties. By contrast, the recent emigrants usually point to the advances in public health and education during the revolution as signs of social advance. They mention the social jump that many of them made when young people from poor families such as theirs were able to study in the university and become well-trained professionals. But then they usually go on to explain that the government, the system imposed on them by Fidel and Raúl Castro, could not accept that such an education has to go hand in hand with the fundamental right to freedom of expression and freedom of association.

From November 2016 to January 2017, Cuba's ONEI (Oficina Nacional de Estadísticas e Información), through its population and demography center, conducted a survey of 42,000 households throughout the island regarding their experience with both internal and international migration from 2008 to 2016 (ONEI, *2018 Encuesta Nacional Migración*). The timing allowed for the impact of the new 2013–14 Cuban law to be felt, a law that liberalized the migration of Cubans out of the island, modifying the very restrictive migration law of 1976. In 2015, the net migration of Cubans (immigrants minus emigrants) was quite negative: -24,684. Since most of the migration continues to be to the United States, this survey gave data on the characteristics of the recent émigrés. The data comes from the head of the Cuban household regarding how many members of that household had moved to another country, temporarily or permanently (not including those working in internationalist missions or studying abroad). Given how the sample was chosen, it is an underestimate, as in some households everyone emigrated (i.e., the household is no longer there). However, the characteristics of the sample offer a good description of the fourth and fifth waves of the Cuban exodus. Of the total population of 9.4 million who were 15 years of age or older, the sample size was 240,042. Fully 77 percent of them had moved permanently. Of those, 43 percent had not returned to Cuba, while 19 percent had returned once, and 38 percent had returned on several occasions, demonstrating the now circular nature of the Cuban migration. Comparing the social characteristics of those who emigrated with those who did not emigrate but were still in Cuba, the survey showed that the émigrés were younger; men, more often than women; White, far more often than Black or mestizo; and, overwhelmingly, the sons or daughters of the head of the household still on the island, or other close family. With respect to levels of education and occupations, those who emigrated had higher levels of education, and more often were professionals, scientists, and managers than those who did not emigrate. Fully 77 percent of those who were living overseas sent some type of assistance to their households back in Cuba—mostly money and medicines. Interestingly, those who remained on the island also helped those who emigrated when necessary, especially by traveling abroad to look after someone in the family that required assistance.

The survey also showed that the remittances Cuban households receive from those who emigrated are first and foremost used for food; otherwise, for medicines; for home repairs; for a cell phone or the Internet; and for electrical appliances. According to the heads of households on the island, the principal motivation for the migration was to improve one's economic circumstances—*superación* (to improve one's lot and surmount obstacles)—as well as to grow closer to the family elsewhere (especially important to women). To improve one's economic circumstances constituted 53 percent of the motivations while familial motives accounted for 27 percent. Certainly, for the new Cubans in the United States who lived the worst economic times on the island, and who still have substantial family there, the economic and the familial are deeply intertwined.

All Cubans who left the island for two-thirds of a century suffered enormous losses: not only of property and status but also of their memories and affective past. They lost those with whom they shared their emotional life: the family they grew up in, the family that would have shared their old age, their classmates, their church friends, their neighbors. Against their will and against their hope, their lives were often shattered. Most left Cuba never to return and had to start a new life and new family in other lands. Though known for their success story, not all achieved success as immigrants. But almost always their children—born in the United States, Puerto Rico, Spain, Costa Rica, Canada, Europe—did benefit from their parents' sacrifice.

In the meantime, Cuba continues to decline economically, not only due to the external embargo of the colossus to the north but also to the internal embargo of their own government, which does not allow sufficient initiative and autonomy to those who live and work on the island. Cuba's economic decline is enormous; its population growth is negative. In the past, sugar was the pillar that held up the economy, but it no longer does. Sugar production has declined precipitously, as Castellanos (2021) emphasizes. In the 1950s, Cuba normally produced 6 million tons of sugar. Despite Fidel Castro's exhorting everyone in the country to become mobilized to cut sugar cane, whatever their usual occupations were, the 1970 sugar harvest never produced the 10 million tons Fidel hoped for. Despite his insistence that the honor of the country rested on it, it yielded only 8.5 million tons of sugar. Castellanos underscores that it also left the economy and the society dislocated. In 2001, sugar production reached only 3.4 million tons, and, in 2005, only 1.3 million tons—the lowest point in the previous 100 years.

Tragically, today the production of sugar is at nineteenth-century levels. As Castellanos highlights, the 2020–21 harvest yielded only 816,000 tons of sugar, similar to the 1891 harvest of 807,000.

Moreover, tourism has declined steeply, nearly disappeared, in part due to the new restrictions imposed by former president Donald Trump and left in place for some time by the new president, Joe Biden. Tourism's decline, however, is also due to the new restrictions on the internal economic relations imposed by Cuba's new president Miguel Díaz-Canel (Pérez-Villanueva and Torres-Pérez 2013, 2015). To a devastated economy arrived COVID-19. One can only hope that the two crises of the economy and the coronavirus pandemic will push the Cuban government to deepen its timid economic reforms.

A painting done by a Cuban *balsero* expressed Cuba's dilemma well. Ricardo Blanco was living in Guantanamo with his wife, after the US Coast Guard rescued them from a treacherous passage on a raft. While waiting to come to the United States, Blanco painted Cuba's dilemma on a sheet for his canvas, a painting that became the cover of Pedraza's (2007) book. In it, Cuba is a white dove gripped by a strong hand wearing a metal glove, so she can hardly breathe. Behind the white dove are both the American and Cuban flags. "They both oppress her," he said. "But she still hopes to fly free."

3

The Bolivarian Revolution on Trial

Causes of the Bolivarian Revolution

Hugo Chávez's electoral victory in 1998 and his transformational presidency became an important topic for the social sciences in Latin America. Indeed, the very idea of a decisive political change in Venezuelan politics captured the attention of many scholars and analysts (Ellner 1997; Corrales and Penfold 2015). From the beginning, three major perspectives guided the theoretical and methodological discussions. Initially, a debate took place regarding the nature of the regime: Was it truly a revolution? Or an expression of social populism? Or classic authoritarianism? Or merely reformism? Another debate ensued regarding the causes and scope of the change. Had Venezuela really broken with the past? For a long time, Venezuela's democratic stability for the 40 years between 1959 and 1999 was considered a *sui generis* case in comparative politics. A third debate developed regarding the role the international context played in shaping the change, specifically the exogenous characteristics of the process (Rey 1992; Kornblith 1997; Coppedge 2005).

Initially, most authors and observers defined the Bolivarian Revolution as reformist and led by a moderate Left. However, the country gradually became a socialist-oriented society as president Hugo Chávez's government attempted to build what he eventually called "the socialism of the twenty-first century" through the electoral system. His heir, Nicolás Maduro, who radicalized the electoral process starting in 2013 after Chávez's death, followed this notion.

In the 1960s and 1970s, Venezuela was not a harbinger of Latin America's political path. For some academics, nothing of significance was happening in the nation, while, for others, the Venezuelan political process was difficult to classify (e.g., Karl 1997). Yet Venezuela was also seen as a successful case of political transition because it was able to overcome the military regime led by Marcos Pérez-Jiménez, a military officer who held power from 1948 to 1958 (Butto 2012). Plus, the country then went on to enjoy many democratic and Constitutional governments. From 1959 to 1999, Venezuela had a democratic regime under several presidencies: Rómulo Betancourt; Raúl Leoni; Rafael Caldera; Carlos Andrés Pérez; Luis Herrera Campíns; Jaime Lusinchi; Carlos Andrés Pérez, a second time; interim presidents Octavio Lepage and Ramón J. Velásquez, who finished the term after Pérez resigned in May 1993; and Rafael Caldera, also a second time (Rey 1992; Kornblith 1997).

Because of these 40 years of democracy, most scholars defined the Venezuelan political system as highly stable, particularly given the government elites' political pact of 1958, known as the Puntofijo Pact, which constituted a limited pluralistic democracy (cf. Myers 2017). A formal arrangement among representatives of Venezuela's three main political parties, they agreed to accept the results of the 1958 presidential election and to support and preserve the emerging democratic regime (Silva-Michelena 1967; Levine 1973). As Zahler (2017, 3) notes, under this pact "elected governments would include members from different parties sitting in the president's cabinet and the legislature," including labor leaders, but they would exclude parties from the far Right and far Left." The multiparty agreement worked until 1961. Thereafter, it was a pact between the strongest political parties at the time, AD (Acción Democrática) and COPEI (Comité de Organización Política Electoral Independiente). It enabled Venezuela to weather the storms of the Cold War and the challenge of the small guerrilla movement in the 1960s while remaining a peaceful constitutional democracy. However, to Zahler's mind, *Puntofijismo* is also one of the root causes of Venezuela's present-day crisis because it resulted both in the lack of government accountability to its citizens and in the lack of a culture of "loyal opposition."

The oil boom that took place from 1963 to 1988 provided the Venezuelan government with extraordinary revenue. In 1960, the annual average price of oil was only $2.30 a barrel, a price that remained steady until 1971, when it began to climb, fluctuating until 1977, when it rose to $14.10 a barrel. It continued to climb steadily until in 1981 it reached $28.87 a barrel, and it remained quite close to $40 until 1981, when it began to decline again. In 1989 the price was $16.87 a barrel, and by 1999, when Chávez was elected, the average price was $16.00 (Petróleos de Venezuela, various years).

In this period of economic prosperity, most Venezuelans saw AD and COPEI as representative political parties that exercised political power effectively, by investing in education, developing industry, enhancing agriculture, and improving public services. Through the national budget, a rather powerful state ably distributed oil revenues among various social groups, such as the entrepreneurs, laborers, middle class, and rural peasants (Karl 1997; Velasco 2015). In addition, civilians exerted control over the armed forces and other pressure groups via AD and COPEI (Levine 1973; Rey 1992). Coronil (1997, 391), however, sees the trading of oil for "the illusion of progress" as a "Faustian exchange." He writes: "As foreign banks recycled petrodollars into loans, the state mortgaged the national subsoil in order to obtain loans to finance its vast plan to create the Great Venezuela. Thus, oil wealth brought debt money." This intensified the pattern of "wasteful investment and corruption that had characterized the use of oil rents from the outset. These combined resources were dissipated in inefficient enterprises, domestic consumption, and capital flight, leaving as their main domestic harvest the highest debt per capita in Latin America and a decimated economy."

By the end of the 1970s, the very stability of the political system was ending. The government had created a client relationship with various social sectors based on its oil revenues, relationship which became known as *el rentismo*. This arrangement was coming to an end due to the growing income inequality among different social classes and groups, the high inflation, a soaring external debt, and an unfavorable rate of exchange. In large part, Venezuela's exceptionalism was also ending because, as Zahler (2017, 3) notes, the ruling parties did not need citizen support as much as they needed "access to petrodollars that could be used to continue ineffective politics, curry favors, and buy votes. Politicians thus were often immune to the pressures from a discontented citizenry." Ideology and policy debates became less important than being able to access oil money.

In addition to these political problems, real economic problems developed when the oil revenues declined. In 1976, the government had nationalized the oil reserves and created a semiautonomous enterprise to run the industry: Petróleos de Venezuela, S.A., better known as PDVSA. However, oil prices began to decline, both internationally and in Venezuela, while the country's oil production began to decline as well. Moreover, political circumstances developed, threatening the democratic governance. AD and COPEI both lost their capacity to inspire vast social sectors due to the growing economic crisis and people's increasingly negative perception of their leadership as corrupt and unresponsive. As Myers (2017, 5) expresses it, "The confluence of factional strife in the governing political parties, economic recession, and perceptions that ruling elites were corrupt and unresponsive destroyed the legitimacy of *Puntofijo*. . . . Before the new century dawned, *Puntofijo* would be no more."

An extraparliamentary political opposition developed, both from the extreme Right, which promoted a liberal and anti-state solution to Venezuela's problems (the Roraima Group and some business executives and liberal ideologues) and from the extreme Left, which promoted a revolution (based on the Marxist-Leninist ideology). The latter included some small parties, such as Liga Socialista, Causa R, Tercer Camino, Bandera Roja, and Tendencia Revolucionaria, as well as some university professors, student leaders, labor leaders, pro-Leftist politicians, and intellectuals (Kornblith 1997; Coppedge 2005).

Thus, the academic discussion lost its optimism regarding the Venezuelan political system, and a more critical perspective took hold. Some pioneering studies during the 1960s questioned the explanation that the country's political stability was due to the Puntofijo Pact. However, these early studies did not have the same impact as the books, research projects, and articles written by many experts on Venezuelan affairs during the following 20 years (Naím and Piñango 1984). They warned about the dire results of the hypergrowth in public spending, the additional credits that resulted in an exaggerated and uncontrollable external debt, and the federal budget's overreliance on oil revenues. They also stressed the dangers of corruption in the public sector, the lack of a true democratic aperture with a citizen-oriented democracy, and deteriorating civil-military relations (Rey 1992; Kornblith 1997; Diamint 2005).

At the same time, the prevailing idea—that Venezuela's foreign policy reflected a real internal consensus—also came under attack. Significant voices emerged warning that Venezuela's foreign policy was hyperactive, and a lack of consensus prevailed on important issues, such as its bilateral relations with Colombia, Cuba, and the United States; boundary issues; and its oil policy and foreign trade.

In 1989, Carlos Andres Pérez was reelected president of Venezuela for a five-year term. Upon coming to power, he applied the Venezuelan version of the "Washington consensus" model, a neoliberal economic program that involved "shock therapy": deregulating the economy, eliminating subsidies for everybody, doing away with price controls, and privatizing state companies. The result was a strong social explosion in February 1989, two attempted military coups in 1992, and Carlos Andres Pérez's departure from the presidency in May 1993—before the end of his term and in the midst of a crisis of political legitimacy. Pérez was replaced by two interim presidents: Octavio Lepage (May 21–June 5, 1993) and Ramón J. Velázquez (June 5, 1993–February 2, 1994), who in turn handed power over to Rafael Caldera (former president from 1969 to 1974, who in 1993 won the presidential election for the second time). Caldera waged his campaign under the banner of recovering the Puntofijo Pact. He went on to govern Venezuela until 1999.

Hugo Chávez was then an army officer jailed for his involvement in the coup attempt against president Carlos Andrés Pérez in February 1992. He was released from prison and went on to retire from the military in 1994. Initially, Chávez refused to participate in electoral politics; however, in 1995, he realized that it was possible to attain power through elections. Chávez developed a socialist revolution using the electoral system. A failed *golpista*, he won the election in December 1998 by an ample margin: with 56.2 percent of the vote. With a populist platform and a rather heterogeneous alliance, he sounded the themes of social justice and nationalism. As Jansen (2011, 82) argues, populism should be understood not as a set of beliefs, but as a set of political practices that "mobilize ordinarily marginalized social sectors into publicly visible and contentious political action, while articulating an anti-elite, nationalist rhetoric that valorizes ordinary people." Thus, when Chávez first came to power, he promised to create a new and better society, especially for those marginalized sectors. His early years were years of idealism, full of promises. At the core of his platform was a call for radical political reform in Venezuela's political life—for a National Constituent Assembly to write a new Constitution to replace the old Constitution of the Fourth Republic and to end the Puntofijo Pact.

In the beginning, Chávez's own party, the Fifth Republic Movement (Movimiento Quinta República), was small and lacked deep roots. For Chávez's political project, the absence of a political party representing the working class and the poor was a problem. This could be seen in the debate a decade later over Chávez's proposal for a unified socialist party and the PSUV in 2007, the party that for many years has controlled Venezuelan politics. In 1998, Henrique Salas Römer, the most important presidential candidate from the opposition, proposed a neoliberal program of reforms and gathered around 40 percent of the vote. In addition to his own personal charisma, Chávez's argument was that the people elected him legitimately and that he enjoyed a popular mandate. As Goldstone (2009) points out, in our contemporary world elections provide the most important source of legitimacy. As in Cuba under Fidel and Raúl Castro, Venezuela under Chávez used the popularity of the incumbent with *el pueblo* together with a favorable international context to conquer the existing institutions and rules.

Flores and Nooruddin (2016) distinguish among different types of legitimacy. Elections do confer legitimacy for the victor, but "that legitimacy has an expiration date." Thus, they call it "contingent legitimacy" to emphasize that, "while elected leaders enjoy a governance advantage over their non-elected counterparts, they do so only temporarily. At some point, their democratic halo dissipates, and they must perform and meet their citizens' lofty expectations or risk squandering their honeymoon period" (81). Therefore, contingent legitimacy needs to be followed by performance legitimacy—the ability to generate public goods. This, however, is hard to generate in countries that inherit what Flores and Nooruddin call low stocks of legitimacy. This happens when the seeds of democracy fall on poor soil, since the country does not have a deep stock of democratic-institutional legitimacy from its experience with democracy in the past. Although Venezuela did have 40 years of constitutional democracy to fall back on, the polity's lack of accountability to the citizenry and the lack of a culture of loyal opposition were problems that plagued the *Chavismo* era. As Zahler (2017, 4) notes: "A key ingredient to the current crisis is that Chávez devised political-economic policies that served to concentrate power on himself and his party rather than to promote economic sustainability."

Chávez's political demagoguery further inflamed the opposition; both sides insulted each other as irrational, self-serving, vile, and anticonstitutional. As Urreiztieta (2013) notes, one of the achievements of *el Chavismo* was the inclusion of *las mayorías populares* (the majority constituted by the common people and the poor) into the body politic as participants. However, at the same time, Urreiztieta highlights, the political subjectivities that this social process developed rested on the antagonism of groups: on conflict, lack of trust, polarization, resentment, threats, and the desire for revenge. Those who dissented were enemies to be vanquished, traitors to the cause. These political subjectivities, she added, rendered daily life hyperideological, leading to a cult of personality of the leader that asks for unconditional surrender. These political subjectivities also weakened the basis for a truly plural and participative democracy based on respect for differences and diversity.

Process of the Bolivarian Revolution

As soon as Hugo Chávez came to power via elections, the new president proposed a different political formula. The old formula of *la decisión por consenso* (decision by consensus) was replaced by the new formula of *la mayoría del pueblo* (majority of the people). Müller (2015) points out that the term "populism" has different meanings or associations in different nations. In Latin America, the phrase *el pueblo* has meant both "all the people"—the body politic—as well as "the common people," the excluded and forgotten. Chávez appealed to the will of the people as their authentic representative. In addition, the master frame with cultural resonance was "the Bolivarian Revolution": a revolution that was authentically Venezuelan, hearkening back to the ideas of Simón Bolívar, the revered patriot of the war of independence. Chávez always referred to Bolívar's legacy in these terms: "Simón Bolívar is the leader of the revolution of this land. He is the leader of the social revolution, the people's revolution, the historical revolution" (Chávez 2009).

Hugo Chávez won the 1998 elections and set himself the task of dividing the history of Venezuelan democracy into two periods: the Fourth Republic (from 1959 to 1999) and the Fifth Republic (from 1999 on), the latter belonging to him. He also began the process of transforming the nation into a new political model: displacing the old elites, establishing himself as a new and prominent player among equals, and promoting a new relationship between state and society.

In its first decade, the Bolivarian Revolution went through three stages. The first stage, from 1999 to 2000, was a period of transition to a new political and economic model of populist democracy under the stewardship of a constitutional process. This stage resulted in the new 1999 Constitution, the relegitimization of the national authorities, the presidential election in July 2000, and the beginning of Chávez's new presidential term (2000–2006). The 1999 Constitution stipulated the principles the Bolivarian revolution preferred for citizen participation in politics: the use of three national referenda and several regional and local ones (Rey 2004).

The second stage, from 2000 to 2004, laid the foundation for the new model. This process was fraught with instability and uncertainty due to the clash between the government and its ruling alliance vis-à-vis a growing political opposition. The period had three turning points. The first was the failed coup carried out against President Chávez in April 2002 by a significant number of military and civilians that took power for 48 hours. The second was the employee strike at the state oil company PDVSA, from late 2002 to early 2003. The third was the presidential referendum recall in August 2004, which was intended to achieve a political, democratic, and constitutional solution to the crisis. The referendum was part of a negotiation between the government and the opposition supported by important intermediaries: the Organization of American States (OAS), the Carter Center, and the United Nations. Both Chávez's government and the democratic opposition chose these organizations. The Coordinadora Democrática (forerunner of the MUD as well as later Frente Amplio) was created to unify the opposition's various political parties and movements.

The third and final stage of the Bolivarian Revolution began in 2004 when the government installed a new, radical political model: a statist model that broke sharply with the past. Moreover, the Venezuelan opposition declined to participate in the December 2005 parliamentary elections, which it tried to boycott. As a result, an absolute majority of Chavistas were elected. The following year, Hugo Chávez was reelected president of Venezuela for the third time, with an extremely large margin of 62.8 percent of the valid votes. Thus, President Chávez obtained the contingent legitimacy to implement his program and did away with many people's previous doubts. In traditional Marxist thought, this was a transition from a national liberal and reformist model to a fully socialist one. Thus, he baptized the new program as "the socialism of the twenty-first century." This was to be a socialism without poverty and an authentically "Third World socialism." Hugo Chávez emphasized that "the capitalist model, the developed model, the consumer model which comes from the North, which it has forced on the world, is falling apart on the Earth, and there is not a planet nearby that we can emigrate to" (Chávez 2011).

Chávez then initiated a constitutional reform proposing that his presidential power be indefinite. This reform was subject to a referendum in December 2007, when it was defeated by a margin of only 1 percent. In 2008, Chávez tried this move again. With the National Assembly then under his control, he was successful. Thus, at present the Venezuelan Constitution does not set term limits on the presidency. This reform was still in place in October 2012 during Chávez's last election as president of Venezuela.

However, the election generated a sharp debate regarding the lack of real democracy in Venezuela. As O'Donnell (2004) points out, electoral democracy can result in a "delegative democracy," with a strong father figure at the helm of the nation whose people are its children more than its citizens.

At the same time, worldwide oil prices were high. The graphs in figures 3.1 and 3.2 show the remarkable rise and fall of oil prices from 1946 to 2020. In 2001, shortly after Chávez assumed the presidency, the price of a barrel of Venezuelan oil was an average of $20.21. Just four years later, in 2005, the average price had more than doubled, to $46.15. Four years later, in 2008, the price had risen to $86.49, nearly doubling again. Just before Chávez's death, in 2012, the average price of a barrel of oil had risen to $103.42. Thus, Chávez was able to use the revenues from PDVSA to fund his vast increases in social spending. The oil revenues also made possible the expansion of the government's social programs, with the goal of redistributive justice (Dunning 2010; Fernandes 2010). After 2013, however, the price of oil began to decline steadily, so that by 2016 it was only $43.29 per barrel. In 2020, the average annual price of a barrel of oil was only $35.93 (Petróleos de Venezuela, various years).

In 2003, Chávez initiated a targeted outreach to the poor in cities and

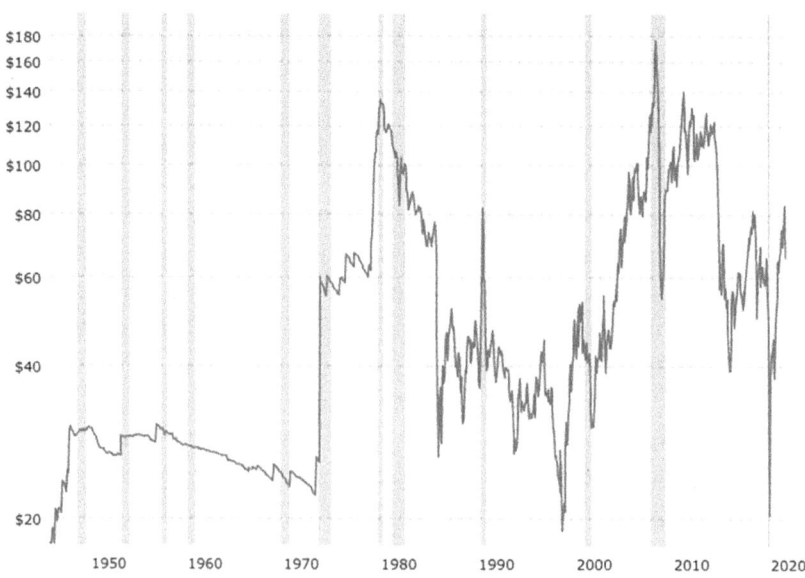

Figure 3.1. World crude oil prices, 1946–2020, historical. (Graph from Macrotrends LLC, https://www.macrotrends.net/crude-oil-price-history-chart-2021-09-09-macrotrends)

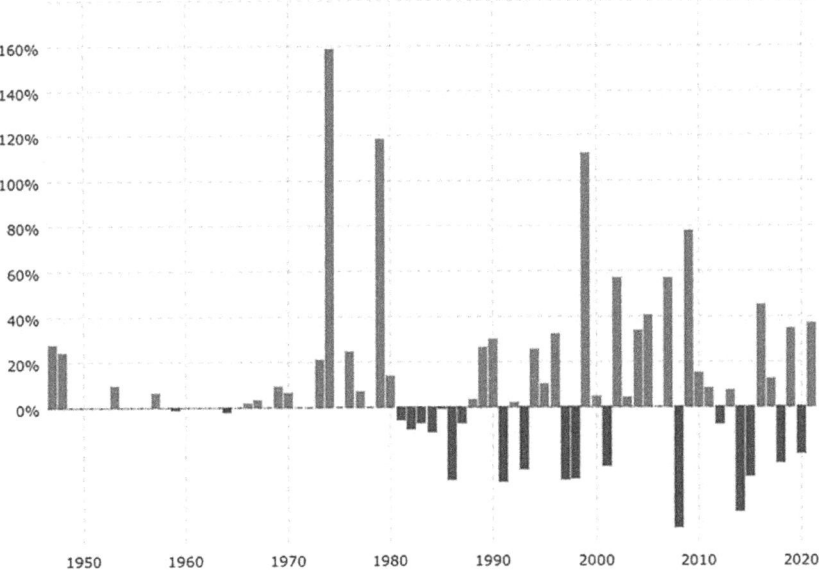

Figure 3.2. World crude oil prices, 1946–2020, by year. (Graph from Macrotrends LLC, https://www.macrotrends.net/crude-oil-price-history-histogram-2021-09-09-macrotrends). These are interactive charts of West Texas Intermediate (WTI or NYMEX) crude oil prices per barrel 1946 to 2020. The price of oil shown is adjusted for inflation using the headline CPI and is shown by default on a logarithmic scale.

rural areas through the institutionalization of the social missions—Misiones Bolivarianas—that took their name from the patriot Simón Bolívar. Among the largest and most important of these missions were Misión Barrio Adentro (primary health care), Misión Milagro (ophthalmology), and Misión Robinson (literacy). Thus, the government provided education, housing, and health care to millions of poor people. These missions, established by the government, in which Cuban doctors and health personnel worked, largely bypassed the old government structures. Their stated aim was to combat extreme poverty and its health manifestations in Venezuela's inner cities, shantytowns, and rural areas. Through the missions, the government aimed to achieve performance legitimacy and garner emotional and political support for Chávez's social project of building socialism in Venezuela, garnering the political loyalty of the people.

Venezuela's socialism was to be built with Cuba's assistance (Chávez 2014a). In 2011, according to Cuba's estimates, there were 51,000 Cuban *colaboradores* (assistants) working in Venezuela, including 31,315 working in the health sector: 11,054 doctors and 10,997 health technicians, as well as

5,000 political workers training revolutionary cadres. In 2020, an estimated 22,000 Cubans still live and work in Venezuela, working in the social missions and other public activities, including the armed forces. This includes the over 2,000 doctors and health personnel that arrived in April 2020 to help with the coronavirus pandemic. This gives evidence of the formidable alliance that existed between Cuba and Venezuela; it still stands though weakened by the severe economic crises in both countries at present.

The missions achieved important results: the poor in shantytowns and urban and remote rural areas felt that they were listened to and looked after (Coppedge 2005; Kornblith 2007; Rey 2004; Fernandes 2010). Thus, the legitimacy Chávez enjoyed changed form: the contingent legitimacy of his electoral mandate became performance legitimacy.

However, none of these large state projects were economically autonomous or sustainable. As Zahler (2017, 5) stresses, *el Chavismo* "used petrodollars to reduce the independence of state institutions and make the citizenry more dependent on the central government." Such a strategy could only function for as long as the state enjoyed an abundance of cash from its oil. Figures 3.1 and 3.2 show the rise and fall of world crude oil prices from 1946 to 2020, the very jagged pattern of very high highs followed by very low lows.

Under Chávez, Venezuela's domestic goals shifted toward redistributive justice; its foreign policy goals also began to change. From 1999 onward, Venezuelan diplomacy developed an agenda that combined traditional concerns with new issues. Venezuela used oil as the means to participate on the world stage and for activism in its hemisphere. It also promoted a new political model based on participatory democracy; launched a new economic model called an "endogenous development model"; and created an ideologically partisan foreign service, as career diplomats were sidelined. Moreover, it actively supported political, social, and cultural antiglobalization groups all over the world (Romero 2006).

Moreover, the Venezuelan political process increasingly relied on the media, particularly the international. Naím (2005, 208) expresses it well: "Both the government and the political sectors that support it, as well as the Venezuelan opposition, have played out their performances—actions and differences—on a global stage. Under their protection, Venezuela's international relations have become geographically broader and more diverse, as well as more intense with non-governmental groups than with other nations' governments."

Venezuela had lived through a politically moderate democratic experience that lasted 40 years (1959–99). Then a group of civilians and military took power with a program designed to reestablish the nation on different principles. During the 14 years of Chávez's mandate (1999–2013) the Bolivarian revolution had three prongs. First, the government chose new elites to displace the traditional elites—parliamentary, bureaucratic, and military. Second, the government strategy expanded its new political majority with populist, authoritarian, and socialist features, taking total control of the state bureaucracy, PDVSA's executives and workers, the social movements of the Chavistas, military personnel, the media, and some social groups, reducing private initiatives in those sectors. Third, the government enjoyed the economic surplus that resulted from oil. However, this deepened society's dependence on its oil revenues.

This paved the way for the government's increased social spending and led to its practice of direct economic transfers for the neediest. Propaganda in favor of the government presented Hugo Chávez's photo in posters and TV and radio stations. The facades of the towering apartment buildings he constructed to house the poor featured his signature under an abstract drawing of his eyes near the building's top. Such social expenditures and visual messages ensured the continuity of the regime. However, the social investments also had an impact on the public sector budget, together with a growing public debt, and early signals of corruption schemes. Moreover, Chávez enabled huge numbers of low-income Venezuelans to become workers on the government payroll and extended direct government benefits to many other poor Venezuelans, as well as the middle class. Most poor people supported Chávez's government and programs at the time because he fed them, housed them, and gave them a voice: in short, he included them (Fernandes 2010). In October 2012, Chávez won the presidency for the fourth (and last) time with 55 percent of the valid votes. While the margin was much less than the 63 percent of his previous election, it was still notable. However, when oil revenues declined, the government was unable to continue with those social programs, so it had to cut or reduce them, losing some of its previous supporters (Corrales and Penfold 2015).

Chávez's mandate continued for 14 years with significant popular support, and at enormous cost to the social groups who refused to back him, as well as to all Venezuelans. An enormous social and ideological polarization took hold of the country (Corrales and Penfold 2015). Today, the political polarization in Venezuela is total, as evidenced by the two sides that violently protested in the streets in 2014 and 2017, and the acrimonious debate in political forums, the media, social media, and the international arena.

At present, one can say that a revolutionary socialist society was not fully attained, not only because of the incompetence and inefficiency of most public policy programs but also because the economy grew based not on citizens' taxes and on domestic and foreign investment but, rather, on oil revenues. Consequently, Venezuela neglected the development of its agriculture, to the detriment of its people, who suffered from scarcity of food.

In fact, the Venezuelan economy revolved around the international energy market: the production and marketing of oil and its derivatives through sales, profits, and losses. Oil supported Venezuela's investments abroad, its rising external debt, and the financial costs involved in international cooperation. But oil was a remarkably unstable commodity, as can be seen in figures 3.1 and 3.2. In 2010, Venezuela's oil revenues constituted 28 percent of its GDP, 95 percent of its exports, 95 percent of its foreign currency assets, and more than 50 percent of its public spending funds (Orro 2009; Ross 2011). In 2019, oil revenues fell by half due to the loss of markets, especially the United States'; the decline in oil production to no more than 600,000 barrels per day in 2019 (in contrast to 3,600,000 barrels in 1997); and the decline in the price of oil.

Despite Hugo Chávez's draw for large sectors of Venezuela's population, a significant sector of Venezuelans refused to accept his plans. The opposition remained committed to democratic resistance and tried several times and by various means to stop his control. At times, they were successful, as could be seen in the parliamentary elections of 2015, when they won control of the National Assembly, as well as in large street protests. Leandro Buzón and Roberto Patiño are two young men that participated in the street protests. Buzón voted for Henrique Capriles, leader of the opposition, and sees the government as a dictatorship. However, he was quite willing to collaborate with the socialist government to help the common people. They founded Caracas Mi Convive, to promote leadership from below—genuine leadership from the community to combat the violence and criminality on the streets of Caracas. These efforts at *convivencia* between the political elite of the PSUV, the Socialist Party, and the common people (*el mundo popular*) sought to build trust, solidarity, and respect among everyone. As Buzón pointed out, this was especially important during the pandemic (in interview by Hugo Prieto [2020]). However, the government did not tolerate the competition between Convive and the missions in the popular sectors and crushed their work in November 2020. Like hundreds of thousands of Venezuelans, Buzón emigrated to Colombia. At other times, the opposition incurred severe losses, as was the case during the 2002 attempted coup, as well as when the opposition refused to participate in the 2005 parliamentary elections (Coppedge 2007; Kornblith 2007; Taguieff 2007; Weyland 2003).

The political order gradually shifted from representative democracy to socialism; it showed signs of the old regime, punctuated by some new features. Elements of the old regime included the strong presidency, the power of the state, the representation of the common people, the political use of public spending, the arbitrary use of oil revenues as a major source of national income, and a weak institutional framework. Newly added to the mix were the declining strength of the key parties, AD and COPEI. Moreover, President Chávez considered himself to be "first among peers": a leader above the rest of his comrades. In addition, the government dismantled the efforts to decentralize the public sector. Other new elements were the statist-socialist orientation of the economy, the Social Missions, and the efforts to create a direct democracy through the new *comunas*, the community councils (Kornblith 2007; Weyland 2003).

The creation of new communal councils, in which the community and workers organized to take power into their own hands, came from Chavez's notion of communal power. The *comunas* had an impact in Venezuela's poor neighborhoods. Followers of *el Chavismo* led and organized them, as they distributed goods and services to the poor. Handlin (2016, 1243) notes that this included "the establishment of mass organizations capable of engaging in campaign activism, distributing resources, and mobilizing voters to the polls during elections."

From 1999 onward, Venezuela's political transition went from democracy to authoritarianism—a peculiar and little-studied case in comparative politics, a field that has largely focused on the opposite political transition from authoritarianism to democracy. Noted, the country has been called an "electoral oil authoritarianism" (Kornblith 2007). Venezuela used to be thought of (along with Norway, Canada, and a small group of democratic, oil-rich countries) as "the exception to the rule," because for over four decades it was able to forestall authoritarianism. However, its sustained economic surplus due to its oil revenues placed Venezuela once again on the agenda of comparative politics. In fact, the country is no longer seen as a model in which oil revenues played a key role in its democratic past. Rather, oil revenues now help to explain the emergence and development of the electoral oil authoritarianism that shaped the nation since 1999. Venezuela is now shifting to a corporate authoritarian model and is facing a profound economic crisis (Corrales and Penfold 2015; Hachemaoui 2012).

Recent analyses that attempted to explain this transition from democracy to authoritarianism repeat the debate that took place during the 1970s. Efforts to explain the 40-year stability of Venezuela's party system ranged from the "pact thesis" (a democratic consensus) to the "oil thesis" (a rent-seeking society). Those who argue that democracy has disappeared from the country resort to the traditional idea of the political agreement reached in the Puntofijo Pact, underscoring that its breakdown was partly responsible for the changes that began in 1999 (Rey 1992). Others focus their explanation on the decline in oil revenues beginning in 1983 that was responsible for democracy's loss of stability, leading to a political vacuum in 1999 that opened a space for Chávez's hybrid regime with his electoral victory (Karl 1997).

Pro-Chávez regime advocates also emphasize that a new social contract developed based on the Bolivarian socialist project, a civic-military union, together with Chávez's leadership and will. Others argue that oil revenues will still lead the country down the same path as in the past, though now the government is a profit maximizer, as it uses that economic surplus to control wealth and to distribute it more equitably. Orro (2009) calls such behavior "petrolism," which helps to explain the stability of the new regime and its popular support from 1999 to at least 2013 (Karl 1997; Romero and Curiel 2009; Dunning 2010). As Orro (2009, 4) points out, "Oil can result in a lot of oil revenues but it also fails to diversify the economy and to create an autonomous work force." Thus, inequality and poverty remain stubbornly high, although Venezuela's leaders struggle to reconcile their Bolivarian message of social justice and equality with the reality of a government elite awash in wealth and privilege (Karl 1997; Romero 2006).

From 1999 to 2013, the Venezuelan regime not only undertook a journey toward authoritarianism but also maintained a double grip on power: de jure and de facto. In the economy, a parallel financial track developed alongside the regular budget—the special funds established by the government. As a petrostate, Venezuela's economic model had some commonalities with those of other Arab oil-producing countries, such as Algeria and Libya (before 2011) and Syria and Iraq (prior to 2003) The revolutionary party captured a dual identification with the state and the revolution. It also entailed an authoritarian coalition, control of the economy, and the absence of democratic institutions capable of exercising control over public spending (L. Martínez 2010; Hachemaoui 2012; Morse 2012; Levitsky and Way 2010; Lindberg 2009).

Therefore, it is not surprising, as Etzioni (2007, 234) points out, that "the government interprets that the country has the right and the ability to transform the world according to their own initiative." In practice, this entailed developing several regional alliances—the Cuban-Venezuelan alliance as well as the alliance with other Latin American governments and movements whose goals were related to the founding of the ALBA (the Bolivarian Alliance of the People). The ALBA is a regional alliance formed with Bolivia, Cuba, Ecuador, Nicaragua, Dominica, and Saint Vincent and the Grenadines that Venezuela sponsored. In Spanish, its acronym means "the dawn." As Puyosa (2019) notes, in the twenty-first century hybrid or authoritarian regimes justify their mandate by the electoral victory the majority gave them but have little respect for the rights of the electoral minority. Typically, they restrict social media communication, democratic organizations, and civil society, as they have done in Russia, Venezuela, and the countries ALBA grouped. Still another alliance was a set of special relations with some nations—Iran, Syria, Russia, China, Turkey, Vietnam, and Belarus. The petroleum refinery in Cienfuegos, Cuba, for example, has a huge sign outside that shows the Cuban and Venezuelan flags side by side, and the title ALBA, with the saying, "Another Latin America is also possible."

Of critical significance is that Venezuela has played an important historical role in the functioning of political and economic alliances outside the Western hemisphere, both bilaterally and multilaterally, with other Third World nations, aimed at reducing superpower control of the international system. Note the country's role in creating the OPEC, as well as the Group of 77 and the Group of 15, political coalitions developed inside the United Nations before Chávez came to power. From 1973 on, Venezuela also participated as an observer and later a full member of the so-called Non-Aligned Movement, in which Cuba also played a crucial role. It was also part of the Group of 20, within the World Trade Organization (WTO).

However, Hugo Chávez's government was uncomfortable with those multilateral processes, seeing them as too neutral in relation to the struggle against imperialism and not radical enough in international relations.

Therefore, Caracas chose to develop a special relationship with nations like Russia, China, Iran, and Cuba; to strengthen ALBA; and to promote a radical multilateralism with rousing calls for disengagement from the West, as could be seen in Venezuela's behavior in the United Nations, with its special agreements with some anti-Western countries and its vote and stance. Chávez's speech at the United Nations in 2006 in which he mocked George W. Bush for smelling of sulphur, like the devil, was unforgettable (Chávez 2006). All of these decisions led Chávez's government to a foreign policy based on two goals: to promote regional relations through its Bolivarian identity, and to confront the US government under the banner of anti-imperialism. As Chávez underscored: "The imperialists see extremists everywhere. It's not that we are extremists. It's that the world is waking up. It's waking up all over, and people are standing up" (Chávez 2005). In the end, Venezuela's international behavior sought to influence the whole world as a form of resistance against globalization, to undermine the United States' hegemony. Chávez's leadership was tested and proven, although it derived from a worldview that was stuck in a Cold War time warp.

After Chávez's death in March 2013, Nicolás Maduro was elected president in April by a narrow margin: 51 percent of the votes. In 2018, amid great controversy over the elections, he insisted that he was reelected. Thus, it is important to consider whether President Maduro has been able to follow Chávez's example. So far, it has not been an easy path.

Outcomes of the Bolivarian Revolution

In the early years of Venezuela's socialist governance, scholars who studied Latin America and the Caribbean looked at it as a case of revolution, though characterized by the key lever of its ambiguity. Beginning in 1999, fundamental changes occurred in Venezuela. After a centrist democratic experience lasting 40 years, a group of civilians, military officers, and retired military came to power with a program designed to reshape a country whose economy was booming into a socialist nation (Hirst et al. 2020).

Venezuela developed a major international presence, not only due to the Bolivarian Revolution but also because it held the world's largest oil reserves, in addition to having significant gas and mineral reserves. The development of the Orinoco Oil Belt, one of the top engineering projects in the world, also contributed to Venezuela's prominence, despite recent setbacks in its oil industry and severe sanctions by the Trump and Biden administrations. Under Chávez's rule, Venezuela sought to maintain its relations with the United States, though in an unstable fashion. Caracas managed to retain the commercial relationship, especially *its* energy contract, and increased trade between the two nations with an asymmetry in favor of Venezuela. In the same vein, President Chávez's government and successive US administrations handled diplomatic frictions and incidents of medium intensity without breaking the bilateral relations between the two (Romero 2006).

However, all this changed in 2007, when the MVR became the PSUV, a "critical juncture" signifying the institutionalization of the Bolivarian, socialist revolution (cf. Tarrow 2018). The PSUV was more revolutionary than the MVR, which unified most of the Chavista parties. Chávez's government and the ruling PSUV developed an anti-American foreign policy. This included denouncing the alleged US interference in Venezuela's internal affairs, reducing Venezuelan oil shipments to the United States, reorienting Venezuela's exports to other oil markets, and blaming Washington for helping the opposition to destabilize the regime.

Venezuela's aim was to become a Cuban-style socialist society. However, significant obstacles rendered this impossible: substantial regime opposition still within the country of those that had not joined the exodus; an economy punctuated by traces of capitalism; and a rent-oriented society based only on oil, its major export. Ultimately, McCoy and Myers's (2004) assertion regarding Venezuela's permanently ambiguous nature is accurate. As they write, the "evidence suggests that the unraveling of representative (though limited) democracy in Venezuela and the transition to a more hybrid regime (one that combines elements of pluralism and authoritarianism, of representative and direct democracy, and of capitalism and statism) are chartering a previously unobserved path of political change" (2).

Hugo Chávez's electoral victories and the advent of a different type of Venezuelan government allowed the country to adopt the Cuban ideological package: a foreign policy that defied Washington, an economic policy based on statism, and populist social measures. Thus, the government's broader goal was to impose a hegemonic project while relying on political continuity, contrary to democratic alternation. In 2008, Chávez changed some parts of the 1999 Constitution, including the change that allowed him to be reelected president of Venezuela without any obstacle.

In President Chávez's final years, the discussion focused on the consequences of applying a socialist model. For some scholars and critics, the move was revolutionary; in the minds of others, it pointed to an illiberal nature. Scholars assumed that the president's charisma, his control of the masses, the high price of oil, and a growing economy would guarantee the country's success (Corrales and Penfold 2015).

Surprisingly, on March 5, 2013, Hugo Chávez died, from cancer, at the age of 58. He chose to have his treatments and surgeries in Cuba, evidence of his strong relationship with Fidel Castro (F. Castro 2013a, 2013b). An emotional outpouring gave way among the Venezuelan people. In April, elections were held between Nicolás Maduro, who inherited Chávez's mandate, and Henrique Capriles, governor of the state of Miranda (serving a second term), for the opposition. Tulio Hernández, from the newspaper *El Nacional*, underlined that the campaign was really between Capriles and Chávez's ghost and memory. Hernández thought Capriles had charisma, but he did not seem capable of the "emotional, seductive, and extensive discourse through which Chávez had re-educated the Venezuelan people" (in Ramírez 2013). Maduro won the 2013 elections by only a small margin (1.3 percent), with the opposition complaining that the elections were rigged. Michael Shifter, president of the Inter-American Dialogue, noted that Maduro and Chávez were not the same, however. In his opinion, Maduro lacked Chávez's charisma, had only partial support among the Chavistas, lacked political experience, and had a tenuous link with the Socialist Party (Ramírez 2013). Additionally, in December 2015, the opposition's parliamentary victory gave them control of the National Assembly, adding to the regime's political losses. These political setbacks went hand in hand with serious internal economic disruption, reduced space for democratic action, a decline in oil revenues, and the increasing criticism of the regime by large numbers of citizens and international actors (Corrales 2015; Mazzuca 2013; Mainwaring and Pérez-Liñan 2013).

At the same time, the oil boom of 2005–13 ended. While it lasted, the Chavista regime was able to survive due to sufficient public revenues; the standard-bearers who came to power could wave the banner of "the socialism of the twenty-first century" (Corrales and Penfold 2015). In his analysis of this tendency, Burchardt (2017) emphasizes that, "thanks to the high revenues from raw materials, it was no longer necessary to settle conflicts of interest through democratic procedures or solve them through negotiations," as the state appeased them through transfers of resources. Burchardt writes: "Conflicting sectors were bought and co-opted. Latin American societies have mutated into outlaw societies in which, although the state initially granted participation to almost everyone in the exploitation of nature, the new nexus was not based on social consensus and cohesion" (119).

What was the cost of these experiences? Is it possible to isolate a variable that explains what gave rise to many Leftist governments in Latin America and the Caribbean—governments that challenged the United States and neoliberalism? Governments that initially wanted to banish representative democracy with new, rejuvenated and tempting formulas ended with many liabilities, including *personalismo*, informality, voluntarism, polarization, public-private corruption, and steep economic decline (Mazzuca 2013; Mainwaring and Pérez-Liñan 2013).

Economic Crisis

In the twenty-first century, Venezuela has experienced a constant economic crisis, particularly from 2014 on. It went from being in the 45th place in the world economy in 2014 to the 90th place in 2020—a precipitous decline. After several years of unstable behavior, economists wondered what had happened. Was the crisis the product of the bankruptcy of the rentier model, the government's statist control policy, the decline of the oil industry, the United States' economic sanctions, or excessive corruption? All of these factors were involved.

Regarding the Venezuelan economy, a look at its national accounts and economic data provides a very negative picture. Beginning in 2014, GDP has contracted, and the contraction continues to grow. In 2014, Venezuela's GDP growth rate was -3.9 percent; in 2015, -6.21 percent; in 2016, -16.5 percent; in 2017, -15.7 percent; in 2018, -19.6 percent; and in 2019, -35 percent (Focus Economics 2020). For 2020, the Economic Commission for Latin America and the Caribbean (CEPAL, in Spanish) estimates that it will be around -26.1 percent (CEPAL 2020a), while other sources give it as still higher, -30 percent (Knoema 2021). International reserves were at a low and decreasing level: $9.9 billion in September 2017, $7.7 billion of which were gold reserves; they were $6.3 billion for 2020. As for inflation, in 2017 it was around 438.1 percent; in 2018, it was 65,374.1, closing at 19,906 percent in 2019 and 2,355.2 percent in 2020 (Knoema 2021).

Along with this, there has been a progressive devaluation of the bolívar in the parallel market. At the end of October 2019, it stood at 22,000 per dollar and, in August 2020, at 268,000 per dollar. As of September 2021, the bolívar stood at 4,100,000 per dollar. Moreover, the unemployment rate stood at 35.5 percent in 2018 (Knoema 2021), and 65 percent in 2020.

In terms of foreign trade, 2006 marked a steep decline in bilateral trade. In 2015, Venezuela showed little change compared to 2012 (the last positive cycle of the Venezuelan economy). The Venezuelan trade balance stood at US $43.1 billion in 2017; $41.8 in 2018; $19.8 in 2019; and $9.6 in 2020. It is estimated to be $8.6 billion in 2020, taking into account the impact of the COVID-19 pandemic (CEPAL 2020b). The export of goods from Venezuela to the United States amounted to $32.1 billion in 2017; in 2018, $31.2; and in 2019, $14.6. In 2020, Venezuelan imports from the United States accounted for $14.4 billion (28 percent of total Venezuelan imports of goods and services in that year), demonstrating the importance of trade between the United States and Venezuela. In 2017, Venezuelan trade was about $11 billion; in 2018, $10.6; and in 2019, $5.2 billion. For 2020, exports are calculated to be around $5 billion and imports in the range of $3.6 billion (CEPAL 2020a).

These changes are due to the decline in the price of oil per barrel as well as in oil production, cash-flow problems at PDVSA, the loss of the US market under president Donald Trump, the increase in external debt (estimated at about $250 billion, including PDVSA debt), and the reduction of foreign direct investment (FDI), estimated at $3.7 billion by 2015 (CEPAL 2020a). According to Berry (2016), Venezuela is "a near basket case because of government mismanagement of economic policy." As Zahler (2017, 6) sums it up: "At this point, in this large country blessed with natural wealth, there is no corner that can escape the spreading indigence." Abject hunger, malnutrition, and crime were the result, pushing Venezuelans to leave their country across the border to Colombia or Brazil, on foot to Central America through the Panamanian jungle, or overseas to the United States, Spain, and Chile. A country that was once a haven for immigrants escaping repression and intolerance in the Old World now sees its people fleeing. In *El Universal*, Olivares (2014) underscores that this diaspora was caused by "the deterioration of both the economy and the social fabric, rampant crime, uncertainty and lack of hope for a change in leadership in the near future." Data from the UN High Commissioner for Refugees (2020) tell us that from a population of 28.9 million in 2019, over 5.4 million Venezuelans are now living abroad–around 18.7 percent of the population. Most of these people are highly educated, but those fleeing also include working class and poor people. Data from the 2019 American Community Survey put the number of Venezuelans living in the United States at 549,256—triple the number of 184,039 in 2010 (US Census Bureau, American Community Survey, 2019). The neighborhood of Doral, outside of Miami, Florida, holds the highest concentration, and is now jokingly called Doralzuela.

Why so much pessimim regarding Venezuela's economy? Because the decline is real. From 2013 to 2017, following Chávez's death, the country saw its main dollar income reduced by more than half, given the fall in oil revenues and the near paralysis in oil production. Add to that the external debt payments, increasing inflation, a strong devaluation of the bolívar, and the increase in unemployment (CEPAL 2020a). What was once a country at the top of Latin America's economies, and a hope for the future, has now become a nation that people flee, seeking a decent life abroad.

President Maduro tried to get around the situation by generating more monetary liquidity, manipulating the price of the dollar, "burning" the international reserves, selling assets, opening the dollar market, and looking for long-term international loans with low interest rates. In addition, the government has allowed a parallel economy to thrive: a black market that supplies 60 percent of goods and services. The resulting economic decline is steep. It robs most Venezuelans of the right to a decent life.

Venezuela's Present and Future

While the armed forces in Latin America have participated in wars against other nations on only a few occasions, their participation in the domestic political process has always been crucial. It has taken various forms, from tutelage of nascent civic republics to direct participation in the formation of military governments and military dictatorships, to coups d'état, military uprisings, and other forms of institutional pressure. Some *caudillos* either used the military in their favor or lost the support they provided (Burggraff and Millet 1995).

The literature on comparative politics in the region has paid a great deal of attention to the role of the military in politics, emphasizing their different forms of participation and their relationship with civilian politicians (whether democratic or not). The emphasis has been on their institutional participation in the structure of the state: training, equipment, security, and, above all, their role as a pressure group (Manrique 1996).

With the advent of the Cuban Revolution in 1959, the role of the armed

Figure 3.3. Venezuela's history and culture, collage by Ivonne Ferrer, Miami, Florida, 2020.

forces took an important turn in their politicization and closeness to Leftist ideology. Long before the Cuban case, in Latin American there were numerous instances of military populism: in Brazil under Getulio Vargas, in Argentina under Juan Domingo Perón, in Peru under Manuel Odría, in Venezuela the attempts of two Left-wing military uprisings in 1962, and in the Dominican Republic in 1965 (Burggraff and Millet 1995). In a radically different way, the armed forces also participated in the establishment of conservative governments, civil or military, amid accusations regarding human rights violations, the exclusion of certain political sectors, and the "colonization" of the institution by conservative movements. Cuba was different in that the old career military disappeared in the wake of the revolution, identified as it was with Fulgencio Batista's dictatorship and forces. This led to the creation of the new, revolutionary armed forces, the FAR (Fuerzas Armadas Revolucionarias). They formed a symbiosis with the leaders of the revolution, who mixed their political and military roles, particularly in the figure of Raúl Castro, who, as minister of defense for 49 years (from 1959 to 2008), guaranteed his brother Fidel the loyalty of the military (Sucre-Heredia 2016).

As in the rest of the region, both de jure and de facto military power were fundamental to explain the various periods through which the republic developed, from the break with Spain in the nineteenth century onward. Even Simón Bolívar, a military man, could not reconcile the political interests of the civilians who assisted him in gaining independence with the interests of the military caste. Statesman that he was, Bolívar still could not achieve their balance when forming independent republics. For example, from 1818 to 1830, he sought to give Colombia a stable foundation for a republic through a strong and unified alliance among Nueva Granada (later, Colombia) and Quito (later, Ecuador). This project earned him much appreciation internationally, but it was also the most vulnerable to the clash between democratic and authoritarian currents—a crucial contradiction that continues to this day (Trinkunas 2004).

In Venezuela, various politicians promoted a political model that involved greater military presence in the government's functions, compared to countries with a stronger civilian tradition. After several governments of *caudillos* that involved few civil intervals, Juan Vicente Gómez led the country between 1908 and 1935. His long reign made him a major focus in the study of Latin American dictatorships, not only in the social sciences but also in literature (Manrique 1996).

Gómez's death was followed by a period of military governments maintaining power with civilian support, which provided a timid opening for the democratic effort that ended with the civic-military coup in 1945. That coup gave way to a frustrated democratic interregnum until another military coup in November 1948, the leaders of which held power until 1958, when the dictator Marcos Pérez-Jiménez was overthrown (Butto 2012). In a few months, a group of civilians and soldiers restored and stabilized the democratic system, based on the Puntofijo Pact, and ousted Pérez-Jiménez (Manrique 1996). Thereafter, until 1999, an elected democratic government was installed, and the role of the armed forces was subjected to norms and procedures that allowed it to act positively as a faithful arbiter. This did not mean, however, that the military presence in the Venezuelan political scene between 1958 and 1999 was invariably institutional and impeccably loyal to democracy. After 1958, attempts at military insurrection in 1958 and in 1960 and two important military attempted coups d'état, known as *el Carupanazo* and *el Porteñazo*, occurred in April and June 1962, respectively. Military officers and subofficers together with civilian political leaders of the most important Leftist parties in the country (the PCV and the MIR) chose the path of armed struggle, bolstered by Cuba's support (Garrido 1999).

A turning point in Venezuela's military history came with the attempted military coups of February and November 1992, in which Chávez participated. After more than three decades of political stability in the country and a military that played an institutional role, close to half the officers and troops committed themselves to these movements, which shook not only the basis of the political system but also the future the military had envisioned (Burggraff and Millet 1995). Hugo Chávez and his allies arrived on the political scene as an antisystem officialdom. In deciding to participate in the 1998 presidential elections, they presented the country with a government program that provided a different role on two levels. First, the military movement of 1992 had become an alliance between Left-wing military and civilians with Left-wing parties and even anti-party sectors—a heterogeneous electoral alliance contrary to the Puntofijo Pact designed in 1958. Second, the military would no longer be just the loyal arbiter of the regime, but an active part of it, keeping and developing privileges and economic gains, interwoven with ideological commitment (Garrido 1999).

Thereafter, the government systematically purged the military of those who did not agree with that perspective. At the same time, the government gave officers who supported the regime responsible occupations in the state bureaucracy and state enterprises. This drew the attention of specialists who analyzed the military's new role, given that it had relied on Cuba's advice since the attempted coup in 1992. In 1994, when Cuba received Hugo Chávez in Havana, with honors as head of state, the link between the Cuban government and the Venezuelan military establishment became evident. In truth, this connection dated back to 1962 (Trinkunas 2004).

As of 2021, after so many years and several military crises, the most dramatic of which was the ephemeral civil-military coup d'état against Hugo Chávez in 2002, the country is living through its worst political crisis, hand in hand with a deep economic crisis, and the international community's alienation, led by the United States.

In this historical framework, the armed forces have ratified their support for the Bolivarian revolution. The crisis strengthened the civic-military union. It has ignored the calls of the opposition and numerous foreign governments who oppose it and indicate the need to begin a political transition. Once again, the armed forces serve as the faithful arbiter of Venezuelan politics (Sucre-Heredia 2016; Trinkunas 2004).

What is the forecast for Venezuela's future? Regarding the economy, it depends on different sectors that operate simultaneously: the subsidized economy, the black market dollar economy, and the informal economy. There is also the institutional economy, which depends on public spending, legal exports and imports, foreign direct investment, and external debt. The government still has dollars, international reserves, and the loan portfolio under control, but it has not been able to stop the enormous growth of the black market, where goods and services are obtained through corruption, cronyism, clandestine overpayment, smuggling, and other illegal practices common in other highly centralized governments worldwide (Corrales and Penfold 2015). In addition, there is the increase in government purchases that closed at a very high level in 2016—60 percent of total imports, accompanied by a sudden gain in the public and private financial system, given the high and evident monetary liquidity (CEPAL 2020a). Moreover, the recent United States' financial sanctions against Maduro's government, PDVSA, and other public banks and enterprises also affects the forecast.

Venezuela's economic situation generates much controversy and various forecasts. Despite divergences, all agree that the country has now reached a real crisis that cannot be resolved unless the basis and instruments of economic policy are rearranged. The macroeconomic picture shows that the balance of payments has a shortage of foreign exchange, a high rate of inflation, and poor economic growth, and that the rent-seeking model has now collapsed (Berry 2016; Bull and Rosales 2020).

Venezuela's future is both uncertain and contradictory. The cards are stacked against a negotiated transition to democracy (Marsteintredet 2020)—uncertain because it is not possible to determine what will happen in the coming months and years. While the government still holds onto power, its stability is in danger. In the meantime, other social processes increasingly play a role: the drug trafficking; the massive exodus of Venezuelans now scattered in a diaspora; and the growing collaboration of the government with Russia and China, as well as Cuba (Hirst et al. 2020).

Of even greater concern, US president Donald Trump threatened to use severe sanctions. Some American decision-makers even indicated that a military invasion led by the Americans is possible (United Press International 2017). In his remarks before the United Nations' 2017 Annual Assembly, Trump asserted that "the socialist dictatorship of Nicolas Maduro has inflicted terrible pain and suffering on the good people of that country." He went on to add that "this corrupt regime destroyed a prosperous nation by imposing a failed ideology that has produced poverty and misery everywhere it has been tried." Moreover, he added, "the Venezuelan people are starving, and their country is collapsing. Their democratic institutions are being destroyed. This situation is completely unacceptable, and we cannot stand by and watch." He concluded: "The United States has taken important steps to hold the regime accountable. We are prepared to take further action if the government of Venezuela continues its path to impose authoritarian rule on the Venezuelan people." While Trump lost the presidency, his sanctions remain in place.

Addressing the question of how populism turns authoritarian, Fisher and Taub (2017) contend that Venezuela exhibits the worst-case outcome of populist governance: institutions have been so crippled that crime is rampant, corruption is nearly universal, and the quality of life has collapsed. Thus, according to Murillo (2016, 6), "the tension created by elections is that majoritarian mandates are often used to confirm plebiscitarian leadership, although minority presidents have also chosen that political style when relying on decrees and concentrating executive power to build electoral majorities."

In a highly polarized society, the explanations for this crisis vary widely.

The external factors (the drop in prices, the embargo) helped, but the problems were mostly caused by internal factors (the domestic economic policies Chávez imposed). The expanding state control of the economy and the restrictions on the private sector are, as in Cuba, a huge cause of the decline.

According to the government and the ruling party, the crisis is due to an economic war. Bolton (2016), then national security advisor to Donald Trump, underscored in his assessment of the various explanations that "the crisis is the result of economic mismanagement and the ideological rigidity of the country's 'authoritarian' Chavista-led government" (in Bull and Rosales 2020).

In either case, the Bolivarian Revolution is in the process of a historic shift. It is clear that the regime no longer enjoys the popular support that it did during Chávez's years. As Levine (2017, 2) aptly describes the situation: "Venezuela is in the midst of a protracted, bitter, often violent, and sometimes deadly struggle to determine what kind of society and government it will have and what kind of future Venezuelans can hope for." The regime wants, above all, to stay in power: "Its principal leaders and enablers (army, national guard, police and political police, and paramilitaries) fear a loss of power which would limit their access to goods and funds, and make them vulnerable to legal and political processes, for example, for violations of human rights, corruption, or drug trafficking." Thus, the authoritarian competitive model has become an authoritarian corporate model, especially since the Maduro government created a brand-new National Constituent Assembly in July 2017, to draft and approve a new Constitution. In effect, it meant to take away the powers of the National Assembly that was under the control of the opposition since 2015. This heavy-handed move only sparked more protests. The opposition is trying to confront el Chavismo by attempting to remove the president by legal and constitutional means, holding new elections, freeing political prisoners, "and restarting the economy by loosening controls and reopening international ties." Moreover, in the last two years, an ad hoc coalition of countries in the region has formed that is opposed to the Chavista regime led by Nicolás Maduro; rather, they accept the president of the National Assembly elected in 2015, Juan Guaidó, as the legitimate representative of Venezuela. This coalition was endorsed by the United States, the Lima Group, and the OAS. In September 2019, this coalition was reinforced by the Inter-American Treaty of Reciprocal Assistance (TIAR) to analyze the case in question.

Beginning in August 2021, in Mexico City, with the support of Norway, a new cycle of talks and eventually some negotiations and agreements began to take place between Maduro's government and a large part of the democratic opposition. After two meetings, the two sides agreed to a common position toward the territorial dispute with Guyana and a common health policy. However, disagreements remain on electoral and judiciary matters—the kernel of democracy.

At present, one can observe a growing internationalization of the Venezuelan crisis. On the one hand, a strategic situation prevails between the interests of the United States and its regional allies who do not want to allow the political and military presence of intermediate powers in the region. Nor do they want to allow the alliances taking place between Maduro's regime and a significant number of countries, such as China, Russia, Turkey, and Iran. On the other hand, the arrival of a growing economy of unregulated mineral extraction has had repercussions in the countries bordering Venezuela via the smuggling, drug trafficking, and human trafficking of people. Amid this, the Venezuelan exodus has become the largest in the history of the region. Estimates say that more than 5.4 million Venezuelans have left the country, particularly affecting their neighbors (UNHCR 2020). The COVID-19 pandemic arrived to accompany these crises, affecting all social life in Latin America and the Caribbean (CEPAL 2020b).

In September 2020, an independent committee of the UN Human Rights Council evaluated the situation of human rights in Venezuela, and recommended that the case be taken before the International Criminal Court. As president of the National Assembly, Juan Guaidó called for the Responsibility to Protect (R2P) thesis and for the reactivation by the US government of the sanctions and threats against the Maduro regime. Maduro, however, refused to move the date of the parliamentary elections on December 6, 2020, and the popular review on December 12, knowing the majority of the opposition would not participate in that electoral event (Hirst et al. 2020). Nonetheless, the results change neither the political picture not the economic crisis. The ruling PSUV party obtained 70 percent of the valid votes and 253 deputies; the opposition obtained only 30 percent of the valid votes and 21 deputies—a clear imbalance of forces. These results were deemed fraudulent by over 40 governments, the Lima Group, the European Union, the OAS, the International Contact Group, and a significant part of the media and social networks, as well as nongovernmental organizations. Abstention was very high both in the parliamentary elections of December

6 and the review of December 12: fully 70 percent. Given the depth of the crisis, people try to distance themselves from the political life, as most polls anticipated. However, the opposition review process motivated some people to become militants, and a small mobilization did take place.

In the new framework in the United States, with the victory of the Democratic presidential candidate, Joe Biden, together with the results of the legislative elections in Venezuela supporting the official results, the future of Venezuela is now under speculation. Clearly, the control the regime has over the country has increased, reducing the possibilities for a short-term change. Paradoxically, this allows for a greater rapprochement between the regime and the moderate opposition. As elsewhere, the Venezuela opposition is diverse. The moderate opposition is composed of Voluntad Popular, Primero Justicia, AD, and Un Nuevo Tiempo, among other organizations that support the leadership of Juan Guaidó and Leopoldo López, under the patronage of the United States. A "loyal opposition" also exists that remains close to the present government and that participated in the parliamentary elections of December 6. A radical opposition also exists on the Right, under the leadership of María Corina Machado and Antonio Ledezma, who believe that regime change can only result from applying force. The radical opposition continues to cling to the geopolitical vision propagated by former president Trump and his advisors for Latin America and Venezuela, including a possible military invasion.

Analysts do not expect that the Biden administration will soon resume the dialogue with Cuba for a renormalization of their relations, closer to what they were under Obama's administration. It is also not likely that the Biden administration will seek to make the sanctions against the Maduro regime more flexible, conditioning them to specific internal changes. However, Biden will face strong Republican opposition in the Senate, in the swing state of Florida, and from the Cuban-Venezuelan lobby that Trump's election boosted. Maduro's regime may seek to defend itself from the charge that it is moving toward full authoritarianism. The opposition may well enter into a political labyrinth. We will see whether it will continue to oppose the regime by extending Guaidó's mandate or whether it will seek to negotiate an electoral solution to the crisis (Hirst et al. 2020). At present, there is *ni paz ni pan*—neither peace nor bread (Romero 2017). More than Venezuela's future hangs in the balance.

II

Cuba's and Venezuela's International Relations

4

Cuba's Foreign Policy

Large Presence, Few Resources

Cuba's Old and New Goals

"Principles are not negotiable," said Fidel Castro during the second Congress of the Communist Party in 1980. This phrase sums up what many analysts see as the cornerstone of Cuban foreign policy: its proletarian internationalism and anti–status quo international behavior (F. Castro 1980).

A study of Cuban foreign policy must begin by distinguishing its two prongs. One prong is Cuba's active foreign policy as part of its long political, economic, and military alliance with, first, the Soviet Union and, thereafter, with Venezuela. The other is Cuba's work to advance the global Leftist movement (Blasier and Mesa-Lago 1979; Domínguez 1978a; Mesa-Lago 1971, 1978; Pérez-Stable 2006; Alzugaray-Treto 2009). Relations between Cuba and the Left in the rest of the world are closely linked with the local role of Leftist parties, movements, and individuals in the world political process. The alliance with the former Soviet Union placed Cuba on the geopolitical stage during the Cold War (Thomas 1971; Blasier 1976, 1983; Brenner et al., 2015; Domínguez 2006). For some years after, its notion of proletarian internationalism dictated Cuba's foreign policy when it sought to determine military outcomes in various African countries. Recently, Cuba changed the way it tries to influence other countries. Its support for revolution has declined while its support for democratic backsliding has increased. Cuba now supports semidemocratic governments that arrived at the helm of political power through democratic elections with a mix of state-run and private economies. In addition, both Cuba and Venezuela now have strong ties with authoritarian governments outside this hemisphere (e.g., China). With Venezuela, there is also strong support for illicit trade, particularly in drugs.

One should not forget that Cuba, though the largest island in the Caribbean, is a small country. As of 2019, the population was 11.2 million and an area of 109,880 km² (42,426 mi²); as such, it is one-third the size of Venezuela's population of 28.9 million, which has a vaster territory, of 916,445 km² (353,841 mi²). However, Cuba has a large presence and regional prestige. As Vital (1971, 77) expresses it, for many years Cuba became "an alternative for governments whose disconnection of the West is the most natural and essential symbol of change." Due to the prestige of the revolutionary process, as well as the stature of Fidel Castro, the defense of the Cuban revolution contributed to creating a political model that was constantly being judged, by both supporters and detractors. Cuba needed to influence its own region, to get support for its own security, and to avoid isolation. The United States and its allies interpreted this in a manner that fluctuated from wanting the country to thrive to promoting its isolation. Avoiding these claims was a revolutionary objective, and the Cubans used diplomatic and political instruments with partisan and ideological goals (Domínguez 1978b, 2004).

One needs to understand the difference between the formal objectives and realistic goals involved in Cuba's foreign policy. The main objectives were:

1) promoting anti-imperialism;
2) allying itself with the Third World, Latin America, and the Caribbean;
3) inserting itself into the world socialist movement through its alliance with the Soviet Union (until 1990); and
4) promoting revolution (Alzugaray-Treto 2009, 2012; Suárez-Salazar 2009; Falcoff 2003; Domínguez 1978a).

Vital (1971), in his *The Inequality of States*, asks whether a small state without protection could really achieve an independent foreign policy. That was Cuba's dilemma for many years: how to achieve an autonomous path within the hegemony of the Soviet Union. From the strategic point of view, Cuba managed to establish a defense system capable of reducing its vulnerability and extending its territorial deterrence. From the standpoint of the economy, Cuban diplomacy established a beneficial relationship of trade with the Soviet Union and the Eastern European countries; they also promoted the exiles' sending remittances to Cuba. Moreover,

Cuban diplomacy sought a beneficial trade relationship with the Soviet Union (until its collapse in 1990) and Venezuela (from 1999 on), even in the midst of the economic embargo imposed by the United States, its historical partner (until 1960). Many who doubted the viability of the Cuban model were long-time critics; others supported the revolution from its inception (Alzugaray-Treto 2009, 2012; Romero 2009; Pérez-Villanueva 2009; Domínguez 1978a; Falcoff 2003).

Cuba's economy is extremely dependent on foreign trade and special economic relations. While sugar rose to become 80 percent of Cuban exports for many years, the basket of exports is more varied today, as it now includes the service sector, particularly Cuban professionals (e.g., doctors, nurses, ophthalmologists) who are working abroad in professional and technical assistance programs. From 1960 to 2003, the Soviet Union and Russia were Cuba's main trading partners, with over 50 percent of its imports and exports. Today, Venezuela holds first place, though China is becoming a contender (Mesa-Lago 2019a; Pérez-López 2017; Pérez-Villanueva 2009). Always it has been a case of dependent development, as specified by Cardoso and Faletto (1977) long ago.

Until 1959, Cuba's relations with the United States shaped its economy. In truth, Cuba was a US-subsidized economy that depended on sugar exports to the American market and imports of American-manufactured goods and services. A popular phrase in the nineteenth century was "Without sugar there is no nation." Cuba was a leading sugar producer for the entire world. This dynamic sector of the economy promoted a cosmopolitan urban life; an emerging manufacturing sector; vibrant small businesses; and good indexes of health, education, employment, and consumption. Cuba was not poor when the revolution arrived, but it was a typical case of growth without development. The monoculture of sugar characterized its economy, along with the presence of a single trade partner, and an unfair income distribution (Mesa-Lago 2012).

The leaders of the revolution sought to overcome these problems, but, after 62 years in power, they have not done so. Most of the efforts to overcome this economic dependence have failed. These include the implementation of an industrial model from 1960 to 1963, the return to the sugar industry in 1963, the "revolutionary offensive" confiscating the small businesses in 1968, the Rectification Process of 1986–90, and other economic experiments (Mesa-Lago 2012).

In the late 1970s and 1980s, the Cuban economy experienced a positive cycle of economic growth, resulting from the expansion of new products for export (nickel, citric fruits, pharmaceuticals); the arrival of international private financing under the direction of the Paris Club; and the flow of foreign direct investment, especially in tourism. However, these peaks were cyclical. Negative cycles of economic decline were due to the fall in the price of sugar and nickel; the disappearance of the Soviet Union's subsidies after 1990; the demise of COMECON, the Eastern European common market; the growth of an enormous external debt; and the rigid US embargo (Mesa-Lago 2012).

The worst period for Cuba's economy was in the early 1990s, after the Berlin Wall fell in 1989 and the Soviet Union collapsed. With his oratorical flair, Fidel Castro euphemistically called it "a special period in a time of peace." Since then, both among Cubans in the island and academics everywhere, these years became known as "the special period." Yet, in truth, it was the harshest economic crisis the country had ever lived through. In just four years, from 1989 to 1993, GDP contracted by -35 percent, close to three-quarters of foreign trade was lost, the deficit shot up to 30 percent of GDP, and professionals and technicians left en masse. Cubans experienced a dramatic decline in personal consumption that for most resulted in constant hunger and illness (Mesa-Lago 1978; Mesa-Lago and Pérez-López 2013; Pérez-Villanueva 2009). With its ties to the Eastern European world totally severed, Cuba also became remarkably isolated.

From the beginning of the revolution, Cuba established a bridge with many countries in Latin America. However, in 1962, Havana had diplomatic relations only with Mexico. In the late 1960s and early 1970s, Cuba reestablished relations with Chile and Peru, as well as with Barbados, Jamaica, Guyana, and Trinidad and Tobago. Diplomatic relations with Venezuela returned in 1974, as did relations with other countries in the region. Fidel Castro traveled to Chile, Peru, Ecuador, Jamaica, and Guyana, establishing diplomatic ties and trade. After the events in the island of Grenada (when the Leftist, pro-Cuba government was overthrown in 1983 and American troops invaded the tiny island) and the crisis of the Sandinistas in Nicaragua (when the Leftist, pro-Cuba government in power since 1979 lost the presidential elections in 1989), Cuba expanded its connections with democratic governments. Gradually, it resumed diplomacy with Argentina, Brazil, and Peru. At present, most Latin American countries have relations with Cuba.

At the turn of the twenty-first century, Leftist regimes resurged, particularly in Latin America and the Caribbean. In Venezuela, the Bolivarian Revolution developed, which entailed a strategic alliance between Cuba and Venezuela. Thus, Cuba's foreign policy managed to regain what it had lost over 40 years earlier and to expand its international activism. In 2006, the 14th Summit of the Non-Aligned Movement took place in Havana, just when the leadership transition from Fidel to Raúl Castro was taking place. In June 2009, the 39th General Assembly of the OAS took place in San Pedro Sula, Honduras, where they decided to do away with the 1962 resolution that excluded Cuba from the OAS (although Cuba did not accept that proposal). Cuba also benefited from the presence of governments like Venezuela's and other Leftist governments at the time, in Argentina, Bolivia, Brazil, Dominica, Ecuador, Guatemala, Honduras, Nicaragua, Saint Vincent and the Grenadines, Uruguay, Paraguay, and El Salvador. In short, Cuba expanded its regional as well as its international presence both bilaterally and multilaterally (in the UN, and as part of ALBA, and CARICOM). Venezuela's aid was critical, as it constituted a major injection of foreign capital in the primary Cuban industries of energy, tourism, and nickel. It was a strategic trade alliance.

From 1994 until 2003, some reforms aimed to open the economy. However, many of these measures were restricted or cancelled under the ideological debate called "the battle of ideas" that took hold in 2004–5, which strengthened the Cuban socialist economy. The government then devalued the Cuban national currency, the peso, and launched the CUP, the *peso convertible*, with a rate of 25 CUP for a US dollar (though with a penalty of $0.83 per US dollar—a penalty that lasted until 2020). Thereafter, the dual currency fluctuated, leading to an intense debate regarding the scope of equality in Cuba. Cuba ended the dual monetary system in January 2021, eliminating the CUC that had been traded 1 to 1 with the US dollar, and devalued the peso to a fixed rate of 24 pesos for 1 dollar. While in the long term this is expected to be beneficial, in the short term it has led to enormous inflation in prices, which is damaging to those who live there and can scarcely find or afford food or pay for their electricity.

In 2006, Cuba began a process of gradual change, through the economic reforms Raúl Castro undertook when he was in power until Fidel Castro's death in November 2016. The hope was that those reforms, together with the new measures taken by the Obama administration, would result in greater openness of the economy. However, since 2016 the reforms have either stagnated or been reversed (Mesa-Lago 2019a).

In 2000, the United States also undertook a number of measures facilitating trade between the two countries, especially after the case of the *balserito* Elián González. On Thanksgiving, fishermen found the young child at sea. His mother had tied him to an inner tube before she slipped away to her death by drowning. Dramatically, dolphins surrounded him. Many in the Cuban American community saw the event as portending a different future, the end of communism; many in the island perceived it as another treason by the Americans, who now wanted to keep the Cuban child. A crisis ensued when Elián's Miami family insisted in keeping him in the United States, though his father back in Cuba insisted on their returning him to Cuba. In the end, under Bill Clinton's presidency, the US government stepped in and seized the child by force, returning him to his father, who waited for him in Washington, DC (Pedraza 2007).

The crisis of the young rafter resulted in a softening of the US embargo toward Cuba, as Congress voted in the Trade Sanctions Reform and Export Enhancement Act, or TSRA (Mesa-Lago 2012; Alonso and Vidal 2013; Pedraza 2007). Today, Cuba's main trading partners are, for imports, Venezuela, the European Union, China, Brazil, Canada, Mexico, and the United States; and, for exports, the European Union, Canada, China, Venezuela, Guyana, Belize, and Brazil (Schöllmann 2015).

Cuba–US Relations

Relations between Cuba and the United States can be divided into several stages. The first was from 1959 to 1961, when the relationship deteriorated due to Cuba's internal dynamics, culminating in a total break in economic and political relations. The second was from 1961 to 1970, when Washington was concerned about Cuba's efforts to expand its revolution to Latin America and the Caribbean, especially through Ché Guevara. The third stage was from 1970 to 1985, when the key issue was the Cuban-Soviet global partnership and the island's proletarian internationalism. The fourth stage was from 1985 to 1999, when the United States focused its interests on Cuban domestic affairs. The fifth stage was from 2000 to 2016, when Cuba returned to the regional scene, making new friends with other Leftist governments. The sixth stage was from 2016 to 2017, with Obama's reopening of diplomatic relations and a significant rapprochement between Washington and Havana beginning in December 2014 (Alzugaray-Treto 2012; Suárez-Salazar 2009; Blasier 1976; Falcoff 2003). A final stage began in January 2017 with Trump's efforts to roll back Obama's measures that favored the Cuban people in the island and in exile (R. Rodríguez 2017). A new stage has opened beginning in January 2021 with the presidency of Joe Biden, who partially rolled back Trump's santions.

Both the United States and the Soviet Union carefully monitored the development of the Cuba Revolution. Surely, it was not easy to lead a revolution in a country so close and so tied to the United States. Ironically, Fidel Castro's triumph rolled in the "democratic wave," when the fall of some military regimes led to the establishment of an increasing number of democratic regimes in Latin America (W. Smith 1987). From 1959 to 1961, Cuba nationalized American companies operating on the island and challenged US foreign policy toward it. Washington suspended the Cuban sugar quota as well as the export of goods and services to the island. In January 1961, Washington severed diplomatic relations with Fidel Castro's regime and, in April of that year, the US government supported the exile invasion of the Bay of Pigs. Thereafter, they traded the exiles imprisoned from the invasion for food and medicine.

When Cuba openly proclaimed itself a socialist nation, it began a special relationship with the Soviet Union. At the same time, the United States defined the Cuban problem as a regional one and aimed to sever Cuba's hemispheric ties. Early in 1962, Cuba was expelled from the OAS, and the United States declared the unilateral economic embargo of Cuba, prohibiting the entry of Cuban products into the country. In October 1962, the Cuban Missile Crisis took place, during which Washington declared a naval blockade of the island. As Pérez Jr. (2015, 298) points out, "After 1962, Cuba pursued an ambitious foreign policy. It extended moral and material support to guerrilla movements across Latin America—in Guatemala, Colombia, Venezuela, Peru, and Bolivia." Cuba pressed its claim for leadership in the Third World.

From the mid-1960s on, Cuba's proletarian internationalism expanded its reach to various parts of the world, particularly in Angola, Mozambique, and Ethiopia. Cuban militancy peaked in 1963 with the establishment of OLAS (Organization of Latin American Solidarity) and the Tricontinental in Havana with its support of several anticolonial wars in Africa, Asia, and the Middle East. As Eduardo Torres-Cuevas (2019) stresses, Fidel Castro's achievement was to place Third World concerns squarely within the Cold War. Cubans actively supported the MPLA. In 1967, Ché Guevara's attempt to spread the anti-capitalist guerrilla movement to Latin America ended

Figure 4.1. The migration of refugees whose exodus is motivated by both political and economic conditions in their homeland can result in waves of migration that are quite distinct in their social composition. Here is a family of Cuban refugees from the first wave of the Cuban exodus, resettled by the International Rescue Committee, ca. 1961. (Photo by Christine Da Cruz via the International Rescue Committee).

when he died in Bolivia, nearly alone, without the direct aid of the Cuban government or the Bolivian military. Müller (2014) notes that El Ché's total isolation is evident in his diary. Certainly, the poor peasants of the altiplano neither answered his call nor came to his rescue. Yet people in Cuba venerate him today as a martyr of the revolution and the legendary hero that schoolchildren are taught to emulate. Toward the end of the decade, Cuban activism in the Third World waned, as Pérez Jr. (2015) highlights, and people in Cuba turned to the reorganization of the economy, particularly after the failed attempt in 1970 to make the 10 million tons of sugar harvest on which, Fidel insisted, the honor of the nation rested.

Early in the history of the revolution, the US government froze Cuban assets and prohibited further financial transactions between the two countries. Moreover, Washington threatened to punish countries that traded with Cuba. In addition, tension ensued regarding the perimeter of the US naval base at Guantanamo, which was still inside Cuban territory (López-Segrera 1989). In 1964, the United States supported the OAS's resolution to declare a diplomatic and economic boycott of Cuba, after which the tensions between the two neighbors again escalated. The United States also engaged in a "secret war" against the Cuban regime. Further, it banned Americans and Cuban Americans from visiting the island and sending remittances to relatives living in Cuba.

From 1970 on, the situation began to open up. The United States' concern regarding Cuba entailed more issues. As the tide of revolutionary governments ebbed in Latin America and the Caribbean and the Cuban-Soviet alliance was consolidated, the United States insistently linked the issue of Cuba with other major points of interest when it negotiated with the Soviet Union (Blasier and Mesa-Lago 1979; Domínguez 1978a). Paradoxically, these were the first steps to resume contact between the two governments. In 1973, Cuba and the United States signed an agreement on aircraft, maritime, and other crimes—the first official bilateral contract for both countries since 1961. In 1974, the US government allowed American companies to sell their products and services to the Cuban government outside of American territory. In addition, they allowed Cuban diplomats in the United Nations to go beyond the 250 miles to which they had been restricted (W. Smith 1987).

Moreover, in July 1975, the OAS lifted the economic sanctions against Cuba that had been enacted in 1964. Although the United States voted in favor of that decision, its unilateral economic embargo against Cuba was not suspended. In 1976, regular US spy planes flights over Cuba were suspended, and, in 1977, President Jimmy Carter lifted the ban on American citizens visiting Cuba. Additionally, both countries signed an agreement regarding fisheries, the maritime boundary, and other matters. In Washington, DC, the Cuban Interests Section was opened in September 1977, attached to what was then the Czechoslovakian embassy (in the former building of the Cuban embassy). In Havana, the US Interests Section opened at the same time, attached to the Swiss embassy. Similarly, small boats could leave South Florida for Cuba legally for the first time since 1961, and a member of Cuba's Council of Ministers, Fernando Vecino, visited the United States with a Cuban university delegation in 1979.

In November 1978, a turning point in US-Cuba relations occurred: what became known as "the dialogue" between the Cuban government and representatives of the Cuban exile community took place in Havana. Despite enormous controversy within the Cuban American community, many of whom saw it as a betrayal, the effort bore fruit. One result was that both governments allowed Cuban Americans to travel to Cuba for family reunification visits, as well as some American journalists, academics, and politicians. Another was that the Cuban government agreed to the release of over 3,600 political prisoners in Cuba's jails, who the United States gradually processed and received (Pedraza 2007; W. Smith 1987). However, the situation worsened again, beginning with the discovery of a Soviet combat brigade in Cuba in 1979, which resulted in the United States reducing the migration as well as the recently developed commercial and humanitarian measures.

In 1980, a massive flotilla exodus ensued from the Cuban port of Mariel, the third major wave of the Cuban exodus. From April to September, over 125,000 Cubans came to the United States by sea, on boats sent by their Miami relatives, who were hoping to bring their family to the island. Toward the end of the outflow, this included Cuba's "social undesirables," whom Fidel Castro called *escoria* (scum). Cuban police forced many of them out of prisons and onto the boats for Miami. This resulted in a heated political controversy. Cuba uses prison terms for a number of reasons: for political prisoners, for those who simply challenge the state, and for criminals that any country would recognize as such. Thus, it was not always clear why those arriving had been in prison. Some were incarcerated for political reasons—what Amnesty International calls "prisoners of conscience." They became *plantados*, refusing to wear the uniform of the common criminals. Some were imprisoned because they challenged the state—deserting the military or being actively gay. Some were in prison for actual crimes, such as larceny, murder, robbery (Montgomery 1981; Pedraza 2007).

Under president Ronald Reagan, given his decisive anticommunist stance, Washington provided funding for the creation of Radio Martí and TV Martí, anti–Cuban government stations with radio programs opposing the revolution. Washington accused Cuba of resuming its revolutionary commitments in Grenada and Nicaragua and of cooperating with the guerrilla movement in El Salvador and Colombia (Domínguez 2006). The situation worsened again in 1982, when the secretary of state, Alexander Haig, and Cuba's vice president, Carlos Rafael Rodriguez, met in Mexico City—the first time since 1960 that two senior officials from both countries engaged in such talks. In April 1982, Vernon Walters, then US ambassador to the United Nations, visited Havana. After discussions with Fidel Castro and other senior officials regarding Cuba's role in the world, they felt that the probability of improved relations was low, despite Barbara Walters's landmark first interview of Fidel Castro in June 1977, "Fidel Castro Speaks." In Walters's interview, which aired on ABC News, Castro disclosed that he had been a communist from an early age, when he was studying law at the University of Havana. Furthermore, he blamed all of Cuba's ills and its lack of freedom on the US embargo. He also insisted that Cuba had intervened in Angola because the MPLA had asked for its help, to defend them from South Africa. He stressed that Russia "is the freest of all countries" but refused to acknowledge the enormous subsidy it gave Cuba (Walters 1977). As the *New York Times* reporter John J. O'Connor (1977) contends, Barbara Walters was at her best when she questioned, confronted, flattered, cajoled, laughed, and reprimanded Fidel.

The situation worsened again in 1982 when Washington intensified spy flights over Cuba and put in place a spy penetration program, expelled two Cuban diplomats assigned to the Cuban Interests Section in Washington, and dismissed Wayne Smith as head of the US Interests Section in Havana due to his firm opposition to US policy. Cuba was accused of being committed to international drug trafficking, the United States reintroduced the issue of Cuba's disdain for human rights, and Cuban diplomats were restricted from entry to the United States. The two countries suspended the migration agreements they had recently signed.

Nevertheless, some initiatives spelled collaboration. Cuba and the United States participated, together with Angola and South Africa, in peace talks in Angola. After the collapse of communism in the Soviet Union and Eastern Europe, Cuba withdrew its troops from Ethiopia in 1989, from Nicaragua in 1990, and from Angola in 1991. Cuba decided to downplay its presence in Africa and Central America as an ally of Leftist governments and political movements, as it had done in the 1960s when Ché Guevara tried to use guerrilla tactics in Latin America and Africa.

Furthermore, the arrival of a new American president in 1989 brought a new hardening of the line with Cuba. George H. W. Bush ordered the tightening of the economic embargo, and American policymakers deepened their contacts with Cuban exile activists. Ships that came from Cuba were banned from entering US ports; Latin American governments were again pressured to reduce their diplomatic and trade relations with Cuba; naval surveillance was intensified; and restrictions were put in place regarding travel to Cuba as well as sending remittances, clothes, food, and medicine. All of this took place in the midst of "the special period": the severe economic crisis in the island that brought so much suffering to the people there after the fall of Soviet and Eastern European communism (Leiva 2019; Brenner et al. 2015; Domínguez 2006).

The fate of the Soviet Union as a historical experience and the collapse of socialist regimes in Eastern Europe resulted in Washington intensifying the economic and political siege of Cuba through the Baker Memorandum of 1989, the Torricelli Act of 1992 (called the Cuban Democracy Act), and the Helms-Burton Act of 1996 (called the Cuban Liberty and Democratic Solidarity Act). Although they challenged the very existence of the Cuban Revolution, they did not have a real effect. Still, under Bill Clinton's presidency (1993–2001), the dramatic case of the *balserito* Elián González in 2000 ushered in Congress's vote to allow the sale, in cash, of food and medicine to Cuba. This commercial agreement is still in place; it made the United States into a major Cuban trading partner.

In turn, the Cuban government acted to prevent further setbacks, preventing the success of a series of human rights initiatives against Cuba in the United Nations, and achieving a majority of its members condemning the US embargo of Cuba—a vote that still obtains. At the same time, Cuban diplomats launched a diplomatic offensive in Latin America and the Caribbean for "normal" relations with most countries, without any ideological stigma. They were successful in doing away with the provisions that prevented charter flights to fly from the United States to Cuba. Moreover, they succeeded in raising the size of the remittances Cuban Americans could send to their relatives in the island ($1,200 per year). They also succeeded in further regulating the exodus of people who wanted to leave Cuba by legal means to live in the United States. Cuban authorities promoted foreign direct investment in the island from Canada, Spain, the Netherlands, and other capitalist economies. They also improved the diplomatic and trade relations with China, Vietnam, and Angola, that had suffered during the years when Cuba was a strong ally of the Soviet Union. Cuba additionally developed programs of cooperation and solidarity in education and health and prevented the European Union from exerting further pressure for human rights in the island (Alzugaray-Treto 2009).

Despite the reorientation of US foreign policy after the events of September 11, 2001, during the two presidencies of George H. W. Bush (2001–9),

Havana and Washington kept the status quo. Title III of the Helms-Burton Act (which prohibited foreign direct investment in Cuba from countries that had diplomatic relations with the United States) was, in effect, suspended. Moreover, the Migration Agreements of 1994–95's "wet foot/dry foot" policy remained in place. However, Cuban Americans' travel to Cuba was restricted to only once every three years. Furthermore, the US government appointed a Commission for Assistance to a Free Cuba, and a coordinator for the transition to democracy in Cuba in the State Department; they published two reports in 2003 and 2006.

During president Barack Obama's administration (2009–13, 2013–17), the balance can only be called positive. When asked to do away with the embargo, Obama rightly replied that only Congress could do so; however, economic, commercial, and consular measures were quickly adopted to make the embargo more flexible. The two governments also resumed bilateral talks on border and security issues along the coasts. In addition, funding for the Commission for Assistance to a Free Cuba was eliminated, as was the transition coordinator. Restrictions on Cuban Americans' travel to the island and their sending remittances were lifted. Nonetheless, Cuban American representatives in Congress thought that Obama had given away too much for too little, as he had not insisted on the release of the political prisoners.

In 2009, Cuba convicted a US citizen, Alan Gross, of espionage activities and sentenced him to 15 years in prison. The Cuban government finally liberated him in 2014. A major change for those in the island began in 2013–14, when Immigration Law 302 began to allow Cuban citizens to travel and return more freely, modifying substantially the very restrictive 1976 Immigration Law 1312. Since then, thousands have gone to visit their families in the United States, as well as Canada, Spain, and Latin America. The Cuban government stipulates that those who leave need to return to the island every two years or they lose their rights as citizens—their property, their health care. For many Cubans living abroad, especially those that are far from the island, as in Spain or Canada, this is an onerous requirement, as the travel is expensive, which prevents them from accumulating savings.

Yet Obama's administration did not break completely with the previous American discourse on Cuba. Washington denounced Cuba's negative handling of human rights, the massive arrest of political prisoners, the crackdown on internal dissent, and the absence of democracy. However, Cuba was pulled out of the list of terrorist countries; the controversial case of the

Figure 4.2. Like all immigrants, Cubans who settled in the United States continued their cultural practices. Here, Cuban Americans are playing dominoes, the most popular game in Cuba and in the Cuban American community, at a city park in Little Havana, Miami, Florida, December 18, 2016 (Photo by Fotoluminate LLC via Shutterstock).

Cuban exile Luis Posada-Carriles, the legendary anti-Castro activist, was frozen; and the five Cubans accused of spying in the United States were returned to the island after being imprisoned for some years. Both countries also reached some bilateral economic arrangements to ease the travel and trade bans. Most important, Washington and Havana reestablished diplomatic relations in 2015. In an extremely moving ceremony in front of the US embassy in Havana, on a clear and sunny day in July, the same marines that had taken the American flag down 54 years earlier handed it over to the young marines to hoist it up. After years of being folded, it finally unfurled, ending a long spell of incomprehension and hostility.

Likewise, the Obama administration supported the initiative to liberalize the travel of Americans citizens to Cuba. However, the administration was not able to end the economic embargo, nor could it close the US military base in Guantanamo. As Obama stressed to the people in the island

Figure 4.3. Hugo Chávez and Fidel Castro, Venezuela's and Cuba's heads of state, respectively, joke at Havana's Karl Marx Theater after joining their medallions, given to them by the students, signifying that the two revolutions would succeed (or fail) together (Photo by Claudia Daut via Reuters).

upon his visit there on March 2016, these actions did not belong to the president, but to Congress. His visit to the island, together with his wife and daughters—the first US president to visit in nearly a century—was immensely popular. He met with leading dissidents and small entrepreneurs, and he delivered a speech on television transmitted to the entire nation. He also appeared on an extremely popular TV show *Vivir del Cuento* with Pánfilo—the leading character that is a social critic while making viewers laugh; he ate in some recently opened *paladares*; and he toured the country for a few days. On the day he departed, Fidel Castro openly criticized him. But Obama had brought the Cuban people hope. After the 2016 elections, however, president Donald Trump started to roll back these measures (Domínguez 2006; Mesa-Lago 2012; Padura 2012).

In sum, for the United States the "Cuban problem" has rested on three premises:

1) Cuba is a socialist country in a region dominated by the US and is only 90 miles from American soil;
2) Cuba developed a close relationship with the Soviet Union and the world Left; and
3) Cuba's foreign policy served the Soviet Union in the Cold War.

Cuba's point of view also rested on three premises:

1) Cuba has the right to autodetermination;
2) Havana has the right to chart its own foreign policy; and
3) Castro's government practices "proletarian internationalism."

Thus, the relationship has historically been traumatic and conflictual. It has been characterized by the absence of diplomatic relations since 1961 (reestablished in 2015), the economic embargo of Cuba since 1962 (though modified in 2000), travel restrictions on US citizens and Cuban Americans, criticism of human rights violations in the island, and claims regarding the Cuban government's expropriation of property from 1959 to 1962.

The result has been a relationship that, at best, is stagnant and, at worst, hostile. Only if Cuba and the United States yielded their maximalist positions could they achieve a compromise and reach a normal relationship—as they tried to do for a couple of years under Barack Obama and Raúl Castro. This entailed a commitment to gradual, bilateral negotiations on critical issues (e.g., migration, travel, food exports, trade, and remittances) while also cooperating to combat the drug traffic in the Caribbean. However, although the international situation did change in the last 20 years, and the Cold War seemed to end, the political and psychological relationship between the two countries did not yield to the new global parameters. Thereafter, both Putin for Russia and Trump for the United States reheated the Cold War. Cuba was, as before, right in the middle.

At present, the situation seems to be at a standstill. On the one hand, the United States has not lifted the economic embargo; Washington maintains the Guantanamo base; and the Cuban American lobby in Congress and in the state of Florida remains very strong, influencing an antagonistic reading of Havana's regime and its relations with the world Left. On the other hand, Cuba has not substantially changed either its domestic or its foreign policy, nor heeded the internal voices of the dissident movement calling for change. As former president Donald Trump remarked many times, the United States had not completed its rapprochement with Cuba (Domínguez 2006; Mesa-Lago 2012; Padura 2012). Seeking, as Trump did, the support of Cuban Americans in Florida, he certainly did not complete it. The new president, Joe Biden, has just begun to undo Trump's extreme sanctions.

Cuba-Soviet and Russian Relations

Cuba's foreign policy is the result of the convergence of three factors. First, there is a negative historical legacy regarding the American presence in Cuban history. It dates back to the Spanish-American War and its aftermath, when the United States granted the people in the island less than total independence, and its *injerencia* (interference) in Cuba's domestic political issues through the Platt Amendment was not welcome. Second, the United States had strong private interests in many sugar plantations and American companies in the island. Third, Cuba challenged the United States through its strong alliance, first with the USSR, then with Venezuela—both countries that sought to undermine US hegemony in this hemisphere and provide a model for another Latin America.

Interestingly, although Moscow recognized the revolutionary government in 1959, at first it gave it only modest support. Cuba had lain within the US sphere of influence and had developed a foreign policy that strove to extend beyond the two major ideological blocks (Blasier 1983, 1976; Torres-Ramírez 1971; Romero 1992). In September 1959, Nikita Khrushchev visited the United States as part of the so-called "spirit of Camp David." In Cuba, the old communists, grouped under the PSP, had no significant leadership posts in the new revolutionary government (Pedraza 2007).

Anastas Mikoyan, an old Bolshevik and revolutionary who had managed to survive several conflictual periods of Soviet history and remain at the top echelons of power, visited Cuba in January 1960. He signed a series of trade agreements that expressed the Soviet vision of competing with Washington. As relations between the United States and Cuba deteriorated, Moscow began to support Havana openly. In July 1960, Nikita Khrushchev, then first secretary of the Soviet Communist Party, stated that the Monroe Doctrine for Americans had "died a natural death." He committed the

Soviet government to defending Cuba, in the event of a US invasion of the island. In those early months of extraordinary conflict, Cuba rapidly integrated into the world communist block.

This integration was strengthened during the October Missile Crisis in 1962, that brought the world to the brink of nuclear war. It made president John F. Kennedy a world hero, obscuring Nikita Khrushchev in his decisive response. In the end, both Kennedy and Khrushchev bypassed Fidel Castro and Cuba in their final agreement. Nonetheless, it altered the international status quo in the Western Hemisphere as it forced the United States to accept the Cuban socialist regime (Pedraza 2007). Although the Soviet Union temporarily lost its credibility as a world power, it gained a beachhead in Latin America and the Caribbean, only 90 miles from US shores (Romero 1992).

Nonetheless, the relationship between Cuba and the Soviet Union was not without conflict. From 1963 to 1969, a controversy developed between the Soviets and the Cubans regarding the kind of socialism practiced in Cuba and its international role. At the time, under the influence of Ché Guevara, Havana espoused the ideologies of moral incentives, economic centralization, armed struggle, and permanent revolution. Quite the contrary, Moscow espoused the ideologies of material incentives, the primacy of the mass party above the guerrillas, the institutionalization of the revolution, and the decentralization of the economy.

This controversy affected the Cuban-Soviet alliance, as Cuba moved away from the Soviet Union. Moreover, the Soviet Union sought an understanding with the United States, as could be seen in their neutral attitude toward the US intervention of the Dominican Republic in 1965. They also sought to expand diplomatic and trade relations in the Western Hemisphere. Cuba, on the other hand, promoted a world revolutionary movement, radicalized its anti-American stance, supported the guerrillas in Latin America, and criticized the antirevolutionary attitude of Moscow (Romero 1992).

Amid disputes with Havana, the Soviets undertook a rapprochement with the region. Despite the United States' implementation of the theory of counterinsurgency, the failure of the guerrillas, and the ambiguous Soviet attitude toward the Third World insurrectional Left, the Soviet Union launched a diplomatic offensive in the region, trying to prevent its isolation. From 1964 on, the Soviet Union began to establish diplomatic relations with Chile, followed by relations with Colombia in 1967, with Venezuela in 1969, and later with most Latin American and Caribbean governments.

Moreover, from the mid-1960s to mid-1970s, a number of incidents supported the Soviet thesis of promoting legal and peaceful ways of effecting revolution—for example, the experience of the military government in Peru as well as the electoral victory of Unidad Popular in Chile and Salvador Allende's rise to power in 1970. These events served to strengthen diplomatic and trade relations with other socialist governments. Similarly, Cuba began the process of institutionalizing the revolution, while making the island a reliable ally of the Soviet Union (Mesa-Lago 1978).

Developing a close political, economic, and military alliance, the USSR consolidated its presence in Cuba, to the benefit of the revolutionary processes in Central America and the Caribbean, as evident in Nicaragua and Grenada in 1979. Although the Soviet Union may not have been directly involved in the development of these and other Leftist governments in Latin America, Havana and Moscow were in solidarity with them and established a linkage that allowed socialism to be reborn in the region.

The United States and its allies, including Venezuela's presidents Rómulo Betancourt (1959–64) and Raúl Leoni (1964–69), sought to contain these efforts. Despite their differences, they pledged to stop the rise of communism in the region under their principle of "No More Cubas." However, other Leftist governments came to hold sway, as in Nicaragua (1979) and Grenada (1983), and some progressive governments developed in the region, such as Michael Manley's effort to achieve a democratic socialism in Jamaica. This led to the use of systematic pressure from Washington and Caracas against any leftist government, compelling them not to deepen their relations with Cuba (Blasier 1983). In Grenada, the government of the New Jewell and the leadership of Maurice Bishop, a pro-Cuban leader who tried to impose a socialist revolution in the island, quickly ended (Valenta and Valenta 1984; Lewis 1987). With Ronald Reagan and his decisive anticommunism in the White House, reducing the influence of communists and Cubans in the region became a top priority. Meanwhile, Cuba also became aware of the limits to its expansion when it met the US invasion of Grenada in 1983 after Bishop's overthrow and death.

In Angola, Cuba played a large military role, first supporting the political party of the MPLA in the Angolan civil war, and then the Leftist postcolonial government led by MPLA leaders in their defense against external attacks (Falcoff 2003; Blasier 1976, 1983; Torres-Ramírez 1971; Romero 1992). Cuba's decision to send troops to Angola in 1975 cannot be explained simply by pointing at their revolutionary commitment to national liberation struggles in Africa; rather, they must be seen in the light of Zaire's and South Africa's actions in that struggle. Cuba sent over 50,000 soldiers to help the MPLA, the most important political movement in Angolan politics, who had governed the country since its independence.

After Leonid Brezhnev's death in 1982, relations between Cuba and the Soviet Union entered a more complex phase in which the latter questioned the former's proletarian internationalism, not only in Latin America but also in Africa and the Middle East. Mikhail Gorbachev's arrival to power in 1985 had a significant impact on Soviet policy toward the Third World. While as president Gorbachev intended to reform the communist system from within, ultimately his reforms—*glasnost, perestroika*, and the "new thinking"—led to the Soviet Union's dissolution. They also provided an important impetus for the emergence of a dissident movement in Cuba at this time, as a new intellectual force began to emerge, such as la Tercera Opción (a third option, different from the governments of Cuba and the United States).

From 1991 on, with the dissolution of the Soviet Union, Moscow started to review the cooperation agreements between Cuba and the USSR, reducing economic aid and military commitments. The declining Soviet activism in the Third World, the critique of the attempt to apply the socialist model in underdeveloped countries, and the reintroduction of the thesis regarding "multiple ways to take power" all reshaped Cuba's international role as part of Russia's objectives. Priority was given to diplomacy, as well as trade, rather than to guerrilla commitments.

Without doubt, Cuban leaders clearly disagreed with *perestroika, glasnost*, and the "new thinking" that sought cooperation with the West and wanted to reduce the Soviet presence in the Third World. Fidel Castro and others insisted that these changes were not right for Cuba, and that the Cuban revolution had a militant role to play with movements in the Third World (Romero 1992). Using what became the major slogan of Cuba's revolution—*Patria o Muerte* (Our Homeland or Death)—Fidel reiterated:

> In this period of confusion . . . we are aware of the tremendous responsibility we have in the eyes of the workers of the world and especially the people of the Third World, of the responsibility of our revolutionary process. We always act accordingly. So, with more rigor

than ever, we say Socialism or death! Marxism-Leninism or death! That's what we mean now, as we have always said over the years: ¡Patria o Muerte, Venceremos! (F. Castro 1989)

Yet, after this, Havana reorganized its relations with Moscow and other former Soviet republics. Moreover, Soviet intellectuals criticized the Cuban economic model and the socialism implemented on the island. In turn, Cuba criticized the new nonsocialist Russia. Kamorin (1989) points out the need for economic decentralization in Cuba. However, in Cuba Fidel Castro underscored that "we belong to the West, according to our geography, but we are Marxist-Leninist and fight for socialism and communism" (F. Castro 1989).

No one imagined that Cuba would find a replacement, years later, for their dwindling special relationship with the Soviet Union (Domínguez 2006; Mesa-Lago 2012; Padura 2012). From 1990 to 1999, Cuban foreign policy experienced one of its most difficult times. Although for years Cuba had avoided its international isolation, led by the United States, after the Soviet Union disappeared, it could no longer receive aid to counter such threats. Nevertheless, in 1999 Cuba found a new ally and a strong support for its economy: Venezuela. Under Hugo Chávez, Venezuela changed the fate of the Cuban Revolution; Havana began to expand its diplomatic and economic relations with other Latin American and Caribbean governments, and Russia restored its relations with Cuba, as they sought to implement new economic deals.

Contemporary Cuba-Venezuela Relations

The fall of the Berlin Wall and the demise of the Soviet Union constituted a great test for the survival of Cuba and its socialist project. Nevertheless, Havana was able to overcome the most difficult moment of its history. Cuba survived, and its foreign policy radically changed. Seeking alternatives, Cuba looked for revolutionary solidarity with Algeria, China, and Vietnam, as well as for stronger economic relations with capitalist countries such as Canada, Japan, the Netherlands, and even the United States, despite the embargo (Mesa-Lago 2012).

For the 30 years during which Cuba was squarely inside the Soviet camp, the notion of proletarian internationalism guided its foreign policy. Alongside, Cuba also engaged in providing medical personnel for humanitarian situations. Militarily, Cuba scored enormous successes in Africa. Beginning in 1966, UNITA (National Union for the Total Independence of Angola) originally fought alongside the MPLA in Angola's war for independence. However, in the civil war that ensued, it fought against the MPLA. In the mid-1970s, when most foreign sources withdrew from Angola, Cuba's troops increased from 5,500 in December 1975 to 11,000 just two months later, in February 1976. UNITA and South African forces attacked the MPLA's base at Cuito Cuenavale. In 1988, the Battle of Cuito Cuenavale, under the leadership of Cuba's admired general Arnaldo Ochoa, ushered in negotiations among all the parties. These negotiations led to the New York Accords in August 1988, granting independence to Namibia and ending the direct involvement of all foreign military in Angola's civil war.

Despite his military victories, General Arnaldo Ochoa fell into disgrace with Fidel and Raúl Castro, who accused him of being involved in the lucrative drug trade. This led to Ochoa's execution in 1989—a decisive moment for many in Cuba (Oppenheimer 1993; Montaner 2001; Pedraza 2007). Roberto Ortega (2007) defected in 2003, after serving as colonel of the Cuban Armed Forces and chief of medical services for the Cuban military. He attended Ochoa's trial. In his view, Ochoa was eliminated due to his enormous popularity with Cuban soldiers in Angola and Ethiopia, as well as to his sympathy for President Gorbachev's reforms in the Soviet Union. Roberto Ortega underscored that "Cuba was one before Ochoa's trial and another Cuba afterward" (in Pedraza 2007). As Domínguez (1997, 9) describes the change in the waning ideological commitment in the public: "The revolutionary process in the '50s and '60s based itself, in part, on the absolute faith that the nation had taken in its hands the reins of history. Today that faith has disappeared, and has been replaced by fear, hope, doubt." The state itself became weaker, having lost both the power it had and the fear it prompted.

When communism collapsed in the Soviet Union and Eastern European countries, Cuba lost the notion of proletarian internationalism that had guided it for a long time. The collapse of Soviet socialism and the historical experience of Eastern European socialism reduced Cuba's influence, both globally and in this hemisphere (Romero 1992; Suárez-Salazar 2009). Thereafter, Cuba continued its programs of assisting developing countries in the areas of health, education, and sports. Over the course of the revolution, Cuba had sent doctors and other health care workers to aid other developing countries where people suffered due to a hurricane, an earthquake, an epidemic. However, these missions were typically small—50 to 150 personnel. With Venezuela, however, the medical teams Cuba sent were extremely large, numbering in the thousands, until at its peak in 2013 there were close to 50,000 doctors, ophthalmologists, and nurses working in Venezuela, as part of Hugo Chávez's Barrio Adentro (Inside the Barrio) program. In 2019, the number declined to around 20,000, though 2,000 more arrived in 2020 to help with the COVID-19 pandemic.

Through various legislative and public policy initiatives, Washington seized the moment of the Soviet Union's disappearance to reduce the scope of Cuba's influence. Both the government and transnational liberal groups began to openly criticize Marxism-Leninism, considering the Cuban Revolution a matter of the past. However, history taught a lesson to those that predicted the demise of the revolution and an end to Cuba's foreign policy.

Amid Cuba's enormous problems, many of them due to the loss of Soviet aid, Hugo Chávez and his followers in Venezuela changed Cuba's international landscape. Venezuela became a key ally of Cuba; with the Bolivarian Revolution, Cuba became the model for Venezuela to follow. At the same time, in Latin America and the Caribbean, there was a major political movement committed to reducing dependence on the United States (Domínguez 2006). During those years, a hemispheric agenda developed based on the foundation of a multipolar world, growing relationships with countries outside the Western orbit, promoting socialism and a regulated economy, and challenging the impact of Washington's neoliberal consensus (Mesa-Lago 2012). Within this framework, Cuba's foreign policy was reduced to a modest regional scenario. The larger job remained Venezuela's, who had the resources to promote business and cooperation agreements with several governments in the hemisphere, using both subsidies and direct aid (Romero 2016). However, no one imagined that Cuba and Venezuela's behavior would change after 2013. Cuba's did when it began to participate internationally, in regional summits and other high-level meetings. Moreover, Cuba was successful in restoring diplomatic relations with the United States and recuperating a relationship with the European Union. A visible change also came about when Cuba helped the Colombian government and the Colombian guerrillas—the Fuerzas Armadas Revolucionarias de Colombia (FARC)—to reach a peace agreement through meetings that took place in Havana, with Raúl Castro as their intermediary.

Clearly, the revolution with Fidel at the helm could not have succeeded without the support of Raúl's military. Yet it is also evident that Fidel and

Raúl did not always see eye to eye. Only after Fidel Castro's death at the end of 2016 did Raúl Castro engage in a coherent program of economic reforms that made a difference in people's lives and aimed to undo the tired Soviet-style system. The forecast was that an economic aperture and the normalization of relations with the United States would buoy the island back up. In addition, the remittances coming in from the generous Cuban diaspora, the import of food and medicine from the United States, the family visits and tourist visits to the island, and the new international investments in the island all resulted in increased production and consumption (Romero 2016). However, Cuba's economic reforms were timid—not robust enough to impel a transition to a market economy and to solve Cuba's economic woes (Mesa-Lago 2012). Many observers pointed out that the reforms moved slowly or were not working. Most Cubans were not satisfied with the outcome. As if this were not enough, Venezuela's support languished. Many Cubans sought to leave the island fearing Washington would do away with the Cuban Adjustment Act, which allowed them to find asylum—hardly an encouraging outlook (Romero 2016).

At the same time, some Latin American countries and the United States called for a political overture in Cuba, as they continued to have sharp differences over its lack of democracy and its human rights violations. Some governments in the region, including the United States, tried pressuring the Cuban government to find a solution to Venezuela's political crisis (Romero 2017). "Venezuela will go the way of Cuba" was a commonly held attitude in the international community. Given the political fragmentation in the region, the Leftist-oriented governments that supported the Bolivarian Revolution found it difficult to develop an expansive foreign policy.

When Nicolás Maduro became president of Venezuela, he confronted quite a different economic scenario, with low international prices for raw materials and a dramatic fall in the prize of oil. Two of Venezuela's main economic and political partners, Brazil (until Jair Bolsonaro became president) and Russia, were living through harsh internal socioeconomic situations of their own. In Russia, the regime suffered from sanctions imposed by the Western powers. China, for its part, continued to be the locomotive of the world's economy, though progressive devaluations of the yuan compensated for the disruption caused by distinct economic bubbles.

Even more dramatic was the situation the allied governments of Iraq, Libya, and Syria faced. Chávez had witnessed the judicial execution of Saddam Hussein, the extrajudicial execution of Muammar Gaddafi, and the marginalization of Bashar al-Assad. Maduro was unable to maintain these alliances. Moreover, other friendly regimes underwent drastic changes in foreign policy. Such was the case of Algeria's introversion due to President Bouteflika's resignation, the turnover of the Iranian government, the overthrow of Robert Mugabe in Zimbabwe, and Iran's apparent nuclear agreement with the P5+1 group (composed of the United States, Russia, China, the United Kingdom, France, and Germany).

The globalization process itself was in crisis, as could be seen in the worldwide economic recession, and the fallen exports in Latin America. The region became increasingly vulnerable, suffering from fewer exports, greater economic risk, and greater financial instability. At the same time, some observers pointed out that multilateralism was under stress due to the growing importance of the new antiglobalization movements. Both Cuba and Venezuela now need to meet the challenges posed by these changes and the pandemic. The fate of the ALBA alliances remains to be seen. Cuba, Venezuela's ideological reference, found itself amid an ambitious overture process with the United States. After the removal of Evo Morales from the presidency in 2019, Ecuador and Bolivia distanced themselves from the Venezuelan economic model and ceased offering political support to Caracas. Bolivia returned to democracy with the election of Evo Morales and the Movement for Socialism (MAS) party in 2020, which does not imply strong support from La Paz to Caracas, as in the past.

Finally, yet importantly, Venezuela's foreign policy became defensive due to the obstacles that confronted the nation. A significant part of the international community withdrew its support from Venezuela, criticizing the regime's failure to maintain a democratic polity, its handling of the economy, and its repression of the opposition. They also decried Venezuela's refusal to find a political solution to the current situation.

Internationally, Chávez's presidency enjoyed extraordinary conditions associated with the power diffusion phenomenon: a supercycle of raw materials; the rise of reemerging powers; and the United States' geostrategic reorientation under Trump, who sought to roll back Obama's gains. High oil prices from 2003 to 2009 granted Chávez the opportunity to experiment with a regional foreign policy that was not completely new, though it had a "revolutionary" ideological orientation. Chávez's government created PetroCaribe with the intention of projecting overseas the economic model promoted by Havana and Caracas. The rise not only of China, Russia, and Brazil, but also of petro-states such as Algeria, Iraq, Iran, Libya, and Syria, permitted a rearrangement of foreign alliances and alignments, with the goal of economic diversification. Finally, given the relatively low importance of Latin America in the American foreign policy agenda, the American presence in two Eurasian operational theatres—Afghanistan and Iraq—as part of its "war on terror" doctrine allowed a more defiant policy across the hemisphere.

Looking at it from Washington's geostrategic standpoint, the change was positive neither for Cuba nor for Venezuela. President Barack Obama proved to be more realistic in practice than in rhetoric (Ferguson 2015). Proposing to be the opposite of his predecessor, he made considerable efforts to limit the presence of American troops in Eurasia, to offer logistic but not tactical support to military intervention operations in the Middle East, and to reinforce the US naval presence on China's periphery under the "Pivot to East Asia" policy. However, contrary to expectations, this contraction did not strengthen positions across the Western Hemisphere. Instead, it seemed to be part of a great strategy of reducing political costs and using force more efficiently. In Venezuela's case, the US government committed itself to imposing selective sanctions, as announced by President Trump. Considering this, an authoritarian centralization model was expected. Its expressed objective was a rupture with the international political agenda of the Western Hemisphere based on human rights, the free market, and liberal democracy. Foreign autonomy was a vehicle through which the Venezuelan government was able to promote authoritarian political values, as well as alliances with other similar regimes.

Such a revisionist doctrine required a huge surplus of funds and a strong centralization of internal political control. In a changing international order, there was no guarantee it could continue over time. It became clear that the government could not sustain it when Chávez died, and Maduro succeeded him. There was, indeed, a permanent contradiction between their efforts to decentralize international political power, inserting themselves in critical counterhegemonic debates, and their tendency to concentrate power and authority in their foreign policy.

Venezuela's foreign policy will depend on the direction that its government takes, on the opposition as well, and on the effectiveness of societal demands. Maduro's presidency has given evidence of episodes of violence and repression. In addition, expectations abound regarding the return of a Democratic president to the White House and his views on

Cuba and Venezuela. Moreover, one needs to take into account the effects of COVID-19 in Cuba and Venezuela, as it exacerbated already existing stresses.

Cuba is still backing the Chavista experience and the government of President Maduro despite the current growing international and domestic criticism of Venezuela. Some Western governments signaled that they wanted Cuba to play a significant role in a negotiation process between the Chavistas and the Venezuelan opposition leaders, but Raúl Castro and others refused to accept this intermediary role and, instead, reaffirmed Cuba's full support for the Venezuelan regime. Possibly, they have no choice since Venezuela became Cuba's benefactor and major source of economic sustenance.

For better or for worse, from 1999 onward, Cuba and Venezuela shared a history of advantage and disadvantage. In the twilight of this bilateral relationship, with the new challenges each must face, an economically and politically shaky Venezuela no longer has the means to sustain the island's economy. At present, this is evident in the long lines at gas stations throughout the island and the scarcity of food in stores. The island is still supporting Venezuela, though it is suffering its own crisis. The question is: For how long and at what price?

5

Venezuela's Foreign Policy

Large Presence, Excessive Resources

Venezuela's Old and New Goals

For most of the twentieth century, relations between the governments of the United States and Venezuela ranged from cool to ambivalent to supportive. American policymakers viewed Venezuela as a country that naturally fell within Washington's sphere of influence. Thus, president Theodore Roosevelt's disdain for president Cipriano Castro (1899–1908) and his alarm at the chaos that accompanied his rise to power did not prevent the Roosevelt administration from coming to Venezuela's aid when European powers blockaded the Venezuelan coasts (Ewell 1996; McCoy and Myers 2004; Polanco et al. 2000).

During the long military leadership of Juan Vicente Gómez (1908–35), who was president three times and who influenced puppet governments in between, Venezuela appeared on American politicians' radar only when they were concerned about petroleum, which proved crucial in World War I and World War II. Venezuela also supplied oil to the United States during the Korean conflict, serving as the largest source of petroleum imports. During the mid-to-late 1950s, Washington supported the dictatorship of Marcos Pérez-Jiménez, assuming that his government would provide the easiest means to secure an uninterrupted flow of Venezuelan oil to the United States and NATO allies.

Pérez-Jiménez's overthrow in 1958 and the arrival of representative democracy to Venezuela forced the US government to rethink its relations with the South American nation. A new form of interaction between the two countries developed, which lasted over 40 years (1958–99). First, building on an axiom that dated from the Gómez era, policymakers in both

Figure 5.1. As part of their alliance, Venezuela supplied Cuba with large amounts of oil, in exchange for Cuban doctors and health personnel. Here a Venezuelan ship carrying the oil is arriving to Havana, having just passed the statue of the Christ of Havana behind it (Photo by Silvia Pedraza).

countries continued to treat Venezuela as unique in Latin America due to its massive reserves of petroleum. These reserves and the Venezuelan government's willingness to supply energy to the United States (at an acceptable price), coupled with Washington's strategic interests in having a secure oil source close to home, led to good and solid relations between the two countries throughout the years of representative democracy, 1958–99 (Ewell 1996; Polanco et al. 2000).

Venezuela was also unique due to its stable political system. In a region characterized by military coups, insurgencies, and revolutions, Venezuela seemed an island of stability under the leadership of the social democrat Rómulo Betancourt, who was president from 1959 to 1964 (Betancourt 1967). However, both Betancourt and his successor, Raúl Leoni, who governed from 1964 to 1969, had to confront the presence of urban and rural guerrillas. Sponsored by the Communist Party of Venezuela (PCV), they had strong ties to Fidel's Cuba and the USSR, as did the Movimiento de Izquierda Revolucionaria (MIR), the extraparliamentary organization with links to revolutionary Cuba. Betancourt and Leoni also had to confront coup d'état attempts from both the Left and the Right, mass protests, and political violence. The armed forces remained separated from political decision-making except for border security and the purchase of military armament. For over 30 years, Venezuela avoided the cycle of "democracy—military coup—dictatorship—democracy" that undermined most Latin American democracies (McCoy and Myers 2004).

Venezuela–US Relations

An important consequence of this Venezuelan exceptionalism was that the US government supported the democratic leadership of Venezuela's main political parties, the social democratic party, AD, and the Christian democratic party, COPEI. Venezuela also succeeded in integrating the majority of the former guerrillas and extraparliamentary fighters into its electoral politics. With the military's acceptance of civilian rule, the country became a model for advocates of democracy in the region (McCoy and Myers 2004; Domínguez and Fernández de Castro 2010; Romero and Corrales 2010).

Successive Venezuelan democratic governments took an oppositional stance toward the United States in only a few instances: when Venezuela adopted an activist role in the UN, the OPEC, and the OAS, and when they disagreed regarding the status of Puerto Rico (as Venezuela supported its independence). Washington was also unwilling to support the Betancourt doctrine: the policy launched between 1960 and 1969 that condemned any coup d'état against an elected democratic government and called for the expulsion from the OAS of any military regime that overthrew a democratic regime. Other disagreements between Washington and Caracas occurred when Venezuela denounced the US military's 1965 invasion of the Dominican Republic and its support for the United Kingdom in its war against Argentina during the 1982 Falkand/Malvinas crisis (Cardozo de Da Silva 1998, 2006).

During the 1970s and 1980s, Venezuela and the United States collaborated to promote democracy and human rights in Latin America and the Caribbean. This cooperation became possible when, in 1975–76, the US government did not oppose Venezuela's nationalization of its petroleum, gas, iron, and aluminum industries. Nevertheless, Venezuelan policymakers found a way to combine the social populism expressed in AD and COPEI with a mixed capitalist-statist economic system that accepted private property, protected political freedom, and guaranteed the rule of law. Venezuelan presidents portrayed their country as a democratic nation promoting democracy, limiting Cuban influence in the hemisphere, and reliably supplying oil to the United States (Myers 1994; Ellner 1997).

Following Hugo Chávez's ascent to the presidency in 1999, Venezuelan foreign and domestic policies proceeded in directions that Washington political circles viewed with skepticism. The first concern focused on the armed forces' open participation in policymaking. Washington was uneasy with the US Leftist orientation of this military faction and feared that its leaders lacked a firm commitment to democracy and free enterprise (Romero and Corrales 2010; Corrales and Romero 2013). The new direction Hugo Chávez took also threatened to interrupt the steady supply of Venezuelan oil to the United States. Additionally, his political efforts promoted a close and special relationship with Cuba and, according to Washington, intensified anti–United States cooperation with "pariah states," such as Iraq, Libya, Iran, Sudan, and Syria. Finally, he supported Leftist political parties and guerrilla movements in Latin America and the Caribbean, in some parts of the Third World, and even in the West (Petrásh 2000).

In his own country, Chávez attempted to reduce American influence. He insisted that his government did not want a confrontation with the United States, but he pursued a set of policies that sometimes flew in the face of cordial relations laid out by previous American administrations. Examples abound. Venezuela opposed America's condemnation of Cuba's human rights violations, the US embargo of Cuba, and other policies against Cuba. Chávez also refused to join the United States in condemning human rights policies in China, Iraq, Libya, Iran, and Syria. Chávez was one of a few international leaders to condemn the 2001 US invasion of Afghanistan. He became one of the most vociferous international critics of the United States, actively campaigning to create anti-American institutions and alliances and fostering close ties with the most anti-American governments on the planet (with Iran, Syria, Libya, Iraq, and Sudan). In addition, Venezuela promoted the concept of "participatory democracy," opposed several efforts by the US government to promote representative democracy in the region, and condemned the US position on human rights matters in Venezuela (Romero 2004, 2018).

Chávez's public attitude toward the United States was contradictory. On the one hand, he showed a desire to continue relations, while on the other hand he was confrontational and seemingly delighted to challenge the country's preeminence in the hemisphere. Such was the case when he opposed the Colombia Plan, created by Colombia and the United States to combat drug trafficking and guerrilla activities, thereby reducing cooperation in drug-related initiatives.

Hugo Chávez and Nicolás Maduro both used brinksmanship—taking a risk until the last moment and then backing down—as a strategy, when they threatened to cut the oil supply to the United States. With this, Venezuela tried to provoke the United States several times, as well as to reduce Washington's influence. They both sought to deepen Venezuela's socialist revolution and to export it to the rest of the continent. Moreover, they assumed that the American superpower was in decline, and that its preoccupation with problems in the Middle East and Asia would entail a desire to negotiate with Caracas. Until 2016, the United States continued its own policy of calculated risks with Maduro's own provocative behavior and responded with appeasement. However, after 2017 an inevitable confrontation arose (Romero 2017). The prospects for a rapprochement with the American government are now dubious. Venezuela has pursued the following objectives: finding allies that can support the soft balance with the United States; buying large supplies of weapons; identifying trading partners that do business through state-owned operations, rather than the private sector; and dealing with foreign governments that are not democratic (Kelly and Romero 2005). However, until 2016, both parties avoided a punitive relationship. Unlike a traditional enemy, Venezuela did not break fully with the United States. Venezuela bought a massive number of weapons, but fell short of a real military threat. While the United States was able to respond with a tough stance to Venezuela, it generally settled into a policy of "Talk softly, sanction softly, and keep watch" (Corrales and Romero 2013). However, when Donald Trump assumed the presidency in 2017, the relationship became a confrontational zero-sum game.

Under Trump and now Biden, Washington recognized the parallel government of self-proclaimed president Juan Guaidó in January 2019 and lent it strong support. Trump also broke off diplomatic relations with Maduro's government in January 2019 and promoted a hemispheric and world alliance against the Venezuelan regime, accusing it of human rights abuses, ties to the drug trade, and a failure to respond to Venezuelans' claims while promoting political violence in the region. The United States also imposed new economic and financial sanctions on Venezuela: it could not trade the new debt, buy or sell bonds in the United States, or to use the Venezuelan cryptocurrency of *el petro*. Moreover, the US government prohibited PDVSA's financial transactions, the circulation of Venezuelan gold on the US market, financial operations involving oil in the United States with third parties (in effect, an oil embargo), and the Central Bank of Venezuela from using its dollar accounts. In effect, the United States has progressively imposed an economic and financial embargo not unlike that which was imposed on Cuba 60 years ago.

A mutual distrust now exists between Venezuela and the United States. Relations with the American government are frozen; most congressmen and the mass media were against Chávez and then opposed Maduro; and a Venezuelan lobby has developed as exile groups in Washington and Miami exert pressure to block any rapprochement between the two governments. It is also important to consider Chávez's perception, now also Maduro's, regarding the United States' presumed intent to reverse the Bolivarian Revolution—a perception that is also shared by part of the Venezuelan opposition.

Before his election on April 14, 2013, Nicolás Maduro hinted at possibly opening a dialogue with the United States. However, once he won the election, diplomatic relations remained stagnant as Washington and Caracas continued to send mixed signals (McCoy and Myers 2004; Corrales and Romero 2013). Now diplomatic relations are severed, and Washington is, with the help of its allies, trying to overthrow the Venezuelan regime.

President Trump hardly needed a serious confrontation with Venezuela, given the precarious security situation in Afghanistan, the uncertainty over Iran's future, the North Korean provocations, and China's and Russia's threats to return to power on the world stage. Nevertheless, the Trump administration responded to pressure from American domestic groups, including the strong presence of the Venezuelan lobby, which does not take kindly to the Venezuelan government's efforts to weaken the United States.

After all, there is no consensus in Washington regarding the root problems in the bilateral relations. Is Venezuela a revolutionary government that includes among its plans confrontation with the "empire" and, therefore, must be fought by any means? Or is it possible to avoid cornering Caracas by offering a nontraditional friendship route? This problem has no à la carte solution and we need to see what comes next. In the meantime, the US government named an ambassador to Venezuela to engage with Juan Guaidó's parallel government. Inside the American embassy in Bogotá, Colombia, there is now a Venezuelan unit led by James Story.

Geology, geography, diplomacy, and institutions all combine to make the US-Venezuela oil trade one of the most truly interdependent trading relationships in the world. Thus, in the event of an economic embargo, Venezuela would not only need to find a new, large, preferably close-by customer for its oil but also a replacement for refining its heavy oil. CITGO, a Venezuelan oil and state company registered in the United States, also plays an important role in Venezuela's refinement of that heavy oil. During most of Chávez's and Maduro's administrations, plenty of talks took place, but little progress was made in building new refineries outside the United States. However, Trump's government froze PDVSA's assets in American banks and ordered that CITGO's profits be diverted to a special account to prevent their use by Maduro's government.

However, Trump's most important decision was its strong support of the provisional presidency of Juan Guaidó as the legal and legitimate representative of the Venezuelan nation. In fact, Washington broke off diplomatic relations with Maduro while establishing diplomatic relations with the parallel government of Guaidó.

As 2021 opened, everyone watched to see how the newly elected US president, Joe Biden, would manage the relationship between the United States and Venezuela. Broken diplomatic relations, minimal trade between the two countries, mutual accusations, many sanctions, a growing Venezuelan community in the United States, and strong support for Guaido's parallel government are some of the negative items on an agenda that will be very hard to overcome in a short time.

Both Chávez and Maduro tried to end Venezuela's dependence on the United States by turning to China and Russia. The ideal outcome would be for China, Russia, and other new partners to replace the United States as a market for Venezuelan goods, as a source of foreign investments, and as a supplier of the expertise currently provided by American companies. However, thus far, this effort has not been successful (Corrales and Romero 2013; Karl 1997; Dávila 2013).

Since 2015, Venezuela has been under the sight of the United States. Both the executive branch and Congress have viewed the recent political events negatively, condemning both the Chavista regime and Maduro's government. US officials—president Donald Trump, senators Marco Antonio Rubio and Bob Menéndez, and former congresswoman Ileana Ros-Lehtinen, among others—criticized the Bolivarian Revolution as never before. Moreover, many public personalities from the press, TV broadcasts, NGOs, and social networks raised serious questions regarding the current situation in Venezuela. They support the Venezuelan opposition and have asked for a return to democracy.

Will the international democratic community lose its patience and punish the Chavista regime? This depends on them. On the one hand, Caracas could press its luck and turn more autocratic, anti-capitalist, and friendlier toward the avowed rivals of the United States and the West. On the other hand, Venezuela could shift its foreign policy approach to a more moderate and diplomatic stance (Dávila 2013; Hogenboom 2012). Might it be possible to reach an agreement with President Biden?

Venezuela-Soviet Relations

In 1945, Venezuela and the Soviet Union established diplomatic relations in the context of the World War II alliance between the USSR, the United States, and the victorious Allies. Due to deteriorating relations between Moscow and Washington and the emerging Cold War, relations between the two countries broke down in 1951. After 1959, under Rómulo Betancourt's government, Venezuela objected to the role the USSR played in Latin America and the Caribbean, the Soviet defense of Cuba, and the Soviet support for the insurgent Venezuelan Left.

In the late 1960s, détente—the political rapprochement between the Soviet Union and the United States—left behind the years of bipolar world confrontation, contributing to reestablishing relations between Venezuela and the Soviet Union in 1969. For the next 30 years, small diplomatic and trade ties characterized these relations. The disappearance of the USSR after 1991 and the formation of the Russian Federation contributed to these developments (Romero 1992). But as soon as Russia reestablished itself as a key player in international relations, it also reestablished relations across Latin America after what Moscow called "the lost decade" of the 1990s. In 2008, Russia traded US $15 billion in the region. Of this, $6 billion was trade with Brazil (40 percent of the total); $400 million was trade with

Cuba; and over $1 billion was trade with Venezuela ($68 million of these funds were Venezuelan imports from Russia, and $320 million were Venezuelan exports to Russia). This asymmetry was due to the military purchases by the Venezuelan government (Bermúdez 2009).

President Chávez visited Russia eight times and signed 65 agreements between Russia and Venezuela. In addition, both governments signed a cooperation agreement regarding the peaceful use of nuclear energy, which would allow Russia to provide technology and build a plant in Venezuela. In 2008, the two countries established a working group that selected Atomstroyexport (which built the Bushehr nuclear plant in Iran) as the company to accomplish that task, and they confirmed their participation in a cooperation agreement. During the 2008 visit of then Russian president Dmitry Medvedev to Caracas, an agreement was signed in the field of controlled thermonuclear fusion; nuclear facility security, development, and construction; and the decommissioning of research reactors and nuclear power plants. Also included was Russian support for the development of uranium in Venezuela. However, Venezuela canceled its nuclear program in 2011, after the Fukushima nuclear accident in Japan (Schwirtz 2009; Dávila 2013).

Rusoro, a Russian-Canadian company, wanted to exploit Venezuela's Las Cristinas gold mine (since 2019 in the hands of the Chinese consortium CITIC) and other gold fields and to develop other mining works. However, in July 2012, after failing to achieve international arbitration against Venezuela at the International Center for Settlement of Investment Disputes (ICSID), Rusoro asked for an agreement with the Venezuelan government for the nationalization of its assets. By September 2009, Russia had extended a loan of $4 billion dollars to the Venezuelan government, part of which the government used to purchase military equipment and services. Both governments also highlighted the creation of the Russian-Venezuelan Business Council and the creation of a binational fund of $12 billion (now a binational bank). Furthermore, both governments developed a project to facilitate bilateral trade transactions in local currencies and created a direct air route to connect the two capitals. They also created a joint venture called Petromonagas between the Russian National Oil Company (NOC), SRL (formed by Gazprom Neft, Russia's gas company), and the Russian companies—Lukoil (that left the project in 2014), Rosneft, TNK-BP, OBP, Surgutneftegaz, and PDVSA. The goal was to invest more than $20 billion for the joint exploration and exploitation of the Junin-6 block in the Orinoco Oil Belt, an area of 448 km². The shareholding was 60 percent PDVSA and 40 percent NOC-SRL. In January 2013, the Russian state company Rosneft bought out TNK-BP and Surgutneftegaz from the consortium, which made Rosneft the senior partner and leader, replacing Gazprom Neft (Dávila 2013).

The high-level Intergovernmental Commission (CIAN) Venezuela-Russia administers all these agreements. In total, there have been 12 meetings of CIAN. Both governments signed a memorandum for the evaluation and certification of reserves in Block Ayacucho 2 in the Orinoco Oil Belt that confirmed that TNK-BP, a Russian-British joint venture, would assist PDVSA in the evaluation and certification of reserves in the Ayacucho block. The Russian company LUKoil also signed an agreement with PDVSA. In addition, representatives of the oil and gas exploration company Russian National Oil Consortium CNP SRL signed an agreement with PDVSA to explore oil and gas areas in the Ayacucho Block 3 and in the Carabobo Block 1, both located in the Orinoco Oil Belt.

In January 2013, the Russian company Rosneft announced that it planned to invest over $10 billion in Venezuelan oil and gas industries. Rosneft and PDVSA signed five agreements, three of which focused on exploration in mature oil fields in the Maracaibo basin and in offshore areas in the Gulf of Paria (gas and oil). Two other agreements created joint ventures in oilfield services and engineering, drilling works supply, and the construction of a factory for drilling units (Dávila 2013).

Venezuela bought 13 Russian thermoelectric machines totaling 350 megawatts that PDVSA used to increase its energy capacity. Both governments agreed to establish a joint venture to transport oil and derivatives and to sign a contract to purchase a compressor extraction plant. The Russian company Rosneft has the right to exploit oil in the Carabobo 2 block, and a joint venture was established with a producer and processor of plantains and bananas. Similarly, the two countries agreed to increase the capital of the Russian-Venezuelan Bank to $4 billion (Corrales and Romero 2013). President Chávez announced in October 2011 that creating "a new organization of 'oil giants'" was under discussion—a step taken to criticize OPEC's price policy and to increase oil production by some members of the organization.

In March 2012, President Chávez congratulated Russia for vetoing the UN Security Council's request to sanction Syria. Paradoxically, Russian rulers warned that unless he rushed reforms in Syria, President Assad should leave power (Corrales and Romero 2013). In the last decade, Venezuela spent almost $16 million strengthening its military—personnel, equipment, infrastructure, education, and logistics. Overall, Venezuela went from being the 39th leading arms importer in the world in 1999 to being the 8th in 2008—a truly remarkable increase in only nine years. After 2007, Venezuela became the third largest buyer of Russian weapons globally, after China and India (Romero and Corrales 2010). As of 2019, Venezuela was buying Russian weapons and military equipment through 12 contracts signed since 2005 for more than $5.4 billion, with the intention of paying cash for $3.2 billion in loans granted by Russia, and with $1 billion and another $1.2 million in the future.

Venezuela bought additional military items from Russia: three Varshavianka Class 3 submarines; 25 Sukhoi-30 MK-2fighter aircraft; 60 attack helicopters, Mi 17B-5, My 26T, Mi 28N and Mi 35M aircraft Antonov transport; an unknown number of Igla-S-24 and S-125 Pechora 2M missiles; and 100,000 Kalashnikov AK-103 rifles. Furthermore, Russia is building a factory in Venezuela to make the rifles and other munitions, a helicopter repair center, and a training center for military aircraft pilots.

Venezuela also bought rather sophisticated Russian weapons, such as an unspecified number of Sukhoi Su-35 aircraft; Il-114 patrol aircraft; Strela-S-300PMU-2 and Tor-M2E air defense systems; multiple mouths shuttle Smerch missiles; and Buk-M1 and M2rocket spears. Other military purchases included: the Antey radar; 2,500 armored combat vehicles type T-72B1, BMP-3 and BMP-3S; 90 T-72 and T-90 tanks; 5P85SE 48N6E2 missile launch vehicles and missile launchers; 3 Project-636 submarines; a submarine-877; and 12 military heavy transport Ilyushin-7. Venezuela also showed an interest in Russian Beriev Be-200 amphibious aircraft; Mirazh patrol boats; a Murena-E mobile coastal artillery system capable of lowering vessels at distances up to 130 kilometers; and more than 50 Russian-made aircraft (Romero and Corrales 2010).

In 2008, President Chávez announced a naval exercise with Russia, which took place November 14–19. Russia contributed two Tu-160 strategic bombers (known as Blackjacks) and Tu-95MC bombers; the nuclear-powered cruiser *Peter the Great* without nuclear weapons on board; the frigate *Admiral Chabanenko*; and an underwater hunter support ship. On September 10, 2008, the Russian government announced that it had placed two Russian Tu-160 strategic bombers in a Venezuelan air base, and they conducted a military exercise in the Caribbean (Alandete 2008).

The June 2009 visit of then Venezuelan vice president Ramón Carrizales to Moscow led to the definitive creation of a binational bank with founding capital totaling $4 billion (the goal was to reach $12 billion) with Russia providing 51 percent of those funds. This development resembled the binational banks Venezuela had created with Iran and China, as well as credit operations signed with Japan, Brazil, and Qatar.

Venezuela also supported Russia during the country's conflict with Georgia. During September 2009, Chávez visited Russia for the eighth time, when Venezuela became the third country in the world (after Russia and Nicaragua) to recognize Abkhazia and South Ossetia, Georgia's breakaway republics backed by Moscow. Moreover, the National Assembly of Venezuela passed a law maintaining the reliability of military agreements with Russia and protecting classified information in the framework of bilateral military-technical cooperation.

Vladimir Putin, then prime minister of Russia, visited Caracas in April 2010. The two nations signed 31 cooperation agreements concerning energy, infrastructure, science and technology, transportation, education, culture, and electric industries. Among these was a memorandum of cooperation between both countries' Ministries of Electricity, especially in terms of planning and engineering. They also signed a new agreement between the Venezuelan Ministry of Energy and Petroleum and Russian NPC for the joint exploitation of the Junín 6. PDVSA reiterated the Russian presence in the development plan of the Ayacucho 2, Ayacucho 3, and Junín 3 Blocks. Upon his return from Caracas, Putin announced that Venezuela wanted to purchase $5 billion worth of Russian military equipment.

In 2011 and 2013, a Russian government delegation visited the country to review a series of energy and military agreements, highlighting the signing of a new credit agreement with Venezuela to increase military purchases of Russian weapons. The rapprochement between Moscow and Caracas revolved around Venezuela's purchases of Russian military goods and Venezuela's support of Russia's international policies. Caracas believed that this support provided Venezuela with a freeway and with independence from the United States. Indeed, Venezuela was a very lucrative market for arms and military technology. Likewise, Russia is a long-term market for Venezuelan energy commodities (Dávila 2013). As Berg (2019, 1) explains, despite the American-led sanctions on Venezuela's PDVSA, oil from the country is still flowing in world markets, often facilitated by Rosneft, which has been accepting Venezuelan crude as a form of loan repayment: "In this way, Russian President Vladimir Putin is playing a role in keeping

Venezuelan dictator Nicolás Maduro afloat." For as long as he does, the current US sanctions will do little to force a change in Venezuela. However, due to the United States' demand, Rosneft pulled out from joint ventures with PDVSA and PDVSA's subsidiary CITGO in 2020.

Although the present relationship between Venezuela and Russia is quite different from the historic relationship between the Soviet Union and Cuba, it does involve a strong political dimension. Venezuela is one of the largest purchasers of Russian arms. However, this investment might have been politically motivated, due to Venezuela's support of Russia and Caracas's wish to break away from the United States. As a result, cooperation between the two governments is bound to continue.

Since 2015, Russia has supported Maduro's government. In 2017, Maduro confronted the Venezuela opposition's combative stance under the leadership of the MUD. The MUD refused to accept Maduro's creation of a National Constitutional Assembly in 2017 and took to the streets to express their disagreement. Russia closed ranks with Venezuela and asked for a political and democratic solution to the country's current situation (Romero and Mijares 2016; Romero 2017). In 2019, Maduro payed a visit to Putin in Moscow and was rewarded with the arrival of more Russian military specialists in Venezuela (Berg 2019).

Venezuela: Same Policy, Different Environment

Three important issues are at stake. First, the growing leadership of the late president Chávez not only limited Venezuelan diplomacy's institutional strength but also raised questions about the government's previous political alliances with nondemocratic regimes in the world. Its leaders perceived such an alliance as a network of loyalties, commitments, affinities, and forms of subordination. Second, the existence of a Left-progressive camp both internationally and regionally was embodied mainly in the ALBA, which Chávez was instrumental in creating. Third, Venezuelan diplomats, who understood their work as committed to the revolutionary cause, became increasingly politicized (Romero 2006; Corrales and Romero 2013).

Oil has historically been the main instrument for Venezuela's inclusion in international relations. This, in turn, has promoted the development of a political culture that regulates the private economy and promotes Venezuelan society's dependence on the state, making the country vulnerable to oil price fluctuations. Since OPEC's inception in 1960, Venezuela has supported their actions. The country has proven reserves of 286,300 billion barrels of oil—the world's largest. It is also important to highlight the role PDVSA has played in the implementation of Venezuela's foreign policy (Blanco 2002; Domínguez and Fernández de Castro 2010; Karl 1997).

With the rise to power of a Left-wing government in 1999, Venezuela not only maintained the international activism of previous governments but also expanded its global presence. It used Leftist radical narratives to oppose liberal Western narratives. The Venezuelan opposition also used the international agenda to influence public debate, constantly complaining about Bolivarian foreign policy (Romero 2006; Corrales and Romero 2013).

To gain political support, the Venezuelan government supported a number of partisan organizations, social organizations, NGOs, and academic networks that are sympathetic to Caracas and in solidarity with its politics. Many of these institutions and groups receive financial, logistical, and ideological support from Venezuela (Blanco 2002; Romero 2006; Romero 2017). Thus, the country embarked on a foreign policy with the key objective to create an anti-American alliance to reduce dependence on the United States. The goal is to promote a new geopolitical map and to gain global leadership (Domínguez and Fernández de Castro 2010; Corrales and Romero 2013).

From 1999 onward, Venezuelan diplomacy tried to use foreign policy to sustain the new regime and support revolutionary movements in the world. Between 2002 and 2004, given domestic circumstances, Chávez's international activism slowed down. After the events of 2002 and 2003—the brief military coup against him and the oil workers' strike—Chávez agreed to international mediation by the OAS, the Carter Center, the United Nations Development Program (UNDP), and a group of friendly governments. After 2004, Chávez's government resumed its international activism as an alternative to the current multipolar context (Cardozo de Da Silva 2006).

When Nicolás Maduro took over in 2013, he pursued the same goals and tasks as Chávez. However, he found that his determination to sustain Venezuela's international standing and the ambitious Bolivarian program of domestic reform were incompatible. Moreover, at present, the opposition possesses more international support than the president, and his government has more domestic troubles and far less world sympathy than in the past (Gratius and Romero 2013). The country had an active foreign policy that tried to develop a dual and unconventional path to power (with less democracy and fewer market-friendly policies) at the same time that it developed a radical international program—the Bolivarian ideology—to export the revolution.

Oil plays a dual role in Venezuela's foreign policy. Structurally, oil is what allows Venezuela to engage in active diplomacy. Now that the technology to exploit the Orinoco Oil Belt reserves exists, Venezuela has become the largest oil depository in the world. Because the state monopolizes the entire energy sector, all the revenue goes directly into the government's coffers. Thus, the state can afford the costs of an active international role (McCoy and Myers 2004; Corrales and Romero 2013).

Since November 2017, when Venezuelan bond tenders were called on to negotiate the restructuring and refinancing of a portion of the external debt, the negative evaluation of Venezuela's economic and political crisis has deepened. In fact, Venezuela is close to defaulting on its bonds. The delay in paying interest and coupons shows that the government needs fresh money to respond to a crisis bigger than the one in 1983, during which former president Luis Herrera-Campins had to devalue 100 percent of the bolívar (Blanco 2002; Romero 2006, 2017).

The country is clearly in trouble. Maduro's government refuses to be rescued by the International Monetary Fund due to the conditions they would impose. The country does not have enough international reserves; oil revenues have been declining for a number of years; and there is too much money supply in the market, creating an inflation rate that is one of the highest in Latin American history. Similarly, debtors ask for an economic adjustment, but the government refuses to apply it. President Maduro expects to overcome the current impasse by accepting the financial support of China and Russia, who continue to support him, and the backing of his own military, as well as Cuba's.

Venezuela is also in the midst of an unprecedented political crisis. In November 2017, the foreign ministers of the European Union approved an arms embargo against Venezuela and other restrictive measures to pressure Maduro's administration. Canada also deepened its economic sanctions, the US government condemned the increasing authoritarianism of the regime and increased its economic sanctions, and many Latin American governments asked Maduro's government to obey the 1999 Constitution and the National Assembly. In addition, the secretary general of the Organization of American States, Luis Almagro, is a major advocate of democracy and a strong critic of Venezuela's government for its human rights abuses and the humanitarian crisis now enfolding. While in 2014 Venezuela's government was able to repress people with impunity, they are no longer able to do so. As Almagro stresses, "In those days, nobody was calling Maduro a dictator. Today he is known worldwide as a dictator" (In Brinter 2018).

Venezuela's regime has not overcome the fierce criticism regarding its legitimacy—an issue that is only now being placed on hemispheric and international agendas. In fact, given that Maduro himself created the National Constituent Assembly (ANC) in 2017 (and closed it in December 2020) without a new constitution, although he insists he won the parliamentary elections of December 6, 2020, his regime lacks legitimacy in the eyes of national and international actors. Nonetheless, beginning in 2021 the relationship between Cuba and Venezuela will probably be tighter than before. The regime created the ANC to duplicate the legislative functions of the National Assembly (AN), which has been under the control of the opposition since 2015. Maduro also lacks legitimacy due to the process and results of the governors' election. The exception is the National Assembly, because it is a constitutional institution. Nonetheless, the two institutions that belong to the regime—the ANC and the Supreme Court of Justice—usurped the National Assembly's functions. Thus, many observers regard the validity of the regime with concern. From the point of view of its legitimacy, the regime is increasingly deficient, both economically and politically (Corrales and Romero 2013).

Until now, it has not been possible to offer an alternative to the many actions that were contrary to the democratic order, such as the failure of negotiations between the government and the opposition, the constant violation of human rights, the unfair cases of political imprisonment, and the detention and persecution of political leaders and members of parliament. Moreover, electoral manipulation by the National Electoral Council has become visible to many, as has the misuse of laws and institutions to favor the regime (Romero 2017). This was evident in the parliamentary elections of December 6, 2020.

Most significantly, the regime behaved undemocratically through the illegal use of the ANC by passing judgments on matters that do not concern it. It has also usurped the functions of the other government branches, such as the direct approval of laws and regulations (a function that belongs to the National Assembly), and the swearing-in of the elected governors (a function that belongs to their respective Legislative Councils as stipulated by the national Constitution). Furthermore, evaluating the president's administrative actions is supposed to be carried out by the National Assembly, not by the Supreme Court of Justice and the ANC.

The ANC's illegal actions provided evidence that Maduro's public management was flawed, since it ignored the powers that correspond to the National Assembly and indiscriminately used those stipulated in the national Constitution. In effect, the government behaves in a sectarian manner, corroding the opposition, manipulating the administration of justice, and using the national budget indiscriminately. Thus, the government chaired by Nicolás Maduro is illegal in nature. The result can only be sanctions by the international democratic community (Romero 2017).

International actors who have supported a media campaign and have denounced the current situation in Venezuela know that these aspects of political reality make a short-term solution difficult (Romero 2017). The regime has not fallen despite the efforts of many: secretary general of the OAS, Luis Almagro; members of the US Congress; the democratic governments' alliance known as "the Lima Group;" and various multilateral entities, NGOs, the media, and public personalities.

Venezuela's crisis has now become a test case for comparative politics. Various contradictory narratives converge. In strategic studies, some ways of perceiving the problem collide. On the one hand, there is the classic military perspective, which prioritizes issues of national security, arms competition, preventive measures, and balance of forces, based on the parameters provided by the realistic tradition. On the other hand, there is the societal perspective, where economic, social, health, cultural, and environmental issues take their place on the agenda, placing stress on the non–state sector, both the multilateral organizations, the media, and the population. Yet another perspective comes from Marxist-Leninist discourse, particularly important since it is the official narrative of some governments who support the Bolivarian Revolution.

The Venezuelan case has drawn attention among global intellectuals and the media as an example of historical metamorphosis—a process that shifted from being a representative model of democracy and Western identity to a hybrid model of illiberal democracy and anti-Western positions. The Venezuelan case is an open process, where three ways of looking at it stand out.

The first way of looking at it stresses the undoing of the political system that prevailed in Venezuela for 40 years, that entailed a total break with the past, in particular with representative democracy. This total break came about when Hugo Chávez, a retired military man, won the presidential election of December 1998 with a fundamentally Left-wing electoral alliance, and took office as Constitutional president of Venezuela. However, this rupture in the political did not equally occur in the economic. *Rentismo*, considered as a way of accumulating *sui generis* capital through the income generated by oil profits, strengthened the Venezuelan public sector, when the decision to start applying socialist policies was taken. Then the state as political actor and the communal experiments became the alpha and omega of the Chavista process, recognizing and protecting the poorest sectors of the population against the upper and middle sectors of Venezuelan society. Social and ideological polarization resulted. Critics of this model warned that this socialist narrative concealed the transfer of power from one type of elites to another, especially regarding the control of the oil wealth and whatever changes might take place in prices and production. According to this vision, from that moment on, the foundations of the political and economic model were meant to be oblique and opaque, intended to confuse others regarding their true intentions, as they led to creating an authoritarian and exclusive system, with high participation from the military. From an international perspective, the regime also based its foreign policy on a break with the past, redesigning the aims and objectives of diplomacy and international trade, according to an alliance with non-Western countries that was radically opposed to the liberal Western alliance with the United States, in particular. Thus, from early on there was a commitment to establish a multifunctional alliance first with Cuba, and later with China, Russia, Iran, Iraq, Libya, Bolivia, and Nicaragua, and to design new forms of integration while shifting away from a hemispheric and Panamerican vision of international relations and regional geopolitics.

The second way of looking at it comes from the thesis that the Venezuelan case reproduces the political situation of the Middle East and Eastern Europe, particularly the authoritarian Arab countries that are Russia's allies and have confronted Israel. To these analysts, Venezuela wants to internationalize its conflict, leading Latin America and the Caribbean to become a "gray zone" of competition between world powers within the new multipolar framework. These analysts also consider that the historical, ethnic, and religious characteristics of the Middle East and Eastern Europe are not applicable to Venezuela's reality.

Yet a third way of looking at it states that the political and economic crisis of the country, together with the growing Venezuelan diaspora and the growing diplomatic ignorance regarding the regime, is such that it justifies the strategic demarcation against Venezuela undertaken by many political actors. At present, these political actors are the United States, the Lima Group countries, many member countries of the OAS, the European Union, the United Nations, multilateral and nongovernmental organizations, and the media. Sanctions are most effective when they are multilateral. "Now that the region has bound itself to a policy of sanctions," Berg (2019) points out, "the United States must work to ensure that countries uphold their commitments." These political actors have united around a critical platform that includes coercive diplomatic measures, such as the recognition of a parallel government represented by the president of the National Assembly, Juan Guaidó, leading to economic sanctions against the regime and military threats. To justify the sanctions, the Venezuelan opposition and the governments that support it classify the Maduro government as a "usurper," given the irregular presidential elections of May 2018. They ignore the electoral victory and apply new concepts to describe regimes in crisis, such as "failed state" or "outlaw state," as well as the concept of the Responsibility to Protect (R2P).

Venezuelan politics has gone through at least three strategic stages: from 1959 to 1999, the stage of representative democracy; from 1999 to 2013, the Chavista mixed stage; and from 2013 to the present day, as an authoritarian regime. Once again, there is speculation regarding the future of *el Chavismo*, particularly after the events of Tuesday, April 30, 2019. On that day, at dawn, a small group of rebel officers and military troops, along with various opposition politicians, placed themselves near the La Carlota military base in Caracas and called for an insurrection against President Maduro, beckoning for the support of the armed forces. However, this action did not prosper. Nonetheless, the event began a new phase in the complex political process at present in Venezuela.

Why was the opposition movement that deepened its ties to the military taking place at this time? One hypothesis is that due to an informant, Juan Guaidó, Leopoldo López, and other opposition leaders knew ahead of time that the government prepared a massive repression for May 1, forbidding the march the opposition had planned in support of Guaidó. Another hypothesis is that a group of infiltrated soldiers deceived the opposition leaders, promising them that, from the moment the march started at the

Carlota military base, they would have the support of all the country's garrisons. Yet another hypothesis is that this operation intended to crack the unity of the military, to deepen the division that would favor Maduro's departure. Finally, there is the hypothesis that the opposition wanted to create a liberated space—a safe haven—to ask the United States and its allies for military support against the regime. This is not unlike what happened in May 2020, when a small number of foreign mercenaries, together with members of the Venezuelan opposition, tried to invade the country through a naval operation against the Maduro regime.

Who lost in this skirmish, and who won? The answer is: both sides. In effect, the government won because it managed to maintain its internal unity, renewing the popular support it maintains to this day. But the government also lost, because the events exposed a fissure in the armed forces that was not evident before. Now Maduro must face the defections, detentions, and scrutiny of officers and professional troops whose loyalty cannot be assumed. In effect, the opposition also won because it renewed the enthusiasm for a real change, and it reinforced its international support. However, it also lost, because the military insurgency did not prevail.

Maduro's government responded to the march the opposition called with violence and intimidation, preventing the various local marches from joining the opposition. Therefore, the United States accepted the call of the Venezuelan opposition, represented in the provisional president, Juan Guaidó, to provide military support for regime change in Venezuela. As former president Donald Trump put it, Washington considered "all options on the table." Clearly, this would lead to only one option: a military solution.

The United States also invited Russia to stop defending Maduro's government unilaterally and to join the coalition that had formed between Washington and other governments, in favor of a transition. However, Venezuela's crisis instead deepened. For *el pueblo*, the possibility to lead a normal life ended. Politically, a resolution to the conflict—a negotiated peace, or a dialogue between the parties—also ended, despite several international efforts, as was the case with the Norwegian government's initiative.

Venezuela's situation is reaching a limit, where the question of power is being played out between the government chaired by Nicolás Maduro and the provisional government of Juan Guaidó, whom the Venezuelan opposition and many governments around the world recognize as the legitimate president. The outcome could resemble a train collision. Furthermore, the crisis has resulted in a massive exodus, a diaspora that already has close to 5.4 million emigrants—around 15 percent of the total population (UNHCR 2021). They have been forced into exile, are now living in neighboring countries (Colombia, Ecuador, Panama, Peru, and Chile), as well as in the United States and Spain. Poverty, hunger, joblessness, displacement, and isolation are the consequences. As Luis Almagro, secretary-general of the OAS underscored, we can count the people in the millions already who "have been forced into exile, those that have suffered extrajudicial executions, human rights violations, hunger or lack of access to the rights of health or life. So we need to protect those people and hope that we may be able to protect them through diplomatic means" (in Brinter 2018). Some can respond to the crisis; others cannot.

Moreover, Maduro's government found itself fenced in by the loss of support of bordering countries. Diplomatic relations broke down with Colombia, the country that has taken in most of the frightened émigrés who crossed that porous border. Estimates from Colombia's Ministerio de Relaciones Exteriores (2020) show the enormous increase in the number of Venezuelans who immigrated to Colombia as the migration crisis evolved from 2014 to 2020. Because many Venezuelans who enter are in transit to other countries, in Colombia they distinguish those who are settled there as migrants who have "the vocation for residency." The growth has been spectacular. In 2014, they numbered 23,573; in 2016, they had risen to 53,747; by 2017 they were 403,702; by 2019, they were 1,771,237; and in 2020 they were 1,764,883—close to 4 percent of the Colombian population. Estimates of the total number of Venezuelans living in all South American countries put the number in 2017 at 629,261, Colombia having the most. Other countries with sizable numbers are Argentina, Brazil, Ecuador, Peru, and Chile, in that order (Ministerio de Relaciones Exteriores 2018, fig. 1). Truly a humanitarian crisis, as the United Nations labeled it.

Moreover, Colombia's government under former President Ivan Duque expressed clear support for the Venezuelan opposition and Guaidó's provisional government, as well as the United States, should a war-like conflict develop. They also consistently criticized the Venezuelan government and provided the opposition with resources and logistical support. Other countries also failed to support Maduro's regime. Guyana voted against the Chávez regime in the OAS and repudiated the Geneva Agreement (signed in 1966 between the United Kingdom, Venezuela, and Guyana, whereby the United Kingdom recognized Venezuela's right to claim part of the territory of Guyana as the former British colony was becoming independent). Guyana also seeks a solution to its border dispute with Venezuela at the International Court of Justice in The Hague. Brazil's conservative government, under president Jair Bolsonaro, has behaved aggressively toward Maduro. However, the most important strategic condition that makes Venezuela a test case is the growing internationalization of the conflict in terms of the increasingly strong contradictions between the United States government and Russia that resembles the Cold War. As Berg (2019) puts it, one conflict "in the United States' own backyard is about to get more dangerous." Washington does not conceal its intention to roll back its former assistance to Venezuela and seek a regime change there. Moscow, however, supports Maduro indirectly, behind the scenes. Only time will tell the outcome of this Venezuelan situation of dual power.

III

Cuba, Venezuela, and the United States:
Alliance and Confrontation

6

The Cuba-Venezuela Alliance

Relations between the Two Nations

Fidel and Raúl Castro and their followers believed that proletarian internationalism—promoting revolution in other countries—could ensure the survival and the consolidation of their regime. Exporting the revolution was a major foreign policy goal, and Venezuela was crucial to the effort Blasier 1976; Chaliand 2008; Chilcote 1970).

In the early 1960s, Fidel Castro not only supported the guerrillas and two Leftist-oriented military coup attempts in Venezuela (April and May 1962), but he also supported the ill-fated possibility of a Leftist pro-Cuba candidate in the Venezuelan presidential elections of 1963. Fidel also resented Venezuela not providing him with oil. Thus, from then on, there was always a Cuban fifth column inside Venezuela. At the same time, the Democratic government of Rómulo Betancourt confronted Cuba and supported Cuban exiles who were social democrats. Moreover, Venezuela denounced Cuba's intervention in their country at the United Nations and the OAS. Caracas was a key player in confronting revolutionary Cuba, as was evident during the 1962 October Missile Crisis (Blasier 1976; Chaliand 2008; Chilcote 1970).

From the early 1970s on, Cuba and Venezuela began to have normal diplomatic and trade relations, which lasted until Hugo Chávez's rise to power in 1999. Chávez and Castro then began a new relationship, deeper than anyone imagined possible. During the 1980s, because of the failure of the socialist experiment in Chile and Grenada, the retreat of the Left on the continent, and its waning presence in the hemisphere, Cuba ceased to be a strategic concern and its social model underwent severe criticism. This situation worsened during the 1990s due to the hardening of American policy toward Cuba as the Helms-Burton Act of 1996 sought to tighten the existing economic embargo. Cuba remained isolated in the region and suffered the severe economic crisis known as "the special period." While many expected Cuba to follow suit and communism to fall, the island survived when Venezuela effectively replaced the Soviet Union as its key ally. As we entered the twenty-first century, Cuba turned to the newly emerging Left in Latin America and the Caribbean: first in Venezuela and later in other places, such as Brazil, Bolivia, and Ecuador. Thus, an old debate reemerged, regarding whether Cuba was a security problem or a model for the Americas (Romero 2006).

Havana had supported the *lucha armada* (armed struggle) in Venezuela during the 1960s, helping Bolivarian Revolutionaries. However, after the failure of guerrilla warfare, the Cuban leadership had to look for other alternative roads to power. With Chávez's coup in 1992, the Cuban fifth column became evident. Cuba helped the Venezuelan movements around Hugo Chávez to take the presidency through an open election in 1998. Then Fidel's long-held dream became true. The golden age of both revolutions was from 1999 to 2012. Fidel and Chávez considered themselves brothers in arms. To help Chávez attain power in Venezuela, Cuba used the same means as its own: leadership (Hugo Chávez), ideology (socialism), and political party (MVR/PSUV) to transform the nation's power structure and values (McCoy and Myers 2004). However, to date, much remains the same. Economic dependence on oil, political vulnerability, corruption, and an inequitable distribution of wealth remain salient features of Venezuela, just as they were in the 1950s. The nation did not achieve the hope the Bolivarian Revolution held out for others.

The contemporary relationship between Venezuela and Cuba can be divided into three stages. The first stage was from the ascension of Hugo Chávez to the presidency in 1999 until 2004. The second was from 2004 until 2013, with the ALBA. The third stage began in 2013. With Nicolás Maduro at the helm, it is still ongoing.

During the first stage, Venezuela's interest in Cuba centered on the convergence and defense of one hope: two similar ideological and political projects joined by an economic and commercial agreement to create a common identity at the regional level. They aimed to circumvent the US economic embargo of Cuba, increase the supply of Venezuelan oil on the island, help Castro's regime to overcome a crippling economic crisis, implement the global Leftist movement, and condemn American military actions in Afghanistan and Iraq. In October 2000, this relationship took a fundamental turn with the signing of the comprehensive Cooperation Agreement regarding trade and commerce. This enabled them to cooperate, promoting the exchange of goods and services—in effect, exchanging oil for doctors. This led Venezuela to sell oil at a fixed, preferential price (US $27 a barrel). In 2002, the exchange entailed sending Cuba 6,000 barrels of oil a day; by 2009, it had risen to 100,000 barrels; and, from 2017 on, it declined to 60,000 barrels. At present, given the economic contraction in both countries, it is only 10,000 barrels of oil a day. Cuba paid for this oil in two stages: half of the payment was made within 90 days after the purchase, and the other half was to be paid over 25 years, including the cost of transportation and insurance.

In exchange, Cuba sent over 50,000 Cuban health workers to Venezuela (doctors, nurses, ophthalmologists, dentists, and paramedics as well as sports sector workers). Initially, this was bartering; from 2003 on, it became payment for professional services. Venezuela pays the Cuban government for their doctors seven times what a Venezuelan physician earns, which is a hidden subsidy (interestingly, this resembles how the USSR paid for Cuban

Figure 6.1. Cuba and Venezuela exchanged doctors for oil. Here Venezuelan patients wait to receive the care of a Cuban doctor in a free health care clinic that was part of president Hugo Chávez's Barrio Adentro (Inside the Barrio) program. The poster shows Chávez saying "7 Years . . . For Now" (Photo by Mario Tama via Getty.)

exports of sugar and nickel). This exchange also led to growing cooperation in the energy sector, massive official Cuban participation in the social missions initiated by Chávez, and bilateral promotion in the Americas.

In late 2004, the ALBA was created. When the comprehensive Cooperation Agreement between Cuba and Venezuela was expanded on December 14, 2004, it stated that "a convergence of positions at a global scale is sought." A key reflection emerged:

> Once the Bolivarian process was consolidated, after the decisive victory in the August 15, 2004 recall referendum and the October 31, 2004 regional elections, since Cuba is in a position to guarantee its own sustainable development, the cooperation between the Republic of Cuba and the Bolivarian Republic of Venezuela will be based, starting today, not only on the principles of solidarity, which will always be present, but also on the exchange of goods and services to the greatest degree possible. (Ministerio de Relaciones Exteriores de Cuba 2000)

Today, the relationship between Venezuela and Cuba runs on two tracks. One is an alliance between two peripheral countries: a South-South form of development assistance. This is a welcome change from the North-South alliances that involve greater differences in power and culture. Two, the relationship entails far more than just a diplomatic and commercial link among countries that share a Latin American history and resemble each other culturally. Their rapprochement is due to oil, revolution, and their common anti-American foreign policy. "Cuba and Venezuela: Two Flags, One Revolution" was the motto that appeared on posters and billboards throughout both countries, denoting their common hope. Their union was also evident in their participation in the ALBA and their significant socioeconomic exchange, whereby Cuba exported its trained personnel, mostly in the health sector, to Venezuela in exchange for crude oil. That oil is critical for the island, as it supplies electrical power to run its industries and transportation. It put an end to the many years when people on the island suffered constant *apagones* (blackouts). Moreover, their collaboration entailed promoting socialism in both nations (Romero 2011).

Meanwhile, Cuba's government issued a statement denouncing the United States' efforts to prepare a military intervention of Venezuela disguised as a "humanitarian intervention." They stated: "The Revolutionary Government reiterates its firm and invariable solidarity with the Constitutional President Nicolás Maduro Moros, the Bolivarian and Chavista revolution and the civic-military union of his people, and calls to all the peoples and governments of the world to defend the peace and to oppose this together, over political or ideological differences, to stop a new imperialist military intervention in Latin America and the Caribbean" (*Granma* 2012).

On June 19, 2018, at the meeting of the National Assembly of People's Power in Cuba, where the new president, Miguel Díaz-Canel, was elected, the government of Venezuela also issued a statement expressing their unconditional support for Díaz-Canel. It noted: "To further deepen our union and face together the challenges and battles for social justice and human development in this troubled world, in the months and years to come" (*Correo del Orinoco* 2018). Shortly thereafter, outgoing president Raúl Castro gave a speech highlighting that "the aggression against the Bolivarian Republic of Venezuela is currently the central element in imperialism's efforts to overthrow the popular governments on the continent, erase social conquests, and liquidate the progressive and alternative models to neoliberal capitalism that it is trying to impose." He underscored Cuba's total solidarity with Venezuela and Maduro's efforts to continue Chávez's legacy (*Granma* 2018). Díaz-Canel's first action as president was to hold a meeting with President Maduro. In turn, that same solidarity was reiterated when Cuba learned the results of Venezuela's election. Cuba's new president arrived in Caracas on May 30, 2018, for an official visit that emphasized two issues: maintaining military stability, and avoiding street protests in Venezuela. Other issues—the eventual OAS condemnation, the radicalization of the opposition, and the economic crisis—were not given a high priority (*Juventud Rebelde* 2018a).

Cuba made numerous public statements of support for Venezuela. When the agreement to renew Venezuela's supply of oil to Cuba was renewed on September 16, 2018, Díaz-Canel underlined that "the Americans do not want Cuba to repeat itself anywhere in Latin America." He also accused the United States of "putting pressure on the peoples of the region to adopt a position contrary to Venezuela" (*Caraota Digital* 2018a). Shortly thereafter, Maduro visited Havana for a few hours, holding several meetings with the Cuban leaders amid rumors about the negative internal situation in Venezuela (*Juventud Rebelde* 2018b). The Cuban leaders went on to declare that fully 219,000 Cuban "internationalists" had passed through Venezuela since the year 2000, during which time 1,468 collaboration projects were completed, 40 more were in process, and 2,170 million medical consultations, 23,900 community doctors, and 12,000 specialists were trained. At that time, 22,000 Cuban collaborators were working in Venezuela, and 55,000 barrels of oil were arriving daily to the island.

President Maduro traveled again to Cuba in December 2018 to attend the expansion of the ALBA's People's Trade Treaty (ALBA-TCP). There he stated that that the countries that made up the alliance "retake the socialist and integrative model to combat the neoliberalism that has been imposed." He asserted that "ALBA has been and will be the only project for the integration of peoples from Latin America and the Caribbean, who know how to reach the life of the poor man to give him love, solidarity, education, life, presence" (Rodríguez-Rosales, 2018).

On January 1, 2019, on the 60th anniversary of the triumph of the Cuban Revolution, Maduro congratulated Cuba and reiterated his commitment to its people "with the total certainty that now is when there is and will be a Cuban revolution to continue illuminating this challenging and complex 21st century" (*El Nuevo Herald* 2019).

Doctors for Oil: The Social Dimension of the Partnership

In the more than 40 years since Cuba's revolutionary government launched its first international aid mission, thousands of Cubans left the island to lend their expertise in health care to the poor in other underdeveloped nations. These humanitarian medical missions won Cuba worldwide admiration (Feinsilver 1993). However, the number of health personnel—whom Cuba considered "foot soldiers," spreading Fidel Castro's goodwill internationally—that Cuba exported increased dramatically after the collapse of the Soviet Union and Eastern European communism (Ojito 2008). By 2006, this form of medical diplomacy took more than 25,000 health care workers to lend their aid in 68 nations. As Calvo-Ospina (2006) writes, "The willingness of the new barefoot doctors to intervene in areas where their local equivalents refuse to go, because of the poverty of their clientele or the danger or difficulty of the access, has persuaded other countries, especially in Africa, to apply for assistance." Cuban doctors, nurses, dentists, and ophthalmologists worked in Latin America, (Bolivia, Nicaragua, and Guatemala); in Asia (the Solomon Islands, Indonesia, and China); and Africa (Zanzibar, Angola, and South Africa). But in all these nations the size of the medical brigades was small—typically 50 to 150 personnel—and their stay brief, mostly for disaster relief (Feinsilver 1993).

Andrea Rodríguez (2014) underscores that while official figures are not public, Cuba sent around 100,000 professionals, mostly health care workers but also athletes, engineers, and even circus artists, to Venezuela since Chávez came to power in 1999. An estimated 31,000 Cuban health workers, about 11,000 of them doctors, were working in the country. By mid-2019, around 20,000 Cubans still lived and worked in Venezuela—a major form of the alliance between Cuba and Venezuela (*Granma* 2018). In the spring of 2020, 2,000 more arrived to help with the COVID-19 health crisis.

Under Hugo Chávez's government, Venezuela welcomed Cuba's medical workers for the Barrio Adentro (Inside the Barrio) program that provided free primary health care for the poor. This was the backbone of Chávez's populist social reforms. In return, Venezuela paid Cuba with oil—from 50,000 to 100,000 barrels a day, filling the void left by the Soviet Union (Forero 2007). These doctors' principal motivation for joining the medical brigades was to improve their dire economic situation back on the island. In Cuba, abject hunger and poverty characterized the lives of most during "the special period" following the collapse of Eastern European communism (Domínguez et al. 2004). An average doctor's salary in Cuba was $25 a month, while in Venezuela they learned they could earn over $250 a month. Not realizing the high cost of living there, this difference in wages enticed most Cuban doctors and health personnel to Venezuela. Other incentives existed. Upon their return, the doctors gained access to a bank account in which the government deposited a monthly sum of $50 while they worked abroad. Furthermore, they could bring back to the island necessary appliances (e.g., a refrigerator, a microwave, an air conditioner). Most doctors returned to Cuba, where their economic situation radically improved. However, the number who defected also increased, numbering over 6,000 in 2019 (Solidaridad Sin Fronteras 2019). For them, it was a dual exodus.

With massive investments in the health sector on the island, Cuba produced solid outcomes in maternal health, infant mortality rate, and life expectancy—outcomes that were particularly impressive for a developing country. However, they also overinvested in the health sector, at the expense of other fields (e.g., engineering). Other countries, such as Chile and Costa Rica, achieved equally impressive results with far fewer doctors. Moreover, in recent years, the push to train more doctors for export to Venezuela often led to lower standards in the training the doctors received.

Health Care in Cuba

Cubans took pride in their health care achievements going as far back as the nineteenth century, when Dr. Carlos Finlay's work on the transmission of yellow fever gained Cuban medicine an international reputation. Throughout the twentieth century, they promoted the development of good quality health care. *La buena medicina* (high-quality medicine) was a source of pride for all Cubans. As Mesa-Lago and Pérez-López (2005, 83) put it: "It is widely recognized that, in the revolutionary period, Cuba significantly improved its health-care services and levels of health, but not as well known is that in 1958 Cuba led Latin America in most of the same health indicators." In comparison with other countries in Latin America that ranked at the top in socioeconomic development, the island had one of the lowest infant mortality rates (deaths under 1 year of age per 1,000 live births) in Latin America. In 1960, the infant mortality rate was extremely low in the United States (25.9) in comparison with the rest of Latin America, even its most socioeconomically developed countries: quite low in Venezuela (58.9), Argentina (59.8), Cuba (64.6), in comparison with the much higher rate in Mexico (103.1) and even more in the Dominican Republic (131.3, twice as high as Cuba's). In 2015, the infant mortality rate had declined in all of those countries—Venezuela (12.9), Argentina (12.8), Mexico (12.7), Dominican Republic (23.5)—but nowhere had it declined as low as in Cuba (5.2), to a rate that is comparable to the United States' (5.8) (Knoema World Data Atlas, 2018). It must be said, however, that in comparison to other developed countries (Western Europe, Canada, and Japan) in 2014 the United States had the highest rate of infant mortality of any: Canada, 4.8; the United Kingdom, 3.9; Germany, 3.2; Sweden, 2.2; and Japan, 2.1 (OECD, Health Statistics 2017).

Nonetheless, in the first 20 years of the revolution, from 1959 through the end of the 1980s, real advances took place in public health. Virtually all health indicators steadily improved. The number of physicians rose from 9.2 to 33.1 per 10,000 inhabitants; hospital beds increased from 4.2 to 5.4 per 1,000 persons; and the infant mortality rate fell from 33.4 to 11.1 per 1,000 live births, while the maternal mortality rate fell from 125.3 to 26.1 per 100,000 live births. Most contagious diseases (e.g., diphtheria, tuberculosis, typhoid fever, polio) were eradicated or became insignificant. Importantly, the gap between urban and rural areas in access to health care facilities and personnel was vastly reduced (Mesa-Lago and Pérez-López 2005, 83–84).

Between 1959 and 1962, when the revolution that initially sought to restore democracy on the island took a communist turn, most of the upper and middle classes left, among them about 90 percent of Cuba's doctors. This refugee exodus constituted such a "brain drain" that in 1963 Cuba barred doctors from exiting. It also began training new doctors, more attuned to the needs of the poor, especially in the rural areas. Starting in 1984, Cuba created the Medicina General Integral, a comprehensive health program that took into account not only the physical ailments but also the social conditions under which people lived in their neighborhood, aiming to prevent illness.

In the early years of the revolution, under the impact of the massive exodus and the US embargo, disease and infant mortality grew worse. Then the revolution aimed to provide access to primary health care for everyone, opening up clinics even in the remotest rural areas and mountains. Thus, Cuba made a massive investment in its health care system—not only financially but also in the sacrifice of its people traveling to the far distant corners of the island, as well as up and down its mountains, to set up the *policlínicos* for their access. Thanks to the generous Soviet subsidy that lasted 30 years, the government was able to spend 7 percent of its GDP on the health sector. Medical brigades who worked overseas were an important part of the solidarity Cuba expressed to many countries who lacked medical personnel or who had to confront emergencies and catastrophes resulting from earthquakes, hurricanes, and the like (Feinsilver 1993, 2010).

As is well known, the two major achievements of the Cuban revolution were its success in expanding health and educational services to cover the entire population, particularly those in remote rural areas. Despite Cuba's abysmal economic record and its violations of civil liberties, these two accomplishments stand. Having trained a surplus of doctors, and guided by an ideology of proletarian internationalism, beginning in 1968 Cuba also began to export doctors as a form of medical diplomacy as well as a form of South-to-South development assistance. Through a massive program of vaccinations, public health workers eradicated many contagious diseases, such as polio, chicken pox, and, particularly, tuberculosis. In a few years they created 18,090 *consultorios* (doctor's offices) in towns, communities, and *barrios*, transforming the face of public health on the island (Fernández and Díaz-Espí 2018). Public health campaigns targeted the infant mortality rate by attending to prenatal care as well as by widely practicing abortion, including very late-term, as a form of contraception. Health indicators continued to improve, and from 1995 on, Cuba ranked at the very top for density of practicing physicians. Data from the World Bank shows that in 2017–19, the number of physicians per 1,000 persons in Cuba was ranked eight, in comparison to Uruguay, with five; Germany, four; Argentina, four; Spain, four; Russia, four; the United States, three; Venezuela, two; the Dominican Republic, two; and Mexico, two (Nationmaster 2018).

The deep economic crisis of "the special period" that resulted from the collapse of Soviet and Eastern European communism spurred this new, massive export of doctors. Today, due to both this export and the contemporary economic crisis, the quality of the health services on the island has truly deteriorated. Fernández and Díaz-Espí (2018), who analyzed the data provided by Cuba's *Anuarios Estadísticos de Salud Pública* (statistical public health annual reports), have underscored the contradiction between the extremely high number of doctors per 1,000 population (7.5, in contrast with Sweden, 4.2; Germany, 4.1; United States, 2.6; Japan, 2.4) and the declining number of doctors on the island. While in 2010 doctors working in Cuba's family clinics were fully 36,478, just a few years later, in 2017, there were only 13,131—64 percent less. At present, the relative lack of health personnel results in dangerously long waiting times for many patients to see a doctor, a situation that has been aggravated further by the COVID-19 crisis. In addition, the scarcity of medicines means that the prescriptions doctors write go unfilled, leaving patients with only a piece of paper in their hands. Frustrated, they can only hope the medicine will eventually arrive from overseas, either via the charity of the churches or their family living abroad. In the past, the notion of the neighborhood doctor and *la medicina integral* had almost a mystical halo to it. Today, that halo has disappeared.

In the midst of the worst economic crisis the country has endured since the 1990s, in the years between 2007 and 2018, health indicators were negative. Maternal mortality became worse, going from 31.1 to 43.8 per 100,000 live births; and the infrastructure of health also declined—the number of hospitals by 32 percent, policlinics by 8 percent, and hospital beds by 5 percent. Additionally, all rural hospitals and health posts were shut down in 2011, and sporadic epidemics of dengue, cholera, and other infectious diseases resulted in many deaths (Mesa-Lago 2019a, updated with official data from ONEI). Cuba confronted the COVID-19 pandemic by manufacturing its own vaccines: Abdala and Soberana 2. Mid-2021, it began to vaccinate its population.

In Cuba, from January 2020 to September 2021, for a population of 11.2 million, there were 818,200 confirmed cases of COVID-19, with 6,919 deaths reported to the World Health Organization. Comparing this with a nearby country of similar size, Ecuador had 507,000 cases and 32,666 deaths for a population of 16.6 million (World Health Organization 2021). To contain the spread of the virus, Cuba closed its doors to tourism and even to family travel from the outside. It also engaged in its ever-vigilant public health measures with health workers who went house by house vaccinating everyone. The country partially reopened its doors to tourism beginning in November 2021.

Cuban Doctors Who Left Venezuela: Economic Immigrants or Refugees?

As part of this research, Pedraza conducted 30 interviews with Cuban health personnel who left the island from 1990 to the present. In Cuba, she did not formally interview doctors, since it is not possible for them to speak freely, without fear, or to have their interviews taped. Instead, she conducted informal interviews and engaged in fieldwork, traveling the full length of the island and speaking with people from all walks of life, as few academics are able to. She also visited a social mission in Venezuela. Among the doctors she interviewed in Miami and Puerto Rico, some had previously been on international missions (e.g., Haiti, Guatemala, the Seychelles Islands, Nicaragua, Venezuela, Brazil, and Mozambique). Other doctors came directly to the United States, while still others went to work in the Venezuelan missions and then defected.

The in-depth, semistructured interviews focused, above all, on the causes of the doctors' and health workers' decisions to leave Cuba and their expectations for the future. They also addressed the actual journey, including their legal status, and focused on the consequences of their decision to leave for the ways in which they were able to adapt; to acclimate to a new life in America; pass a new set of exams for foreign-trained doctors, and regain their occupations as doctors, ophthalmologists, or nurses; or to find a new occupation. The interviews also covered their relationship to Cuba and their family on the island through contact, travel, and remittances. Many of the doctors spilled blood, sweat, and tears in one of the revolution's best efforts, only to become disappointed and politically disaffected.

The Cuban health personnel added to the substantial immigration to the United States in recent years—the very large fourth and fifth waves of the exodus. The American Community Survey (2019) gives us data on the rather large growth in the number of Cubans in the United States. In 2000, it was 1,241,685; in 2019, it was 2,381,565—fully 1.2 million more in just this decade (Méndez-Pupo 2021). Since the economic and political conditions worsened substantially in 2021, in that year and the first few months of 2022 a record number of Cuban migrants arrived to the United States: 145,389— the largest yearly record in the last 60 years. Mostly, they arrived crossing the southern border.

The interviews Pedraza conducted searched for the reasons for their defection, knowing that, for contemporary émigrés, the political and the economic are, often, inseparable. While as health workers they all shared the same class and occupations, their social characteristics (age, gender, race, and religiosity) made a difference. Most were young; close to half of them were women; and their race or ethnicity represented Cuba's multiracial society (White, Black, mulatto, mestizo). The interviews sought to capture both the positive and negative aspects of the doctors' experiences as idealists called upon to help the poor, and as people caught in a web of poverty, social control, and family separation. Of the 30 interviews, 15 were with health personnel who worked in Venezuela, and 15 were with those who worked elsewhere (in Guatemala, Nicaragua, the Seychelles Islands, West Africa, Haiti, and the Dominican Republic). The latter helped us to see what was distinct about the experience in Venezuela. While the sample was too small to allow for quantitative inference regarding the various types of émigrés, the interviews do allow us to illustrate their motivations. They shed light on two fronts: on the contemporary Cuba-Venezuela alliance, and on the difference between medical diplomacy (in which Cuba engaged in the past) and this enormous export of Cuban doctors and health personnel to Venezuela. Simply put: humanitarianism motivated the medical diplomacy; politics motivated the massive medical exodus.

Despite its small size (11.2 million people), in recent years Cuba ranked fifth as a top immigrant-sending country to the United States, after Mexico, China, India, and the Philippines—all very large countries (Wassem 2009). That fact alone speaks to the scale of the Cuban exodus. Moreover, of the four major types of immigrants identified by Portes and Rumbaut (1991), these Cuban health workers exemplify three: refugee, professional, and labor migrants. Only entrepreneurial migration was not presesnt, since they were all health personnel. Refugee migration refers to the motivation of many of these doctors who left Cuba not only to improve their lives but also as the result of their political disaffection. Professional migration refers to the medical skills and training they brought with them, which many were able to utilize afterward while serving populations in the United States, depending on whether or not they attained new American credentials. Labor migration refers to the conditions under which they worked in Venezuela, including the role the Cuban government played as labor exporter of medical workers. While the emigration from Cuba was voluntary, when they were working in Venezuela they owed their travel and their wages to the Cuban state, who paid them. Moreover, their supervisors watched them closely, did not authorize them to move freely, and kept their passports from them. This also involved their transportation from Cuba to Venezuela in great numbers, through daily flights from Havana's José Martí airport to Caracas's Maiquetía airport. Moreover, the Cuban government put in place a vast infrastructure that allowed the health workers to spread throughout many cities and small towns in the Venezuelan provinces and rural areas. Without doubt, they were serving the underserved. And, since the two governments exchanged them for crude oil, they became a commodity. This gave rise to a controversy: "Is Cuba's 'Army of White Coats' Medical Diplomacy or Contemporary Slavery?" headlined an article by Karra (2021) from Cornell's College of Business.

Doctors who decided to leave Cuba to work on an international mission went to many places; others deserted directly for the United States. Many made their way to Miami not only because there is the major Cuban settlement but also because president George W. Bush established the Cuban Medical Parole Program (CMPP) to expedite their entry, a policy appropriately named Barrio Afuera (Out of the Barrio) (Carrillo De Albornoz 2006). It lasted until January 12, 2017, when President Obama ended it just as he was leaving office. In the 13 years it was in place, Barrio Afuera benefited around 9,000 Cuban medical professionals: doctors, dentists, nurses, medical technicians, and sports trainers. At present, it is estimated that around 4,000 Cuban professionals live in other countries, particularly in Colombia, without legal status, in a legal limbo that does not allow them to work or travel (Solidaridad Sin Fronteras 2019). Solidaridad Sin Fronteras (SSF) is working with Florida lawmakers to reestablish the CMPP. Despite the end of the American medical parole program, doctors are still escaping Venezuela (Pentón 2018).

The interviews also sought to assess whether this US policy was an incentive for them to desert or simply facilitated it (Ceaser 2007). Many of the Cuban doctors and health personnel who were able to enter the United States did so thanks to the legal assistance of Solidaridad Sin Fronteras. The Cuban American National Foundation (2007) as well as El CID—Cuba Independiente y Democrática (Cuba Independent and Democratic) also helped them. At present, the former Cuban doctors are working in many communities—not only in Florida but also in North Carolina, Kentucky, Tennessee, New Mexico, New Jersey, Colorado, California, and Arizona. Their spread is due to the recent US resettlement policy for refugees, particularly those who did not have family in the United States. Some were able to pass the series of extremely difficult tests that enable foreign doctors to practice in the United States; others did not but were able to obtain licenses to work as physician assistants, nurses, and technicians.

For scholars who study revolutions, Cuba's medical brigades are also interesting because they capture what is positive and negative about life under communism, about daily life in a totalitarian society (Inkeles and Bauer 1959). Positively, doctors who joined the medical brigades were often driven by the idealism the Cuban Revolution always sparked in many, to be of service to others, not unlike that which swept through well-educated Americans during the beginning of the Peace Corps. On the island, all Cuban health workers were trained in a social medicine whose aim was to bring good medical care to the poor. Negatively, doctors who joined them had their freedom severely curtailed. In Venezuela, they were constantly watched; Cuban officials held their passports; their families were kept back in Cuba as hostages for their return; and part of their salary was deposited in a Cuban bank account, but only for those who did return.

Moreover, for those who deserted, the government placed painful obstacles in the way of family reunification. The government did not grant them the visa to return to the island to visit their family, and their immediate family was not allowed to leave the country for quite some years. These work conditions led many to call the workers "indentured servants" (Association of American Physicians and Surgeons 2009). Still others called them "slaves in white coats" (Montaner 2005).

Venezuela's state-run PDVSA oil company paid for the program, pouring as much as $28.8 billion into Barrio Adentro from 2003 through 2015. The Cuban government earned over $11.5 billion a year from the work of its professionals abroad (Pentón 2018). Cuba clearly realized that selling the services of its health personnel abroad was a major advantage. Moscow had played the role of economic *salvavidas* (life preserver); Venezuela then played it, in relay. By 2012, Cuba's health workers were in 66 countries, with Venezuela and Brazil at the lead. As Fernández and Díaz-Espí (2018) and Méndez-Pupo (2021) underscore, the extremely low salaries they earned on the island constituted the major spur to their leaving the island. Thus, they accepted the dire economic and social conditions of their work abroad, as well as the severe restrictions on their freedom, and the reality that the Cuban government retains 70 percent of what the host countries actually paid for their services. In 2017, the Cuban government earned $11.4 billion from the export of these services; only $428 million went to pay for the costs of public health on the island. The results were an incline in contagious diseases, and a decline in health personnel, hospital beds, hospital infrastructure, *consultorios* and *policlínicos*, and medicines in pharmacies.

Few realize the costs of migration for these doctors. Given the imposed separation from their family back in Cuba, they arrived alone, knowing that, if they defected, for fully seven years the Cuban government would not allow them to return, nor would they permit the children left behind to be reunited with them in exile. Moreover, most of them were young: socialized and educated in the values of the revolution—with Fidel as a father figure and El Ché as a role model, from the time they were children. Hence, it is quite likely they would also feel alienated from a large part of the Miami community, especially the early exiles, who had little sympathy for them. Thus, theirs was a double alienation: from Cuba and from Miami. Since they left so much family behind, the recent Cuban émigrés engaged in various forms of transnationalism, unlike the early exiles (Basch et al. 1994; Pedraza 2006, 2022).

The social and political conditions of life in Cuba, particularly during "the special period," were so harsh that they affected the doctors in several different ways. The interviews allowed us to identify three major types of motivations:

1) Some doctors left Cuba to work on internationalist missions as economic immigrants, to earn a better salary and return to Cuba with savings and with the *electrodomésticos* they were allowed to bring back (e.g., refrigerators, washing machines, microwaves). When they left, they fully expected to return to Cuba. Other doctors hoped Venezuela

would be like a *balsa*—a springboard to the better life they longed for. We call them economic immigrants.

2) Some doctors left Cuba, where they were profoundly disaffected politically, wanting to live somewhere where they did not feel corralled, with a different set of values and democratic institutions. We call them refugees.

3) Some doctors changed their attitudes, deeply influenced by their experiences while living and working in Venezuela. Initially, they left Cuba for Venezuela as economic immigrants, but, after living and working in Venezuela, they left for the United States as political immigrants. We call them both economic immigrants and refugees.

Economic Immigrants

Odelaisys Enriquez was an example of a doctor who left Cuba for Venezuela as an economic immigrant. She was searching for a way to improve her meager life on the island by the promise of a better salary and help for her family if she worked in an internationalist mission. In her early twenties when she left Cuba for Venezuela, Odelaisys was there only a month because, from the beginning, she intended to use the medical mission as a springboard to leave Cuba for another country–a safer jump than on a *balsa*. In effect, she had no other way to leave Cuba. She had no immediate family in the United States to claim her; she had not won the visa lottery; and doctors could not leave the country until the government functionaries gave them *la liberación*, the written permit. Thus, only an international medical mission could open the way to a different future.

The economic crisis was at the root of her decision to leave. Odelaisys began her residency specializing in anesthesiology, as part of an honors program—Movimiento María Inés Manfroi—for students who excelled not only academically but also socially and in sports, as well as politically, as members of the Young Communists League (Unión de Jóvenes Comunistas). Like all Cuban youth, she had engaged in *la doble moral*, hiding her true feelings behind a mask of acquiescence.

Odelaisys's aspirations had always been to come to the United States, to find "a better quality of life." She recalled how once she was bicycling down a street and, when she stopped at a light, in the mirror she could see an older European man together with a young Cuban girl—clearly someone who came to Cuba for sexual tourism. She could hardly look at them, thinking about what the future held for her daughter, for only $30. "Such is the reality of life in my country now," she said. Her daughter was constantly on her mind. "Once she asked me for an ice cream and I could not buy it for her. Professionals in Cuba earn less than a taxicab."

Recently divorced, Odelaisys went to Venezuela alone, leaving her daughter behind, as the Cuban government required. Through the Internet, she found her best friend in Cuba, who had deserted, and who put her in touch with Julio Cesar Alfonso, the director of SSF in Miami. A Venezuelan man working with SSF helped her and others: putting them up, helping them obtain the Venezuelan exit visa while they worked in a bakery, and then getting them to the bus terminal. He also gave her courage: "Just remember that you are only one step away from your freedom," he emphasized. Odelaisys was one of the first doctors to benefit from George W. Bush's policy of "Out of the Barrio," facilitating the escape of Cuban doctors and health personnel by having them processed quickly—in her case, in only two months. "In Cuba, life really changed in the'90s when the Soviet Union collapsed and 'the special period' ensued," she stressed. "In Cuba people thought about nothing other than what are we going to eat tomorrow.... People have now realized this is not what they were promised."

When she first came to Miami, Odelaisys worked as a medical assistant. She soon found a partner who made it possible for her not to work but to concentrate on her studies to pass the medical exams, knowing that she was young enough to start life again. For her the greatest sorrow was that the Cuban government would not allow her daughter to join her, nor could she visit her. Aware that she was deeply depressed, she added, "Not a day passes by that I don't cry."

Refugees

Isaac Rivery also left for Venezuela to escape Cuba. After being educated in a military career, he went on to specialize in physical therapy. A single mother of two who hardly had the time to discuss politics raised him; his father was never estranged from the family, but he never discussed politics either. Above all else, Isaac's father followed the principles José Martí bequeathed the nation in the nineteenth century. As part of Cuba's merchant marine, he traveled widely. Nonetheless, from quite a young age, Isaac became profoundly disaffected about the conditions of life in Cuba, as he observed the privileges of social class. Most of his friends were in the military but were neither for nor against the government; they simply searched a decent economic life with a good salary, clothing, a *bolsa* full of food, and good appliances for their homes. While in Cuba, people admired and truly respected doctors, though economically they were never adequately rewarded "They were like magicians," he stated. "From nothing, they accomplished something." As a physiotherapist, Isaac's first medical diplomacy tour was to Pakistan, when he almost jumped ship. "In Cuba," he said, you live like "*un miserable* [a miserable person] not only economically but also morally, spiritually," as everything revolves around money (prostitution, drugs). "The best values crumble."

When the opportunity came to work in Venezuela, Isaac prepared his escape carefully and took leave of his mother knowing it would be many years before he would be able to see her again. Aware that he would never return to Cuba, Isaac did not expect to enter the United States, but imagined he could leave Venezuela for Ecuador or Colombia, or perhaps even remain in Venezuela. However, after almost a year there, though working quite far away from the American embassy, he was able to attain a US visa and desert as a political refugee. The Cuban officials constantly watched their every move. He had become very close friends with Fidel Alejandro Turrón—one of the first to arrive and one of the first to desert. The Cuban officials were looking for him all over Venezuela to return him to a prison in Cuba for being a traitor to them. Once his coworkers knew of their friendship and that Isaac planned to leave Venezuela, they marginalized him—did not want to be near him, spoke ill of him, avoided him. At the airport, Cuban and Venezuelan authorities harassed him, though all his paperwork was in order, causing him enormous anxiety as he missed several flights.

Once in the United States, Isaac realized that he had to start over from nothing. Obtaining a physiotherapy credential would only take four years in Cuba, while in the United States it would be around seven, more like a PhD, so he gave up on a medical career. He took classes at Glendale Community College in Phoenix for an associate degree in mechanical engineering and did quite well in the ESL classes, so much so that his effort was featured in one of their newsletters. At the same time, he was working in maintenance for an apartment complex of 350 units. He took great pride in his beautiful American wife, who had a master's in education from the University of Arizona and was on the faculty at Northern Arizona University. "We started from zero," he noted, but they soon went on to have their own home, a car, a good life. "She dances like a Cuban," he said, and "speaks Spanish Cuban style." They had a small child.

In Cuba, he was alone, never involved with dissident groups. In the United States, he wanted to help the cause of democracy in Cuba, together with other Cuban Americans, provided that what they planned to do was morally sound and nonviolent. Like many other Cuban Americans, Isaac leaned more toward the Republican Party, because the Democratic Party at times reminded him of the socialists and communists in Cuba. At the time of the interview, he had not yet voted for anyone. When asked about his attitude regarding the US embargo, he explained that the conflict was between the two governments and the exiles, and that it is *el pueblo*, caught in the middle, that suffers. "Cuba does not have an economic problem; it has a political problem. It is the political problem that has the economy *revuelta*, upside down," he asserted. He would return to Cuba to visit his family, and he planned to always help them and the country, but "this is my home."

Frank Vargas also left for Venezuela as a *trampolín*: a springboard to a better life. He was profoundly disaffected politically and wanting to escape—truly a refugee. Tall, handsome, with dark hair and dark eyes, in his early thirties, Frank had first served in the Cuban marines for a year, where he had his first negative encounter with the military. He then went on to study medicine under the faculty in the Calixto García Hospital in Havana for five years. Thereafter, he began two years of social service as a doctor, part of the FAR, in the unit that watched over Raúl Castro. From 2000 to 2001, he also worked in what had been Radio Escucha de Lourdes, a Soviet radio electronic base that was being dismantled in an area developed for the Universidad de las Ciencias Informáticas, specializing in computer communications.

Like many young people in Cuba, Frank had profound disagreements with his father, who was completely convinced that communism was a good system. An engineer specializing in videos, his father worked editing Fidel Castro's speeches for television—an operation he supervised for 15 years, making sure they came across as well as possible. A committed revolutionary, as a young man he had been in the reserves at Playa Girón, ready to combat the Bay of Pigs invasion. Their generational differences were profound. Frank felt caught between what his father thought and what he had actually seen, which his father could not understand. A young man who liked women, his troubles began due to the law that prohibited Cubans in the military from having relationships (love or friendship) with foreigners.

Cuba had given asylum to many Leftist *guerrillas* from other Latin American countries, and Frank had grown close to an attractive Colombian *guerrillera* who lived in the same apartment building as his mother, while working for the CDR (Committees for the Defense of the Revolution). Frank insisted that they were simply friends, and that he wanted to learn about her and about Colombia, to break the isolation in which Cubans lived. Because of his father's work, he had seen how they edited foreign films to take out parts they thought Cubans should not see. However, in 2003 Raúl Castro himself expelled him from the FAR and took away his rank of lieutenant. When his father learned about it, he cried, which only turned Frank further against the government. For the last four months of his social service, Frank was sent to work in the Cristóbal Labra clinic, where he suffered other disappointments. Hoping to specialize in internal medicine, he was glad when they transferred him to the Luis Díaz Soto naval hospital.

Nine months after he was expelled from the FAR, Frank's father died, of a heart attack, which his father's boss tried to blame on his confrontational behavior. However, Frank insisted that might have been true if his father had died soon after he was expelled, but not nine months later, and that there was a history of cardiac arrest in that side of the family. Another love relationship with another young Colombian woman resulted in her becoming pregnant. He knew how difficult it would be for his son to be able to leave Cuba and enter the United States, so he encouraged her to return to Colombia to give birth to their son. Born in Barranquilla, Colombia, at the end of 2006, his son bears his name.

Frank realized that the only way for him to leave Cuba was to join an internationalist mission. He applied to leave for Venezuela, thinking that, once there, he would find his way to Colombia to meet his son. However, the doctor in charge of bringing his case to the committee for review failed to do so. When Frank asked to be let go from the naval hospital, they refused his request. Thus, his only alternative was to intentionally fail the exam at the end of the first year. Since they made him retake it, he failed it twice. The faculty decided to put him under psychiatric care, arguing that he was going through a difficult period due to his father's death (though his father had died two years earlier). With his insistence, they sent him to work in the Camilo Cienfuegos clinic and to take the course in intensive therapy offered at the Salvador Allende hospital. At last, in April 2008, he left for Venezuela.

In Venezuela, Frank lasted only a couple of months, after being sent to work in the state of Zulia, 12 hours from Caracas. The supervisors told all the doctors that they could not engage in relationships with Venezuelan women, and that Venezuela housed thousands of Cuban military personnel to watch them so they would not desert. He went to work in the *barrio* called Pueblo Nuevo El Chivo, in the Venezuela city of Maracaibo. While in Cuba, as a doctor he had earned around $573 Cuban pesos a month—around US $22. Since he was single, his mother was supposed to receive the extra $50 CUC a month awarded to those working in a social mission. She never got it.

At the Centro de Diagnóstico Integral where he worked, Frank became interested in another young woman who worked there cleaning, nicknamed "la Pacha." The center's Cuban director told Frank not to go near her and transferred him to a clinic in the Santa Rosa de Lima port—a town so small that there were only ten to 12 *casitas*, and mosquitoes everywhere. Frank felt utterly alone. His neighbor, loyal to Chávez, prepared Venezuelan *arepas* (corn bread) for him to eat. Most of the townspeople worked as anglers, and five patients at most would come to see him in a day. However, his supervisors told him he had to write in the ledger that he had seen 25 patients a day—the kind of institutional lie he had become familiar with in Cuba. Moreover, his supervisors told the townspeople that in that area none of Chávez's candidates had won and threatened them with withdrawing medical assistance unless they voted for Chávez. Thus, Frank realized that, "rather than a medical mission, the mission was really political proselytism, telling *el pueblo* to vote for Chávez." He no longer wanted to continue working there and decided to leave for Colombia. He was truly sorry to leave la Pacha, but did not tell her he was leaving. "Because in Venezuela, as in Cuba, one could not be certain of who was who," he explained. Initially, he had planned to return on a furlough to Cuba, to bring his mother a washing machine, but when he saw how badly they treated the appliances bound for Cuba, he decided it was not worth it.

With the help of Venezuelans who were anti-Chávistas, he was able to defect. After traveling a long distance by bus and by taxi, they eventually crossed the border in a car. His friends asked him not to speak, so no one could tell from his accent that he was Cuban. Bribing the border guards also eased the way. In Colombia at last, they told him: "Now you can talk; now you are free." A few days later, when the news of his desertion reached Cuba, those who knew him said, "Anyone else but him."

Eventually he made his way to Bogota, where he spent 15 months helping a doctor in a clinic. During the interview, he looked at his father's photograph and said, "You were so wrong." In Colombia, he met his son, but the mother chose not to accompany him to the United States. When he arrived in Miami on August 13, 2009, television cameras filmed his arrival, as Julio Cesar Alfonso from SSF greeted him. All his experiences turned him into a refugee.

Elizabeth Rojas-Elías's work as an ophthalmologist in Venezuela changed her—from someone who only had doubts into a refugee. For Elizabeth the experience in Venezuela was just the last stage of a gradual and cumulative process that was already taking place. A pretty young woman in her early 30s with beautiful green eyes and light-colored hair, Elizabeth had always lived for her beliefs. She had studied in Manzanillo, Granma province and in Bayamo. After becoming a doctor, she specialized in ophthalmology. Highly skilled, in Bayamo she was in charge of doing cornea transplants. Elizabeth had previously joined an internationalist mission in Guatemala, in San Antonio de Ilotenango, Quiché province, where she had worked with the poorest of the poor.

A very idealistic person, even when her mother, father, and grandparents all left Cuba, Elizabeth remained alone with her husband because she still believed in the revolution, still wanted to be a revolutionary and to sacrifice herself for the best it had to give. But, witnessing the gap between what the leadership said (asking for the sacrifice of the workers, such as herself) and what they actually did (benefit from the system), she lost her political faith. Her experiences in Venezuela completed her process of disaffection. She worked in Operación Milagro (Operation Miracle), operating on patients who suffered from cataracts or from pterrigio, but did not do corneal transplants. To be able to, one needs to have a bank where eyes are stored, and this was not available in Venezuela.

Venezuela paid Cuba based on statistics, not on what was happening in the clinics. The doctors had to fulfill a certain quota of patients cared for, a certain number of medicines given, so Cuba could be paid with barrels of oil. Thus, often the supervisors pressured the doctors to operate on patients that did not really require the operation. To Elizabeth, this was contrary to the best medical practice and to her beliefs. When she aired this in meetings, her supervisors accused her of not being sufficiently revolutionary, to which she would reply: "I am a revolutionary, but this is not right." She added, "Their concept of revolution was wrong, because the revolution should mean to advance, to progress, to evolve. It should not mean to lie, to practice the *doble moral*." Struggling as she was with her values, eventually she realized that being far from family was not worth it, not for something that lacked a true basis. "You must abandon your family for a long time," she said, "a sacrifice that you can never recuperate."

While she was working in Venezuela, the Cuban government reduced the doctors' stipends and benefits. The extra $50 CUC a month that the family in Cuba received while they worked in Venezuela disappeared, as did the $25 CUC they were supposed to receive for life. They expected a raise in salary to $200 and then $300 a month during the second and third years of their stay overseas, but this was curtailed. Bringing appliances back home when they returned also came to an end. At the same time, her husband back in Cuba had little work. Self-employed as a locksmith, during the best of times he earned $350 pesos a day; however, when she worked in Venezuela in 2011–12, thousands of Cubans were let go from their jobs as a measure to reduce government costs. "*El pueblo* suffered this in the extreme. Now they had to spend their little money on some bread, rather than a new lock, making my husband's salary about $10 pesos a day. Also, he was no longer receiving the extra funds for her working in Venezuela." Again, when she raised these issues at meetings with other colleagues and supervisors, they branded her a counterrevolutionary. "I was not, in truth, against the revolution," she insisted, "nor against the process, but against the measures they were taking, which were not helping the people to improve their lives."

Moreover, Elizabeth's work in Venezuela left her fully disillusioned due to the corruption of her supervisors. One day, she had been working as usual from 8 a.m. to 9 p.m. or 10 p.m. at night, operating on patients' eyes, after which she was also expected to clean the office, for no extra pay. Due to her fatigue, she slipped on the wet floor and cut herself with a surgical knife on the floor. Not knowing which patient had been operated on with it, there was a possibility that she could end up with the HIV virus, so they got her started on the antivirus treatment for three days. On the fourth day, she was supposed to go to a Venezuelan doctor for the remainder of the doses, but she was unable to because her supervisors chose to use the car for something else. Only on the fifth day could she get to the clinic, where the Venezuelan doctor informed her that continuing the treatment for a month was now pointless, because if the virus were to enter her system, it had already done so. Fortunately, that virus has a very long period of incubation, and the tests thereafter were negative. "But I suffered from my supervisors' negligence.... Their ideals were not deeply rooted; they simply benefited from their jobs and worked with *la doble moral*."

Elizabeth was able to leave Venezuela from Yaraquí, three hours from Caracas. A Cuban refugee from the early years of the exodus helped her. A member of a Cuban exile organization, from time to time he had engaged in conversation with her criticizing Fidel and communism, to sound her real thoughts and feelings. However, afraid of others—as Cubans usually are—she thought he might be prompting her to speak against the system, in order to denounce her. In fact, he wanted to help her. "Your worst enemy is usually right in your *misión*, looking to see where and when you make a mistake so as to denounce you to your boss, to gain some sort of advantage, to take your place away." Their lives were very circumscribed—for example, they had to be back where they lived no later than 6 p.m., and they were not allowed to talk with Venezuelans. "The whole time I was in Venezuela I felt like I was in a prison," she said. After nine months, Elizabeth decided to call him and to take advantage of his offer to help her. Knowing the location of the key that locked the three doors in their apartment, in the middle of the night, while everyone was sleeping, she made her way out, to where he was waiting for her. She was afraid that he might be from the Cuban state security. But, three hours later, they were in his home, and his wife greeted them with a special *arroz con pollo* (chicken with rice). Yet she could hardly eat.

Later, when she went to the American embassy to ask for a visa, she found other friends there. They turned pale when they saw her; when she deserted, they were still in the mission, working. After she left Venezuela, many others left as well. SSF helped her, and, when she arrived in Miami, Catholic Charities was waiting for her. After eight years of separation, she was finally able to join her mother. At the time of her interview, in Phoenix, Arizona, she was working as a medical assistant and studying to pass the medical exams for foreign doctors, while trying to bring her husband to join her. In Cuba, many of their former friends had left him; he felt marginalized.

After her experiences in Venezuela, Elizabeth realized that she had spent her life following an empty ideal. She understood that her work in Venezuela as a doctor had an economic role (Cuba received oil, which put an end to the *apagones* when the electricity often went out); a health role (Venezuela received well-trained doctors who helped the poor); and a political role (Chávez received their electoral support). This last became clear. When she operated on patients with cataracts, upon seeing clearly once again, they typically exclaimed "*¡Gracias a Dios!*" (Thanks be to God!). She then had to say: "And to Chávez!"

Otto Sánchez clearly stated that, for him, economic and political motivations were inseparable—welded together as one. Otto went to work in Venezuela as an economic immigrant trying to improve his conditions on the island, particularly because he had a child who was quite ill. Somewhat heavy but jovial, a mixed-race Cuban who was partly Chinese, while in Cuba he had been a lieutenant in the militia of the armed forces, the Milicia de Tropas Territoriales. In Venezuela, he practiced primary health care, with the advantage that he could rely on medicines to cure the patient, unlike in Cuba, where they had disappeared. He was part of Barrio Adentro and worked under dangerous conditions. When he first arrived in Venezuela, he proselytized the Cuban health care system as the best in the world, emphasizing its very low infant mortality rate. That was not hard to do, because he believed it. He noted that in Cuba the network of medical attention reached across the length of the island, to cover the vast majority of the population through their access to the policlinics. However, the real goal of the health system, he came to see, was to maintain the political system: to keep those who governed in power.

Otto was part of the suit in 2011 led by the Cuban American Miami lawyer Pablo A. De Cuba against the Cuban government for the conditions of slavery in which doctors worked. He underscored that their labor benefited others, but not them or their families; that it was coerced, driven by the extreme economic necessity that prevailed in Cuba; that it was the result of the fear that characterizes Cuban relationships. Moreover, he underlined that the government separated them from their families, who were held hostage in Cuba until their return; that they had to turn their work into a form of propaganda; and that their daily lives in Venezuela were a form of imprisonment. They were forbidden to go out in the evenings and were not allowed to socialize with Venezuelans. Always they were under the surveillance of the *seguridad del estado* that were part of the *misiones*, monitoring their attitude. Doctors' movements were always circumscribed: they had to tell their supervisors where they were going, and their guards held their passports. They were threatened with not allowing them to send remittances to their family in Cuba; with not seeing their family again unless they behaved well. In addition, they were used as strikebreakers, because they did not know the labor conditions in the country. Altogether, these strictures deprived them of personal identity.

As a doctor, Otto felt that, although he was curing people, which is what he always wanted to do, he was not himself: "I had to tell the patient that he was being cured thanks to Chávez and to socialism. 'If you vote for Chávez, you will always have this.' Yet I knew that was not true because it was not true in Cuba. When you fool someone else, you deteriorate morally, as a person. Chains come in many forms." Otto emphasized that the goal of these social missions was to introduce in Venezuela "the same poison that Fidel introduced in Cuba": dividing the society against itself, fanning the hatred of one group against another. "Those who were born slaves suffer less than those who were enslaved," he argued, "because those who were enslaved knew what it meant to be free."

Otto also felt that the Cubans had taken jobs away from Venezuelan doctors; in Cuba, they were told they would be sent to work where there were not enough of them. Actually, they were placed in remote areas where Venezuelan doctors were asking for better compensation due to the danger and violence there, which had been the case for Otto. Shortly after his arrival, he had seen the Venezuelan doctors in the strike called *la huelga de los sartenes* (the strike of the frying pans). He realized how they were being used to replace the labor force that was protesting, rather than listening to their demands for better working conditions.

After six months of living and working under these conditions, Otto left Venezuela, illegally crossing the border with Colombia, with a backpack that contained only two pairs of pants, two T-shirts, and a bar of soap. A good friend of his had been caught before; he had spent a year in a Venezuelan prison. Otto left before the Barrio Afuera legislation that facilitated their entry to the United States, so he did not benefit from it. He spent some months performing whatever jobs turned up: washing cars, mowing lawns, working in a pizza house. Later, in Miami, he became vice president of SSF to help those who defected. He knew he could not return to Cuba because doctors who deserted were not given the visa to return, as punishment for their transgression. However, he hoped to one day be able to return to a new Cuba, a democratic Cuba, and to help that society prosper.

Both Economic Immigrants and Refugees

Julio Cesar Lubián originally left the island with every intention to return, as an economic emigrant who aspired to make more money, save money, and come back with a better life. The idea of deserting Cuba developed gradually out of his experiences in Venezuela. Much older than the others, Julio Cesar was 47 years old when he arrived in America. He came from a working-class, mulatto family. His father, Carlos Lubián, was politically very active in Cuba, first fighting against Batista's dictatorship, then Fidel Castro's. But Julio hardly knew him; since his father became a political prisoner, when his parents divorced his mother did everything she could to separate him from that family—probably to protect him.

For all his life in Cuba, Julio had fervently believed in the revolution. After studying medicine in Havana he went on to do the two years of social service the government expected of everyone by becoming the medical doctor for a unit of the armed forces. Afterward, he taught a course at the University of Havana and began work toward a doctorate in medical science, with a thesis on arteriosclerosis among the elderly. Then he was mobilized—that is, the Young Communists League, the Communist Party, and the labor union informed him that he had to go to Venezuela. Initially he refused, but they let him know that he would be resettled elsewhere, and his medical degree might be withdrawn. He said, "They forced me to join to fulfill the agreement they had signed with Chávez for close to 31,000 doctors a year in exchange for crude oil."

Julio went to Venezuela hoping to solve his economic problems in Cuba with a larger salary. In Cuba, he earned only around $565 pesos—about $25 a month, the typical salary for a doctor. While Cubans do not pay for housing, or for electricity or water, $25 is still not enough to cover food, clothing, and transportation, which are expensive. Thus, working in a medical mission overseas was an attractive option. The first three months Julio was supposed to be earning $100 CUC a month, deposited in his bank account in Cuba, for his return. His family was also supposed to receive monthly payments of $50 CUC for his service overseas. However, Julio called it a "ghost account" because he never saw the money. The government pressured Cubans to return with negative incentives: by depositing part of their salary in a Cuban bank account, to be accessed only when they returned; and by retaining their families. Positive incentives also existed, as when the government paid Julio to return to Cuba on a vacation, and he was greeted at the airport with much fanfare and a bottle of rum—the welcome for *un internacionalista*. Misión Patria was created alongside the medical mission so they could take back to Cuba a television, a DVD player, and a camera.

In Venezuela, he began to work near the city of Cumaná, in a poor seaport of fishermen and agricultural workers, as part of the Barrio Adentro program. Part of a small medical brigade, they were under constant surveillance by the Venezuelan National Guard, which was armed "with a real gun with real bullets," he said. Also, the Cuban embassy held their Cuban passports. A few months later, he was taken to work alone in the fishing village of Cariaco, where he began to assemble a pharmacy with the medicines he received from Cuba. Later he went to a clinic in the small town of Soledad de Cariaco. Having worked with the Cuban armed forces in the past, he knew how Cuba's *seguridad del estado* worked, similarly to Venezuela's state security: they monitored whether he had opened up the clinic, and what he did there.

A tall and attractive mulatto, Julio was an idealistic person who loved his profession and took great satisfaction in helping others. However, he stressed that Chávez created Barrio Adentro not only as a medical infrastructure but also as a political infrastructure of people that spread his message, to garner the support of the common people. Cuban health personnel were expected to point out to Venezuelan patients that their renewed health was due to *la revolución bolivariana*—Chávez's revolution. Chávez insisted it was patterned not after communism but after Simón Bolívar, the founding father. However, Julio emphasized, this revolution was really a continuation of Cuban communism by another name; as in Cuba, it was to be won through improvements in health, education, and sports. Real social improvements did take place, but they also served to hide everything else the government functionaries were doing. He believed that Chávez had won the elections thanks to the work of the Cubans in the social missions. At a time of enormous political turmoil, Chávez was able "to win with pride—thanks to our labor."

"Remember this," Julio urged. "Behind all of this, over and beyond helping the poor, is a political agenda. Chávez's government wants to show the rest of the world that another revolution resembles the Cuban revolution and will continue that same history. Venezuela carries enormous weight because it is the second Latin American country where the revolution took hold." The Cuban government also wants to solve its economic problems, he added. After the Soviet Union collapsed, Venezuela replaced it, keeping Cuba afloat.

Julio went on to become part of the new program called Misión Milagros (Miracle Mission), the miracle being the return of eyesight to people who suffered from cataracts and pterrigio. Misión Milagros won many people over to Chávez's side who did not realize that the real cause of their eye problem was the social conditions where they lived: cooking with wood and charcoal, the smoke caused their eyesight to deteriorate. Julio was in charge of overseeing 30 *casitas* a day and finding ten people to send from this rural area to Cariaco, to Cumaná, to Caracas, and then to Cuba to be operated on—all at enormous cost to Venezuela.

Julio lived for close to four years in Venezuela, through several programs: Barrio 1, 2, 3; and Misión Milagros. Clearly, going to Venezuela was not a gateway for leaving Cuba; rather, the decision to leave rooted and matured while he worked there. During this time, he saw what life in Cuba was really like: the elite lived incredibly well and lacked nothing; there was a new class; and the common people below were struggling and suffering. "In Cuba they point the finger at the slaves that capitalism, indeed, creates," he said, "but they never acknowledge the slaves that communism also creates."

After four years, Julio went to the US embassy in Caracas, where he asked to be considered a political refugee. He was giving up a good future, he knew, deserting Cuba. Having worked in Misión Milagros, he could easily have returned to Cuba to become the director of a hospital, with a car and other comforts, but the gap between ideology and reality had grown too wide. In the end, he stressed, thousands and thousands of Cuban health workers in Venezuela were engaged in occupying a nation, as in a war.

His interview took place in Miami, where he was living inside a garage, under dire conditions. "Everything has a price," he stated. "Liberty has a price. For some, the price is their life; for others, prison; for me, my family." He had not yet found a steady job. However, in Venezuela he had established a relationship with Elizabeth, a lovely Black woman from the Venezuelan working class, with whom he had a daughter. Her family's help while there had made it possible for him to leave Venezuela, hoping she would later join him, as she did.

Miguel Jiménez was another doctor who left Cuba for Venezuela as an economic immigrant, and then left Venezuela for the United States as a refugee. At the age of 45 when he arrived in the United States, he left Cuba for Venezuela in 2003, not as part of Barrio Adentro but as part of the Medical Sports Mission, a team that served as an advisor to Venezuela's National Institute for Sports, as their doctor. In Cuba he had specialized in sports medicine and was the medical doctor for Havana's metropolitan baseball team—work in which Miguel took great pride. Given his specialty, in Cuba his salary of $675 pesos a month (about $27) was somewhat higher than the norm. In Venezuela, he earned around US $333 a month, also higher than average.

Initially his motivation for leaving Cuba was purely economic. Like most Cubans who worked overseas, he wanted to solve his economic problems but had every intention to return. In Cuba, he had adapted to life "as is," he said, mostly by centering his life around his work, which gave him great satisfaction, and his family, whom he treasured. As a Cuban Jew, he practiced his religion quietly. While he worked in Venezuela, his family in Cuba received his full medical salary.

The Cuban government forbid close relationships with Venezuelans, particularly romantic ones. Nonetheless, Miguel fell in love with Cristina, a lovely, petite girl, when they were both working in the Center for Handicapped Children. They married, and he fully expected to return to Cuba with her. To that end, he kept it all above board, making certain that everyone in his medical mission, in Cuba, and in the Cuban consulate knew it. However, only a week before they were due to leave, the vice-consul informed him that for her to return with him to live in Cuba as his wife, they would have to pay US $5,000. The shock was enormous: he was being plainly disregarded as a human being.

Given his age, Miguel had lived during what he referred to as the "romantic era" of the revolution, the early years. His father was utterly convinced of the importance of the revolution. Many young Cubans were imbued with idealism: they went to cut sugarcane in the countryside to help their country, and they went to work overseas in international missions to help others. "Today that idealism is gone," he concluded. Cubans go to work overseas to improve their economic situation, and the old generation, like his parents, who gave everything for the revolution, feel lost and betrayed by a cause that is no longer theirs.

Given the importance of his work, he had to be *integrado* into the institutions of the revolution. He was a member of the Central de Trabajadores de Cuba (the national Labor Union), of the UJC (the Young Communists League), and the Communist Party. In the 1970s and 1980s, the romantic stage had given way to a more lax and economically stable stage, thanks to the assistance of the Soviet Union. In truth, Miguel said, he began to realize the errors of that way of life after he left Cuba, not before. Like most Cubans, he lived "in a state of inertia" where no one protests. In addition, he was involved in multiple activities, which, he recognized, were a form of escape: parachuting, karate, guns, even raising purebred dogs for sale. When the chaotic exodus of Cubans from the port of Mariel took place in 1980, Miguel was 18 years old and part of *la turba*: those who attacked and insulted those who were leaving, though he fell short of throwing eggs at them. He felt he was part of the system, and he wanted to return to his work, his neighborhood, his family, and the life that—despite all it lacked—was, to him, a happy one.

Miguel did not intend to desert the country; rather, the Cuban government turned him into a deserter. He left the Cuban Medical Sports Mission and remained in Venezuela for two more years, working in a private medical clinic, in occupational rehabilitation. "For me, Venezuela was like a school," he said. "I not only fell in love in Venezuela, I fell in love with Venezuela." There he encountered another way of life: a better standard of living, more freedom, and democratic politics. Miguel stressed that in Cuba, in meetings, all decisions are unanimous; if people dissent or abstain, others turn around and look at them, considering them traitors.

By contrast, in Venezuela, it is common for people to dissent and to say what they have to say, and nothing happens to them—a right that Venezuelans defend, even under Chávez. This democratic way of living prompted his own transition. "In Venezuela there really is an opposition," Miguel stressed, "that expresses itself in various political parties. Cuba had no such opposition. It emigrated." In Cuba, his "democratic vocation," as he called it, was suppressed for so long due to the "conformism" of life there; in Venezuela, his "democratic vocation" began to emerge. Given his age, and as the economic mainstay of his family, which soon included two children, Miguel did not plan to take the foreign medical graduate exams. "I left Cuba for Venezuela as an economic immigrant," he said. "I left Venezuela for the United States as a political immigrant."

The interviews showed a range of motivations for leaving: some were economic immigrants, some were refugees, and some made the difficult attitudinal transition from economic to political émigrés due to the experiences they lived through while working in Venezuela. All gave evidence of one of the strongest aspects of the Cuban-Venezuelan alliance: all showed that both economic and political factors entered into their decisions to, first, join the international medical brigade, and, second, to leave Cuba altogether, painful as that decision was. With much effort, and not without sorrow, they gradually remade their lives in America. Invariably separation from family, whether physical or political, caused them great pain. Caught in the web of conflicts between the nations where they lived and worked, they suffered.

7

The Impossible Triangle

Cuban Americans: A Divided Community

After more than 62 years of migration from Cuba, the process of political incorporation of the Cuban American community in the United States is impressive. It became extremely concentrated in Florida, particularly in Metropolitan Miami, where approximately two-thirds of Cubans live. Therefore, it has power at the ballot box. Over the years, it has had a large number of elected officials: representatives in Congress, in the House and Senate both; state governors, as well as city mayors; and many other prominent public officials. Most were second-generation Cuban Americans, citizens born in the United States; some were the "1.5 generation" immigrants who came to the United States while still quite young and grew up with its language, culture, and political life. Nearly all were affiliated with the Republican Party. Over close to 40 years, in the House of Representatives Cuban Americans had Lincoln Díaz-Balart (R, now retired), Mario Díaz-Balart (R), Joe García (D, former), Carlos Curbelo (R, former), David Rivera (R, now retired), Ileana Ros-Lehtinen (R, now retired), María Elvira Salazar (R), and Carlos A. Giménez (R), all for Florida; James Devereux (R) for Maryland; Albio Sires (D) for New Jersey; and Alex Mooney (R) for West Virginia. In the Senate, Cuban Americans had Ted Cruz (R-TX), Mel Martínez (R-FL, now retired), Bob Menéndez (D-NJ), Marco Antonio Rubio (R-FL), and John E. Sununu (R-NH). In local government, a number of the mayors of Miami and Hialeah were of Cuban origin, including Carlos Alvarez, Joe Carollo, Manny Díaz, Tomás Regalado, Carlos Hernández, and Francis X. Suarez. In Florida's state government, Cubans had a governor, Bob Martinez (now retired), and Marco Antonio Rubio, who was speaker of the Florida House of Representatives before becoming a twice-elected US senator. In addition, there have been various cabinet members, such as Carlos Gutiérrez (secretary of commerce) and Mel Martínez (secretary of housing and urban development, who came to America as part of the Operation Pedro Pan). Moreover, in 2021, president Joe Biden appointed Cuban American Alejandro Mayorkas as secretary of homeland security. The exile community's political incorporation is also evident in its exercise of diaspora politics. The Cuban American National Foundation has been a strong lobby since its founding in 1981, during the Reagan years, by Jorge Mas-Canosa, and his son, Jorge Mas-Santos, continued his work, though with a more moderate stance.

The pervasive stereotype is that the Cuban American community is a bastion of conservatism. Yet the Cuban migration is not monolithic now, if it ever was. It is divided by the various waves of migration, the contrasting attitudes of the "old" exiles versus the "new" immigrants, its party identification, age, and birthplace. Certainly, there is a split in the exile community between hard-liners and moderates, divisions reflected in their political attitudes toward Cuba's society and regime, voting patterns, and the many exile political organizations founded by Cuban Americans.

Waves of Migration

As we have seen, the Cuban exodus is composed of five major waves over 62 years. The first wave was Cuba's elite and professionals; the second, the petite bourgeoisie; the third, the working class and artists from the Mariel harbor; the fourth, the *balseros*, or rafters; and the fifth, those who walked from Ecuador through Central America, and who crossed the Mexican border to the United States. The waves entail differences in the migrants' social characteristics: in class, race, gender norms, and religious beliefs, as well as in attitudes, particularly political. Their varying political stances are the result of their very different lived experiences and memories, and they express very different relationships to the *patria* (homeland) they left behind. They are also the result of very different processes of incorporation into American society (Pedraza 2007). Over time, the dramatic changes the Cuban Revolution underwent interacted with the social characteristics of those affected to produce markedly different processes of political disaffection.

After more than 62 years now of revolution, and its many different political and economic cycles, the Cuban American community is very heterogeneous, contrary to the monolithic way in which most Americans view it. It is composed of what E. F. Kunz (1973; 1981) calls different "vintages" (as in the wine of this year versus the wine of that year). The "vintages" are groups of émigrés that underwent very different processes of maturation in the Cuba they were impelled to leave. For the many waves of immigrants that reside in Metropolitan Miami, the Cuba of their memory and desire is not the same Cuba.

Miami Cubans' Political Attitudes and Voting Patterns

Due to the various historical moments through which the exiles lived—their different "vintages"—the various waves have consistently differed in their attitudes toward Cuba. The Florida International University Cuba Polls (FIU Polls), conducted by Guillermo Grenier and Hugh Gladwin (2018) were first carried out under the auspices of the Cuban Research Institute (CRI) and now by the Steven J. Green School of International and Public Affairs. Through a random sample of Cubans 18 years old or older, the pollsters tracked their data for many years. Beginning in 1991 (with two polls in that year), many more polls followed in 1993, 1995, 1997, 2000, 2004, 2007, 2008, 2011, 2014, 2016, 2018, and the most recent 2020 poll carried out by Guillermo Grenier and Qing Lai: fully 29 years of attitudinal trends, sampling Cuban Americans living in Miami-Dade County. The 2020 poll was conducted from July 7 to August 17, some months before the November 2020 presidential election. Thus, we have a good demographic picture of the differences in attitudes toward Cuba at crucial moments in the US-Cuba relationship; we can see how trends have changed or remained stable over time. The various waves of the exodus are well approximated by the FIU Polls' data, which are presented separately by the year the migrants left Cuba: 1959–64 (the first wave), 1965–73 (the second wave), 1974–80 (the Mariel exodus), 1981–94 (the fourth wave of the *balseros*), and 1995–2020 (the most recent).

Sharp differences obtain between the "old" and the "new" Cubans. For the sake of simplicity, here we use the term "old" to refer to Cubans who left the island in the first two waves of the exodus (1959–73), when Cuba was in the process of transition to a new society that reorganized itself according to a communist blueprint. They describe themselves as "exiles"—literally, people who were banished against their will, and whose exodus was not motivated by the search for a better life but constituted an escape from an intolerable new order. As new Americans, they took pride in building a life in America, particularly in Miami. These "old" Cubans founded a vast institutional community, rich in restaurants, churches, clinics, neighborhood associations, bookstores, art galleries, and schools. They often replicated the institutions they had lost, naming them after the ones they remembered (e.g., Ayestarán restaurant, Versailles restaurant, La Habana Vieja restaurant, Los Violines nightclub, Hoy Como Ayer nightclub, La Moderna Poesía bookstore, La Casa Bacardí Institute for Cuban and Cuban American Studies).

We use the term "new" Cubans to refer to those who left the island in the last couple of waves of the exodus, particularly after the collapse of communism in the Soviet Union and the Eastern European countries (1989–2020). Since many were born and raised in the new communist nation, they do not usually describe themselves as "exiles" who were banished from their homeland. For most of them, their exodus was motivated by a meld of political and economic circumstances (inseparable as they are in communist societies). However, their consciousness was marked by the dire circumstances they lived through, the hunger and want they experienced during "the special period." They remain in close contact with the people and places they left behind (Eckstein 2009). In these comparisons between "old" and "new" Cubans, we focus on the extremes: those who knew *la Cuba de Ayer*, and with true nostalgia still long for it, capitalist and democratic, and those who knew only *la Cuba de Hoy*, the communist Cuba that replaced the Cuba of old, where life was sometimes a nightmare but also held bittersweet memories.

As of 2019, the Cuban-origin population had grown to 2.4 million, including more than half (1.3 million) who were born on the island. Of the foreign-born, 58 percent were US citizens—a rather high rate of naturalizations. As is well known, the level of education in this population is high. Among those 25 years old and older, among all Hispanics only 16 percent have obtained at least a bachelor's degree (or higher) or professional degree, compared with 27 percent of Cubans. Fully 38 percent of second-generation Cuban Americans (born in the US) have that level of education (Noe-Bustamante et al. 2019).

The most recent publicly available FIU Polls—for 2014, 2016, 2018, and 2020—were each conducted under very different political circumstances. The 2014 poll was taken between February and May 2014, before the reestablishment of relations with Cuba was announced on December 17, 2014, and the reopening of the two embassies that took place the following summer, in 2015. The 2016 poll was conducted in the summer of 2016, under

Obama's presidency, and shows substantial support for his initiatives, particularly for the reopening. The 2018 poll was the first one taken after President Trump's inauguration, with the 2020 poll taken at the end of his term. The last two show substantial retrenchment in attitudes.

An important caveat: we must note the demographic shift that lies behind these numbers. Already in 2014 and 2016 most of the first-wave Cubans (who left between 1959 and 1964) and the second-wave Cubans (who left between 1965 and 1973) were deceased, as this early exodus of people who made the original decision to leave Cuba was quite mature when they left the island. Due to the process of dispossession of the upper and middle classes, those who left Cuba in these early waves were in their middle years: the median age for Cubans who left during that period was around 38 years old (Fagen et al. 1968). A Cuban who left Cuba in 1960 at the age of 40 would in 2014 be 94 years old—either deceased or too old to participate. Thus, the early waves of Cuban immigrants represented in these data are really their children, what is often called the "1.5 generation": those who grew up and were educated in Cuba, socialized in the cultural patterns and values of the *la Cuba de ayer* (depending on their age when their parents left). They then came to the United States, where they began or completed their education (again, depending on their age at arrival). Often, they underwent a process of resocialization to American culture, values, and institutions, though much attenuated by the influence of the Miami cultural enclave that did its best to preserve the old Cuban culture, language, and values (García 1996; Portes and Bach 1985). Still, while reading these data it is important to recognize that those who left Cuba between 1959 and 1973 are both Cuban and American, unlike their parents, who are no longer with them.

Political Attitudes

The FIU Poll data consistently tells us that the vast majority of Cubans in South Florida agree that the US economic embargo of Cuba has not worked. However, dramatic contrasts obtain between the waves. Fully 68 percent of the "old" exiles (1959–79) favored continuing the embargo, in contrast to only 40 percent of the "new" immigrants (1995–2018) as well as 40 percent of those not born in Cuba (FIU Poll 2018, fig. 3).

In 2014, overall, a rather large majority of Cubans living in Miami-Dade County favored the US reestablishing diplomatic relations with Cuba (fully 68 percent). However, among the "old," less than half (40–47 percent) favored it, while 80 percent of the "new" arrivals (double) favored it (FIU Poll 2014, fig. 4).

Over the years, support for the embargo steadily decreased. Comparing the results of these recent polls with earlier polls, Grenier and Gladwin highlight the fact that support for the embargo declined from a high point of 87 percent in 1991 to a low of 48 percent under Obama in 2014—a dramatic change, close to half. In 2018, while 68 percent of the "old" immigrants still favored the continuation of the embargo, only 40 percent of the "new" did, as was also the case for young Cubans (18–39), who strongly opposed the continuation of the embargo (65 percent) (FIU 2018 Poll, fig. 3). However, in 2020, at the end of Trump's presidency, support for the embargo rose to 60 percent (FIU 2020 Poll, fig. 5). Much had changed during those years. As Stack Jr. puts it in the foreword to the last poll, "The policy shifts initiated by President Obama in 2014 disappeared. Old hostilities, dating to the Cold War period, now dominate relations between the two neighbors." Still, large differences can be observed among age groups, with close to two-thirds of the older Cubans supporting the continuation of the embargo, in marked contrast to less than half of those not born in Cuba. Even so, around two-thirds of all respondents supported the temporary suspension of trade sanctions on Cuba during the COVID-19 crisis, and close to three-quarters supported the sale of food and medicine to Cuba (FIU 2020 Poll, figs. 6–9).

Party identification also changed. With a history of the worst excesses of communism behind them, Cuban Americans distrust Left-wing politics and were drawn to the Republican Party. Navas (2018) underlines the importance of the Cuban American vote in 1980, "when Cuban Americans helped lift Ronald Reagan over Carter by 17 points in Florida to win the presidency." Since then, Florida has been a crucial state for winning the presidency, a fact that speaks to the importance of the Cuban vote (and, more generally, the Latin vote). Yet, pushed by their children and grandchildren, their vote for the Democratic Party was steadily increasing. As Navas (2018) notes, "Nearly half of Cuban Americans in Florida voted for Obama in 2012, a titanic shift from the 78 percent of the vote won by George Bush in 2004"—only eight years earlier. However, in 2020 the proportion registered as Republican went up to 53 percent, a retrenchment under Trump (FIU 2020 Poll, fig. 2).

These trends are also the result of another major demographic shift in the Cuban community: a decline in numbers from the early exiles to the recent immigrants, and from the generations born in Cuba to those born in America. In recent years, the "old" exiles declined (due to normal mortality and low fertility) while the "new" immigrants inclined (due to recent immigration). Thus, the attitude shifts here expressed over time are the result of the shift in volume from early immigrants to recent immigrants, and in both cases from the generations born in Cuba to those born in America. Fully 44 percent of the Cuban American population in Miami-Dade County arrived after 1995. However, many of them are not yet citizens; thus, they are not included in the data on voting patterns. The community is much larger than the electorate, and they exert their influence on American life in different ways. We can expect that in the next few years, when more of the "new" Cubans become citizens, their impact on electoral results will be much greater.

Transnationalism

As they did yesterday, today immigrants engage in transnational behavior across two or more nations (Basch et al. 2004; Pedraza 2006, 2022). Most immigrants keep ties with the family, friends, and neighbors they left behind and still hold in their hearts and minds—familial and social transnationalism. They live life in a dual social field, in America and in their homeland, depending on the strength of their identities, their memories, the ease of travel, their capacity to remit money, and their political engagement. Some immigrants keep ties with political or communal associations back home (Pedraza 2006). In *Sinews of the Nation*, Lainer-Vos (2012) focuses on examples of two diaspora communities who send money home to their homelands—Ireland and Israel—which were embroiled in highly contentious nationalist struggles, to demonstrate how organizations in the diaspora serve to forge national movements. Certainly, over the years, Cuban exiles tried to support grassroots dissident movements on the island, with varying success. Yet, as Tarrow (2001, 2) emphasizes, mass-based transnational social movements "are hard to construct, are difficult to maintain, and have very different relations to states and international institutions than more routinized international NGOs or activist networks." Greater success can be achieved through international institutions that "serve as a kind of 'coral reef,' helping to form horizontal connections among activists with similar claims across boundaries" (15). Ironically, these international institutions are created by states, usually powerful ones. Thus, Tarrow contends, the distinction between international relations and domestic politics needs to be challenged.

In the Cuban American community, many of the "old" exiles opposed these normal forms of behavior, especially traveling and sending remittances back to the island. To them, those who engaged in this behavior were simply supporting the Castro regime and buoying it up economically. Registered voters were asked how likely they would be to vote for a candidate who supported the reestablishment of relations with Cuba. Around 58 to 60 percent of the "old" immigrants responded they would not be very likely to do so, in contrast to only 39 percent of the "new," who overwhelmingly supported the rapprochement (FIU Poll 2014, fig. 5). In the same vein, support for unrestricted travel by all Americans to Cuba rose: from 44 percent in 1991 to 69 percent in 2014, though falling to 57 percent in 2018 and 54 percent in 2020, again due to Trump's influence (FIU 2020 Poll, fig. 17).

Remittances show dramatic contrasts. While 60 percent of Cubans who immigrated prior to 1995 did not send remittances to Cuba, 66 percent of those who immigrated after 1995 did (FIU 2020 Poll, fig. 22). The "old" Cubans think these activities prop up the Cuban government, so they do not engage in them. In addition, most of the early exiles have next to no family on the island, since, over the years they either gradually brought them to the United States, or they lost touch with those who believed in communism and remained behind. The recent exiles, however, still have a great deal of family in Cuba, and they feel it is their responsibility to help them. At times of emergency, such as after hurricanes, "old" and "new" Cubans alike collaborate to send help through the churches, particularly in Miami. This kind of assistance began under the leadership of Father Francisco Santana, who founded Fe en Acción (Faith in Action) in 1993, to send medicines to Cubans on the island who were ill—around 160 pounds a month. Since then, both Protestant and Catholic churches play a leading role in sending clothing and food and then distributing them on the island via a network of priests, nuns, and ministers. The Jewish Cuban American community also substantially helps Cuban Jews on the island.

Voting Patterns

The FIU Polls also constituted the first empirical attempt at measuring the actual Cuban vote in a presidential election—for a Republican (John McCain or Mitt Romney) or a Democrat (Barack Obama). Both in the 2008 and 2012 elections, Obama gathered one-third of the Cuban vote: 35 percent. However, as Grenier and Gladwin point out, more important is the time trend.

Cubans' naturalization rate is quite high: around 87 percent of the total in 2020 (FIU 2020 Poll, fig. 35) and naturalized Cubans are quite politically engaged. Among those who were US citizens, there has been an enormous decline in the proportion of registered and voting Republicans: from 70 percent in 1991 and 68 percent in 2007 to slightly over 53 percent in recent years. The number of registered and voting Democrats first increased from 16 percent in 1991 to 29 percent in 2014, but then declined substantially, to 23 percent, in 2020. Most notable in both the 2018 and 2020 polls was the large number of people who identify as Independents, which is also a national trend. Among Cuban Americans in 2016, the Independents amounted to 29 percent; in 2018, 30 percent; but in 2020, they declined to 24 percent, again a retrenchment in attitudes (FIU 2020 Poll, fig. 42).

Once again, the differences in waves of migration are stark: only 17 to 18 percent of the "old" exiles (1959–73) voted for Obama, but twice as many, 40 to 42 percent of the "new" Cubans (1981–2014), supported him (FIU Poll 2014, fig. 17). The 2020 poll asked Cubans whom they intended to vote for; fully 59 percent expressed their intention to vote for Trump, while substantially fewer intended to vote for Biden—25 percent. Among the "old" Cubans who immigrated prior to 1995, support for Trump hit a high of 71 percent, while among the "new" who immigrated after 1995 it was only 56 percent. Among those who were not born in Cuba, less than half (46 percent) intended to support Trump (FIU 2020 Poll, fig. 38). The FIU Polls thus give us an excellent attitudinal map of the Cuban community in Miami-Dade County, showing us how it has changed over time, particularly as the demographic composition of the community changes.

President Trump's election results are also interesting. The Pew Research Center based its estimate on the Florida exit poll done by Edison Research for the 2016 presidential election that said 54 percent of Cuban voters in Florida voted for Donald Trump (R), while only 41 percent voted for Hillary Clinton (D). This contrasts sharply with the voting pattern of other Latin voters in Florida, where only 26 percent voted for Trump while 71 percent voted for Clinton (Krogstad and Flores 2016). Comparing the most recent election results for Florida with other groups, Cubans voted for Donald Trump at about the same rate as non-Latinos (in Florida, mostly Anglo Americans): 54 percent of Cubans versus 51 percent of non-Latinos. But

Cubans voted markedly differently than other Latinos, only 26 percent of whom voted for Trump and 70 percent of whom voted for Hillary Clinton. Trump's promises to be tough on Cuba, erect an impregnable border wall between Mexico and the United States, and deport more of the undocumented no doubt drove these wedges.

At present, Latinos constitute around 20 percent of Florida's eligible voters, 50 percent of whom are Cubans and Puerto Ricans, in nearly equal numbers. The increasing number of Puerto Ricans that moved to Florida recently was aggravated by the destruction caused by Hurricane Maria. Thus, in the future, the voting patterns of Puerto Ricans (who lean Democratic) and Cubans (who lean Republican) may well cancel out each other's votes, negating the political influence of both. However, such an effect will not be immediate, as Puerto Ricans who lived on the island are not familiar with American party politics and may need some time to understand them.

Yet, until Trump's election, the time trend showed Cuban Americans moving toward the Democratic Party. However, the 2016 presidential and the 2018 midterm elections reversed that trend. Several issues seem to be at stake. One is that, for many Latinos, the recent election brought conflicting issues to the table. Many dislike Trump's anti-immigration discourse, his insults toward Latinos, and his administration's family separation policies. However, they also abhor what they see as the Democratic Party's obsession with abortion, especially salient since Catholics and Evangelicals—both pro-life groups—are an important part of their constituency (Associated Press 2018). Second, Trump's stance toward Cuba became more hardline over time, garnering more support among Cuban Americans. Moreover, the GOP threw mud in the face of Democratic candidates by characterizing them as extreme far-Left socialists. One must remember that, by definition, a refugee community is a wounded community. In Miami, the wounds of humiliation endured by many Cubans under the revolution are still open. These characteristics serve to alienate Cubans from the Democrats. As Carpenter (2018) asserts, "These strategies are particularly effective at gaining support from older Cuban-Americans who have an aversion to any socialist or communist candidate due to their firsthand experiences with the worst of Castro's regime. . . . GOP characterizations of Democratic candidates as sympathetic to communism and socialism have proven effective." Still, the Cuban vote was solidly red in the 2016 presidential and the 2018 midterm elections. Among other Latino voters, the trend was reliably blue. In South Florida, most of the Latino vote does support the Republican Party, which houses not only Cubans but also Colombians, Nicaraguans, and Venezuelans (Martínez 2020). In a battleground state like Florida, where elections can be decided by small margins, the Latino vote of this conservative pole does count, as we saw in the last presidential election.

Exile Political Organizations

Over the decades, Cubans built an extraordinary number and variety of Cuban-American institutions. If we look at the political organizations that Cubans founded in Miami, however, we get a different map. The many organizations that have sprouted over the years are sharply divided into two wings: the Right, who call themselves *los intransigentes* (see Pérez 1992), and the Left, who call themselves *los moderados* (see Duany 2015). Outside these two major factions lay a small group of radical Cubans who strongly supported the revolution, including Francisco Aruca, the late Max Azicri, the late Lourdes Casal, and the remnant of the Brigada Antonio Maceo.

The numerous organizations representing *los intransigentes* and the Republican Party include: the original Cuban American National Foundation (la Fundación, founded by the late political leader of the Cuban American community Jorge Mas-Canosa); the Municipios del Exilio; Cuba Independiente y Democrática (el CID, founded by the late political prisoner Huber Matos); la Brigada 2506 (founded by the survivors of the Bay of Pigs); Unidad Cubana; la Junta Patriótica Cubana (founded by the late political prisoner and political leader Andres Vargas-Gómez; el Comité Cubano Pro Derechos Humanos; M.A.R. (Mothers Against Repression, founded by Sylvia Iriondo and other Cuban American women); el Directorio Democrático Cubano (Orlando and Janisset Gutiérrez, founders); el Presidio Político Histórico Cubano (founded by many former Cuban political prisoners); Vigilia Mambisa; and Alpha 66. One must also include the elected representatives of the Republican Party itself, such as the brothers Díaz-Balart (Lincoln, now retired, and Mario, now in Congress), Ileana Ros-Lehtinen (now retired), and former representative Carlos Curbelo. While New Jersey senator Robert Menéndez belongs to the Democratic Party, with respect to policies and issues pertaining to Cuba he consistently votes with this group. *Los intransigentes* continue to oppose the normalization of relations between the United States and Cuba, seeing it as *una traición* (a betrayal), giving dictators (Fidel and Raúl Castro) what they want in exchange for nothing, especially not the end of the dictatorship and the arrival of true freedom. Their policy choices are to continue the US trade embargo, the Helms-Burton Act, and restricted travel to Cuba, until such a time as free elections in which all people can participate take place in Cuba. In the same vein, most of them strongly disapprove of President Obama's visit to Cuba, though they are pleased that he met with the representatives of civil society—Cuba's dissidents, meetings that did not take place even during the earlier visits of any of the three popes.

The organizations that represent *los moderados* and the Democratic Party include: the Cuban American National Foundation, with its currently more nuanced position (under Jorge Mas-Santos); el Partido Demócrata Cristiano (Marcelino Miyares, now Andrés Hernández-Amor, founded by the late José Ignacio Rasco and Rafael Warry Sánchez); el Partido Liberal (Carlos Alberto Montaner, now Elías Amor Bravo); el Partido Social Demócrata (Enrique Baloyra and Lino Bernabé-Fernández); el Partido Cubano Democrático Socialista (founded by the late Jorge Vals); the Committee for Cuban Democracy (el CCD); the Cuban Democratic Alliance; CubaNow; Raíces de Esperanza; Cuban Americans for Engagement (CAFE); the Miami Cuban Democrats Organization (Hector Caraballo); and the Cuba Study Group and Consenso Cubano (Carlos Saladrigas and now Ricardo Herrero, directors). Moreover, there are some elected representatives of the Democratic Party, such as Joe García, former US representative for Florida's 26th Congressional District, succeeded by the now former Republican Representative Carlos Curbelo, and senator Bob Menéndez (D-New Jersey), on social issues other than Cuba (e.g., on immigration).

Los moderados applauded the normalization of relations between the United States and Cuba, seeing it as an end to a bankrupt foreign policy of confrontation that achieved nothing in over half a century, as well as sending positive cultural influences to Cuba. As President Obama himself expressed it, "Let's try something new." Their policy positions were for an end to the US trade embargo and to restricted travel to Cuba. Most *moderados* think that Obama's new *apertura* served as an impetus for democratic change (see Oppenheimer 2003). In the same vein, they were pleased when secretary of state John Kerry and President Obama visited Cuba and gave speeches that spoke plainly and forthrightly about the value of democracy as practiced in America.

The thousands of Cubans who donated their time; labor; financial support; and expertise as professionals, ministers, philanthropists, staff, activists, and so forth, and whose commitment to Cuba compelled their engagement, sustained this vast institutional structure. As vital as this community has been in the past, however, it is now poised for a generational decline, a weakening of its institutional force.

One reason for the imminent decline is the marked contrasts between the "old" and "new" Cubans, with their contrasting attitudes and experiences. Another reason is the passage of time, which has brought new generations of Cuban Americans born on American soil, whose attitudes toward Cuba and the salience it holds in their lives is not the same. Numerically, the "old" Cubans are shrinking while the "new" Cubans are growing, and young Cuban Americans are coming to the fore. Thus, the future portends a decline in the numbers of those who are engaged with Cuba.

It was the "old" Cubans who founded all these organizations, in which the "new" Cubans scarcely participated. This lack of participation seems due to a number of reasons. First, it is due to the deep divide and mistrust that exists between them. The "old" Cubans feel that the "new" Cubans lent their support to and upheld the communist revolution, helping it to succeed, while the "new" Cubans feel that the "old" Cubans were insensitive to the real problems of inequality on the island that spurred the social revolution. Likewise, the "old" Cubans simply fail to realize that the "new" Cubans were born after the revolution was consolidated, and that, in a totalitarian society, little could be done to chart an independent course. All cultural patterns are learned behavior that responds to social circumstances. Gómez et al. (2008) studied the values and attitudes of the "new" Cubans recently arrived in Miami. They found that more than 85 percent of their subjects evidenced mistrust toward political systems and government institutions. Thus, one can understand that the "new" Cubans will not be very engaged.

Second, the low engagement can also be attributed to the lack of grassroots organizations expressing an independent and autonomous civil society in revolutionary Cuba. Several generations of Cubans grew up on the island unable to express their political *voice*, whose only choices were to be *loyal* or to *exit* (Hirschman 1970). Like all cultural patterns, this is learned behavior that persists over time, even when the original circumstances no longer obtain.

Third, it is due to the excessively political nature of life in Cuba. For two-thirds of a century, people on the island were asked to be vanguard workers, to donate their Saturdays to the *emulación socialista*—the political effort of socialist emulation—by caring for emergency patients in a clinic, cutting sugarcane in mobilizations, and, recently, vaccinating people against COVID-19. As a result, most recent immigrants arrive in America wanting to do nothing more with the little spare time their low-wage jobs allow them than to watch television, play with their computers and smart phones, and spend time with their families, while helping their loved ones who remained behind in Cuba by sending their remittances.

Be that as it may, unless the "new" Cubans go on to found their own organizations—a task for which they are culturally not well suited—in the not too distant future the exile community will be far less political and politicized than it has been for the last two-thirds of a century.

Age, Generations

With the inexorable passage of time, the "old" Cubans from the immigrant generation will give way to the new generations of their children and grandchildren. Despite the early Cubans' efforts to preserve Cuban culture, these new generations are now American—for better and for worse. Younger Cubans are splitting from their parents and grandparents on politics. While close to 50 percent of Cubans aged 60 or over returned to Cuba, 72 percent of those not born in Cuba have done so (FIU 2020 Poll, fig. 20). In 2018, older Cubans (76 and older) were overwhelmingly registered as Republicans (76 percent), while only 35 percent of younger Cubans (18–39) identified as Republicans (half), and fully 40 percent identified as Independents (FIU Poll 2018, fig. 15). Their political attitudes regarding Cuba and their voting patterns are the same as those of other millennials, for whom Cuba is not a major issue. The 2020 FIU Poll tells us that around 50 percent of those not born in Cuba oppose the continuation of the embargo (fig. 5), and over 70 percent favor the sale of food and medicines to Cuba by US companies (figs. 8–9). They also overwhelmingly support the reestablishment of diplomatic relations with Cuba—77 percent (FIU 2018 Poll).

With the continued demographic decline of the "old" exiles, the Cuban American community will be increasingly bereft of the political organizations mostly operated at present by "old" Cubans, with the participation of few "new" Cubans. Possibly, they may have even fewer young Cuban Americans, who lack the felt sense of a life lived on the island. Thus, one of the major divides in the Cuban American community today is generational.

198 · Part III. Cuba, Venezuela, and the United States: Alliance and Confrontation

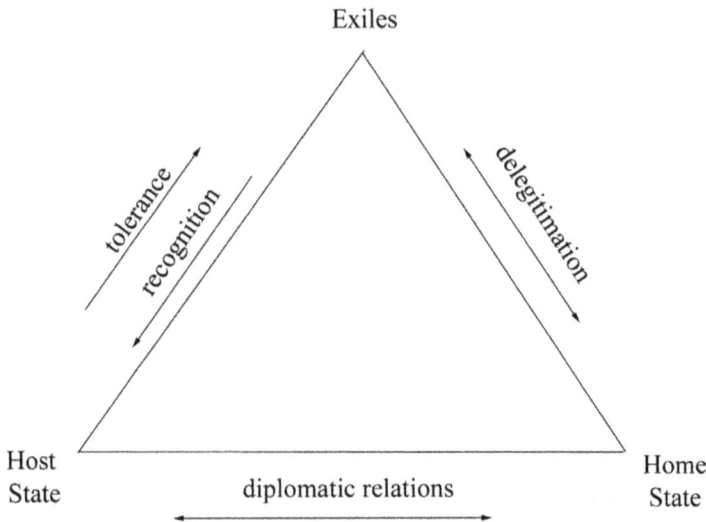

Figure 7.1. The notion of the impossible triangle (Dufoix 2000) says that the relationship between the triangle's three sides—the homeland government, the host government, and the exile community—is inherently unstable and conflictual.

The Impossible Triangle

For the many years since the United States began to provide refuge to Cuban émigrés, a triangulated relationship developed between the United States, Cuba, and the exiles that can best be understood with Dufoix's (2000) notion of an "impossible triangle" (see fig. 7.1). As a concept, the triangle has appeal because it has to do with whose side one is on, as well as with the loyalty or treason that result from belonging to different political communities. Because the triangle that develops is so conflictive, both the home (Cuba) and the host (United States) societies are involved in intelligence, counterintelligence, and espionage—all activities that regularly involve the exiles. Thus, as Dufoix points out, a great deal of uncertainty exists in the exile community regarding, as Cubans say, in Spanish, *quién es quién* (who is who). Little trust exists even among collaborators, who often see one another as possible traitors. At times, this even extends to close family members.

Building on Shain's *The Frontier of Loyalty* (1989), Dufoix (2000) calls the relationship that develops between the home regime, the host regime, and

Figure 7.2. Cuban Americans at a rally at Versailles restaurant in Miami's Little Havana. Here a woman is holding a photo of *La Caridad*, Cuba's patron saint, at the rally in support of protesters in the island, July 11, 2021 (Photo by Fernando Medina via Shutterstock).

the exile community (Miami's Cubans) an impossible triangle—impossible because the host stage cannot recognize, tolerate, or encourage the exiles politically, thus legitimizing their existence and their political goal, and at the same time support diplomatic relations with the home state. To this notion of the impossible triangle, we add that one has to pay attention to the split within the exile community: in the Cuban case, between the hardliners and the moderates. The host state responds according to its own political tendency: in the United States, Democratic or Republican. The host state has to side with one *or* the other but *cannot* side with both at once. Only when there is an actual war between the two states does the impossible triangle disappear, as the host state and the exiles stand together against the home regime. At such times, governments in exile are recognized. Such was the case during the Bay of Pigs 1961 exile invasion of Cuba. However, at times the war is not an actual war, but a war by another name—as is the case with the US economic embargo of Cuba.

Betrayal of the Exiles

Because the triangle is impossible most of the time, on several occasions the exiles felt betrayed by the host state when its relationship with the home state became more important than its relationship with the exiles. The first major betrayal was at the Bay of Pigs, at the hands of a Democratic administration under John F. Kennedy, who tried to "hide the American hand" in the operation, which could hardly be hidden (Pedraza 2007). As a result, Cuban exiles turned in droves toward the Republican Party. Electoral data is not available to confirm this, since in the early 1960s Cuban exiles had not yet become citizens, nor did they aspire to become so, still imagining their situation to be temporary and the return to a democratic Cuba imminent. However, participant observation and in-depth interviews with veterans of the Bay of Pigs supports it. The relationship that developed between the early waves of the exiles and the Republican Party was cemented later when President Reagan, through his anticommunism, strengthened the modern conservative movement.

The other major betrayal took place nearly 40 years later, in 2000, under president Bill Clinton's Democratic administration, with the youngest rafter: the *balserito* Elián González (Pedraza 2000, 2007). That incident took place just a couple of years after Cuba's downing of the two airplanes manned by the exile group Hermanos al Rescate on February 24, 1996. They intended to distribute very small leaflets with the articles from the Universal Declaration of Human Rights over the city of Havana. The result was the Cuban military caused the death of the four young pilots.

After this incident, President Clinton sided with the exiles and signed the Helms-Burton Act, legislation the Cuban American National Foundation (CANF), under Jorge Mas-Canosa's leadership, lobbied through Congress. The Helms-Burton Act was CANF's greatest triumph, though it depended on a notion of dual citizenship, asserting that, as Cubans, those who were dispossessed of their property by the Cuban government were entitled to restitution as Americans, in American courts (Smith 2000, 146; cf. Roy 2000). Tony Smith (2000), who has analyzed ethnic group lobbies and the influence the most successful can have on their host governments, points out that the CANF was at its most influential in the two presidential elections in the 1990s. They were one of the ethnic lobbies that could muster at least $1 million in targeted campaign contributions and 250,000 votes in selected congressional districts. For a long time, they were also the "voice" of the Cuban American community.

Another major betrayal came during the Elián González case. Elián, a six-year-old child, was found by fishermen on Thanksgiving Day 2000, tied to a tire floating at sea in the Florida Keys. A child that tugged at one's heartstrings, Elián's family nearly tore his fate apart. After his mother died at sea, on the island his father claimed him, but his uncle's family in Miami sought to keep him, since, they argued, his mother had drowned trying to bring him to a land of liberty. Moved by the tragedy of the Cuban family split apart by the continuing exodus, as well as by the economic interests of American farmers, Congress eased the embargo. They allowed the sale of food and medicine to Cuba—commerce that is still in place, making the United States one of Cuba's major trading partners in the new millennium.

Also under Bill Clinton's presidency, when the Cuban American community rallied behind Elián's cause, the United States withdrew its support

Figure 7.3. After the reestablishment of US-Cuba relations, ground crew welcome one of the first American flights. They hold American and Cuban flags near a recently landed JetBlue airplane at the Abel Santamaría International Airport in Santa Clara, Cuba, August 31, 2016 (Photo by Alexandre Meneghini via Reuters).

from the exiles, who sided with Elián's family in Miami. Thus began a saga that made the little boy the center of a struggle between Cuban exiles in Miami and the Cuban government on the island.

In Miami, Elián became a symbol of communism's harm, a standard borne by the opposition. Sylvia Iriondo, president of M.A.R., expressed it well: "In that child, we saw all the pain and all the suffering of 41 years. Elián symbolizes the pain of the Cuban family, the Cuban families that throughout 41 years of oppression have been divided by one man and one system" (in Bikel 2001).

The Cuban government also seized the opportunity to politicize the event. They insisted that the child was Cuban, and that his father wanted him to return to Cuba, to grow up with him there. Always able to pull the masses out on the streets, Fidel Castro demanded a mass mobilization, and Cubans were rounded up to participate at their workplaces and in their neighborhoods. In Cuba, Elián became a symbol of the inhumanity both the United States and the "Miami mafia" (as Fidel Castro repeatedly called the organized exiles) were capable of toward Cuba. Throughout the island, one could see posters depicting Elián's plight. One showed him behind polka-dot bars, reading *Salvemos a Elián* (Let us save Elián); another showed him looking sad, reading *Liberen a Elián* (Free Elián). Elián was said to be *secuestrado*, or kidnapped (Pedraza 2000, 2007). As Dufoix (2000) notes, both the exiles and the home country engaged in delegitimation of the other.

While the exiles made the cause of the *balserito* a political one, about not returning to Cuba a child that escaped communism at the cost of his mother's death, President Clinton, attorney general Janet Reno, and immigration commissioner Doris Meissner failed to recognize the exiles' claim. Instead, they sided with the Cuban side of the triangle, insisting that the issue had to be depoliticized since it involved only the return of a child to his father. In the end, police seized the boy by force from his uncle's home in Miami. He was returned to his father, who was waiting for him in Washington, DC, over the protests of a large part of the Cuban community who adamantly wished to save the boy from communism. Father and son returned to Cuba right away.

Elián's case had important consequences. One consequence was that the American people grew sympathetic toward the plight of the Cuban people on the island, their poverty and want, sympathy that helped to ease

Congress's trade restrictions against Cuba. For the first time, through the Trade Sanctions Reform and Export Act (TSRA), the embargo was softened, and the House of Representatives—by the extraordinarily wide margin of 86 to 8—agreed to allow the sale of food and medicine to Cuba during Elián's very last days in the United States. This was a fundamental shift in policy: the first US agricultural sales to Cuba in 38 years (Radelat 2000). Under TSRA, agricultural products and medical supplies have been the two exceptions to the long-standing embargo. US exports to Cuba presently constitute around $300 million—a very large share of Cuban exports—mostly in sales of poultry, soybean meal, corn, feed, and fodders (US Department of Agriculture 2015). Looking at US trade with Cuba, with no imports, we see that, in 1998, prior to Elián's arrival, total trade exports amounted to only $3.6 million. Thereafter, it rose: in 2000, to $7.0 million; in 2004, to $404.1 million; in 2007, to $ 447.1 million. At the end of George W. Bush's administration, it reached its peak, at $711.5 million in exports. In recent years, it has declined substantially, even during the Obama thaw: in 2014, to $299.2 million; in 2016, to $241.8 million; though in 2018 it went back up to $269.7 million and $283.9 in 2019 (US Census Bureau, 2020).

Yet another consequence of *el balserito* was the massive flight of Cuban Americans away from the Democratic Party. This impact can be seen when contrasting the results of the 1997 and 2000 FIU Polls in Miami-Dade County. The polls showed that, of the registered Cuban voters, 33.5 percent voted for Bill Clinton in the 1996 presidential election; in 2000, that percentage more than halved, down to 14.9 percent—the *voto castigo* (revenge vote), as it was called, to punish the Democratic Party for the betrayal involved in the Elián González case. George W. Bush's campaign benefited from this electoral shift, with 63.8 percent of the Cuban vote in the Miami area going to him. Sergio Bendixen, a Miami-based pollster, points to the revenge vote as the main reason for the increase (in Schneider 2001).

In the more recent presidential and legislative elections of 2014, 2016, 2018, and 2020, despite very different candidates, Cubans in Miami-Dade (FIU Polls) or Florida (PEW Research Center) mostly voted Republican, but at much lower rates. Until recently, it was the proportion voting Democratic that changed, with a dramatic increase. In the 2020 presidential elections, Democrat Joe Biden got 66 percent of the vote in national exit polls, on par with Hillary Clinton's 65 percent in 2016. However, incumbent president Donald Trump picked up Florida's 29 electoral votes, for which the Cuban vote was decisive. In Florida, Cubans voted 56–41 for Trump, compared to an even 49–49 split among non-Cuban voters. By contrast, Puerto Ricans in Florida voted 31–68 for Biden (Sonneland 2020).

War by Another Name

In his analysis of the impossible triangle, Dufoix (2000) also observes that the attitude of both the home and host country toward the exiles expresses a different logic. In the case of the host country (the United States), the predominant concern regarding the exiles is keeping an eye on them. At times of war, surveillance can turn into detention and internment. In the case of the home country (Cuba), the predominant concern regarding the exiles who reside elsewhere is neutralizing them. Cuba is aware that, while they successfully externalized their dissent, they also created a substantial opposition abroad, a new political actor.

As Dufoix (2000) stresses, on a continuum of politics at one end and war at the other, exile politics are closer to war (seeking the overthrow of the regime) than to what is usually called "politics" (the art of bargaining, compromise, and negotiation). Over more than 60 years, exile politics ranged from war-like to open war. The American government also engaged in a war by another name: the trade embargo. This policy has remained in place because the intransigent "wing" of the exiles insisted on it, despite a widespread lack of support among the international community, which consistently votes against the embargo at the United Nations, as well as from the moderate wing of the exile community. Examples of real war abound: the Bay of Pigs invasion, among other forays into Cuba organized by groups such as Alpha 66. Examples of war by another name include the trade embargo; the exiles' denunciation of Cuba's human rights violations before the United Nations; and the culture wars in Miami, when Cuban musicians such as Los Van Van come to play and are met with enormous hostility, reminiscent of the *actos de repudio* in Cuban political culture. Even when exile politics most resembles normal politics (e.g., the creation of the Cuban American National Foundation, whose goal was to lobby the US Congress), its intent was also war-like (the passage of the Helms Burton Act tightening the embargo's screws).

Though united in its rejection of Castro's communism, the Cuban exile community is more heterogeneous than most imagine, embracing a wide range of political expression across the various waves of the exodus and the two major factions in the organized political community: the moderates versus the intransigents. The two major groups share the goal of promoting the return to a democratic government in Cuba, but radically disagree with respect to the means. More often than not, their attitude toward one another is acrimonious and contemptuous.

Both "wings" practice political transnationalism, helping the dissidents in Cuba. *Los intransigentes* see war and open confrontation with the Cuban government as the instrument to achieve that end, with violence as an inevitable prelude. As the late Andrés Vargas-Gómez—then president of Unidad Cubana—emphasized, "Castro will never sit at a negotiation table to negotiate his exit from power" (in Pedraza 2007, interview). These exiles help the internal resistance in Cuba and those dissidents such as Marta Beatriz Roque that deny the present Constitution and propose a return to the 1940 Constitution. By contrast, *los moderados* see constructive engagement with the Cuban government, a dialogue, as the way to a negotiated, peaceful transition to democracy. As the late José Ignacio Rasco—founder of the Partido Demócrata Cristiano (PDC)—explained, "a dialogue is necessary to attain real reforms that will usher in a transition without concessions, violence, or fanaticism" (in Pedraza 2007, interview). Thus, it is only sensible for these exiles to seek nonviolent alternatives to develop in Cuba. They support those dissidents, such as the late Oswaldo Payá of the MCL, as well as Guillermo Fariñas and José Daniel Ferrer of UNPACU, groups that work within the limits of the present Constitution. While they wish to preserve the advances made in education and health care, they propose real changes, particularly the release of political prisoners; supporting self-employment; and electoral, parliamentary democracy (Payá 2001, 2018).

Many analysts have complained that the quality of the opposition in Cuba is poor. However, in the absence of rights, freedoms, rule of law, and due process, it is remarkable that they have been able to hold out for so many years. In a country where there is no free press, where the government and the *seguridad del estado* (state security) marginalizes and jails opposition leaders while threatening and excluding from the body politic those who support them, and where there is a lack of open, political debate, dissidents can hardly flourish. Nonetheless, they have stood their ground. Those in the United States and elsewhere who support them practice a form of political transnationalism. These days, that entails helping them through the Internet, social media, and other virtual tools.

Dufoix's (2000) notion of the "impossible triangle" is an insightful way to make sense of the organization of exile politics by showing the inherent instability and change that takes place between the three sides of the triangle that poses distinct dilemmas for each. However, we add that the Cuban case tells us that divisions within the exile community must also be considered, especially as the host state responds to them. The US government can side with one or the other wing of the exile community, but not with both at once. When the United States sides with the Cuban government or *los moderados*, as Obama did, *los intransigentes* feel betrayed. When the United States opposes the Cuban government and sides with *los intransigentes*, as Trump did, they feel recognized, but *los moderados* despair. Hence, the triangle remains impossible.

To *los intransigentes*, the recent reestablishment of relations between the United States and Cuba spearheaded by Obama was just another betrayal by an uncaring American government that, yet again, took the side of the Cuban government. They were far more satisfied with Trump's meeting with them in the Manuel Artíme theater, in the heart of Miami's "Little Havana," in June 2017, when he praised the former political prisoners in their midst and promised he would take a tougher stance toward Cuba.

No doubt *los intransigentes* were satisfied with President Trump's new sanctions that John Bolton, then national security advisor, announced at the Bay of Pigs veterans site in Miami, on the very date commemorating the day of the invasion nearly 60 years later, on April 17, 2019 (Wilkinson 2019). The new sanctions were aimed not only at Cuba but also at Venezuela and Nicaragua, which Bolton called "the troika of tyranny." They included doing away with the "people to people" travel category started by former president Bill Clinton; lowering the amount of remittances that may be sent from overseas; canceling domestic airlines flight to cities other than Havana; and ending cruises traveling to the island, which dated from former President Obama's policies. The sanctions also included unearthing some of the provisions of the Helms-Burton Act regarding the right to litigate over confiscated property, provisions the US government had never executed. Before his presidency ended, Trump's sanctions also included prohibiting American companies from doing business with the Cuban firms under GAESA (Grupo de Administración Empresarial, S.A.)—the group of business enterprises controlled by the military. He also closed all Western Union offices through which the exiles sent remittances to their families. Remittances could only be sent through the *mulas* (mules) that sell their services in the exile community, taking money and goods with them when they travel to the island. That travel is now more difficult than ever, however, aggravated by the spread of COVID-19. Sixteen months after becoming president, Biden at last reversed these extreme sanctions.

To *los moderados* the reestablishment of relations under Obama was a harbinger of hope, a new politics that might serve to empower the Cuban people so they could take the future in their own hands. To them, Trump's many efforts to undo Obama's legacy was a return to an old and failed politics.

During the first 20 years of the Cuban Revolution, the government called the exiles "traitors" and prevented them from returning to Cuba. Most of the early exiles did not try to return, since to them travel to Cuba was supporting the regime. Moreover, there were no avenues to send anything, such as money or medicines, from the United States to Cuba. Therefore, only exiles who resided in other countries, such as Spain or South America, were able to use some forms of communication with the island to help their families. Thus, among the "old" Cubans, transnationalism was unable to develop. The situation changed beginning in 1979, when, as a result of the dialogue between the Cuban government and representatives of the exiles, family reunification return travel to the island began to be allowed and has never ceased.

Increasingly, Cuban Americans began to distinguish between targeting the Cuban government and targeting the transnationalism of their fellow Cuban Americans. Nonetheless, as the FIU Cuban Poll data show, the "old" Cubans, who have little or no family left on the island, continue to disapprove of return travel and well as sending remittances to Cuba. Such is not the case among the "new" Cubans, who have a great deal of family still on the island and travel to see them and send them medicines and monetary help.

By contrast, Venezuelans who left their country were always able to return and able to help those left behind. Thus, Venezuelan émigrés were able to be part of transnational exchanges. In the new millennium, as Duany (2018) shows, both among Cubans and Venezuelans the extent of all forms of communication rose extraordinarily: travel, phone calls, letters, and emails. As a result, the number of remittances also rose dramatically. Somewhere between 30 to 40 percent of the Cuban community in Miami send them to the island. Estimates of remittances vary, though not widely. Since Cuba does not publish data on remittances, estimates come from source country statistics. Luis (2019) estimates that in 2017 they were about

$2,248 million for cash remittances and $6,034 million including in-kind transfers; Morales's (2022) estimates for the same year are $3,575 million for cash remittances and $6,565 for total remittances.

The remittances mostly support consumption, but they also capitalize or help to sustain a small enterprise, for self-employment. This has turned the émigrés into key economic actors on the island. Despite the US embargo, Duany (2018) points out, the émigrés and their remittances contribute enormously to the daily life of a large part of the island's population: "Cuba's economy could scarcely survive were it not for the massive flow of remittances the émigrés send." At present, three pillars hold up Cuba's economy: the immigrant remittances, the export of professionals, and tourism. Duany concludes: "It is not an exaggeration to say that the future of the Cuban nation depends, in large part, on the economic remittances between the immigrants and their land of origin." Yet, toward the end of Trump's administration, it became nearly impossible for Cuban immigrants to send remittances to help their families. Though expectations regarding Biden ran high that his administration would return to Obama's policies, the new president moved slowly.

The need to help Cuba became crystal clear when, in July 2021, massive protests took place in the poorest neighborhoods of Havana and Santiago de Cuba and continued throughout the length of the island for a week—evidence of the desperate nature of life in Cuba for so many. While some wanted to attribute the protests solely to economic deterioration, the protesters made the political nature of the protests clear. They held up signs that told everyone "@SOSCuba" and chanted not *Patria o Muerte* (Our Homeland or Death)—Fidel Castro's favorite slogan—but instead *Patria y Vida* (Our Homeland and Life). The song "Patria y Vida" became a hymn that criticized what Cuba had become, using the image of a game of dominoes that is *trancado* (stuck), so Cubans are unable to play further. The lyrics tell everyone that the government has the domino that says "5–9" (the 1959 revolution) while *el pueblo* has the domino that is a double two (the hope that life will change in Cuba in 2022). The lyrics also captured the sorrow of life in Cuba today, when it mentioned the tears mothers cry as they watch their children leave.

"Patria y Vida" is a form of both social and political transnationalism, as musicians who were in the US together with those who were in Cuba wrote the reggaeton. From Miami, Yotuel Romero sent the ones in Cuba *la maqueta* (the model). Also outside the island were Gente de Zona and Decemer Bueno. Inside the island, the musicians collaborated. They knew they would be the ones to pay the costs, as Eliexer Marquez "el Funky," who arrived a few months later in Miami, underlined (in Pedraza 2021, interview). On the island remained Luis Manuel Otero-Alcántara and Maykel Osorbo, both of whom are political prisoners that Amnesty International has declared to be "prisoners of conscience." Turning Fidel Castro's *Patria o Muerte* upside down, Afro-Cubans on the island and in exile were able to give everyone a compass for the struggle against a repressive government in Cuba.

Given the dire situation, in early fall 2021, Biden's administration extended humanitarian aid. Flights carrying thousands of pounds of medicines in sacs began to depart from the United States, particularly Miami, for major cities all around the country. In this effort, Cuban Americans and the churches were centrally involved.

Still the tragic history of the Cuban Revolution, its exiles, and the American government continues to replay itself. Only time will tell which side of the triangle, and which side of the Cuban American community, will prevail.

Venezuela's Developing Exile

Venezuelans in Florida and in other American states are developing a sizable exile community, and a young one—only about 20 years old, they are also engaged in a process of political incorporation. In recent years, Venezuelans were pushed to leave their country by the increasingly deteriorating social and economic conditions, making food and medicines scarce; the political instability; and the violence—both street crime and political unrest. Since 1990, the Venezuelan-origin population has grown more than fivefold, going from 49,000 to 248,000 between 1990 and 2013, growing to 383,841 in 2018, with the proportion that is US-born getting larger (López 2015; US Census Bureau, American Community Survey 2019). From 1990 to 2000, Venezuelans were the second-fastest-growing group of Latinos in the United States, growing by 157 percent in that decade, followed by enormous growth again thereafter (Sanchez-R. 2011). By 2008, the number of Venezuelans admitted to the United States was over half a million. Those who were able to obtain permanent resident status grew from 2,498 in 1999 to 10,514 in 2008, indicating a desire to stay. As of 2019, the number of Venezuelans in the United States was 549,256—half a million (US Census Bureau, American Community Survey 2019).

Overall, Venezuelans in the United States are young and well educated, particularly in the age range of 25 to 44, the labor force range. Data from the American Community Survey (2019) show that 29.3 percent of the early immigrants hold a bachelor's degree, and 21.4 percent have a graduate or professional degree—in other words, about 51 percent have a high level of education, in contrast to the overall US population, only 27.1 percent of which has a similar level. A very large proportion—43 percent—are concentrated in professional and managerial occupations, in contrast to only 34 percent of the US population in that social class. As is typical of a refugee exodus in its early years, the Venezuelan immigration is highly selective: young, well-educated professionals predominate. In recent years, low income and poor people have been leaving the country (Sanchez-R. and Aysa-Lastra 2013), and continue to do so, in these COVID-19 times.

In 2017, Venezuelans led in asylum applications in the United States, substantially more than the second place held by China (Brocchetto et al. 2017). Today, most of the community is legal or protected by the Temporary Protected Status (TPS). As with other new immigrant groups, Venezuelans are engaged in transnational exchanges involving sending remittances to the family back home, traveling back, and communicating regularly with those left behind, while also influencing them. Sanchez-R. and Aysa-Lastra (2013) have collected data on the formation of immigrant organizations among South American immigrants. Among them, Venezuelans founded quite a number of organizations, particularly in the last 20 years or so. Most of them are sociocultural organizations whose aim was to help Venezuelans integrate to life in the United States (e.g., student associations, neighborhood associations), followed by transnational organizations that link life in the immigrant community with the homeland via NGOs in Venezuela that seek to assist the people left behind.

In the United States, the areas with the greatest concentration of Venezuelans are the Northeast (particularly New York City), Florida (Miami, Tampa, Orlando), and Texas (Houston, Dallas). In Miami, they are very concentrated in the suburbs of Weston and Doral. Although their naturalization rates were originally low (Barkan 2013), they have risen. Their concentration in Doral has already allowed them to elect a Venezuelan-born mayor, in a city bursting with Venezuelan immigrant politics. Moreover,

Juan Guaidó has a representative in Washington, DC, Carlos Vecchio (recognized by the American government as the Venezuelan ambassador to the United States), and another Venezuelan politician living in Bogotá, Julio Borges, who was in charge of Guaidó's international affairs. Both Carlos Vecchio and Julio Borges are opposition leaders in exile whom Washington recognized as the legitimate representatives of Venezuela's government, shortly after Guaidó took an oath to assume the presidency on an interim basis in January 2019. There they argued that dialogue between Maduro and the opposition—the tactic endorsed by Mexico, Uruguay, the Vatican, Norway and some liberals in Congress—"does not put Venezuela on the path to free and fair elections" (Daugherty 2019).

At present, Venezuelan politics includes the significant associations that developed between the government of former president Trump and other American politicians, mostly Republicans, and the Venezuelan leadership in exile. The opposition to Maduro organized itself as a lobby in Washington, hoping to influence the decisions of the US government—Congress, the White House, and diplomats around the world—to support Guaidó's interim government and push for regime change in Venezuela. Their message has been consistent: dialogue with Maduro is a waste of time, and international pressure is a key ingredient in helping Venezuela accomplish their goal of free and fair elections (Daugherty 2019). Thus, Guaidó appointed over 15 ambassadors (most of them as "representatives") of Venezuela in exile.

Vecchio underlined that there are "three types of pressure to be exerted now. One is internal pressure, people out in the streets. Then we have pressure from the National Assembly, the only legitimate democratic institution in the country. The third is international pressure" (Daugherty 2019). Vecchio also met with former vice president Mike Pence and with seven members of Congress from both parties, including South Florida representatives, as well as a group of US senators, including Florida's Marco Rubio and Rick Scott. The Cold War and the mentality that accompanied it have returned. Dan Coats, former director of national intelligence, called Venezuela "a danger to American interests" and stated that the US government expects Cuba, Russia, and China to "prop up the Maduro government," motivated not only by their international alliance but also by Venezuela's oil. Trump's secretary of state Mike Pompeo also announced that the US government would provide $20 million in humanitarian assistance. Getting it to the desperate people was the most pressing issue. Since the situation has not improved, Venezuelans continue leaving the country en masse. It is forecasted that by the end of 2022 it may well be 7 million Venezuelans living abroad, one-quarter of the total population.

Martínez (2020), together with the Public Opinion Research Laboratory of the University of North Florida for *El Diario*, has presented the first survey of 1,665 Venezuelans regarding the Venezuelan vote in Florida's elections. In August 2020, among registered voters, 16 percent identified with the Democratic Party and 21 percent identified with the Republican Party, with fully 61 percent not yet being affiliated with either. All three groups, however, strongly supported former president Trump's economic sanctions against Maduro's government. Even more, 86 percent believe that the United States should take military action to remove Maduro from his post. Fully 70 percent supported Trump's reelection, as they saw him as a good ally to achieve democracy in Venezuela. While 95 percent of the registered Republicans said they would vote for Trump (as one would expect), even 53 percent of registered Democrats said they would. Most Venezuelans recognize Juan Guaidó as the legitimate president and the leader of the opposition, except for a radical Right group that does not like Guaidó and calls for a US military invasion of Venezuela. While overall the number of Venezuelans who can vote in Florida is only around 60,000 (in contrast to around 600,000 Cubans and 190,000 Colombians), as Martínez underscores, together with the other Latinos who will cast most of their votes for the Republicans—the Cubans, Colombians, and Nicaraguans—the Venezuelan vote can be decisive, as part of a conservative pole. It can make a difference in the gap between candidates, or even in reversing a tendency in the small congressional districts.

Depending on how long the Venezuelan exile lasts, it is reasonable to expect that it will gradually follow the path of political incorporation that Cuban Americans sowed and for which their high levels of human capital prepare them. Yet, like other recent immigrants, most carry in their hearts the dream of return to a better reality back where their hearts call "home." An attempt at negotiation and compromise is now taking place in Mexico. Who wins will seriously influence the development of this rather new Latin immigrant community in Florida. In the meantime, what was once one of Latin America's most prosperous nations lies broken and suffering.

8

Crisis in Cuba

Revolution and Reform

Economic and Political Crises

Both Cuba and Venezuela are living through extremely deep crises. In Cuba, the economy is dismal; in Venezuela, it has collapsed. Inequality has risen dramatically—in Cuba, both of class and race; in Venezuela, of class, with enormous political polarization. Moreover, in Cuba, the exodus continues, not only to America but increasingly to other lands, drawing particularly from the young. In Venezuela, the exodus is now a humanitarian crisis. The Cuba-Venezuela alliance that bolstered both revolutions remains politically strong; however, its economic underpinning is now weak. In Cuba, the revolution is now an old revolution, housing distinct political generations, as well as a growing dissident movement, with new challenges to the government's political legitimacy. In Venezuela, the crisis of political legitimacy manifests itself in the dual power of two heads of state. The economic sanctions imposed by former president Trump deepened the economic crises.

Economic Crisis and Economic Reforms

For over half a century, Cuba relied on the twin leadership of the two Castro brothers: Fidel at the helm of government, Raúl at the helm of the military. Through their joint leadership, Cuba managed to survive the deep economic crisis that intensified with the collapse of communism in the Soviet Union in 1989 and that Fidel dubbed "the special period." Cuba lost its benefactor and its economic lifeline, particularly serious given its isolation from the rest of the world. That crisis reached its peak in 1989–93, when

GDP contracted by one-third (Mesa-Lago 2011). The food shortages were so severe that one could see signs of famine in people's faces; people also became more vulnerable to disease. The summer of 1994 saw the *balseros* crisis, when over 36,000 rafters put out to sea to leave Cuba.

The crisis of "the special period" ushered in a period of economic reforms from 1993 to 1996, to strengthen the role of the private sector in the economy. The government legalized the use of foreign currencies (the euro and the dollar) and promoted foreign direct investment (in joint ventures between Cuba and Spain in hotels for tourism). Moreover, the government began to allow private economic activity, expanding self-employment. Suddenly very small restaurants called *paladares*, mostly for tourists, appeared inside people's homes. The government also broke up the large state farms, converted them into cooperatives, and established private farmer's markets where farmers could sell their extra produce of fruits and vegetables after meeting their quota to the state. As Mesa-Lago and Pérez-López (2005, xi) point out, these measures "undertaken reluctantly by the Cuban leadership, were sufficient to stop the contraction of GDP and bring about modest economic growth." However, the Cuban leadership aborted the market-oriented reforms, probably because they feared the reforms would weaken their political control. Even more, in 2003–4, they took steps to reverse them, recentralizing the economy and eliminating the limited spaces opened to private economic activity (Pérez-Villanueva and Torres-Pérez 2013, 2015). Along with this retrenchment came increased repression for the dissident groups that, through nonviolent means, sought to effect change. While Fidel remained at the political helm, and articles signed by him reflecting on Cuba's condition regularly appeared in *Granma*, unbeknownst to most a leadership transition from Fidel to Raúl was gradually taking place.

Mesa-Lago and Pérez-López (2013, 2005) assess Cuba's economic and social performance from 1990 to 2012, comparing it to 1989 (the year before the crisis) and 1993 (the trough of the crisis). They show the slowdown in economic growth between 2001 and 2004, concluding that, although external factors contributed to it, its root cause was "politically motivated paralysis of essential structural reforms" (2005, xiii). The social services—particularly education and public health, which had proved paramount in the success of the Cuban Revolution—steadily deteriorated (Mesa-Lago 2011). However, the strong alliance and friendship between

Fidel Castro in Cuba and Hugo Chávez in Venezuela served to buoy up the island.

Raúl Castro's new government again underwent a cycle of pragmatic reforms that began with a national dialogue provoked by the 6th Congress of Cuba's Communist Party in 2011 and the *Lineamientos* (Guidelines) to put in place its major policy objectives in the 7th Congress in 2016 (R. Castro 2016). As Feinberg (2016, 28–29) notes, it was a lengthy document containing 313 points on a broad range of topics "rife with internal contradictions" that led one to "imagine the fierce internal debates between orthodox planners and reform advocates." The guidelines were more about *what*, rather than *how*; thus they were not a coherent national development model. Feinberg writes that the guidelines were reminiscent of the "tepid reform documents" common in socialist Eastern Europe in the 1970s and 1980s, which included "nods in the direction of market mechanisms and nonstate management" that were repeatedly "subsumed under genuflections to the hegemony of socialist planning." Nonetheless, the guidelines began a process of reforms that made a difference in people's daily lives, particularly allowing the growth of the small-business private sector and the market mechanisms as well as a wider opening to foreign investment and international tourism. The result, Feinberg observes, soon became evident:

> Commercial districts in Havana were increasingly dotted with new restaurants and small retail outlets, often located within owners' homes. Licenses were issued for private taxis, barbershops, and beauty salons, even as many middle-class professions (lawyers, engineers, architects) were still excluded from private practice. By 2014, over 18,000 rooms in family homes and apartments were being offered as bed and breakfast-style rentals, constituting up to 30 percent of the supply of lodging available for international tourism; and more than 1,700 private restaurants were improving the island's culinary offerings. (32)

However, in 2017–18, the conservative faction in the party gained ascendancy over the reform advocates and froze the reform process, reversing some measures. Moreover, to date, the authorized private activities do not include the white-collar professions, such as doctors, lawyers, and professors that often moonlight in the more profitable occupation of driving a taxi, particularly for tourists. Mesa-Lago (2018) captures the voices of change in Cuba from this emerging small-business sector, voices that often emphasized the obstacles to growth in the excessive taxation and arbitrary bureaucracy they were subjected to.

Perhaps the major accomplishment was the rejuvenation of the party's Central Committee and the greater representation of women and Afro-Cubans among its members. The size of the state sector also declined, from 81 percent to 71 percent, while the private and cooperative sector increased. Raúl Castro emphasized that this did not mean a return to capitalism, lauding the successful economic reforms in China and Vietnam. Raúl remained as first secretary of the party until 2021. He appointed his chosen successor in the party leadership: Cuba's new president, Miguel Díaz-Canel.

Raúl also turned to tourism to lift Cuba's economy. An avalanche of tourists arrived in Cuba to witness the allure of a beautiful Caribbean island and a "tropical socialism." In 1990, Cuba received only 340,000 international visitors. In 2016, a record 4 million tourists visited Cuba (for a nation of 11.2 million people), including some 140,000 US residents (not Cuban Americans). In 2018, 4.7 million tourists visited Cuba, though in that year the number of overnight visitors declined, and it was cruise tourists, who leave little revenue behind, that increased (Spadoni 2019). In 2020, with the arrival of the coronavirus, the government closed the door to all tourism as well as shipments of goods to Cuba (including the mail). While this helped to prevent the spread of COVID-19 inside Cuba, it further damaged an already dismal economy. The situation became even worse when the US president Donald Trump imposed new sanctions. Trump curtailed travel to the island by American citizens, restricted the remittances sent by Cuban Americans, canceled the already popular cruise ships to the island, and drastically reduced airline flights. For an economy dependent on tourism and remittances, the closing of the door to the island by both the Cuban and American governments was devastating. The new US president Joe Biden has just reopened the door to the island.

However, despite those fresh policies, Cuba's economy failed to grow. Since 2016, the Cuban economy has stalled. As Mesa-Lago (2019b) explains, "The island's economy is neither efficient nor competitive." Simply put, for the last 60 years Cuba has relied on substantial aid and subsidies from a foreign nation (first the Soviet Union, then Venezuela) and has been unable to finance what it imports from what it exports, generating appropriate,

Figure 8.1. Beginning in the 1990s, record numbers of balseros (rafters) fled from Cuba to the Florida shores on makeshift rafts. Here Juan Carlos Pérez-Corredoso signals to a rescue plane. Pérez and four of his companions survived six days of December seas. One rafter died (Photo by Hector Gabino via *The Miami Herald*, December 26, 1993).

sustainable growth. Mesa-Lago notes the enormous aid Cuba received from the Soviet Union from 1960 to 1990—$65 million, triple the total amount of aid that Latin America received from Kennedy's Alliance for Progress. Venezuela also aided Cuba. At its peak in 2012, Venezuelan aid, subsidies, and investment amounted to $14 billion, or close to 12 percent of GDP. Yet, despite the staggering foreign aid subsidies Cuba received, the economy's performance was dismal. To Mesa-Lago and other analysts, the Cuban economic situation is—in large part—the failure of the "inefficient economic model of centralized planning, state enterprises, and agricultural collectivization its leaders have pursued despite the failure of these models worldwide." Raúl Castro's reforms sought to tackle Fidel's legacy of economic disaster head on, by enacting a series of market-oriented structural reforms. However, these policies were timid and incomplete. To Mesa-Lago (2019a), there have been too many restrictions, disincentives, and taxes, which impeded the growth of the private sector. Domestic capital accumulation has been insufficient, which is an obstacle for economic growth. In 2014–18, the annual average was 97 percent of GDP, vis-à-vis 25 percent in 1989, which remains the government's unmet target. Direct foreign investment has also been insufficient: $500 million annually vis-à-vis the official target of $2.5 billion a year (Mesa-Lago 2019a).

Mesa-Lago (2019a) argues that the market socialism model—which proved far more successful in China and Vietnam, still under Communist Party rule—could provide a way out. In both China and Vietnam, the government allowed farmers to sell their products to whomever they wanted, at prices set by supply and demand. In Cuba, they must sell them to the state, despite the constant food shortages. In both China and Vietnam, self-employment in the private sector was an important engine of economic growth. In Cuba, the *cuentapropistas* (self-employed) are extremely important for tourism, one of the pillars of the economy. But they are heavily taxed and seriously restricted. Yet Raúl Castro's successor, president Miguel Díaz-Canel, only promised "continuity" with the existing economic model, failed as it has been. Feinberg (2020, 250–51) emphasizes that, rather than providing the long-suffering population "a strategic vision that might light the way towards a brighter future," the new president "showed little inclination to risk new measures. Rather, the government has devoted itself to managing a grueling austerity, reserving scarce foreign exchange to import the essential foodstuffs and energy that the economy is failing to produce on its own." Moreover, the new Cuban Constitution (approved in February 2019) did not introduce any significant changes to the model of centralized planning and state dominance over the economy. Fear of returning to capitalism, they say, guides their reluctance to engage in these sorts of reforms that proved so successful in China and Vietnam. Fear of losing power and of retribution must also underlie their reluctance. Throughout the island, billboards now show portraits of Cuba's heroes of the war of independence against Spain, Carlos Manuel de Céspedes and José Martí, followed by Fidel and Raúl Castro, followed by Miguel Díaz-Canel. The image is titled *Revolución—Somos Continuidad* (Revolution—We Are Continuity).

Raúl Castro took over the presidency of Cuba in 2006, due to a gravely ill Fidel, aged 80. Raúl started the debate, together with members of the Communist Party and the National Assembly, regarding the need to reform some laws, public policies, and economic practices to correct the worst effects of the centralized economy. Since the "revolutionary offensive" of the late 1960s that penalized private initiative on the island, the private sector was almost nonexistent. After the severe crisis of "the special period," the people clamored for changes, as did economists, academics, and other analysts inside and outside Cuba. Thus, Raul Castro's government initiated them, as he repeatedly stressed, "*sin prisa pero sin pausa*," or "without haste but without pause" (*Economist*, September 15, 2012).

From 2006 to 2014, Raúl Castro introduced various reforms, and an economic opening took place that allowed for the legal development of the non–state sector that, in truth, already existed clandestinely as an informal economy typical of all Latin American countries (Centeno and Portes 2006). After Raúl Castro became president of the Council of State, then first secretary of the party, and then president, with the support of the reformists within the party, he was able to introduce important changes. Among the most important were that, beginning in the summer of 2010, the government authorized the self-employment of *cuentapropistas*, in particular jobs on a government list of approved occupations (Ritter and Henken 2015). Ritter and Henken tell the story of the rise, fall, and rebirth of the *paladares* (small restaurants) from 1994 to 2014 (245–96). Originally approved for only 12 chairs, many *paladares* had distinct personalities that made them quite popular, such as La Guarida and El Hurón Azul. Now *paladares* are approved for 50 chairs. Ritter and Henken state that the "thick web of legal restrictions" on these *paladares* and on self-employment in general were so great and taxes so high that they "often overshadowed the benefits of legal status itself," forcing them to utilize "informal strategies or to go into outright clandestine existence to make a living" (245). While they did not result in the creation of new jobs, as initially hoped, they did result in the growth of an extensive underground network of *jineteros* (hustlers) that guided many a tourist to better places to eat and drink, as well as to sexual services. As of June 2014, the government legalized or expanded 201 occupations, among them the *paladares*.

Recognizing the important role that the Catholic Church has played in Cuba all these years, in 2010 Raúl Castro also met with cardinal Jaime Ortega. They began a process, which also involved the government of Spain, whereby 166 political prisoners would be released from jail. This included the 52 remaining from the 75 arrested during "the Cuban Spring," in the 2003 protests. Many of them left Cuba for Spain. Their imprisonment gave rise to Las Damas de Blanco (The Ladies in White), dissident women that every Sunday, fully dressed in white and holding a flower, leave from the Church of Santa Rita to walk throughout the streets of Havana, peacefully protesting the imprisonment of their husbands, brothers, and sons.

Another important reform came about when the government also guaranteed the distribution of idle state-owned land (usufruct) for a specified time to individuals, cooperatives, and state entities. Moreover, the government boosted nonagricultural production, as well as service cooperatives, allowing private taxis and other forms of transportation. Cubans were also allowed access to hotels and restaurants where, until then, only foreign tourists had access—a practice that had left many Cubans feeling humiliated. With respect to the unpopular rationing booklet, known as *la libreta*, many food items were eliminated. Moreover, the government allowed the sale of homes, which had been forbidden since 1960. Additionally, the government did away with the restrictions preventing Cubans from traveling abroad (see Mesa-Lago and Pérez-López 2013, table 6.1). Ritter and Henken (2015) stress that the reforms allowing the reemergence of the self-employment sector were motivated by Raúl's plan to lay off 500,000 rather unproductive state workers. Raúl hoped they would be absorbed by the new non–state sector (i.e., the private sector, though never referred to as such). That, however, was not the outcome.

Raúl's reforms were supported by reformers within the party loyal to his way of thinking and opposed by the orthodox members of the party loyal to Fidel's way of thinking. Such efforts initiated important changes but in the past were subsequently reversed (e.g., with the Rectification Campaign that followed the 3rd Congress of the Communist Party. They involved not only self-employment but also other issues, such as the liberalization of farmer's markets. Yet this time there was to be no reversal. As Raúl himself observed: "The steps we have been taking and shall take towards broadening and relaxing self-employment are the result of profound meditations and analysis and we can assure you this time there will be no going back" (R. Castro 2011).

The excessive red tape involved in implementation; the exaggerated state interference; the absence of a wholesale market; the difficulties in acquiring inputs; the lack of access to the Internet; the dual currency; and the very low incomes and wages—all were obstacles that rendered the reforms less fruitful than hoped for (Mesa-Lago 2012; Ritter and Henken 2015). Feinberg (2020, 256) argues that Raúl Castro's greatest achievement was in foreign affairs, where he succeeded in diversifying Cuba's diplomatic and commercial relations around the globe: "Cuba had been a colony of Spain, a dominion of US capital, a cog within the Soviet-dominated COMECON system. Now, for the first time in its 500-year history, Cuba had escaped the grip of a single world power." However, Feinberg also emphasizes that the "tragedy of Cuba's external relations is that its productive structure has proven unable to take advantage of its diplomatic prowess.... No international economic strategy will work unless Cuba can transform itself into a more efficient and reliable business partner. No amount of geopolitical influences will provide Cuba with the capital and technology it needs unless it creates a more welcoming investment climate. And no international alliances, by themselves, will loosen the balance of payments pressures until Cuban farms and factories churn out products that can compete on international markets" (258).

In 2020, COVID-19 arrived to a devastated economy, further deepening the crisis (Torres 2020). Thus, a series of modifications were decreed that aim to correct and expand the reforms that for 14 years were insufficient to substantially improve the economy. The independent economist Oscar Espinosa-Chepe (2011) notes that the changes in Cuba were few, limited, and late. Among the welcomed changes were doing away with the list of approved jobs for the *cuentapropistas* and lifting the penalty from the American dollar when exchanging it (a penalty that the European euro never had). As 2021 opened, the government engaged in currency reform. The convertible dollar—the CUC—disappeared, leaving only the traditional Cuban peso and the US dollar. Much confusion now reigns with the currency reform that is said to be preliminary to other economic reforms. Spiraling inflation immediately resulted, making it impossible for most people to buy food and other scarce goods. Only a few months later, beginning on July 11, 2021, Cuba witnessed the largest protests ever in its history, particularly in the streets of Havana and Santiago de Cuba, which house the largest Afro-Cuban neighborhoods. The protests became known as 11J. They expressed both economic and political suffering, as Cubans who participated in them called for jobs and food as well as freedom and democracy.

Rising Inequality: Class and Race

In recent decades, social inequality continued to grow in Cuba (Espina-Prieto 2004) between the haves and the have-nots that also had a racial dimension. The exodus always had a racial dimension, too, as White Cubans disproportionately left the island (Aguirre 1976). Therefore, so did the remittances the émigrés sent. Blue's (2007) survey of Havana residents assesses the impact of the 1993–96 economic reforms on the rising racial inequality in Cuba. She found that the increased access to education—the structural means through which the revolution once equalized the income levels of various sectors of the population—had lost its equalizing force, while differential access to state employment, self-employment, and remittances from abroad resulted in rising racial inequality on the island. Given the large size of the Cuban American population, flows of remittances increasingly flowed back to the island to help the family left behind. These remittances aggravated the division between the races on the island, since Afro-Cubans did not have as many family members living abroad to help them.

De la Fuente (2001, 2019, 2020) has long studied the issue of race in Cuba from the early part of the twentieth century until the new millennium. Always he emphasizes that the Cuban Revolution had important impacts on issues of race, eliminating the structural racism of the past, and opening new opportunities, particularly through the enormous expansion of the educational system and the public health system, to Black and mixed-race Cubans. Data from the recent censuses of Cuba in 1981, 2002, and 2012, comparing the educational levels of White, Black, and mixed-race Cubans, show that, over time, the race differentials became very low, as education improved for all races, as did life expectancy, resulting from good public health. Twenty years after the triumph of the revolution, by the 1980s Cuba had become a more racially equitable society. By the new millennium, racial disparities in education and in professional jobs were few. Thus, Cuba became a more racially equitable society than most multicultural societies. However, as De la Fuente (2020) underscores, by the 1990s racially differentiated effects became immediately and painfully visible. White Cubans mobilized to exclude Black Cubans from the burgeoning tourist sector. To appeal to the tourists, racist beauty standards—called *una buena presencia* (a nice look)—became a requisite to acquire good jobs. Moreover, racist attitudes continued to flourish, as epithets, discourses, and practices could again be seen and heard. Today there is an absence of Black Cubans in the tourist sector, as well as in the private, non–state sector, where jobs pay well (approximately one-third of all jobs), contrary to the public sector jobs that pay very little, which prevents the accumulation of resources.

Thus, De la Fuente (2020) wonders whether racism could coexist with equality. This is particularly salient since the government insists on portraying the Cuban people as mestizo in a land where there is no racism, and all forms of racism are understood, as befits the Marxist ideology, as "vestiges of the past." Increasingly, however, among activists that take an anti-racist stand, those that are part of an Afro-Cuban movement contest the notion that racism is a vestige of the past and point out that racism is institutionalized, producing unequal outcomes.

Even more, in the last decade, the municipal university system that expanded opportunities for all to be educated in the *municipios* and was in place from 2000 to 2010 came to an end. As a result, there has been a rapid and massive whitening of the university system. De la Fuente (2020) also brings to bear other data than levels of education and health, showing that the proportion of Cubans living in tenements in the major cities of Havana and Santiago is quite low among Whites, much higher among mestizos, and rather high among Blacks. As Hernández (2020) points out, those living conditions are abysmal, as people go without running water or decent bathrooms. De la Fuente concludes that three factors combined to produce massive racial inequality in Cuba today: a history of unequal race relations, the impact of remittances, and the retreat of the public sector that until the 1980s functioned as an agent of equality.

After the frontal attack of the Cuban Revolution on inequality since 1959, today there is massive inequality in Cuba of class and race that cannot be hidden. Yet it is largely ignored in the official statistics. This led the Afro-Cuban scholar Esteban Morales-Domínguez (2018) in his presentation to the United Nations to call for ONEI to publish statistics that are more meaningful regarding the relationship of race—the reality of skin color—to multiple social indicators. Evidence also comes from the survey Hansing and Hoffman (2020) conducted with over 1,000 respondents throughout the island that showed the restratification taking place. Their results indicated that, since wages are extraordinarily low in the state enterprises, access to hard currency has become key. However, given the racial disparity in the exodus over time, White and Black Cubans have highly unequal access to family remittances. These spur not only different patterns of consumption, but also different possibilities for investment (e.g., start-up capital and goods) in the newly emergent private business sector. As Hansing and Hoffmann (2020, 45) conclude, "With much less access to financial capital, goods, and mobility, Afro-Cubans are being clearly disadvantaged. In the current restratification of Cuban society, this racial bias is turning back one of the proudest historic achievements of the Cuban revolution."

The impact of differential family remittances is aggravated by the tendency of the tourism industry—hotels and restaurants, in particular—to hire White Cubans, imagining that the tourists prefer them. Writing as the editor and publisher of the *Casa de las Américas* in Havana, Zurbano (2013) highlights the fact that after nearly 60 years of revolution, racial inequality still persists in Cuba. Two different realities diverged: "The first is that of White Cubans, who have leveraged their resources to enter the new market-driven economy and reap the benefits of a supposedly more open socialism. The other reality is that of the black plurality, which witnessed the demise of the socialist utopia from the island's least comfortable quarters." The fact that racism is never openly discussed, he adds, only makes it flourish. Zurbano acknowledges that the first decade of the revolution, the 1960s, "signified opportunity for all," and that the 1980s produced a generation of Black professionals, such as doctors and teachers, "but these gains were diminished in the 1990s as blacks were excluded from lucrative sectors, like hospitality." Now, in the twenty-first century, it is apparent that Black Cubans are "underrepresented in universities and in spheres of economic and political power," while they are "overrepresented in the underground economy, the criminal sphere, and in marginal neighborhoods."

The spontaneous protests of July 11, 2021, which lasted a week, came out of the poor neighborhoods of Havana and Santiago de Cuba. The large Afro-Cuban participation was evident. Thus, some observers thought race was a major issue in the protests. Moreover, for many years Black Cubans have been at the forefront of the dissident movement, as with Orlando Zapata, who died in prison; Manuel Cuesta-Morúa, with the Arco Progresista movement; Dimas Castellanos, independent journalist with *Diario de Cuba*; and Guillermo Fariñas with UNPACU.

Even more, the writers of "Patria y Vida," the song that became the banner of the July protest movement, were also Afro-Cubans. However, it is important to realize that they were not saying "Black Lives Matter"; they were saying "Cuban Lives Matter." Both the San Isidro movement and the *Patria y Vida* movement that issued from it asked for a dialogue with the government and for real political participation—for democracy and freedom for all Cubans, for real social and political citizenship. "Patria y Vida" is a clear expression from Afro-Cubans, who, in this reggaeton, captured life in Cuba. It also gave voice to the suffering of the Cuban people. As is typical of this musical style, the song is quite free with its lyrics, which entail a social critique. Written and played by both Cuban immigrants and Cubans on the island, together they gave everyone a compass for the struggle against a repressive government in Cuba.

Cuba's International Relations

Cuba's Continuing Exodus

The contemporary exodus from Cuba that began when the economic crisis of "the special period" became a political crisis has never ceased. It reached its apex in the summer of 1994. That July, some Cuban families left in a small tugboat called *13 de Marzo* to cross the dangerous waters standing between Cuba's north coast and the Florida Keys. Due to the actions of the Cuban Coast Guard, who directed powerful shoots of water at the tugboat, it capsized, and 41 lives were lost. People in Cuba were outraged. Fidel replied by telling the people that the gates to their departure were open, as he ordered the Cuban Coast Guard not to detain them as illegal emigrants. This gave way to the enormous, chaotic fourth wave of the Cuban exodus, the *balseros*: thousands of rafters who tried to cross the Florida Straits in July and August. The US Coast Guard rescued over 36,000 *balseros*, who were housed in a tent city in Guantanamo until, over a couple of years, immigration officials gradually processed them to come to America. The summer of 1994 culminated in Cuba with the massive street protests in Havana on August 5, which was called *el Maleconazo*, as they mostly took place along the seaside wall of the Malecón (Pedraza 2007). That summer's suffering culminated in a sermon by a small-town priest, José Conrado Rodríguez, in Palma Soriano, on September 8, the day that Cubans commemorate the feast day of their cherished patron saint, la Virgen de la Caridad (Our Lady of Charity). That day's homily consisted of his reading a letter he had written to Fidel Castro:

> For over 30 years, our country engaged in a politics at the base of which was violence. This politics was justified because of the presence of a powerful and tenacious enemy only 90 miles away, the United

States of America. The way we confronted this enemy was to place ourselves under the power that for years confronted it, the Soviet Union....

While the Soviet Union gave massive assistance to our economy and our arms race, Cuba gradually fell into a state of internal violence and profound repression.... The use, within and without our country, of hatred, division, violence, suspicion and ill will, has been the main cause of our present and past misfortune.

Now we can see it clearly. The excessive growth of the state, progressively more powerful, left our people defenseless and silenced. The lack of liberty that would have allowed healthy criticism and alternative ways of thinking caused us to slide down the slippery slope of political will and intolerance towards others. The fruits it bore were those of hypocrisy and dissimulation, insincerity and lying, and a general state of fear that affected everyone on the island....

We are all responsible, but no one is more responsible than you. (Rodríguez 1995)

The letter also called for a peaceful, negotiated agreement through the process of a national dialogue among the major political actors—the Communist Party, the churches, the dissident movement, as well as Cubans in exile—and called for a popular referendum. To date, this meeting of the major political actors to negotiate Cuba's future has not taken place. Many in Cuba and in exile applauded Father José Conrado's action, which expressed their sentiments. However, many in the Church leadership did not support him, thinking that the Church had to gain strength first before it could engage in political action.

The *balseros* crisis gave way to President Clinton signing a new migration accord with Cuba, as part of which he devised the "wet foot/dry foot" policy that shaped the fourth wave of the Cuban exodus. This policy was in effect until President Obama overturned it just before he left office, arguing that US immigration policy should treat Cubans the same as all other immigrants wanting to come to America. While the Cuban Adjustment Act remains in place, it is increasingly difficult for Cubans who manage to enter the United States to be granted political asylum, as they need to give evidence of a well-founded fear of persecution. Nevertheless, the fifth wave of the Cuban exodus, mostly over land, has developed in recent years.

Today Cubans leave the island not only for the United States, crossing the border with Mexico, but also for many other nations in South America (Ecuador and Panama, in particular), the Caribbean (Guyana, in particular) and Western Europe (Spain, in particular). The exodus has simply never ceased.

Three Popes Visit

A watershed moment in the history of the revolution came with Pope John Paul II's visit to Cuba in January 1998 (cf. Morello 1998). His visit not only strengthened the Catholic Church and affirmed the religious beliefs of the people, it also made it possible for Cubans to begin to speak freely. In a visit that lasted a full week, over four masses across the full length of the island his messages were quite clear: do not be afraid; the destiny of your nation is in your own hands. In Santiago de Cuba, the pope symbolically crowned La Virgen de la Caridad, the patron saint. The Cuban people accompanied him in song, to the tune of "Virgen Mambisa,"—the Lady to whom Cuba's patriots who fought for independence from Spain in the nineteenth century prayed. Monsignor Pedro Meurice, archbishop of Santiago, gave a stirring sermon in which he emphasized that the Cuban nation lived both on the island and in the diaspora. The Church's commitment, he asserted, is with "the poorest of the poor," adding, "And the poorest among us are those who lack liberty." The event was a moving reunion of the Cuban people with themselves—a newly found tradition. Thereafter, the churches began to fill.

Given its perennial state of crisis, from 1998 to 2016, three popes came to Cuba. In March 2012, the second pope, Benedict XVI, visited the patron saint in her shrine of El Cobre, in Oriente. Not in good health, his visit was short—only three days. At El Cobre, he prayed, leaving the future of Cuba in her hands. His message was one of hope and reconciliation, of gradual change. In Havana, a huge mosaic on the side of a government building portrayed La Virgen de la Caridad, and on many streets the signs read "Charity Unites Us," using her name together with the notion of charity. Both Raúl Castro and the Catholic Church saw Pope Benedict's visit as a success (Miroff 2012).

The third pope, Pope Francis I, visited Cuba in late September 2016, shortly before Fidel Castro died at the end of November. Immediately thereafter, Pope Francis visited Washington, DC, where he celebrated the rapprochement between both countries under Barack Obama and Raúl Castro. However, in comparison with the two popes before him, his visit delivered little. As Miroff (2015) notes, "Pope John Paul II's visit in 1998 put

Christmas back on the Cuban calendar. When Pope Benedict XVI arrived in 2012, the Cuban government made Good Friday a national holiday. Both men brought to the Catholic Church a bigger role in Cuba's public life. Pope Francis?" Indeed, Pope Francis simply brought no new concessions for the Church. This at a time when, amid the weakening of Cuba's safety net, the Church had stepped in to help *el pueblo* in many ways: opening day care centers and health clinics, providing needed medicines, cooking free meals for the elderly, and assisting disabled children. In addition, as Miroff points out, the visit was a notable contrast to Pope Francis's American trip, during which he addressed controversial political topics like immigration, climate change, and the death penalty. None of the three popes who visited Cuba, however, met with the dissidents. Nor did they meet with representatives of the Afro-Cuban religion, known as Santería, which is a large part of popular religiosity in Cuba today (Pedraza 2007). Both groups felt excluded. Still, Pope John Paul II's visit was a watershed in the island's history. Showing great knowledge of Cuba's history, in his sermons he urged Cubans not to be afraid, but to take the reins of history into their own hands, to carve their own future. To this day, people remember his visit as marking two epochs: before his visit, when they hardly spoke to anyone about their true feelings and thoughts, and after, when they began to do so regularly.

Cuba–Venezuela Alliance

Despite the deep economic crises in both Cuba and Venezuela, their alliance has never ceased, given its political importance to both nations. Little by little the Venezuelan process is becoming more like Cuba's, as if in a symbiosis that opens the door to a totalitarian model and in which each provides the conditions for the other to continue existing. However, as we showed earlier, the number of Cuban doctors and health personnel sent to work in the social missions in Venezuela has vastly declined, from a peak of around 50,000 to now only 20,000. Likewise, given the collapse of its economy, Venezuela's contribution to the island's economy has halved. In 2000–12, Venezuela was supplying around 100,000 barrels of oil a day to Cuba; in 2013–16 that became around 65,000. By 2017, it was 43,000 barrels a day. In 2019 and 2020, it has declined even further. Neither country can now uphold the other; their alliance can no longer be viewed as a real alternative by the rest of the world, a critique of capitalism, as Fidel and Chávez had hoped.

US-Cuba Relations

A turning point came with the restoration of diplomatic US-Cuba relations under President Obama that the US government severed in 1961 during the Cold War over half a century earlier (LeoGrande and Kornbluh 2015; LeoGrande 2015). Cubans on the island, and many on the mainland, greeted the July 2015 rapprochement with hope. Secretary of state John Kerry underscored that "U.S. policy is not the anvil on which Cuba's future will be forged," since Cuba's future is for Cubans to shape. However, he stressed, "we remain convinced that the people of Cuba would be best served by genuine democracy, where people are free to choose their leaders, express their ideas, practice their faith; where the commitment to economic and social justice is realized more fully; where institutions are answerable to those they serve; and where civil society is independent and allowed to flourish" (US Embassy of Uruguay 2015). Yet, as he has done repeatedly, Raúl Castro defended the primacy of the one-party system, which, he said, could not be challenged (R. Castro 2016). He argued, "If they manage someday to fragment us," in the name of bourgeois democracy, "it would be the beginning of the end" (Pérez Jr. 2015, 353).

Overall, despite their profound differences, US presidents George W. Bush, Barack Obama, Donald Trump, and Joe Biden all followed the traditional line of conditioning the lifting of the embargo on the implementation of real democratic reforms in Cuba, particularly freeing political prisoners and engaging in electoral democracy. President Obama, however, took the different tack of restoring diplomatic relations with Cuba, together with Cuba's president, Raúl Castro, who announced it in December 2014. Obama's measures had a significant impact on Americans' travel to Cuba. Working with data provided by Cuba's MINTUR (Ministry of Tourism) as well as ONEI, Spadoni (2019) shows the dramatic rise in tourism to Cuba from 1990 to 2018. In 1990, the number of tourists was only 340,000; in 2000, it was close to 2 million; in 2014, it jumped to 3 million; in 2016, close to 4 million tourists a year descended on the island, reaching nearly 5 million in 2018. While Canada remained the largest source country, with 28 percent in 2018, the United States came in a close second, with 21 percent (including both Cuban Americans and other Americans). Not including Cuban American travel for family reunification yields the same basic results. Tourism grew almost sevenfold in just three years from 2014 to 2017—an avalanche.

Wanting to undo Obama's legacy and to deprive the Cuban state of dollars, Trump's measures brought this avalanche to a halt. Trump prohibited American companies from doing business with firms owned or controlled by GAESA (the Cuban military's holding company). He ended the travel to Cuba by cruise ships authorized by President Obama and the individual people-to-people travel and visas that President Clinton initiated. Trump also curtailed the airline flights (e.g., Delta, American, Jet Blue) by permitting them to fly only to Havana, rather than to various cities on the island. The result was a dramatic drop in tourism to Cuba. In April 2020, due to the COVID-19 pandemic, the government closed all airports and ports. While Trump also wanted to empower ordinary Cubans by funneling dollars to their small-scale entrepreneurial activities, the emergent *cuentapropista* sector on the island, the data also show a negative impact on those who depended on tourism. Now, Cubans fear for their future, given both the harsh response of their new leader, president Miguel Díaz-Canel, toward the recent protests and the growing dissident sectors on the island, as well as the new efforts on the part of the United States to isolate Cuba. Throughout his presidency, Trump sought to dismantle Barack Obama's legacy on all fronts: domestic and international (R. Rodríguez 2017). Halfway through 2022, Biden began to dismantle Trump's sanctions.

A key difference between the revolutionary processes in Cuba and Venezuela lies in the size and role of the Cuban exile community in the United States and its ability to lobby Congress and to influence life on the island. Given its large size, and particularly the number of people that left the island since the beginning of "the special period," remittances increasingly flowed back to the island to help the family left behind. Trump was quite able to court the Cuban American vote. All Cuban Americans want the return of democracy and elections to Cuba, in addition to the free expression of opinions and free association. However, this community is divided between *los intransigentes* (those who think one should not give an inch to Cuba's communist government) and *los moderados* (those who think that through dialogue and negotiation one may attain more). The former identifies with the Republican Party, the latter with the Democratic Party.

Initially, Trump did not dismantle much. Two years later, Trump's policies became far more restrictive. In April 2019, new sanctions were announced that went further, tightening restrictions on travel and remittances to Cuba, reversing the engagement policies from the Obama era. Travel for Cuban Americans to visit their family remained unchanged, and the new limits on family remittances remained generous. Nonetheless, the administration blew the dust off of the Helms-Burton Act, since several of its original provisions passed under President Clinton in 1996 were never implemented. Trump's measures meant that lawsuits in US federal courts would be allowed for those seeking compensation for properties confiscated by the Cuban government after 1959.

The United States delivered the message that Cuba's support of Maduro's regime would entail a real cost. John Bolton, then national security advisor, expressed it in a speech in Miami, delivered on April 17, the anniversary of the Bay of Pigs invasion, at the site of the veterans: "In no uncertain terms, the Obama administration's policies toward Cuba have enabled the Cuban colonization of Venezuela today" (in Gámez-Torres 2019).

President Trump also stressed he would not ask Congress to end the commercial sanctions with Cuba until the political prisoners were liberated and free elections held. As was to be expected, Cuba's President Raúl Castro insisted that they would not allow themselves to be pressured, that they would not make political reforms to negotiate economically with the United States. Thus, both countries returned to the chess game that for many years was frozen in these two positions (Erisman 2017).

Strangely, late in the summer of 2017, a sizable number of personnel in the American embassy in Havana, as well as a few in the Canadian embassy, reported that they were victims of "sonic attacks" that made them gravely ill (Entous and Anderson 2018). Trump then took a tougher stance, which resulted in the American embassy in Havana having virtually no personnel, and the Cuban embassy in Washington, DC, running with rather reduced staff. This situation was aggravated by the COVID-19 pandemic. Cubans on the island can hardly obtain a visa to travel outside of Cuba, as it involves traveling to a third country where the interview at the American embassy takes place, adding enormously to the cost and anxiety involved. Thus ended the lively two-way flow of communication established in recent years among relatives and friends on both sides of the Gulf waters. Biden is now reopening the American embassy in Havana and supplying it with an adequate number of personnel.

In our view, Cuba deserves to have a system of free elections, more than one political party, and the expression of parliamentary conflicts and disagreements that we understand constitute the practice of democracy. To many Cubans from a moderate persuasion, Obama did not ask enough from Raúl, although he did open the door to a new relationship that means a great deal to Cubans who live on the island. It is also possible that Trump asked for too much. The Cuban people are, as always, caught in the middle. They continue to suffer from the system under which they live, despite the efforts and the courage of so many dissidents and political prisoners. They also suffer from American sanctions, despite their wish to be good neighbors.

Political Crisis and Political Legitimacy

Cuba's crisis is also the crisis of a revolution that is now quite old. After the passage of 60-some years, and the dramatic changes that accompanied the many stages of the revolution, distinct political generations formed (Pedraza 2016b). Following Mannheim's (1952) suggestion, the concept of political generation is useful because it considers people who, in their transition to adulthood, their coming of age (roughly 18 to 25 years old), were deeply influenced in their political attitudes by the dramatic historical events they lived through, events that marked their consciousness and their lives. Several analysts have used it fruitfully to study the Cuban revolution. Aguilar-León in his *Cuba: Conciencia y Revolución* ([1959] 1972) applies the concept to examine the political generations that were present when the revolution was originally fought. Zeitlin (1966) borrowed Aguilar-León's analysis of the various political generations in Cuban history to analyze the response of the Cuban working class to the triumph of the revolution. Pedraza (2007, 2016b) employs it to scrutinize the political generations on the island and in exile at the dawn of the twenty-first century. Based on participant observation, fieldwork, and in-depth semistructured interviews, Pedraza (2016b) identifies four major political generations. For the sake of brevity, only the first and last generations will be contrasted here. At present, members of these generations live side by side in Cuba, more often than not in the same household.

The "Generation of the Glorious Revolution" consists of people who came of age at the start of the revolution (1950s and early 1960s). They made the revolution through their own efforts and substantial sacrifices fighting in the mountains or the urban resistance, assisting those who were part of the struggle. Today they are in their mid-70s to mid-80s or older, often in positions of leadership in the Communist Party, government, or major cultural organizations. Mesa-Lago (2020) notes that the reluctance of the party at present to engage in real structural reforms to benefit the economy might well be the result of the opposition of the old guard. Pedraza's interviews with those who participated in the struggle and glory of the revolution indicate that this generation, no matter how poor the country has become, still sees communism as a good system that looks after the poor and gives women and Black Cubans their rightful place in the nation. While not blind to the dismal economy, they blame it solely on the US embargo. This generation has never really handed over the reins of power to the next generation; they still dominate most institutions. For example, when Miguel Díaz-Canel formally became president, in his acceptance speech he let others know that Raúl Castro would still be making the major decisions.

The "Generation of Disbelief" consists of people who are now in their 20s and 30s, including many who were born during "the special period." For them, the glory of the revolution is only a story their elders told them, a sign painted on one of the many billboards along the empty highways. All their lives they have known only poverty and want, as well as the wish to be free. Most of them seek to leave, as the island's economic and social deterioration means they have lost hope, cannot see a better future, and have little sense of *la Patria*. Demographic change is inexorable, and it will not be long before the old guard disappears, necessarily giving way to the newer generations. Sad to say, some young Cubans are no longer willing to try to shape the island's future. The revolution's old age, coupled with the weak economy, created a crisis that runs much deeper than the naked eye can see. Young Cubans who leave simply say, "There is no future in Cuba." The decline of Venezuela's support only exacerbates this crisis.

Fidel Castro's passing marked the end of an era in Latin America. He abdicated power in 2006 due to his declining health and died on November 25, 2016, aged 90, after the leadership transition was completed. Back in 1959, Fidel had departed Santiago de Cuba in a victorious caravan across his country, ending in Havana. Almost six decades later, his remains were carried on the same journey, in reverse. Commenting on his legacy, just as his remains arrived to Santiago de Cuba, Pedraza (2016a) underscores that Castro's most enduring legacy will inevitably be that of David vs. Goliath: "He was the young, bearded revolutionary from a small island who took on the enormous Goliath of U.S. capitalism and American hegemony. That is the stuff of dreams."

But it was not a dream for everyone, and real disagreements remain as to whether he was David or Goliath (Pedraza 2016a). The image of Castro as David was first established during the victory of the government forces over the exiles' American-sponsored invasion at the Bay of Pigs. This image was reinforced repeatedly as Fidel threw verbal stones at his superpower neighbor while he relied on the support of, first, the Soviet Union, and then Venezuela. Over the next half century, Fidel repeatedly lobbed his slingshot at the United States. Every time, he blamed all of Cuba's economic ills on the US embargo, rather than taking responsibility for his government's policies that failed to deliver prosperity to Cuba. Every time, he turned the massive exodus from a problem for Cuba to a problem for the United States. Cubans who succumbed to his charisma and passionate oratory, which painted the suffering of the present as necessary stepping-stones for a better future, bought into this, particularly those who benefited from the initial advances of the revolution and who lived through Cuba's early phase of civic glory.

Cubans who fought against Fulgencio Batista's dictatorship in the 1950s, who risked their lives in the undertaking, and staked themselves on the revolution almost invariably remain attached to it. They lived through Cuba's civic joy at the end of the dictatorship, and they followed Fidel when he veered from a revolution originally fought to restore political democracy to a different revolution that sought to bring communism and socialism to the island.

To many of those who benefited from the expansion of education and public health services, Fidel Castro remained an admirably defiant figure even after his death. These advances cannot and should not be overlooked, especially as they were the product of tangible sacrifices made by the Cuban people day in and day out. Many previously illiterate Cubans learned to read during a literacy campaign launched at the beginning of the revolution. Many poorer Cubans in rural areas, and from urban working-class backgrounds, experienced a remarkable jump in social status due to improved education and health care.

However, to many Cubans, the David long ago morphed into an ugly Goliath. As Castro continued to blame all of Cuba's economic ills on the US embargo rather than taking responsibility for his own policies, many Cubans sought a new life in the United States. Among the failed policies was Castro's attempt to mobilize Cuba's population to cut sugarcane in 1970. He exhorted everyone—doctors and peasants alike—to go to the countryside with the goal of a 10-million-ton sugar harvest, all the while insisting Cuba's honor was at stake. The enormous mobilization failed to accomplish his goal, leaving Cubans exhausted and humiliated.

Ultimately, Cubans paid dearly for the social advances under the Castro regime. Their meager salaries have plunged the vast majority of the population, including professionals, into poverty. Even the well educated are left struggling to put food on the table, to *resolver* (make ends meet), legally or illegally. Cubans also paid for Castro's achievements with a lack of liberty that constrained both their efforts and their souls, stunting the island's economic development. Families were torn apart when the lack of liberty and economic growth pushed so many to leave their home country.

What difference will Castro's death make to his legacy? For a long time, Cuba was like a slow-moving chess game where the pieces struggled to move. Now that the king has moved, other pieces have room to move, too. We are beginning to see their moves.

To most Cubans that live in the United States today—as well as the many scattered all over the globe—Fidel was no David. But this was also true for many in the dissident movement inside Cuba who risked their lives in the decades-long struggle to restore electoral democracy to Cuba, even in the face of government crackdowns.

The new dissident movement in Cuba began to develop among young people in the mid-1980s, many of whom had studied in the Soviet Union and other Eastern European countries. It grew out of their firsthand knowledge of communism and their attempts at *glasnost* and *perestroika* to reform communism from within. Today, the dissident movement includes numerous groups. All of them espouse nonviolence as means and end. Some of them have religious roots. Dagoberto Valdés-Hernández's efforts have taken the shape of two magazines: first, *Vitral* (the image of a stained glass window that refracts many colors as the light passes through), now *Convivencia* (to live together with tolerance) (Valdés-Hernández 1997, 2014). The MCL, part of the Christian Democratic movement worldwide, gained the largest following inside the island, under the leadership of Oswaldo Payá (2018, 2001). In 2002, their *Proyecto Varela* handed the National Assembly of Popular Power the thousands of signatures they had collected throughout the island—far more than the 10,000 signatures the 1976 Cuban Constitution stipulated were necessary for citizens to introduce a real change. Likewise, four leading dissidents together wrote *La Patria es de Todos* (The Nation Belongs to All), representing the full gamut of race and gender in Cuba (Vladimiro Roca, René Gómez-Manzano, Félix Bonne-Carcasés, and Marta Beatriz Roque). All of them called for a plebiscite in Cuba so that Cubans could freely elect their government. As Payá expressed it, "Let no one else speak for Cubans. Let their own voices be heard in a referendum" (Payá 2001). He was confident that change could be achieved in Cuba from within and that the darkness of night would not last forever—the title of his last book (2012). But on July 22, 2012, he met a sudden death in Bayamo from an accident that many believe was not really an accident. Of all the dissidents, Las Damas de Blanco most captured the international eye. The ladies march every Sunday throughout Havana, all dressed in white, holding a flower in their hands, asking for the release of their husbands, sons, or brothers, who were imprisoned due to their dissent over a one-party authoritarian society, challenging the state with their visible and constant presence. Recently, they have met not only with insults but also with beatings. UNPACU (Patriotic Union of Cuba) is another major social movement that has spread across the island. One of its leaders, Guillermo Fariñas, has engaged in numerous hunger strikes, particularly calling for the government to give the people access to the Internet. Years ago, in Santiago de Cuba, its leader, José Daniel Ferrer, was imprisoned and is now an Amnesty International "prisoner of conscience." *Somos Más* (We Are Many More) issued from young students who debated the premises of the government. Together with independent journalism, such as Yoani Sánchez's and Reinaldo Escobar's *14yMedio*, they are now a voice inside Cuba. All are marginalized, derided, insulted, and isolated. It is to their credit that they have remained steady and defiant. Their presence, as well as the recent demands from artists and intellectuals, continue to push the regime to enact serious reforms (Castellanos 2017).

On November 27, 2020, an unprecedented event took place as around 400 mostly young artists and intellectuals, led by the Movimiento San Isidro, protested for days in front of the Ministry of Culture in Havana. Their main demand was greater freedom of expression in Cuba for all its citizens and respect for political dissenters. They demanded a real dialogue with the government as well as participation and representation in their nation's political institutions. While the government has tried to dismiss them, they can no longer be dismissed. Univision's Spanish-language news anchor, Jorge Ramos, interviewed an important participant, Tania Brugera, a well-known artist and activist. Brugera emphasized that none of this could have happened without the new social media. In the past, she stated, many people made courageous gestures and demands but no one knew about it; now everyone learns about it. Thus, a collective movement was able to take shape. Soon after this interview, the Cuban government ended the dialogue with the artists and called them "mercenaries." The 11J protests followed eight months later.

Just a couple of weeks after the San Isidro sitdown, in their Christmas greeting to all Cubans, Cuba's new cardinal, Juan de la Caridad García-Rodríguez, together with the two other archbishops and nine Catholic bishops, highlighted the suffering of the island's people. They attributed it to the economic crisis, the COVID-19 pandemic, and the natural disasters—leading people to be fearful and anxious. At the same time, they stressed, this gave everyone the opportunity to practice compassion and charity toward one another (Conferencia de Obispos Católicos de Cuba 2020). The cardinal and the bishops also underscored the need for a dialogue among all Cubans, as Father José Conrado had called for in 1994. They stressed that, just as Christ's nativity is seen as the harbinger of good news, they itemized what would constitute the good news of the season for Cubans:

> Good news for Cubans would be that we should not have to search outside of our country for what we should be able to find inside; that we should not have to wait for those above us to give us what we could and should create ourselves from below. . . . Good news for Cubans would be that all blockades should cease—external and internal both—but, instead, our people's creative initiative should be set free, and the productive forces and laws that support our people's creative initiative should also be set free, so they can play a leading role in their own life.

Calling for a national dialogue and for both the domestic embargo of the government as well as the US external embargo to end is a remarkably political statement on the part of the Catholic Church that, in the past, remained politically uninvolved. Always an important presence on the Cuban scene, the present crisis has now turned the Church into a major political actor.

9

Crisis in Venezuela

Revolution and Reform

Economic and Political Crises

In the last decade, Venezuela has suffered a deep economic crisis, mostly due to low oil revenues. This is the result of a decline in oil production (an average of 450,000 barrels per day in 2020) together with a decline in the price of oil (an average of US $28 per barrel), the extremely high rate of hyperinflation (estimated at 3,500 percent in 2020), and a loss of economic growth (a contraction of GDP by 90 percent). This extreme situation was aggravated by the arrival of COVID-19, the steep decline in trade relations with the United States, and the economic sanctions Trump applied (Velásquez 2021). In addition, the dollar exchange rate deteriorated to $1 millon bolívares for a dollar in December 2020 and $3.3 million for a dollar in July 2021. Moreover, gasoline is now scarce, as are other oil industrial products. The gap between the salaries and earnings of most of the population and the price of food, social services, and health services is now quite wide.

How do Venezuelans survive? Depending on their social class, there are four ways to face the rising inequality. Some Venezuelans are supported by the government's social policies, but with declining efficacy. Other Venezuelans participate in an informal economy that allows them to buy and sell goods and services in US dollars. Still other Venezuelans depend on the remittances sent by relatives and friends living abroad. Others, particularly working-class Venezuelans, leave their country for another—across a bridge, across an isthmus, across the sea—in search of a better life.

Puente (2021) characterizes Venezuela's deep-seated economic crisis as a historical macroeconomic collapse. As he points out, in the last five years it has experienced a tremendous GDP per capita contraction, which he puts at a loss of 47 percent and the IMF puts at 35 percent in 2019 and 25 percent in 2020—the worst in South America, coupled with hyperinflation. Puente notes that Venezuela's GDP today is smaller than that of the Dominican Republic and Costa Rica. This economic collapse is homemade, as it began prior to Trump's sanctions and the arrival of COVID-19. While the crisis runs deep, its human and natural resources must still be taken into account. The state still has international reserves; trade with its partners continues; part of the middle class goes on doing business; and the service sector still works. Many workers and poor people continue to depend (as they do in Cuba) on the government's meager subsidies, as well as what they can reap from the informal economy (Velásquez 2021).

Venezuela's economic situation is the combination of several failures: the state-socialist-oriented economic model, which limited private initiatives and investments and failed to provide economic incentives; the US embargo and economic sanctions under Donald Trump; and the current crisis of the international oil industry (low production and low prices for many years now). International assistance, trade with nontraditional partners, and the existence of an informal economy prevent Venezuela from becoming "a basket case" (Berry 2016).

Rising Inequality and Political Polarization

As president, Hugo Chávez wanted to use his electoral support to radically change institutions and political practice. The reforms that he put in place were intended to constitute revolutionary change—the Bolivarian Revolution—and to create "the socialism of the twenty-first century": a socialism without poverty. While he lived, this plan was effective, given his efforts to create redistributive justice for the poor, based on Venezuela's oil revenues.

But the year 2013 dealt *el Chavismo* two serious blows. First, Hugo Chávez's death on March 5, 2013, after having been to Cuba to receive medical treatments, was an enormous loss for the revolution. Second, the economy began to stumble and decline at an accelerated rate, although it is now has some growth. The "socialism of the twenty-first century," the new model that Chávez fervently offered not only to Venezuelans but also to all of Latin America and the Caribbean, lost ground.

Nicolás Maduro assumed the role of president of Venezuela in March 2013, during a steep economic decline that alarmed many, along with the military's increasing role, and the resurgence of the opposition. Today, among those who still are Chavistas, many are anti-Maduro. Others became totally disenchanted with the Chavista illusion. Still others simply failed to be motivated by the promises of the new leadership. From the moment that Maduro assumed the presidency, the ordinary citizen began to live in a crisis: direct transfers declined, access to cheap and subsidized dollars became difficult, rising inflation made a stable income impossible, and securing one's daily bread became arduous. Thus, a flood of Venezuelans emigrated from the country. As previously discussed, the estimates are that over five million Venezuelans now live abroad. Most of those who left were not only tired of the Chavista political model but were also afraid of economic corruption, rampant violence and street crime, and their lack of future.

Finally, the symptoms of a serious malaise—poverty, violence, and insecurity—broke through. Elections gave a clear signal about the mounting numbers of citizens who opposed *el Chavismo*, as evidenced by the MUD candidates' impressive victories in the December 2015 Parliamentary

Figure 9.1. Nicolás Maduro, Venezuela's president, with his wife Cilia Flores and defense minister Vladimir Padrino-López, in a military parade. Caracas, Venezuela, February 1, 2017 (Photo by StringerAL via Shutterstock).

elections. However, the coexistence of powers (the government and the opposition) inside the National Assembly (AN) ended, and electoral authoritarianism took over (Flores and Nooruddin 2016, 95). *El Chavismo* put an end to any dialogue with a National Assembly controlled by the opposition. Thereafter, the Supreme Court of Justice removed a significant part of its power.

The straw that broke the camel's back was the government's attempt in 2017 to convene and install the National Constituent Assembly (ANC) to alter the Constitution, deepening the Chavista project and putting the seal of approval on its authoritarian-corporatist model of government. The election of ANC members in July 30, 2017, upset international observers. Most international multilateral organizations, governments, and nongovernmental organizations criticized the government, condemning its human rights violations and echoing the opposition's denunciation of Venezuela's loss of democracy. They accused Maduro's government of operating outside the law, systematically violating human rights while increasing the number of political prisoners, and reducing the institutional spaces the MUD obtained democratically in the AN as well as among governors and mayors. Amid this extreme polarization, the efforts of many governments (such as Norway and the European Union), international organizations, and world personalities (including António Guterres, secretary-general of the United Nations) to promote a dialogue between the government and the opposition failed. Many governments closed ranks either against or in favor of the Chavista regime. In addition, Luis Almagro, the general secretary of the Organization of American States (OAS), openly criticized Maduro's government; with the help of the majority of its members, Almagro discussed the current Venezuelan domestic situation and applied some sanctions. As a result, Maduro decided to leave the OAS (Marsteintredet 2020).

From a domestic point of view, the tendencies that already existed in 1999—extreme political polarization and increasing authoritarianism—were exacerbated. The government elite increasingly controlled the institutional, electoral, and judicial processes. Thus, the balance of powers and the exercise of "fair play" that every democratic model demands was lost.

The opposition, for its part, has not responded well to the government's excesses, despite retaining the parliamentary majority in the AN since December 2015. The opposition could have successfully carried out a nonbinding popular referendum to reject the ANC in July 2017. In addition, it could have participated in other regional and local elections: for governors in October 2017; for mayors in December 2017; for council members in December 2018; and in the advance presidential elections of May 20, 2018, as well as in the parliamentary elections in December 2020. Yet only a small part of the opposition participated in those elections, breaking with the majority decision. All the while, the ruling PSUV party had an electoral advantage, particularly as abstention ran high in all the elections.

The ruling party's candidate, Nicolás Maduro, and his allies insisted they won the presidential election of May 20, 2018, with 68 percent of the valid votes, leaving the opposition candidates with 32 percent but with a high degree of abstention (54 percent). Thus, Maduro was sworn in as the reelected president before the ANC on May 24, 2018. The opposition considered this a farce, particularly since, according to the 1999 Constitution, the presidential term was supposed to begin on January 10, 2019. The AN ignored Maduro's swearing in and called for a new presidential election.

Venezuela confronts significant domestic and external problems. The deepening economic crisis, enormous exodus, and the lack of international support created a fireball that constantly threatened the regime and the nation's stability. Political actors around the world emphasized that the humanitarian crisis called for international humanitarian aid. They labeled President Maduro a "dictator," characterized the Venezuelan state as "on the verge of collapse," and classified Venezuela as a "failed state." According to this narrative, these labels are necessary to rescue the country under the principle of the "Responsibility to Protect" (R2P)—a United Nations initiative to end conflicts in the Third World and other places, such as the former Yugoslavia. However, this situation has also generated concern regarding the extent of external political and military interventions when it comes to the internal affairs of a nation in conflict.

The Venezuelan government countered this international sentiment by insisting the situation was the result of the conjunction of a media campaign and an economic war against Venezuela. A sizable part of the domestic opposition sought to cut off the country's foreign trade, its external debt policy, and the flow of its energy and mining investments, while also discrediting it internationally. Most of the Venezuelan opposition created a political platform to act in coordination with external political actors to promote regime change. In turn, the Venezuelan government defended itself with support from countries like Cuba, Bolivia, China, Iran, Russia, and Turkey.

The Venezuelan crisis is more than a media conflict based on bitter mutual accusations. Objective conditions lead to classifying the nation as in a state of precollapse: hyperinflation; lack of food and medicines; breakdown of public services (power shortages, lack of water, lack of waste collection); crumbling communication channels; and insufficient transportation, together with hunger, emigration, and social unrest. The situation is extreme.

It is worth mentioning that between the months of September 2017 and January 2018, several dialogues between the government and the opposition were held in the Dominican Republic. However, they achieved neither a roadmap nor the signing of an accord for the future of the nation. Since these initiatives failed, the democratic international community stepped forward in the media, to judge and criticize Venezuela. Numerous organizations assessed the situation and condemned the presidential elections of May 20, 2018 as illegitimate: the UN, the EU, the OAS, and Mercosur, some of the countries involved in the failing UNASUR, CARICOM, the Lima Group, and over 60 governments worldwide, including the United States, that sanctioned Venezuela's leaders and institutions.

By contrast, most of the ALBA's members opposed this international interference in Venezuela's internal affairs. However, in 2018, Ecuador exited the ALBA, due to Maduro's inaction in the face of the migration crisis, according to its government. Cuba observed in silence. Bolivia moved with diplomatic prudence and decided to exit the ALBA after president Evo Morales left power. However, it returned to the ALBA with Bolivia's new president, Luis Arce. Nicaragua did not get involved, as president Daniel Ortega faced the opposition accusing him of exercising unlimited repression.

The 14 Latin American countries that are part of the Lima Group judged Maduro's government negatively, repudiating his domestic and international actions by not accepting his presence at the 8th Summit of the Americas held in Lima in April 2018. Furthermore, in May 2018, the secretary general of the OAS, Luis Almagro, opened an investigation into President Maduro at the International Criminal Court (ICC). The OAS cannot send a case to the ICC, but a member country that has signed the Rome Statute may. Thus, five Latin American countries supported this proposal (Argentina, Colombia, Chile, Paraguay, and Peru) along with Canada and France. This is a preliminary step to the ICC's opening a formal investigation (Hirst et al. 2020). Argentina later dropped out of the proposal.

Venezuela's International Relations

The Exodus: A Humanitarian Crisis

Nothing had greater impact worldwide than the massive flow of Venezuelans who left their home country, again demonstrating the important role an exodus can play. It is estimated that over 5.4 million citizens have left the country, including more than 1 million Colombo Venezuelans (United Nations High Commissioner for Refugees 2020). The Venezuelan diaspora has become a problem for its neighboring countries, particularly Colombia, where the number of Venezuelans reached 1.8 million in 2020 (Ministerio de Relaciones Exteriores de Colombia 2020). A meeting was held in September 2018 in Quito, Ecuador, attended by representatives of 13 Latin American countries and the OAS to discuss the regional situation generated by this humanitarian crisis. They declared their commitment to coordinating a regional response.

The General Assembly of the United Nations also criticized Maduro's regime and favored humanitarian aid. The UN Human Rights Council approved the report on promoting and protecting human rights in Venezuela. As UN High Commissioner for Human Rights Michelle Bachelet (former president of Chile) told the UN Human Rights Council, her office had "documented numerous human rights violations and abuses by security forces and pro-government armed groups, including the excessive use of force, killings, arbitrary detentions, torture and ill-treatment in detention, threats, and intimidation." She added that the Venezuelan authorities failed to acknowledge the extent and severity of the health and food crisis that had driven millions of people abroad since 2015 (in Nebehay 2019).

At the same time, Colombia and Guyana politically distanced themselves from Venezuela. Colombia left UNASUR and became the main supporter of Venezuela's radical Right opposition, allowing them to operate from Colombian territory. Relations between Venezuela and Colombia deteriorated, to such an extent that observers speculated about possible armed conflict between them. With Guyana, the situation became worse due to the end of the bilateral negotiations between Guyana and Venezuela regarding Venezuela's claim to part of the Guyanese territory, the Esequibo, under the Geneva Agreement of 1966. This dispute passed to the jurisdiction of the International Court at The Hague.

US-Venezuela Relations

Venezuela's relationship with Washington also continued to deteriorate. Given the radicalization of the political process and the international alliances President Maduro's government established, contrary to the interests of the US government, the United States broke diplomatic relations. The United States confronted Venezuela in several ways. First, it formed a coalition of governments, hemispheric and international, capable of confronting the country by raising the costs of its actions. Second, it developed a comprehensive sanction plan directed at representatives of the regime. Starting with President Maduro himself, the sanctions reduced the financial and credit capacity of PDVSA and other institutions to stop Venezuelan oil shipments to the US market, at the same time that it banned US financial transactions using the Venezuelan cryptocurrency, the petro. Third, via a media campaign, the United States supported Venezuela's radical opposition, which pleaded for a US military intervention. A turning point was reached that could result in either more sanctions to push for a negotiated regime change, or a hemispheric military action led by the United States. As former president Donald Trump put it, "All options are still on the table."

Trade relations between the United States and Venezuela totally broke down. After several decades of being Venezuela's main trade partner, Washington moved away from Caracas due to political and ideological differences. At present, the US government has broken diplomatic and economic relations with Venezuela. In August 2019, it opened a Venezuelan Affairs Unit inside the American embassy in Bogotá, Colombia, and recognized the government of Juan Guaidó as the legitimate representative of Venezuela to the United States. Thus, it applied multiple sanctions to the Maduro government and to PDVSA, which also affected trade. In the first half of 2020, US-Venezuela trade closed at $0.57 billion—an insignificant figure given that it had reached over $55 billion in 2011, still under Chávez. In that year, oil exports to the United States reached $44 billion, and the United States remained Venezuela's leading trade partner, with 46 percent of the total in 2011. It is estimated that in the second half of 2020, the trade between the two countries did not exceed $0.28 billion (US Census Bureau 2020b). In 2019, Venezuela exported 500,000 barrels of oil per day to the United States; in 2020, it was next to none. Venezuela's break with the United States has been slower and more complex than Cuba's, as commercial exchange has continued, especially the daily shipment of barrels of oil to the American market via PDVSA's subsidiaries, including CITGO. That relationship no longer exists (Bull and Rosales 2020). Since Joe Biden arrived at the White House, everyone expected US relations with Venezuela, as well as with Cuba, to change. Until now, nothing has changed with Venezuela.

Political Crisis and Political Legitimacy

Dual Power

Both the government and the opposition lack the will to engage in a negotiated agreement that addresses the deep political and economic crisis in Venezuela. Meanwhile, the international democratic community presses for a political solution to the situation but lacks the capacity to carry it out.

On January 10, 2019, the situation was further aggravated by Nicolás Maduro's inauguration before the National Constituent Assembly. Days before, members of the Lima Group, the United States, and several European countries stated that they considered his claim of victory illegal and they would not recognize his mandate. At the same time, they urged that the

Figure 9.2. Juan Guaidó, president of Venezuela's parallel National Assembly in 2015, speaks to the people at a rally in Caracas, Venezuela, January 23, 2019 (Photo by Ruben Alfonzo via Shutterstock).

executive power be delegated to the person elected president of the AN, as stipulated in the Constitution. On January 23, 2019, Juan Guaidó was sworn in as interim president of Venezuela.

This proclamation resulted in a dual power scenario and deepening of the political crisis. Various options were proposed to make this transition effective, including a humanitarian intervention, and even a direct US military invasion. Fully 57 governments recognized Juan Guaidó as president of the AN and the only legal and legitimate head of state. To counter the trend toward military intervention, Juan Guaidó called several political rallies and toured several South American countries, where he was welcomed as president of Venezuela. Guaidó tried to route the humanitarian aid (food and medical supplies) sent by the United States, Canada, and other countries to the western border at the Tienditas bridge (connecting Cúcuta, Colombia, with Ureña, Venezuela). Initially, Venezuelan troops blockaded the bridge, but, eventually, the Venezuelan government accepted the arrival of humanitarian aid channeled through the Red Cross and the United Nations.

Despite the blockade, President Maduro felt confident that he had sufficient internal and external support to remain in power. He refused to surrender, believing that his time had not yet arrived, and portrayed himself as "the victim of imperialist aggression." He also relied on the support of China, Russia, and Cuba, among others. Cuba's counsel was fundamental at that time moment, as it had been since 1999. Cuban advisors, with their social psychological and conflict management skills, played a role in handling the media. For Cuba, the main objective is to avoid the United States invading Venezuela; other issues are secondary.

Meanwhile, shipments of crude oil from Venezuela to the United States declined dramatically from 650,000 barrels a day in December 2018 to 200,000 in April 2019—one-third less in slightly over a year, and virtually none in the year 2020. Furthermore, the US government began to deposit the money from oil purchases in a trust for Guaidó's government. As PDVSA moved its international offices from Lisbon to Moscow, the United States put its letters of credit for Venezuelan oil purchases on hold. Moreover, Maduro knew that by the end of the year he would no longer have enough resources to remain in power unless he received substantial help from China, Russia, Iran, and Turkey. Oil tankers were stranded in the Gulf of Mexico and Venezuela; bilateral contracts were frozen; and there was a ban on the sale of products derived from oil from the United States to Venezuela. CITGO, the US oil company owned by PDVSA, passed into the hands of the Venezuelan opposition. The expectation was that PDVSA would collapse without it.

In short, the Venezuelan crisis resulted from four interrelated conditions. First is the growing number of illiberal regimes worldwide (Weyland 2013). Second is the world's multipolar geopolitical rearrangement in which the United States, China, and Russia compete with each other through other countries. Third is the economic and social crisis that polarized Venezuela and rendered it politically fragile, with a situation of dual power played out on the streets. Last but not least, there is neither an enabling environment nor a negotiator with the patience and skills to bring groups in violent conflict with markedly different perspectives to the negotiating table and, ultimately, to an accord. Such was the role that former US senator George Mitchell played in Northern Ireland's peace process. At present, the chances for a peaceful and democratic solution to the Venezuelan crisis are slim.

In the new millennium, Venezuela is part of a democratic regression worldwide that has manifested itself in the growing violation of human rights, the loss of the rule of law and separation of powers, and the violation of the full electoral and institutional process in a democratic polity (Puyosa 2019). These are considered fundamental in solving the problems of representation, pluralism, and participation.

Under Chávez and Maduro, Venezuela has been a serious critic of globalization, Western values, and liberal capitalism, developing not only an anti-Western alliance with other countries (e.g., China, Russia, Cuba, Turkey, and Iran) but also building new alternatives with like-minded countries (as with ALBA). Thus, from the perspective of the West, Venezuela now threatens their geopolitical security.

The architects of the Russian Revolution were familiar with this situation of "dual power," in which two powers coexisted, competed for legitimacy, defined themselves as the nation's legal government, failed to recognize each other, and were supported by different foreign governments (Lenin 1964; Trotsky 1992). Maduro's regime considers the provisional government of AN president Juan Guaidó illegal and illegitimate. Guaidó, in turn, defines Nicolás Maduro as a "usurper" of the president's office. At the same time, there is rampant deinstitutionalization, as corruption, drug trafficking, smuggling, and the crime-driven economy have replaced the institutional channels and public actors recognized by the law.

Nonetheless, Venezuela's case remains, thus far, unique in that there has been no civil war; each political actor is recognized by part of the international community; the government retains a monopoly of the military's legitimate use of violence; and there is not a state of generalized rebellion. Moreover, the armed forces have not yet tipped the balance, as they did at other times in Latin America. Most of the military power, especially the top brass, remains united and obedient to Maduro's regime. Only if the military were to divide could this situation of dual power change (Hirst et al. 2020).

At the same time, ordinary Venezuelans must dedicate their daily lives to surviving, confronting the social calamities that are now part of their daily life, and bearing the high cost of living. Survival prevents them from engaging in open political confrontation with the government. Maduro has been playing with time at a very high cost: the US government has been enforcing an economic embargo that deepens day by day with new punitive measures. Trump's sanctions clearly intended to squeeze Maduro's government: suspending American flights to Venezuela and the use of US credit by the Venezuelan state and individuals, including credit cards issued in the United States; sanctioning third parties that trade with Venezuela, including Russian and Indian companies; and prohibiting further oil, gas, and mineral negotiations.

To this situation, COVID-19 arrived. Though the numbers are not high by international standards, cases of coronavirus are increasing in Venezuela. As of mid-2021, Venezuela had 237,000 cases and 1,674 deaths for a population of 28.5 million, with a real scarcity of vaccines. For the sake of comparison with a nearby country of similar size, Peru had 1,984,999 cases and 186,757 deaths for a population of 33.3 million (World Health Organization 2021). Venezuela's cases seem remarkably low, particularly given the enormous economic crisis that can only lead to greater contagion.

The political life continues to be torn in two. The opposition around Guaidó is ever more radicalized, labeling the regime as "dictatorship," "genocide," and "usurpation" and the opposition as "rebellion" and "legitimate defense." However, most of the opposition simply does not know what to do: whether to support a mass insurrection or military outbreak, whether to participate in the coming presidential elections in 2024 or simply to wait for better times to come (Lander 2018; Jácome 2018). The government, for its part, cannot hide the health crisis that grows exponentially, the lack of discipline of the people in the face of successive calls for a quarantine, and the extraordinary development of an informal economy. The government is also failing to provide basic services, such as water, electricity, gas, gasoline, and health care, as well as identity services (e.g., passports, identity card, death and birth certificates, as well as public registry, notaries, and courts). This has resulted in a parallel society that, together with the circulation of the dollar, serves as a buffer against the severe crisis. However, that cushioning is not effective enough in the face of the massive spread of the virus, the reduction of public revenues, and the commercial and financial effects of international sanctions. These sanctions are not only against PDVSA and its subsidiaries and against public finances, but also against companies, entrepreneurs, and financial services linked to the regime (Magdaleno 2018). The United States and its allies are, thus, effectively boycotting Venezuela's regime, increasing the burden of continued destabilization, so as to declare Venezuela a failed and outlawed state. Some of the opposition believes that this will serve to justify an invasion combined with a popular insurrection—though, twice, a military operation against the regime (in April 2019) and a frustrated naval operation (in May 2020) failed.

Why is Venezuela in a state of inertia? First, the regime feels supported by foreign governments, by the armed forces, and by the PSUV militancy itself, and by the paramilitary groups that support *el Chavismo*. Second, the regime has still shown itself able to contain the protests of the people with its repression and surveillance. Moreover, many Venezuelans are not politically active, but simply try to survive the crisis and the pandemic, ignoring the political reality, feeling estranged from all political actors (Vera 2018).

As for the opposition, it remains deeply divided between those who accept the electoral legitimacy of the regime, those who remain open to a new negotiation, and those who are in favor of a military invasion from the outside. Each of these trends has its pros and cons. The opposition that until recently agreed with the regime placed some deputies in the new National Assembly. However, this opposition is not representative and lacks the trust of others. The opposition that remains open to negotiation (represented by Guaidó) has the advantage that it is recognized as a true opposition, has international support, and manages its own finances, though it is struggling for the country's representation amid the dual government. However, this has led to a very sectarian position, rejecting outright participation in parliamentary and other elections and in any peaceful negotiations (such as the talks sponsored by Norway), while not rejecting the sanctions. Most negative about this line has been its lack of a firm position. It openly calls for a military invasion by the United States and its allies, as the only solution possible to the present stagnation. Thus, at present there is neither a negotiation, nor a civil war, nor a military insurrection from within, nor a military invasion from without. Everyone is waiting for "something" to happen (Magdaleno 2018). And the international support for each of these internal actors has declined, as foreign governments have now turned to confront the pandemic.

On July 5, 2020, the minister of defense, Vladimir Padrino-López, made a statement that increased the tension in the Venezuelan opposition. In what has been called a "turning point" in the institution's well-known lack of neutrality, Padrino-López warned the opposition: "As long as there is an armed force like the one we have today—anti-imperialist, revolutionary, Bolivarian—they will never be able to exercise political power in Venezuela." This has been interpreted in two ways. On the one hand, the FANB, the National Armed Forces, have been certified to play an active role within the dominant coalition in power. On the other hand, an electoral solution to the country's problems through elections is not now encouraged (Jácome 2018).

Data from the 2020 national survey on the circumstances of their lives, *Encuesta Nacional de Condiciones de Vida* (ENCOVI), conducted by the Andrés Bello Catholic University, indicates that Venezuela has regressed in all its social indicators. It ranked the country among the five poorest in the world. With 80 percent of its people unable to access the basic food basket, 96.3 percent of households and 51 percent of the population lack adequate protein intake, 30 percent of children suffer from malnutrition, and 44 percent of adults lack employment. In addition, the total population fell to 28 million, given the exodus of millions of young Venezuelans. In the meantime, the vast majority of Venezuelans struggle in the face of the crisis or accommodate themselves to it. To subsist is to be unable to act, waiting for government aid or humanitarian aid (Vera 2018).

Many analyses are superficial, as journalists unquestioningly accept the government's and the opposition's propaganda and have no contact with the poorest social sectors. This makes it impossible to observe how Venezuelans move in a parallel country, which continues to grow day by day. If there is no gasoline, they get it on the black market; if they buy it subsidized, they resell it. If there is no electricity, they use domestic gas or firewood to cook. If they hold a formal job that pays them little, they seek to make a profit reselling food and gasoline. They also engage in illicit activities: drug trafficking, theft, contraband, or resale of stolen goods, such as automotive parts, jewelry, clothing, and electrical devices, or they profit from buying and selling dollars. This parallel country grows in particular amid the lower-middle-class and working-class, peasant, and rural sectors. When they leave the country and try to seek asylum, arguing that they are forcibly displaced refugees, the receiving countries view them with suspicion (Lander 2018). Most Venezuelans are engaged in solving everyday problems by alternative routes to the formal economy (Magdaleno 2018; Bull and Rosales 2020). But, in truth, the lethargy and social anomie are due to the control of the government over the movements of the people, quenching demonstrations with repression (including cold, bloody executions of alleged criminals). Therefore, the protest rates are low. The regime still has the capacity to prevent and suppress any initiative against it.

The contradictions between the two parallel governments are intensifying. On the one hand, Maduro's regime insists on not negotiating with the opposition regarding the next elections. On the other hand, Guaidó's provisional government uses the thesis of administrative continuity, upholding the idea that it is a provisional government for as long as Maduro's "usurpation" continues. Maduro has developed a strategy that allows him to sustain himself in power, gradually opening up the regulations derived from the pandemic, and insisting that Guaidó's initiatives are illegal and supported by only a small group of conservative governments. Guaidó hoped that around the time of the parliamentary elections, a popular uprising and a military insurrection would take place simultaneously. It did not happen.

Diplomatically, despite Guaidó's recognition by 57 governments, including the United States, the Maduro government is still in power, in what Washington defines as a "stand-by" situation, due to the serious difficulties President Trump experienced during the elections. Similarly, the victory of the MAS party and its candidate Luis Arce for president in October 2020 gave Maduro oxygen. It also reinforced the new coalition of Left-of-center governments of Mexico, Argentina, and now Bolivia and Chile. As a result, a peaceful and prompt solution to the Venezuelan crisis is not possible at present. Most Venezuelans hope that in the near future a new opportunity for a political negotiation will appear. Meanwhile, the political vacuum further separates the skeptical citizen from political life and reduces people's attention to public affairs.

Venezuelans have become accustomed to emergency and cope with it according to their social class. Upper-middle-class citizens with greater purchasing power have entrenched themselves in their homes, with sufficient dollars to maintain high levels of consumption, spending in supermarkets and special minimarkets stocked with imported products. In addition, the most daring pay up to US $7,000 to leave or enter the country—by land or air, via private or official planes, and via clandestine transportation.

The middle class and lower middle class depend on the growing foreign exchange market, the remittances that arrive from family overseas, their savings, and sales of their own goods. They cannot cope with the situation with their completely devalued salaries or pensions, so they try to restrict their consumption. Their opposition to the regime continues to grow.

The lower class has suffered the most, lacking not only food but also water and electricity. They have taken the path of emigration. Lacking a fair salary or employment, without resources, 80 percent of the more than 400,000 people who have left Venezuela since April 2020 come from this sector. It is projected that by December 2022 this will include one million new émigrés.

Yet another sector depends on government assistance and international aid. They have the most contact with the informal and criminal economy, as they trade with dollars and engage in the sale and resale of food, as well as in trafficking drugs, stolen goods, and smuggling. Thus, Venezuelans have adapted to this kind of "parallel economy" where wage earners lose but those in the informal sector win. The government is aware of this and has no plans to combat the dollarization because it has neither enough foreign exchange nor the capacity to reform the monetary policy. Thus, they ignore what is happening. In fact, banknotes in bolívares are scarce, as are low-denomination dollars, though the government allows the free circulation of dollars.

The reality of the informal economy is that there is another layer of business persons, contractors, high officials, and toll collectors who benefit through corruption, official contacts, and commercial ties, especially with their links to the oil market and mining activity. Taking advantage of the situation, they climb socially; corruption endures.

Future Scenarios for Both Revolutions

It remains for us to ask: What are the possible scenarios for Cuba and Venezuela at this juncture?

For Cuba, a first scenario consists of maintaining the status quo inherited from Fidel and Raúl Castro, in which the highly centralized state and the power of the Communist Party remains the same, controlling domestic politics while supported by unconditional international allies, such as Venezuela. The dismal economy in both countries makes this scenario unlikely.

A second scenario projects structural changes in the economy but without changes in the political institutions: the Sino-Vietnamese path. The Communist Party would reach the conclusion that economic reforms must be deepened, allowing private foreign investment and *cuentapropismo*, together with a delimited amount of private property in home ownership, to diversify the market of goods and services, but without contemplating a political reform. This is partially the present trend, though short of what Vietnam and China have done.

A third scenario would come about if the Cuban Revolution were to emerge from the general crisis of its economy with a leadership vacuum in the government, while the US government punishes Cuba for supporting Venezuela. This could even be accompanied by a social explosion, in which large numbers of Cuban citizens would protest, asking for regime change and an open economy. The social protests of 2020 and 2021 may be harbingers of this scenario.

For Venezuela, a first scenario would entail President Maduro staying in power through applying more coercion, with a low probability of regime change. The economic crisis would worsen; the opposition would increase significantly, both internally and internationally; and, together with the Catholic Church and other sectors of civil society (trade unions, NGOs), they would continue to criticize and challenge the regime through international and domestic initiatives. This is the present trend.

A second scenario is based on the possibility that Maduro's government might lose definitively its internal and external support, ushering in regime change. A political transition might take place via a new presidential election under the surveillance of the international community. This could happen.

In a third scenario, a military coup might take place, together with humanitarian assistance, backed by the United Nations or an American-led military intervention. This is unlikely.

In a highly polarized society, two different narratives exist regarding current events in Venezuela. To the advocates of the Bolivarian Revolution, the fault lies with the United States, the oligarchy, and the Venezuelan Right, together with the Latin American and European Right, all of whom have not let up in their attempt to destroy the achievements accomplished by Chávez's Bolivarian Revolution and Maduro's government. To its enemies, the Bolivarian Revolution is now at its lowest point. Unfortunately, the economic situation has affected working people and the poor—the very people who were the base for the revolution (Bull and Rosales 2020; Marsteintredet 2020).

Still an Alliance

Venezuela has continued to support Cuba, and Cuba has continued to support Venezuela. On January 1, 2018, on the 59th anniversary of the triumph of Cuba's revolution, Nicolás Maduro issued a *comunicado*, congratulating Cuba on its achievements. He emphasized that the two revolutions were linked "by the emancipatory legacy of Martí and Bolívar, and they have sealed their indissoluble alliance with Hugo Chávez and Fidel Castro's historical embrace. The union of our revolutions yielded historic fruits in the construction of ALBA, Petrocaribe, and CARICOM. It has been at the vanguard of the struggle for a multipolar world, and will continue to grow deeper" as their new economic, political, social, and cultural projects will result in the well-being of the rest of the world (Maduro 2018).

However, 2017 saw Venezuela's GDP contract by around -20 percent, while inflation rose to 2,500 percent. Venezuela continues to rely on its reserves in oil, mining, and gas, as well as its economic collaboration with Cuba, Russia, and China. It continues to hope it will get through these difficult times until the price of oil rebounds on the world market. However, as Abadi M. (2017) has underscored, the present economic crisis is not the result of the fall in the world market price of crude oil but actually pre-dates it. Thus, an unexpected increase in the price of crude oil would give Venezuela's government much-needed oxygen, but to really exit the present economic crisis would require profound reforms of the economic model.

Despite their unwavering support, tensions and conflicts now exist between Venezuela and Cuba. The sources are various. First, the amount of oil that Venezuela sends to Cuba declined steeply in 2019—from 110,000 barrels a day in 2012, to only 43,000 barrels a day in 2017, to only around 10,000 barrels of oil a day now; moreover, it seldom arrives on time. Second, the number of Cuban professionals under contract to work in Venezuela is now only 22,000 workers, down from 51,000 at its peak. Third, Venezuela's investments in Cuba have come to a complete stop. While in 2014 the commercial exchange of goods between both nations surpassed $7.3 billion, by 2016 it was only $2.2 billion. In 2018, Venezuela again became Cuba's first trade partner. Since then, China has alternated with Venezuela for that spot. Last, Havana worries about the deteriorating relations between Caracas and Washington, while in Latin America aversion to Maduro continues to grow.

As in 2018, Raúl Castro recognized the critical situation in which the Cuban economy finds itself, given the passage of Hurricane Irma, the low world price for nickel and sugar, the lack of financial liquidity, the low productivity of Cuban enterprises, the economic crisis in Venezuela, and the deteriorating relationship with the United States. In 2019, the Cuban economy grew by only 0.5 percent. Estimates for 2020 are worse: CEPAL estimated that the Cuban economy would decline by -3.7 percent in 2020; the *Economist* Intelligence Unit estimated it to be by -8.0 percent and -11.0 percent in 2021.

Real political reform is not on the agenda, only a continuation of current policies and political structure. The government continues to lack an economic policy that can lift it out of stagnation (Mesa-Lago 2019b). In his analysis of the economy after six decades of revolution, Mesa-Lago shows that it has always been a very dependent economy: first on the United States (52 percent of total exports); then on the USSR (72 percent), and then on Venezuela (44 percent). At its peak in 2012, Venezuela's trade of goods and services was $16 billion—21 percent of Cuba's GDP. By 2017, however, it was half that amount, $8 billion—12 percent of GDP. Mesa-Lago and Vidal-Alejandro (2019) judge this decline to be one of the key causes of the economic crisis at present on the island.

Similarly, sugar used to be the mainstay of the Cuban economy: 75 percent of exports and 22 percent of GDP (Echevarría 1995). Now sugar has been replaced by professional services, exporting health workers (80 percent of exports—12 percent of GDP), treating them as a commodity. Only remittances increased from virtually none to around $3,000 million in cash, the second major source of hard-currency revenue, after the export of professional services, which is first. And population growth fell from 2.1 percent to -0.2 percent, as the exodus continued and Cuba became a rather old nation. In fact, the island has the oldest population in the Western Hemisphere (Mesa-Lago 2020; Mesa-Lago and Pérez-López 2013).

These were profound changes. Constant has been Cuba's "incapacity to generate appropriate, sustainable growth, and to finance imports without substantial foreign aid-subsidies," as Mesa-Lago (2019a) emphasizes. Even focusing on just the new millennium shows an abysmal picture. In 2006,

Cuba's GDP growth was 12.1 percent; by 2009, it had declined to 1.4. It remained quite low thereafter, fluctuating around 2 percent, declined to zero in 2014, up to 4.4 in 2015, and again declined to a very low rate thereafter, close to only 1.0 in 2016. While in 2017 and 2018 it rose to the low figure of 2 percent, in 2019 it was less than 1, and the forecast for 2020 is no higher. The inefficient nature of the economic model—centralized planning and state enterprises that predominate over the market, together with a collectivized agriculture—can be seen even when one takes 1989 (when the Soviet Union disappeared and "the special period" began) as the base year, since most economic indicators are now below that base. In 2018–19, the output of sugar was 82 percent below that of 1989. Likewise, in the key sectors of agriculture, cattle, and fishing, output in 2018 was below the 1989 level. The Cuban economy is stagnant: industrial production in many sectors remains below 1989 levels, and the sugar harvest is no longer a source of pride. Moreover, average wages in the inefficient state sector where most Cubans work are around US $40 a month; imports of merchandise (particularly food) far outstrip exports; foreign direct investment is at remarkably low levels; and young people seek to leave the island (Mesa-Lago 2019a; Feinberg 2020). Today, according to official Cuban statistics, national per capita GDP stands at $7,800, well below the $14,900 that is the average for Latin America and the Caribbean. Data from the United Nations Development Program (UNDP) Human Development Report for 2019 show that other small countries far surpass Cuba's productivity in the region: Chile, Uruguay, the Dominican Republic, Costa Rica, and Jamaica. Jamaica and El Salvador register levels comparable to Cuba's; only Haiti is worse (Feinberg 2020, 253). Havana has grown dilapidated, with much of its old stock in serious disrepair. Its beauty can still be seen in those areas of Old Havana that the late Eusebio Leal-Spengler, the municipal historian of the city, painstakingly restored, leading it to become a UNESCO World Heritage site. After Leal-Spengler's death, given the enormity of the economic crisis, the restored area remains small; however, it offers a glimpse of what Havana could once again be: "With smart urban planning, Havana could regain its place among the world's most beautiful and livable spaces," notes Feinberg (2016, 214). Clearly, its people suffer. In Cuba, the large educated middle class that resulted from Cuba's heavy investments in education and health during the 60-plus years of the revolution lives like poor people live elsewhere in the world: they lack good food, attractive clothing, decent housing, necessary appliances, critical medicines, and reliable transportation.

But much of that middle class has chosen to migrate, due to the "push" and "pull" that guide those decisions (Lee 1966). The lack of these lifestyle supports and political liberty "push" many Cubans to leave the island. Their families and friends who already live abroad also "pull" them with the promise of family reunification and a better life.

Yet Cuba does have sufficient resources—human and natural—to be able to achieve sustainable economic growth. Feinberg (2016) argues that Cuban agriculture could produce an abundance of export crops (tobacco, coffee, sugar, citrus fruit, organic vegetables, and animal husbandry) to feed both its own population and the rising number of tourists. Cuba's tourist industry could expand beyond the sun and surf tourism to other forms of tourism: ecotourism, adventure tourism, aquatic tourism, and medical tourism. An economically sustainable society would encourage the young who today seek to leave the island to remain and contribute to its future. However, as Feinberg (2020) claims, "two binding constraints must be released before the island can blossom." One is to put an end to the conflictual relationship with the United States, so that both nations can trade freely and Cuba can engage with its powerful neighbor to the North with confidence. The other is for the Cuban government to "finally break free of the shackles of the anachronistic central planning" (262) so that it can not only tolerate but also celebrate the emergence of a private sector. In addition, the Cuban government could grant real administrative autonomy to the efficient state-owned firms that can partner and invest together with multinational firms from around the world. While we concur with Feinberg that these are the two constraints that must be released for the island to deliver a decent future to its people, we think it is unlikely to be achieved in the absence of political democracy and respect for human rights.

While most scholars agree by now that the ideal goal of development is "growth with equity," as Amartya Sen (1999) expresses it, Corrales (2012) shows that Cuba presents us with the dilemma of "equity without growth." Historically, Latin America managed economic growth but could be faulted for the lack of social inclusion of the poorest classes. Revolutionary Cuba, however, managed the social inclusion side of the equation by providing education and health services fairly well and fairly universally; however, under the revolution the island has barely registered economic growth. At present, it is caught in a deep decline. Corrales underscores that different authoritarian regimes make different claims to fame: delivering extraordinary economic growth (China), national rebirth (Russia), economic efficiency (Singapore), religious rule (Middle East), and military might (North Korea). Cuba's claim to fame has always been equity and social inclusion, despite the lack of economic growth. Corrales argues that, rather than an achievement, this model is "a sign of grave malaise" (158). Plotting the average number of years of schooling of a country's workforce in 2000 by the country's average annual growth rate per capita for 85 countries showed Cuba to be the most salient outlier (Maddison 2001). The revolution invested in high levels of human capital and by the 1970s had achieved them, with demonstrably good quality. Precisely because of this achievement, an obstacle must be in the way, he emphasizes, to prevent that human capital from spurring economic growth. Corrales contends that this obstacle was the combination of the state's restrictions of property and political rights. They remained even after the substantial reforms of the *Lineamientos* (Guidelines) put in place by Raúl Castro's government in recent years.

To demonstrate his argument, Corrales compares Cuba's and China's development models. In the 1970s, both countries shared the same model: state control of the centralized economy with significant restrictions on property and political rights. The results were similar: equity without growth. But in 1979 China changed its model, liberalizing the economy externally and internally. Externally, China began to attract foreign investment by putting tax breaks and policy incentives in place; internally, China began to grant property rights for individual citizens.

By contrast, Cuba's economy became more global but not more liberal. Thus, since 1980, their development models diverged. Corrales compares them with respect to two quite different industries: the bicycle industry (which relies on menial skills) and the Internet (which relies on high skills). Thus, he argues that Cuba's restrictions on property rights hurt its economic growth. Cuba's command economy impairs productivity and investment because the state makes insufficient economic investments and targets them rather narrowly, and because the state penalizes, rather than encourages, the ingenuity of its citizens, who remain under its tight control, often opting out of new ventures, as a result.

Looking at the bicycle industry, Corrales (2012) notes that the US embargo cannot be faulted for the moribund state of the Cuban bicycle industry, despite the lack of reliable transportation on the island. Though lacking trade with the giant to the north and access to its market remains a constant problem, Cuba did have healthy trade relations with some of the world's largest steel exporters (Russia, China, Germany, Brazil, and Venezuela). Thus, the US embargo did "not seem to have been as powerful as Cuba's own restrictions." Looking at the Internet industry, until quite recently Cuba was isolated from this significant form of communication. While China restricted Internet content, it did not restrict access. Cuba, by comparison, did both—restricted access and engaged in censorship. As Corrales puts it, "Information technologies (IT) are not a development panacea, but it is hard to imagine an economy today achieving international competitiveness with its back turned on this revolution" (169). Fearing the political consequences of unbridled access to the Internet, the government's political and economic repression are responsible for Cuban citizens' lack of access. At present, Cubans' access is freer than in the past, but the availability of independent forms of journalism is still blocked by the government. Corrales concludes that the process of substantial economic reforms that began under Raúl Castro's *Lineamientos* needs to go further, liberalizing economic and political rights, so that Cuba's achievements in human capital can begin to spur economic growth. At present, Cuba not only has problems with growth but also with equity, as its system of social expenditures has deteriorated further—all the more reason why achieving economic growth is crucial for all its people. Without it, the social gains of the revolution become social losses.

Throughout this book, we have focused on the changes in Cuba's and Venezuela's economy, on their economic history over the course of the two revolutions. This is particularly apt since in both societies a socialist and communist ideology resulted in a thorough restructuring of economic life. As Sewell Jr. (2010, 147) points out, the historical study of economic life has had a strange career: precisely in the years since 1980, when globalization, deindustrialization, repeated financial crises, and soaring economic inequality should have made obvious "the need for a deeper historical understanding of modern capitalism's dynamism and perversity, historians have largely abandoned the historical study of economic life while economists turned economic history into a branch of mathematical development economics." Sewell concludes that, at this time, when transformations of economic life are indeed having powerful, even determinative, effects on our own contemporary history, historians (and, we would add, other social scientists) can "construct a more powerful and meaningful history by re-embracing the study of economic life" (166). Sewell concludes that we should use the analytical tools of history to investigate the longue durée of capitalism. We concur, and add that we should also use the analytical tools of the social sciences "to investigate the constraints, the compulsions, the enablements, and the long-term dynamics" (166) that have shaped not only capitalist societies for the past four centuries but also socialist and communist societies for now over a century. We hope our study contributes to this goal.

In the end, Cuba and Venezuela's contemporary crises run so deep that we cannot say (as people often do, when alluding to a particular crisis) that they are at a crossroads. The image simply no longer applies. Rather, we think that a better image is that they are standing at the edge of a precipice. This leaves us with a question: How is it possible for their governments to continue to hold onto power in the face of these deep-seated crises? The answer must be that they cannot.

Both governments could engage in economic reforms that would encourage their citizens' economic enterprises. Yet economic improvements may only come about as the result of a political transition. Velásquez (2021) recently called for a multilateral approach, including international actors close to Cuba and to Venezuela, such as Norway, Spain, Turkey, Russia, and China. Such was the case of the Contadora-Esquipula experience in Central America in the mid-1980s: a multilateral initiative launched by Colombia, Mexico, Panama, and Venezuela to deal with the military conflict in El Salvador, Nicaragua, and Guatemala, while reducing the US military presence and perspective. Such a multilateral group, over numerous meetings, did not call for total surrender, as Donald Trump's administration did, but brought new, positive proposals to the table to solve the violent conflict. Together, they achieved peace in Central America. With this model in mind, the multilateral approach—including Latin American, European, and Asian countries—may be the best way to promote political reforms in both Cuba and Venezuela that, ultimately, could deliver economic growth for its people.

10

One Hope, Two Realities

Comparing the Two Revolutions

While scholars who study revolutions have long called for cross-national comparisons (Skocpol 1979; Goldstone 1982), few comparative analyses have been carried out, with most focused on European cases, seldom centering on the developing world, as we do. Yet it is not easy to compare the Cuban and the Bolivarian Revolutions, as their origins, processes, and outcomes were rather different (cf. Tilly 1981). Here we conclude by comparing the revolutions according to their similarities and differences and articulating the generalizations that may be applicable to other cases.

Similarities

The road to revolution clearly passes through inequality—especially of social class and race, but of gender and religion as well. However, that inequality is insufficient to usher in a revolution unless a charismatic leader articulates it with an ideology that promises a better tomorrow, speaking to and for the masses. This populist leadership guides the revolution, giving it an anti-elite thrust.

The study of populism has recently become popular precisely because it encompasses regimes both of the Left and the Right. Yet distinguishing the two is also important. Both rely on an ideology that speaks to the masses, explaining their frustrations and inspiring them to be part of an important social project, giv ing their lives and their suffering meaning. Their ideologies are embedded in the institutions they create and foster. However, they differ in that populist regimes of the Right harken back to the past, expressing a nostalgia for what they deemed was a better yesterday; populist regimes of the Left look ahead to the future, wishing to create a better world for tomorrow.

Both Cuba's and Venezuela's revolutions succeeded, in part, because of their attractive socialist ideology, which explained the social inequality in their midst and promised to bring about a more just society in the future. Both appealed strongly to the marginalized social classes and races. However, here also sharp differences obtained, as Smilde (2021) underscores. Cuba's populist ideology is that of a totalitarian society with an articulated ideology, while Venezuela's populist ideology is that of an authoritarian society with only a "mentality" that orients its policy. Smilde puts it well: "The difference is that an ideology has concepts and analyses that are fairly well developed, while a mentality rests more on root images, metaphors, and sentiments" (10). Fidel and Raúl Castro, together with Ché Guevara, took the well-articulated ideology derived from Marxist-Leninist principles that issued from the history of the Soviet Union. Hugo Chávez's ideology was, first and foremost, "Third-Worldist," rooted in anti-imperialism while secondarily valuing electoral democracy and basic civil and political liberties. Under Nicolás Maduro, only the anti-imperialist thrust still stands.

Even more important than the ideas it articulates, ideology is expressed not only in ideas and sentiments but also in institutions created. Analyzing the French revolution, Sewell Jr. (1985) notes that the revolutionary ideology was expressed not only as the ideas guiding the revolutionaries but also as the institutions in which all aspects of social life became embedded. Revolutionary leaders in both Cuba and Venezuela totally restructured their economy and society, led by a group of revolutionaries whose communist and socialist ideology led them to want to create a better world. Neither nation achieved that hope.

Both revolutions entailed a fundamental break with the past—the defining feature of a revolution. However, the social transformations went far deeper in Cuba. Issuing from an armed struggle in the mid-1950s that sought to depose the unyielding dictator, Fulgencio Batista, the Cuban Revolution initially garnered enormous support across all social classes and races. Its violent, armed struggle was the only road Batista's dictatorship left open. Thereafter, massive nationalizations took place in the early 1960s of all the large industries and institutions controlled by American and Cuban elites. At the end of the decade, the nationalizations added the small-business sector, placing most economic enterprises in the centralized hands of the state.

Both revolutions depended on a charismatic, populist leader. In Cuba, Fidel Castro was the messianic figure at the helm of the government, supported by Raúl Castro at the helm of the military. Under Fidel's leadership, Cuba became the first socialist and communist nation in the Americas. Rooted in *caudillismo* and the anti-elite thrust of populism, its appeal was also coupled with an anti-American nationalism. In Venezuela, Hugo Chávez was also a charismatic leader, but he gained the presidency in 1998 through the electoral system, which has always remained in place. The revolution he sparked was originally characterized (if rather ambiguously) as "the Bolivarian Revolution." Those who study revolutions need to acknowledge that the path to revolution need lie not only through guerrilla warfare and armed insurrection but also through the electoral system. Thus the pace of change was much slower. Sewell Jr. emphasizes that revolutions are also defined by their ideological ambitions. Chávez's ambition was to create the Bolivarian Revolution gradually, through the electoral system. The Bolivarian Revolution was based on the distribution-oriented oil income; it involved the synchronization of the civic and the military; and it depended on the exercise of the electoral majority. After Chávez's several electoral successes, the revolution gradually became transformed into the deeper vision of "the socialism of the twenty-first century": a socialism without poverty. During his presidency, thanks to the high price of oil, Hugo Chávez was able to effect reforms to support the poor, who rewarded him with their belief and support. After his death and Maduro's inefficient presidency, together with the steep decline in the price of oil worldwide, Venezuela's socialism has come with substantial poverty and want.

Both revolutions took place at a particular historical conjuncture, in a particular geopolitical theater. In Cuba, that was the Cold War. Cuba's relationship to the United States—the hegemonic presence in the hemisphere—was a critical element in the revolution's success. However, a strong opposition began to develop, most of which fled the island, seeking American support. The failure of the exile-led and American-trained invasion at the Bay of Pigs in 1961 turned the mass of Cubans leaving the island into a flood. The exodus has never ceased and now consists of five distinct waves (Pedraza 2020, 2007; Amaro 1981). When the failure at the Bay of Pigs consolidated the revolution, Fidel Castro declared himself to have always been a Marxist-Leninist, contrary to his earlier assertions that the revolution was not red but "green as the palm trees of Cuba" (F. Castro 1959a, 1959b). Thus, the Cuban revolution was consolidated in a rather brief time span (Amaro 1977). Cuba then shifted its economic and political allegiance and dependence from the United States to the Soviet Union. With the Soviet Union and Eastern European countries as its economic lifeline and benefactor for the next 30 years, Cuba recast all its institutions on the blueprint of Soviet communist institutions. That alliance, with the generous support it entailed (monetary subsidies and professional training), enabled Cuba to survive the repeated attempts by Americans and exiles to undermine the revolution.

The geopolitical setting of the Cold War shaped both Cuban and Venezuelan history, most certainly, through both American and Soviet interventions. We contend that American and Soviet history were also shaped by the Cold War and their mutual forms of aggression. An incident such as the October Missile Crisis in 1962 tells that story well, as does the fact that the United States inherited a very sizable part of Cuba's population. The impact of the Cuban revolution on Soviet history is a story yet to be told.

Both revolutions involved the circulation of elites. Since both populist revolutions articulated an anti-elite thrust, the old political and economic elites had to be replaced by new ones. Through a process of nationalization and strong popular support, both revolutions featured elite displacement, replacing the old elites with new elites willing to carry out their new socialist vision. Both entailed the state's social control. Both revolutions enjoyed enormous popular support from those they sought to represent and benefit—the poor, the working class, peasants, women, and racial minorities, though also from the middle classes who believed they would create a better future for all. Both also generated enormous opposition from those most affected and dispossessed—the middle and upper classes, though also from those in the working class, racial minorities, and peasants who did not believe in their promises.

Both revolutions took place in the developing world, albeit in two rather modern and prosperous (though highly unequal) nations, in a hemisphere where the hegemonic presence of the United States was always critical. The geopolitical theater where they unfolded was key, as that was the stage for the drama that was played out. With Cuba, from the early 1960s on, the American government clearly sought to undermine the revolution by breaking economic and diplomatic relations, establishing the trade embargo, and supporting the opposition, including the exile invasion. With

Venezuela, the American government did not clearly seek to undermine the revolution during its early years. Yet it is important to realize that Venezuela went through a couple of transitions, as Smilde (2021) underscores. When Chávez was president, Venezuela made a transition from populism to socialism; when Maduro was president, Venezuela made a transition from socialism to authoritarian *Chavismo*. Only then did the United States break economic and diplomatic relations and supported the opposition, both inside the country and in exile.

Both the Cuban and Venezuelan governments railed against the United States, fanning the flames of an anti-American nationalism that was at the center of their policies. They also established an anti-American foreign policy, while seeking new international alliances. This "Third-Worldist" thrust portrayed the problems of the Global South as stemming from imperialism, economic and political relations between the hegemonic North and the global South that undermined its sovereignty. Both Fidel Castro and Hugo Chávez portrayed themselves as representing *el pueblo* and the Third World.

Both revolutions undermined dissent by persecuting their opponents, including jailing them as political prisoners; exerting pressure on the courts; and taking over the independent institutions of civil society, in Cuba, or stifling the news media, in Venezuela. Both revolutions involved a transition from a strong, charismatic leader at its forefront (Fidel Castro in Cuba, Hugo Chávez in Venezuela) to another far less charismatic leader that inherited their predecessor's hold on power but could not equally speak to or for the hearts and minds of the people (Raúl Castro in Cuba, Nicolás Maduro in Venezuela). That leadership transition took place very slowly in Cuba, after 46 or so years, while in Venezuela it was swift, after only 14 years. In both revolutions, the leader portrayed himself as the father of the nation; thus, the actual death of the messianic leader on whom the masses had placed their hope resulted in his being genuinely mourned. Fidel Castro's death captured the imagination of the world and marked the end of an era in Latin America. Real disagreements remain as to whether he was David or Goliath.

Of utmost importance, both revolutions relied on each other to deepen the social transformations they effected. From Chávez's victory in 1998 onward, the historical link between Venezuela and the United States was gradually replaced by a strong link between Venezuela and Cuba (Chávez 2014a, 2014b). In effect, both governments intended the strong friendship and alliance between Fidel Castro and Hugo Chávez to support both revolutions, helping both to succeed. The "golden years" were from 1999 to 2012, when they marched together as brothers in arms. In Cuba, the alliance served to buoy up the island that suffered the enormous hardships and want created by "the special period." In Venezuela, the alliance made possible the presence of thousands and thousands of Cuban doctors and health personnel to work with the poor, curing their physical and social ailments, in exchange for their political support of Chávez.

Both revolutions exported their best product to forge that formidable alliance, trading Cuba's medical doctors, nurses, and ophthalmologists for Venezuelan oil. When Venezuela replaced the Soviet Union as the island's benefactor, this entailed not only military collaboration and training but also the exchange of the services of medical workers for Venezuelan oil. The oil kept Cuba from the constant loss of electricity and power—the *apagones*

Figure 10.1. A Cuban woman wearing a face mask as a precautionary measure against the spread of the coronavirus walks by a banner with pictures of leaders of the Cuban War of Independence—Carlos Manuel de Céspedes and José Martí—and leaders of the revolution—Fidel Castro, Raúl Castro, and president Miguel Díaz-Canel. The banner reads "*Somos Continuidad*" (We Are Continuity), signifying that the leaders of the revolution continue the tradition of the War of Independence. Havana, Cuba March 3, 2021 (Photo by Yamil Lage via Getty Images).

Figure 10.2. A man waves a Cuban flag during a demonstration against the government of Cuban President Miguel Díaz-Canel, Havana, July 11, 2021. Thousands of Cubans took part in rare protests against the communist government, marching through a town chanting, "Down with the dictatorship" and "We want liberty" (Photo by Adalberto Roque via Getty Images).

(blackouts)—from which it suffered and made the new expansion of the tourist sector more viable.

Cuba's historical mainstay as a nation was sugar; however, faced with the lack of productivity of the sugar sector, Fidel Castro closed nearly half of the mills. With Fidel's influence waning due to his old age, after the 6th and 7th Party Congresses, Raúl Castro began a series of pragmatic reforms. Today, the three pillars on which Cuba's economy rests are: the remittances from the émigrés, the export of professional health services, and the arrival of international tourism.

Cuba's extension of its social services, particularly education and public health, had proved paramount in the success of the revolution. In recent years, however, they continued to deteriorate steadily, particularly due to the lack of essential structural reforms (Mesa-Lago and Pérez-López 2013).

Through an alliance that was both political and economic, both revolutions were mutually dependent and kept each other afloat.

Both revolutions generated a massive exodus of refugees who fled elsewhere. Cuban refugees overwhelmingly fled to the United States and secondarily to Spain, while Venezuela's mostly fled to neighboring Colombia and secondarily to the United States; both were looking for political and economic freedom. Both revolutions issued a diaspora that in time became a significant political actor, influencing American electoral outcomes as well as foreign policy. The exiles of both revolutions sought to influence political conditions in their homeland, through invasion, insurgency, education, propaganda, and dual political representation in international bodies. With Cuba's exiles, in due time (after some 30 years), that ever-growing diaspora also began to influence the island through its remittances. In the recent presidential elections, Venezuela's exiles joined with many Cubans, Nicaraguans, and Colombians in casting the majority of their votes for the Republican Party. These electoral alliances with other immigrants that are refugees from communism or socialism will continue to shape future political outcomes. While each alone could hardly be influential, together they constitute a conservative electoral pole in South Florida that will continue to impact future elections.

Differences

A revolution entails the rise of some and the downfall of others, as well as the exile of many. In short, it is a process with victims and beneficiaries. In Cuba, the political polarization of the society was due both to the internal opposition (called the counterrevolution) and to external processes (the United States, the USSR). In Venezuela, the political polarization was solely the result of internal processes. Nonetheless, President Trump seemed quite willing to play the role of *el imperio* (the empire) that Nicolás Maduro tried to attribute to him. But the fact remains that nothing equivalent to the exile invasion of Cuba organized by the Americans has yet occurred in Venezuela, though Trump's economic sanctions were devastating and helped to cripple the economy, much like the US economic embargo of Cuba.

Two consequences flow from these issues. First, because it largely went into exile and lost its effort to recuperate Cuba via the invasion, Cuba's internal opposition rapidly lost the significance it originally had. This was not the case in Venezuela. During the early years of the revolution, under Chávez, the Venezuelan opposition largely remained inside the country and continued to challenge the revolutionary leadership through organized party politics and its electoral base. Second, Cuban leaders quickly achieved complete political control of the state and of civil society. At the start, the independent institutions of civil society—the newspapers, television, radio, churches, religious schools, labor movement, and electoral system—all fell into the hands of the new Marxist-Leninist government, who fully controlled them. By contrast, in Venezuela, civil society never collapsed, as the independent media never ceased to exist; it continued to express the opposition, which also continued to express itself through the democratic institutions that remained in place.

In Cuba, the opposition to Fidel and Raúl Castro in the early 1960s took the form of armed struggle; in the mid-1980s, it became a nonviolent dissident movement inspired by *glasnost* and *perestroika* in the Eastern European communist world. While the dissident movement continues to exist and to grow, it still lacks strong popular support, as it is the object of severe repression by state security, which deters others from joining. In Cuba, the government has controlled nearly all of the media for more than 60 years, which has asphyxiated the development of an independent civil society. Most recently, Cubans are beginning to carve out some autonomy from the state as the use of the Internet and social media begins to spread. Massive protests have been the result.

In Cuba, for two-thirds of a century, the economy and the polity were and remain totally dependent on external aid (for trade, subsidies, investment, cooperation, and now also remittances). This total dependence has not been true of Venezuela, whose leaders retained a large—though not total—political control of the public sector. Due to its oil revenues, the revolutionary government was not mainly dependent on external aid.

Both revolutions relied for their success on the military, but the military differed. In Cuba, the armed forces—FAR—emerged after the demise of Batista's armed forces; in effect, the government left behind the old army, which had been carefully trained in military schools, and started from scratch. Particularly since the 1970s, they functioned rather autonomously. In recent decades, the military also went on to play a major role directing the economy. As an economic enterprise, they were also quite capable. As a political enterprise, they earned enormous prestige both within Cuba and in international military campaigns waged efficiently overseas (Domínguez 1978a, 1978b; Brenner et al. 2015). The Cuban military leadership lived its best moment when Raúl Castro, for many years minister of defense, became Cuba's president. Moreover, under GAESA, high-ranking military leaders are also leaders of the Cuban Communist Party (Veiga-González 2013; González-Mederos 2013). The military became major actors that steer the Cuban economy. By contrast, in Venezuela, the armed forces were gradually controlled by the new revolutionary leadership. The first step taken by Hugo Chávez (who issued from the Venezuelan army) in military politics was to reincorporate the men that sided with him in the military insurrections of 1992 into the new government. In addition, he invited some retired army officers to participate in Venezuelan politics as leaders of public institutions and to be members of the Movimiento Quinta República that he founded and that afterward became the Partido Socialista Unido de Venezuela (Langue 2002). Thus, from Chávez's arrival, there was an avalanche of military personnel, active and retired, who joined the leadership of the Bolivarian Revolution. The military had initially become divided by the new revolution. While many officials refused to support the new government, some remained neutral, some asked to be let go, and some joined a conspiracy against it. Their opposition came to an end with the detention and expulsion of many. Thus, the government controlled the military institutions, who benefited from massive purchases of arms and from receiving better advantages than others in the state bureaucracy (Burggraaff and Millett 1995). At the same time, a program of ideological training began that departed from the neutral and apolitical nature that previously characterized the military (Romero 2009).

In both countries, the Constitution was transformed, making it a new source of power. Originally, the Cuban Revolution inherited the 1940 Constitution. Through institutional change the Constitution was reinterpreted and overcome until in 1976 the new socialist Constitution issued, after the Cuban Communist Party (PCC) held its 1st Congress, fully 17 years after the triumph of the revolution and 11 years after the refounding of the Party (Domínguez 1978a). Thereafter, Cuba promulgated two other Constitutions: one in 1992, and another in 2019. While some genuine reforms obtained, all aimed at keeping the PCC in power. By contrast, in Venezuela, Chávez originally inherited the 1961 Constitution, which ipso facto gave way to the 1999 Constitution of the new revolutionary regime. Since the latter hardly constituted a socialist Constitution, it was also reinterpreted and overcome in 2006.

In the international arena, profound contrasts also obtain. In Cuba, the revolution developed within the context of the Cold War, where Cuba went on to play various political roles (in Latin America as well as in Africa) to help the Soviet Union win. For the revolution to survive, in the first decade Cuba established a strong alliance with the Soviet Union and close diplomatic ties with other socialist experiences—in Europe, the Third World, and elsewhere—that shaped its foreign policy goals. In Cuba, the citizen-soldier developed (Mesa-Lago 1971; Domínguez 1978a, 1978b). This alliance became a cornerstone for the survival of the new regime (Blasier 1976; Domínguez 1978b). By contrast, Venezuela's revolution took place in a different geopolitical theater. It began *after* the Cold War ended, when communism collapsed in the Soviet Union and the Eastern European countries. The first decade of Chávez's revolution took place in the context of a changed world dynamics: the new globalization together with a far less rigid, post–Cold War international scenario. While relations between Venezuela and the United States deteriorated, this did not result in a new bilateral alliance with a different power (Corrales and Romero 2013). In fact, there was no longer a Soviet Union that could intrude, support, assist, or demand, nor was there an American effort to stop or redirect the revolutionary process, as with Cuba.

Although Venezuela's revolution had the support of the international Left, they had also changed, becoming more diverse in perspective and less controlled by Moscow than in the past. Thus, in the beginning there was not a definitive break between Venezuela and the United States. Twenty years later, however, Trump's sanctions against Venezuela entailed a diplomatic break as well as the nearly total decline in their trade. As a kind of Cold War returned in the new millennium, and the charismatic figure of Hugo Chávez left the scene, Venezuela's revolution also went on to develop within the context of a new Cold War, as Donald Trump and even his successor, Joe Biden, fanned its dying embers.

Regionally, Cuba found great resistance in Latin America and the Caribbean, when it established its alliance with the Soviet Union. This was expressed in the hemispheric trade embargo and the regional associations that excluded Cuba, such as the OAS. In Latin America, only Mexico continued to respect Cuba's new path and maintained trade and other relations. Thus, Cuba was isolated in its own hemisphere. By contrast, Venezuela was not isolated, nor did it find strong opposition from Washington (Alzugaray-Treto 2009; Domínguez 1978b). With the exception of the attempted civil-military coup against Chávez in 2002, in its first 15 years the Venezuelan regime did not experience a serious threat, either from other governments, multilateral actors, or from its own civil society, including the media. This changed under Maduro's regime after 2013, particularly since the Venezuelan opposition grew large, both inside the National Assembly and on the streets, where protests and violence took place. Some international bodies, other governments, and some NGOs began to openly criticize Maduro's government for its violation of human rights, and its effort to reduce the spaces for democracy. Therefore, in the international arena, Venezuela operated with a great deal more flexibility and suffered far less antagonism than Cuba. Venezuela simply did not experience threats like those of the Cuban Missile Crisis in 1962, the US economic embargo, or the expulsion from the OAS in 1964, nor was there a Bay of Pigs—an exile invasion backed by the Americans. Venezuela simply did not experience a direct confrontation with America or with the West, though that changed when former president Donald Trump arrived, precisely when the economic and political situation plummeted.

Last but not least, Cuba was always what its strong supporters inside the island always called it: *una nación asediada* (a nation besieged). It was always under the pressure of an economic embargo, and in political isolation. In our view, the American embargo served both to undermine and strengthen the Cuban Revolution. It undermined the revolution because it cut commercial, trade, and diplomatic relations with the United States and many other nations that followed suit. It strengthened the revolution because its leaders were never accountable for the mistakes they made, for their failed policies, which were invariably blamed on the embargo (Pedraza 2007). By contrast, Venezuela did not suffer a similar economic embargo under Chávez's presidency (Corrales and Romero 2013). However, the situation changed after Maduro refused to engage in a dialogue and to agree to an electoral solution to the deep-seated crisis. At that time, Trump did cut diplomatic and economic relations and went on to progressively issue financial and economic sanctions that do resemble Cuba's embargo.

Domestically, the contrasts in political history loom large. In Cuba, the revolution issued from a dictatorship: Fulgencio Batista's. It involved the swift transition from authoritarianism to totalitarianism. Its characteristics were economic statism, one-party rule, the lack of an autonomous civil society, and absence of freedom. Kirkpatrick (1979) makes a valid distinction between authoritarian and totalitarian societies. In Cuba, the one made the other possible. Batista's dictatorship rendered the institutions of civil society weak. Moreover, he refused to engage in elections as a solution to the deep political crisis in the country. Thus, with enormous speed, in a very short time, Cuba was able to eliminate the institutions of the *ancien régime* and to put in place a centralized state with a minimal private sector (Amaro 1981). After two waves of massive nationalizations, at the end of the first decade of revolution the island had only a few remnants of a capitalist economy and a larger proportion of state-owned enterprises than anywhere in the Eastern European communist world (Mesa-Lago 1971). By contrast, the Bolivarian Revolution issued after a long democratic experience of 40 years, involving the transition from a democratic polity to an authoritarian regime. Moreover, capitalism survived to a large extent. While Venezuela developed a centralized state and controlled the military, the government did not eliminate the capitalist economy. The economy, which revolved around oil, survived, and the government continued to depend on it, while the private sector continued to play a significant role (Corrales and Penfold 2015; Smilde 2021).

Stark contrasts are evident in their opposition movements. In Cuba, the opposition was externalized as a massive exodus out of the island resulted that also served to externalize its dissent. That which remained within and participated in the armed struggle was labeled "the counterrevolution." It suffered death or political imprisonment when vanquished. Eventually, a nonviolent dissident movement did emerge that held its own and provided a democratic vision for the future, though it remained at the margins of the society. By contrast, in Venezuela, the opposition largely remained within and was able to express its dissent through the existing democratic institutions: the media, elections, and parliamentary power.

While legal transformation through constitutional reform did take place, the changes sought to keep Chávez in power without restrictions and to control the rest of the state powers and the regulations regarding elections (Brewer-Carías 2012). Under Maduro, the opposition organized itself through the coalition of different parties in the MUD. Thus, they took control of the AN, the legislative branch of the Venezuelan state.

President Maduro and the PSUV refused to recognize that opposition victory and established an ANC to write another Constitution that would express socialist programs and policies and keep him in power. Most recently, the PSUV again took control of the AN, as a significant proportion of the opposition did not participate in the elections. As Flores and Nooruddin (2016, 95) point out, when conditions make it hard or even impossible for those in power to govern, many governments resort to electoral malpractice to secure reelection—a form of electoral authoritarianism. Democracy thus stagnates or suffers. Such has been the Venezuelan case.

Social identities of class, race, religion, and gender are part of all social movements as well as revolutions, but which are the most salient may well vary. In Cuba, both race and religion were key to the revolution's development. The appeal of the Cuban Revolution to the marginalized particularly attracted Afro-Cubans, whose skin color had rendered them more socially distinct and excluded than in Venezuela, where a much larger proportion of the population was of mixed race. In Cuba, religion was more important than in Venezuela. While both nations were predominantly Catholic, the head-on confrontation that took place in Cuba between the Church leadership and the revolutionary leadership did not take place in Venezuela. When Fidel Castro expelled the priests and nuns from the island, he not only silenced the once-dominant Catholic Church for a couple of generations, but also eliminated the opposition that had found refuge and support in its midst. After many years, from the 1990s on, religion did once again begin to play an independent role; today, it has begun to play a political role as well. Likewise, in the recent protests that pervaded the streets of Havana and Santiago de Cuba in July 2021, Afro-Cubans' demands for better economic conditions but also liberty and democracy came to the fore. Race and religion mattered far more in Cuba than in Venezuela.

Political rights also entailed profound differences. In Cuba, the democratic system of elections and parties collapsed almost immediately, under the weight of Fidel Castro's charisma and the weak civil society left behind by seven years of Batista's dictatorship. As De la Torre (2020) underscores, following Max Weber (1978), charismatic leaders validate their authority at mass meetings where "the leader is recognized and acclaimed by followers." Fidel Castro excelled at precisely this type of communication with the masses in a public arena, with speeches that often lasted for hours yet had his supporters' undivided attention. In a crucial speech on May 1, 1960, at a massive May Day demonstration in the Plaza de la Revolución, Fidel asserted that elections were unnecessary because the people had already chosen: "*This* is democracy. The Cuban revolution is democracy. . . . Our enemies, our detractors, ask us about elections. . . . The presence of such a large crowd is the best proof that the revolution has fought for the people" (F. Castro 1960). To Jorge Valls and other members of the opposition organized in the universities as the Directorio Estudiantil, the legal order—the notion of political rights as the normative underpinning of society—collapsed then (in Pedraza 2007, interview). Following Laclau's (2005) analysis of the logic populism entails, De la Torre (2020) emphasizes that "the logic of populism is anti-institutional." Populist leaders create strong emotional and political identities, and politics becomes an antagonistic confrontation between two camps: the people versus the oligarchy. All demands for change unite under the name of the leader, who has a redemptive mission. The leader's charisma is the revolutionary force of history (Weber 1978). Such messianic leadership assures the people that the new society they are building will be a better world. René Cifuentes, a very young man who came from Cuba in the Mariel boatlift in 1980, underscored that "everything was always based on the future"—a future that never came (in Pedraza 2007, interview; in Domínguez 1985, interview). Thus, in Cuba an opposition that could continue to operate democratically—through the legal framework of elections based on universal and secret vote for plural political parties, recognizing the autonomy of the opposition and the government—ceased to exist, as did the legal recognition of dissent. The result was a one-party system. The merger between the Cuban Communist Party and the Cuban state itself was expressed in the single figure of Fidel (Pérez-Stable 1999). His followers felt that he was the father of the nation: a paternal figure that would deliver them from poverty, racism, and a life at the margins. Gradually, the political system took on the features of Eastern European communism. With the Cuban government's military victories, first, over the external exile invasion at the Bay of Pigs and, thereafter, over the internal counterrevolution in the mountains of Escambray, most of the political opposition that engaged in armed struggle was decimated early on, in the 1960s. It was not until the mid-1980s that it returned, though in a new form, as a nonviolent form of dissent. Cuba's new dissident movement grew largely under the influence of *glasnost* and *perestroika* in the Soviet Union and Eastern Europe, as well as of the social movements for civil rights in America.

By contrast, in Venezuela, even though many people consider that they are in the presence of an odd case of electoral authoritarianism turning into corporate authoritarianism, to date the opposition has not been outlawed. Rather, in recent years, it has continued to grow in significance, due to Nicolás Maduro's inept control of the political and economic system and the growing economic crisis. Part of the opposition participates in elections; it is represented in the National Assembly; and it is legally organized in political parties. Nonetheless, freedom of expression is somewhat limited, and the human rights record has a real deficit (Corrales and

Romero 2013). There are genuine obstacles to the exercise of democracy in Venezuela. The new governing elites developed some novel mechanisms of political control, such as the formation of the *comunas*, the partisan control of the government, and the strong influence of the executive branch on electoral power and the judiciary. However, Venezuela did not establish a one-party regime (Corrales and Romero 2013). As Ezrow and Frantz (2011, 1) express it, in Venezuela "parties and legislatures provide a means through which dictatorships co-opt potential opponents, distribute rents to supporters, and mitigate elite conflicts."

In economics, differences abound. In Cuba, in just a few years, through massive nationalizations, the government became the nation's economic body. The highly centralized economic model of the Soviet Union provided the blueprint for Cuba's economic system as the island took on the features of Eastern European communism. Cuba adopted communist institutions, such as the budget, public spending, private consumption (via *la libreta*, the rationing book), the licit forms of employment, the wage structure, the forms of investment, the exchange rate policy, and the external debt (Pérez-Villanueva 2009; Mesa-Lago 1978). Its proportion of state-owned property was the highest anywhere in the communist world. By contrast, in Venezuela, in the first decade of the Bolivarian Revolution, the government did not exert full control over the Venezuelan economy. From 2006 on the government did make strides in developing a socialist economy through the nationalization of many big enterprises, such as CANTV (the telephone company), the Banco de Venezuela, and SIDOR (steel and iron). It also created the *comunas* and other forms of a socialized economy. But it is also true that most of the private sector and the foreign private investment sector remained untouched (Corrales and Romero 2013).

The economic growth of the two nations contrasts sharply. In Cuba, under the revolution there has been a constant lack of economic respite. Looking at the macroeconomic indicators (e.g., GDP, material resources, and currency reserves), we can see that in Cuba the economic cycles were very pronounced, with few years of economic expansion and overall a low and declining per capita income (Mesa-Lago 1978; Mesa-Lago and Pérez-López 2013; Pérez-Villanueva 2009; Domínguez et al. 2004; Domínguez 1978a). Moreover, in Cuba the economy was mostly dependent on the generosity of the Soviet Union. The Soviet Union gave Cuba a subsidy that buoyed the island for 30 years during which Cubans lived decently, without great poverty or wealth. It also gave Cuba the assistance of Soviet professionals and technicians to man its industry on the island. And it trained thousands of Cuban students in various occupations in their countries. Cuba repaid this economic largesse with support for the Soviets' political ventures in the Third World. By contrast, in Venezuela, after the first few years, Chávez's regime mostly showed positive economic indicators and significant economic growth, thanks to the high revenues brought by the country's crude oil when its price on the world market was quite high. However, after Chávez's death, from 2013 on, the Venezuelan economy began a steep decline just as the price of oil declined and Maduro's ineptitude took over.

Dependence on another nation did not mark Venezuela's course: its oil revenues always assured its economic independence. By contrast, Cuba has always charted a dependent course: first, on the Spanish; then, on the Americans; then, on the Soviets; then, on Venezuela. As a result, in Cuba people now joke, Who will come next? In Cuba, the Soviet bailout had both positive and negative consequences. Positively, it ensured the survival of the revolution; negatively, it helped to form an economically weak state with a downward trend in both production and distribution (Blasier and Mesa-Lago 1979; Mesa-Lago 2020). Moreover, together with the US embargo, it kept the Cuban government from facing up to its errors in policy. The result was the disaffection of large sectors of the population, whose only hope became to leave the country. Few vestiges of capitalism remained in Cuba, but dependence marked its course. By contrast, in Venezuela, economic independence shaped an economically strong state with an upward trend in both production and distribution, and a large private sector still untouched that handles most of Venezuela's imports. This is not, however, the case for exports, nearly all of which are handled by the state oil company PDVSA. In its first decade, the Bolivarian Revolution tried to control the economy and private enterprises—but without success. Thus, the Venezuelan economy remains capitalist (Corrales 2006, 2015).

Venezuela's steep economic decline has had consequences for Cuba. The number of barrels of oil Cuba imports daily have steeply declined—from 100,000 in 2000, to only 43,000 in 2017, to only 10,000 in 2020. The number of Cuban doctors and health personnel working in Venezuela has also declined drastically—from a peak of 51,000 *colaboradores* in 2011 to less than half, 22,000, in 2020. Moreover, their real wages have fallen drastically, given the hyperinflation as well as rampant theft, and the lack of medical supplies. At present, Cubans no longer look forward to working in Venezuela, as they did for many years.

The United States became punitive in dealing with both countries, but it took much longer for that to be true in Venezuela's case. Under Obama, Cuba benefited from restoring the political relationship and from the avalanche of tourism that followed. Those on the island also benefited from Obama and his family's visit, as they showed a genuine interest in the people and its culture. However, Trump rolled back the reforms that took place during Obama and imposed severe restrictions and sanctions on both governments. The sanctions affected the transportation of goods and people, and the balance of trade in both countries. In Cuba, this also affected its import of consumer goods from Venezuela. Cuba imported food, construction materials, clothing, household appliances, computer equipment, medicines, and medical equipment from Venezuela. At present, they are all quite scarce on the island. After President Obama's positive moment from 2014 to 2016, which was greeted with enormous enthusiasm in Cuba, under President Trump Cuba experienced a "rollback." Trump reactivated the dormant parts of the Helms-Burton Act, which allows American citizens to sue the Cuban state and Cuban companies for the return of their assets confiscated by the revolution. He also imposed severe restrictions on investments in Cuba. Moreover, he reduced the size of the remittances Cuban Americans can send to their family annually, diminishing the purchasing power of Cubans on the island, particularly to attain food. He also eliminated Western Union. In addition, he did away with the airline flights to provincial cities and restricted the tourist trips by American citizens via cruises and airplanes to different points on the island. His measures had an impact on the entry of capital to Cuba and caused a contraction in foreign investment (Pérez-López 2017).

Cuba's economy remains dismal. Venezuela's current economic crisis also aggravates the Cuban situation. Venezuela's financial problems (a negative balance of payments, the hyperinflation, and the devaluation of the bolívar) have all affected the growing foreign currency deficit, which also reduces Venezuela's capacity to pay for Cuba's subsidies (Carranza 2021). The United States' sanctions have definitely contributed to the low state of Cuba's economy. However, the main problem comes from the highly centralized, statist economy that refuses to implement a program of private and mixed properties to achieve significant growth in its exports so that these, in turn, can finance its imports (Mesa-Lago and Vidal-Alejandro 2019). Thus, Cuba's economy presents an extraordinary deficit for 2020, with a GDP that declined to -5 percent, and the fiscal deficit at -8 percent—a bleak picture, indeed (Palacios 2019). How do people on the island survive? By the remittances they receive from the family abroad, and from the parallel economy of the black market, the use of the American dollar, smuggling, and illicit food sales (Mesa-Lago and Vidal-Alejandro 2019). Torres-Pérez (2020) contends that the COVID-19 crisis should not be used to avoid making the real structural changes that are long overdue; rather, it should serve to spur the will to put the changes people need into effect. Yet, as Velásquez (2021) points out, an economic transition may not be possible in the absence of a political transition.

The exodus of their people is also a critical difference. Both social processes involved the sharp political polarization of the people—by the major social cleavages of class, religion, gender, and race. In Cuba, that entailed the exclusion of a legitimate opposition, as people could no longer participate, either politically or economically. This resulted in a massive exodus over 62 years and five waves (Pedraza 2020). The impact of such a massive exodus was twofold. On the one hand, it involved the externalization of dissent, which enabled the revolutionary government to achieve greater legitimacy and grow politically stronger. Fidel Castro was well aware of this function, as he repeatedly expressed it. In 1971, when the airlift to the United States of the refugees was thought to be ending, he stressed that "socialist Cuba would be better off in the long run if she got rid of 'small bourgeois elements,'" people that would never become true revolutionaries. "He called them *gusanos* (worms)" (in Volsky 1971). Similarly, in 1980, when faced with the exodus of 125,000 Cubans from the harbor of Mariel, he explained the benefit of externalizing dissent: "I think that those of them remaining here are people with whom we can work better, much better! . . . So we need not worry if we lose some flab. We are left with the muscle and bone of the people. We are left with the strong parts" (F. Castro 1980). On the other hand, such a massive exodus also entailed serious losses. First, it meant the loss of the talent, resources, and skills that define the middle-class—professionals who no longer contributed to the development of Cuba's economy and society but went on to make their contribution elsewhere, in the United States (particularly in greater Miami, in the rest of Florida, and in New Jersey), on the island of Puerto Rico, and in other countries (especially Spain, Venezuela, and Costa Rica). Aware of the "brain drain" taking place, Cuba's government dismissed those who planned to leave with contempt. They barred doctors from deserting the country, as well as other technical and professional people whose skills were deemed necessary, and young men of military age (18 to 26). Second, it meant the loss of the salutary challenge that a legitimate opposition can bring, prompting an internal dynamic for change, even when they fail to win in electoral politics. Such is the meaning of the concept of *loyal opposition*, which is important in exercising a genuine democracy (Flores and Nooruddin 2016).

In Cuba, the exodus had multiple impacts. Politically, it helped to consolidate the revolution. Economically, it caused great harm. Spiritually, it resulted in what well-known Cuban writer Leonardo Padura (2015a, 308) calls "the island's broken heart: Cuba is now a country that suffers from a deep fracture in its spiritual soul" between those who left and those who stayed—a fracture that cannot be easily mended. From the island departed a significant number of people who worked in the cultural sector and shaped its spiritual life. In any society, Padura (2015b, 322) argues, they shape the cultural atmosphere as they "produce work that is inspired by daily experiences there" and they leave a legacy through their words, their works "by means of a necessary accumulation of visions and opinions." While the work of those still on the island is often censored, and they express themselves at great risk, as Padura writes, risks and censorship have also been "a challenge to the imagination," resulting in interesting work. By contrast, in Venezuela, such a massive exodus did not take place in the early years of the revolution under Chávez. The nation itself was not as fractured. In the first dozen years of the Bolivarian Revolution, most of the opposition remained in the country. The exodus really quickened after 2013, when Maduro took over, and the economy went on a downward spiral, bringing large numbers of Venezuelans to the United States (Noe-Bustamante et al. 2019a). The Venezuelan exodus to South American countries (especially Colombia) is now extremely large, constituting a true humanitarian crisis. As is often the case in a refugee exodus, the refugees' levels of education are quite high, though increasingly the exodus includes the poor from the cities and rural areas. Spiritually, the exodus now also weighs heavily on that nation's soul. The esteemed Venezuelan writer Alberto Barrera-Tyszka explains that the diaspora in Venezuela has a strong emotional impact in a country that was not a country of emigrants; it was a refuge for those who arrived looking for liberty and economic opportunities. "There is a change in our identity, in the DNA of the Venezuelan. . . . Now we must learn to be emigrants," he mourns (in García-Marco 2017).

Contrary to Cuba, in Venezuela both democratic politics and the capitalist economy survived. Its large oil resources yielded both business opportunities and rising personal incomes and living standards: the economy was healthy at least until 2013. Venezuela was a society with oil at a time in world history when it was arguably the most prized possession of any nation. Hugo Chávez hoped this would result in "a socialism without poverty." That hope has not come true. Then the price of oil on the world market began to decline steeply, and Maduro's inefficient administration took hold of the government. The economy plummeted until, as Puente (2021) notes, it entered a state of macroeconomic collapse. Under a different administration, perhaps Venezuela's natural resources (oil, gas, minerals) will allow it to rebound in the future. By contrast, in Cuba neither democratic politics nor the capitalist economy survived. Cuba lacked oil—or another coveted economic resource—that could allow it to remain economically autonomous. Its dependence on the Soviet Union assured the survival of the Cuban revolution as a communist revolution and allowed Cuba to circumvent the United States' economic embargo. Cuban revolutionaries hoped that this would result in a more just society with great equality. That hope has not come true. Coupled with the loss of the middle class, the revolution's survival came at the cost of its living standards, which declined to extremely low levels, making it a society whose communism meant the spread of poverty.

Exit-Voice Relationships

Analysts have questioned whether a massive exodus—such as the one that took place from East to West Berlin, from Spain or Turkey to Germany, or from Haiti or Cuba to the United States—is a hindrance or a help to the development of civil society via the use of social protest. Social scientists have approached the question through the analysis that Hirschman (1970) first introduced in his *Exit, Voice, and Loyalty*. Firms, organizations, and political parties provide benefits or services; Hirschman argues that when the quality of the benefits or services they provide deteriorates, the *loyalty* of its members is threatened. The members can then express themselves by using one of two options: they can choose to *exit* (simply leave), or they can use their *voice* to organize and protest, calling for change.

In this early work, Hirschman (1986) asserts that the pattern can best be characterized as a simple hydraulic model: deterioration generates the pressure of discontent, which will be channeled into *voice* or *exit*. The more pressure escapes through *exit*, the less is available to foment *voice*.

Moreover, Hirschman notes, those who exited cannot promote recuperation. Hence, the question becomes whether a massive and unabated exodus constitutes the use of the *exit* option to such an extent that it serves to impede the use of *voice*, which is necessary to develop a civil society.

As Pérez-Díaz (1993, 57) sums it up, civil society is a *type* of society that combines markets, voluntary associations, and a public sphere that are outside the direct control of the state—what Havel (1986) calls the "independent life of society." In totalitarian societies, both of the Left and the Right, those intermediate associations effectively cease to exist as they are either abolished or silenced by the all-encompassing government, so the state becomes the sole owner, administrator, judge, and political party. That same government often goes on to organize some of the intermediate associations—such as the professions, press, television, labor unions—which then lack independence from the government; hence, they do not qualify as part of civil society.

Considering the relationship of *exit* to *voice*, Pedraza (2014) has shown that various *exit-voice* relations developed over time. Four different theses can be derived from this: a massive exodus impedes the use of voice; those who exited helped voice to develop; those who exited became the voice; and both exit and voice increased in tandem (Pedraza 2013).

A Massive *Exit* Impedes the Use of *Voice*

The first thesis was well expressed by Valdés-Hernández (1997), who clearly saw the massive and permanent exodus of Cubans as an impediment to the development of civil society. The exodus resulted from the lack of political liberty as well as the restriction on economic initiatives Cubans were allowed to undertake. Phrased in Hirschman's terms, the use of the *exit* option became an obstacle to the development of *voice* in the country.

This thesis is common among people on the island, especially those who, like Valdés-Hernández, struggle to help build the new civil society. Such efforts take the form of developing intellectual alternatives, such as his own effort with the magazines *Vitral* and *Convivencia*, or strengthening an institution such as a church or synagogue as an alternative way to think and live. To those on the ground who struggle with the renewal of the minds and hearts of the people, the exodus is a bloodletting—a vital loss of people who could help develop the new civil society.

In Cuba, many people exercised either the option of a false *loyalty* or the option of a lived *neglect*—what Cubans call *la doble moral* (the dual morality)—or they seek to be as uninvolved in the political process as possible. Either way, they were unlikely to become involved in the development of civil society, even if they remained in Cuba. Using Wright's (1976) terminology in his analysis of political alienation and political participation, they were "assenters": a spectator to someone else's game. By contrast, dissenters either stayed or left Cuba only after exercising their *voice*—for example, involving themselves in the dissident movement, founding a new human rights organization, or participating in the development of a new alternative through their church or synagogue, or becoming an independent journalist. Doing so, they suffered the costs: lost their jobs and many of their friends, and doors closed behind them until they ended up in prison or living in intolerable conditions. This "pushed" them to leave, which they did after giving to the development of civil society all they could.

Those Who *Exited* Helped *Voice* Develop

In his analysis of the transition to democracy in Spain after Franco, Pérez-Díaz (1993) espouses the opposite thesis, as applied to the emigration of men and women who were laborers from Spain, a periphery country in Europe, to the core European countries of Germany, France, the United Kingdom, England, Switzerland, and Belgium. The émigrés lent their labor to the industrial sector (working in factories) or the service sector (working in hotels and restaurants) in these developed countries. As the migration increased, it became an all-pervasive learning experience. Spaniards were exposed to other ways of accomplishing things in all spheres of life, which were more efficient than their own. They also rapidly learned to appreciate a more comfortable standard of living and increased freedom of movement, more opportunities to prosper, and less subjection to authority. They learned from and identified with the people of Western Europe, their institutions, and their culture, developing a new democratic identity.

In analyzing the impact of the exodus on the development of civil society in the homeland, the question of the return is crucial. In this thesis the exodus was a midwife to the development of civil society because the émigrés lived and worked for many years in societies that were politically democratic and pluralistic. Living there, they underwent a "democratic apprenticeship." Most important, they returned, bringing their newfound political culture back with them, which contributed to the development of the peaceful transition out of Franco's Spain, as well as to being governed in a pluralistic fashion in the years that followed, when democracy was institutionalized and consolidated. Phrased in Hirschman's terms, those who first used the *exit* option underwent a democratic apprenticeship where they lived and worked, developing a new *loyalty* to democratic values and forms of participation. When they returned, they brought back what they had learned and exercised their *voice*, influencing the development of a new political culture and civil society there, at a time when Spain was growing economically and becoming part of the European Union.

In the Cuban case there was such a democratic apprenticeship but time—the passage now of two-thirds of a century—took a toll. Those who left in the early years of the exodus and were adolescents or adults when the revolution began in the 1950s cherished their memories of life in Cuba—people who led a very comfortable life in a country of great beauty and vitality. If they could, they would return. But they will not be able to. Too much time has passed, and they will die in exile.

Moreover, despite glowing memories, the passage of so much time also means these exiles put deep roots in other lands, where another culture, often another language, is dominant, as in the United States, exerting strong pressures to assimilate. Generations of their children and grandchildren were born in another soil and culture. For the most part, the second and third generations have little interest in returning to Cuba. They feel culturally inept in handling their parents' and grandparents' culture and find it difficult to understand and fit in that world. An exception may be Cubans of the "1.5 generation": those who grew up in Cuba during their formative years and acquired a deep attachment to its culture and history yet were young enough when they arrived abroad to be resocialized in another culture and history. Their hybrid nature and their *loyalty* to both worlds may allow them to serve as a bridge at a time of transition.

The recent immigrants could return because much less time has passed, and fewer "roots" were put out elsewhere. However, their own memories may impede it. Contrary to the early exiles' nostalgia, the recent exiles' memories are often traumatic, resulting from the lack of comfort in Cuba, the hunger and the poverty they knew, the marginality they experienced when their loyalty was questioned, and the isolation they felt when denied the expression of their real feelings and convictions. For many of the recent exiles, their way of coping with a past that lacked dignity was to close the door on it, forever. Many of them, though young and able, will not return to Cuba, but will go on to make new lives, wherever they settle.

Still, if a successful transition to a democratic society were to take place in Cuba, accompanied by international assistance, and some measure of real economic growth, the more recent émigrés and some of the early exiles' children may well return. With the democratic learning entailed by living and working overseas—in the United States, Spain, Canada, Venezuela, France, Sweden, and Costa Rica—they may influence the institutionalization and consolidation of democracy.

Those Who *Exited* Became Its *Voice*

A different thesis comes from the work of Laguerre (1998), who analyzed the role that Haitian immigration played in the United States. With Haiti's long history of political repression, the immigrants exercised what he called a transnational diasporic citizenship and became the missing political center: between the government, on the one hand, and the atomized, inarticulate masses, on the other. This informal diplomacy meant they spoke not on behalf of their government but on behalf of themselves or their organizations (*ambassadeurs du béton ou sans cravate*). They helped to establish civilian control over the military and funded cherished social projects back in Haiti, both of which strengthened the development of civil society on the island. Phrased in Hirschman's terms, when the civil society in the homeland has effectively disappeared and the people there remain too atomized and marginalized to constitute it, those who first exercised the *exit* option may end up becoming the ones who constitute its *voice*.

Both *Exit* and *Voice* Increased in Tandem

Yet another thesis comes from Hirschman's (1993) later work, when he applied his initial conceptual scheme to the German Democratic Republic (GDR) in 1989. That was the year in which a series of social movements developed in rapid succession in Poland, Hungary, East Germany, Czechoslovakia, Bulgaria, Albania, Yugoslavia, and Romania that resulted in the collapse of the communist world in Eastern Europe, and the demise of the GDR. In his earlier work (1970, 1986) Hirschman had argued that a basic seesaw pattern existed between *exit* and *voice*: the more of one, the less of the other. But, 23 years later, when he examined the GDR up close during *die Wende* (the turn, as it was called), he was forced to conclude that in the last year *exit* and *voice* had "worked in tandem" and reinforced each other, "achieving jointly the collapse of the regime" (1993, 177).

In the end, Hirschman (1993) reformulated his initial thesis because he saw that the course of events over the 40-year life of that state (1949–89) comprised a large variety of *exit-voice* relationships. While, over the course of time, the easy availability of *exit* did undermine the development of *voice*, other relationships also obtained. For example, in 1961, with the building of the Berlin Wall, authorities sought to repress both *exit* and *voice*. And in 1989, the last year of Eastern European communism, *exit* and *voice* worked in tandem, reinforcing each other. In our view, in recent years, they have also worked in tandem in Cuba, and we can expect them both to continue to increase.

Moreover, in Cuba the government itself (as in the GDR) was quite conscious of the basic seesaw pattern of *exit* and *voice* and chose to consciously manipulate the *exit* option to undermine the *voice* of dissent. The exodus of the dissidents in the 1990s was the result of the government's selective policy of forced *exit* that pushed the *voice* of many of its critics out of Cuba and barred others from returning home. The result of this forced *exit* policy was palpable. Amnesty International (1992) issued a special Country Report on Cuba titled *Silencing the Voices of Dissent*, which featured many of Cuba's most prominent dissidents. Just a few years later, virtually all of them were living outside of Cuba, in exile.

However, the availability of *exit* was not the only reason why *voice* was less likely to emerge in East Germany than elsewhere in the Soviet-dominated Eastern European countries. Hirschman noted other major reasons, which have parallels in Cuba. First, East Germans had no independent institutions, like the Catholic Church of Poland, to sustain them in a struggle for autonomy from the all-powerful communist state. That, until very recently, was also true in Cuba. Second, many East Germans initially embraced the ideology of the state due to the catastrophic historical episode they had just lived through: Nazi Fascism. That ideological advantage, as Hirschman (1970) called it, was also the role that Batista's dictatorship played in the initial acceptance and popularity of the Cuban revolution, in promoting the loyalty of the majority of Cubans in the early years of the revolution. Third, East Germany played a similar role for the Soviet empire in its contest with the West during the Cold War, as evidenced by the presence of Soviet atomic missiles there. That was equally true in Cuba, which played a similar role for the Soviet Union throughout the Third World. In exchange for this role of exporting revolution to Latin America and Africa and of contesting the United States, the Soviet Union subsidized the Cuban economy very generously, mitigating the impact of the US embargo.

Thus, until the 1990s, one could arrive at the same conclusion regarding

Cuba as Hirschman did regarding the GDR: that the direct obstacles to *voice*—that is, to any political movements of resistance or dissidence—were enormous. Adding them to the undermining of *voice* by the real or imagined availability of *exit* to the West, jointly these produced an *exit-voice* balance that was tilted against *voice* and in favor of *exit* (1991, 183).

Yet, in Cuba, in the 1990s, during the crisis of "the special period" we witnessed the increasing use of both the *exit* and *voice* options in Cuba, as was the case in the GDR at the end. For example, in the summer of 1994, *exit* and *voice* were expressed in multiple ways, reinforcing each other. The *exit* of the dramatic *balseros* crisis was the immediate result of *el Maleconazo*—the first large *voice* event on record—when a rather large riot took place in central Havana, protesting the economic conditions in Cuba as well as the lack of liberty. The riots themselves were preceded by the most tragic *exit* event: the tugboat incident in mid-July, when over 40 adults and children died as the Cuban Coast Guard overturned the small boat with powerful jets of water. On September 8, when Cubans celebrate the feast day of their cherished patron saint, Cubans witnessed yet another clear expression of the incipient use of *voice* in Cuba when Father José Conrado Rodríguez was emboldened to act amid the crisis. His sermon was a letter to Fidel Castro, asking him to take responsibility for the dire situation in which the country found itself and calling for a negotiated solution to the crisis to be found by the government, the churches, the exiles, and the dissidents (Rodríguez 1995). That meeting never took place. Yet Father José Conrado never lost his belief in the importance of a national dialogue.

In recent years, when a new dissident movement emerged, both White and Black Cubans, men and women, participated in it. This new movement is characterized by its nonviolence in strategy and approach, following the social movements spearheaded by Mahatma Gandhi, Martin Luther King Jr., and César Chávez. Its inspiration also came from the worldwide human rights movement that found its earliest expression in the United Nations' Universal Declaration of Human Rights as well as the Czechoslovakian intellectuals' Charter 77 (Havel 1986). The dissident movement not only grew but also matured, seeking to provide an alternative vision of a democratic society in Cuba. Among many documents, two in particular stood out: *La Patria es de Todos* (The Nation Belongs to All) and the *Proyecto Varela*. Though different, both projects called for a plebiscite—a national referendum—so that Cubans could freely elect their government. They demanded five forms of change in Cuba: the right to free expression and a free press; the right to free association; amnesty for political prisoners; the right to form small, private enterprises; and a plebiscite law and general elections. Using the vocabulary of *voice* to express it, Oswaldo Payá summed it up: "Let no one else speak for Cubans. Let their own voices be heard in a referendum" (2001). For his role as a human rights activist in promoting peaceful change within Cuba, the European Parliament awarded Payá the Sakharov Prize in 2002.

Shortly after Payá's return to Cuba, in March 2003, the Cuban government arrested and imprisoned 75 dissidents, around 40 of whom had collaborated with the *Proyecto Varela*, gathering the thousands of signatures required by the government, and many others who worked as independent journalists. Amnesty International adopted these 75 as "prisoners of conscience." They were jailed with extremely long sentences for their peaceful opposition, in an incident which began to be called "the Cuban Spring," after its European counterpart. This gave rise to the birth of Las Damas de Blanco. Cuban women amplified the echoes of their dissidence with another dramatic *voice* event: a quiet protest that has gone on for years. As the wives, mothers, and sisters of the 75, they dress in white, often wearing T-shirts bearing the photo of their loved one. Holding a single flower, they quietly set out for a walk every Sunday after attending mass at the Church of Santa Rita in Havana, making their peaceful protest visible to all.

When President Obama ended the "wet foot/dry foot" immigration policy just before he left office in January 2017, he did shut off a valve of escape from Cuba. Immediately thereafter, the exodus of *balseros* became only a trickle. This may well be a factor in the recent upsurge in protests in Cuba, including those of the Movimiento San Isidro on November 27, 2020, and the July 11, 2021, protests. Both were *voice* events that demanded that the government engage in a dialogue with them and that called for real political incorporation. So was "Patria y Vida," the song that became the banner of the protests, expressing the suffering of the Cuban people and presenting their demand for a future with dignity. President Díaz-Canel denied them both, calling them "mercenaries" and insisting the protests were illegitimate. That he bears no connection to *el pueblo* also spurred the protests.

Just before these protests erupted, Father José Conrado had again argued for the importance of a national dialogue to try to solve the crisis in Cuba. However, the massive crackdown on the protesters, who were jailed and beaten by the Boinas Negras (Black Berets) police, made such a national dialogue impossible. Many of the participants were jailed and condemned to many years in prison.

Hirschman (1970) also appealed to the concept of *loyalty*, which delays *exit* as well as *voice* when there is a decline in the performance of an organization, party, or nation to which one belongs. But when the decline passes a certain threshold, the voice of the loyal members tends to become particularly vigorous. However, in this instance the *loyalty* was no longer to the government, but to the nation, as was true for Father José Conrado. For Cubans, that was precisely the symbolic meaning of naming the call for a national referendum after Father Felix Varela, their nineteenth-century hero.

President Miguel Díaz-Canel denied the protesters' demands, blamed the protests on the American embargo, and, in the name of "the revolution" that needed to be defended, unleashed the military tanks and the police on the protesters, jailing hundreds of people and beating many. While the embargo has continued, it can hardly be blamed for the protests, as it is an old and constant ingredient that cannot be said to be the cause of these recent protests. Other factors seem more important. One is the current economic crisis that resulted in negative economic growth. This was aggravated by the recent, drastic reform of the currency, which resulted in spiraling inflation, making food and medicines beyond the reach of most Cubans. As we have seen, the three pillars on which the island's economy rests are: the remittances of the émigrés, the export of the professional health services, and the arrival of international tourism. Recently all three have declined to the point where they no longer hold up the island's economy.

Moreover, only in the last four years Cubans have, for the first time, had real access to the Internet, not only to see what the rest of the world is like, but also to communicate with one another with ease. This is quite an important ingredient in the mix that led to these massive protests. Before, when people challenged the government or the police on the streets, no one else knew it, so they did not trigger a collective response. Now, with access to the Internet, everyone knows what everyone else is doing. Clearly, the government recognized this, as during the protests they immediately responded by cutting off access to the Internet.

The leadership change in Cuba is another important factor. The new president, Miguel Díaz-Canel, was chosen by Raúl Castro, not by the people. And he lacks the charisma, the capacity to communicate with the hearts and minds of the people, that Fidel Castro had. In the past, Fidel Castro was able to use his charisma to blame Cuba's crises onto the United States. Díaz-Canel instead responded with massive repression, for everyone all over the world to see, on television.

Even more, former president Trump left in place some sanctions that have made a negative difference. For example, Trump closed all the Western Union offices in Cuba, making it impossible for Cubans who live in poverty to receive help from their family in the United States, Spain, Europe, or Latin America. Until then, island Cubans received clothing, food, medicines, and money from their close relatives and friends abroad, who lifted them out of their poverty. Donald Trump destroyed the capacity of the Cuban exiles to help those on the island. Sixteen months after his arrival, the new president Joe Biden began to progressively lift those sanctions. As the new secretary of state, Antony Blinken said at the beginning of Biden's term, given more pressing commitments, neither Cuba nor Venezuela were a priority. He added that US policy toward them was being closely examined.

Last, but not least, the COVID-19 pandemic has made a real difference. In the United States, it was partly responsible for Trump's electoral defeat after only one term, because people could see that the coronavirus crisis had not gotten better but worse. Thus, no one believed any longer that the government could be counted on to help them. The pandemic had a similar effect in Cuba.

All of these factors together have created a massive upheaval in Cuban society. Now we begin to witness another massive exodus from the island—on rafts and on foot, crossing the border. However, if we listen to the protesters, we do not hear them saying that they want to leave the country and make a better life elsewhere; we hear them saying that they want an end to the dictatorship, to a government that is unresponsive. During the July 2021 protests, down by the seaside of the Malecón, we could hear Cubans shouting *¡Libertad!* (Freedom). This may well be the beginning of a revolutionary situation.

Social scientists often wish they could separate the impact of one variable from another in predicting a particular outcome, so one could say that it was due to the currency reform, or to the lack of charisma of the new leadership, or to Trump's harsh sanctions, or to the spreading coronavirus, or to the dwindling help from Venezuela. New political actors have come to the fore: the Church and the youth. But in reality it is due to all of this coming together, creating what people now popularly refer to as "a perfect storm" (Pedraza 2021).

Theoretical Contributions

Our comparison of both revolutions leads us to conclude that there are important similarities between the two, similarities that speak to what a revolution is. The differences are due to the social characteristics of their people, their nations' social and economic resources, their historical trajectories, their international scene, and to historically contingent events.

Some scholars believe that revolutions cannot be predicted. Goldstone (1993, 132), analyzing the revolutions that took place in the USSR and the Eastern European countries between 1989 and 1993, contends that we should have been able to predict them, if we had used "a conjunctural process-based theory of revolution." The focus of his theory is not so much on the causes but on the historical processes and events through which they cumulatively developed. In predicting the origin of these revolutions, he lifted three basic conditions that converge:

1) the loss of effectiveness of the state, its inability to command resources or obedience;
2) the alienation of the elites and intellectuals from the state; and
3) the mobilization of the population for protest actions.

We concur that all three of these conditions were present in the onset of the Cuban and Venezuelan Revolutions. But our own comparative analysis of these two revolutions leads us to add that, particularly in developing countries of the Third World, for the revolution to become established as the new status quo and to continue surviving as a revolution, three other factors are also critical:

4) the charismatic, populist leader that wields an ideology that attracts the masses;
5) the international context, the geopolitical theater that served as a foil against which the revolution defines itself, and
6) the exodus of the opposition, that serves to externalize dissent.

Our comparative study has thus contributed to the study of social revolutions. Our larger theoretical contribution also consists of emphasizing that the study of revolutions needs to pay attention to the study of migration. The marriage of the two may well issue impressive insights.

Writing in 1940, in exile from fascism in Germany and Europe, the German writer Thomas Mann (1940, 22) equated fascism and communism as "false revolutions" that suffer from an extreme collectivist ethos, in which individual morality and truth go to ruin. Instead, he defended social democracy, as we do, as the society that maximizes individual freedom and economic justice.

A Democratic Future?

We hope the analytical exercise involved in this book will enable a better understanding of both social processes—Cuba's and Venezuela's revolutions—as these continue to unfold, and of the success and failure of social revolutions more generally. We stress that particularly when considering revolutions in the developing world, analysts need to take into account the key roles the international context and a massive exodus can play. We conclude with Merleau-Ponty, who, writing in the mid-1950s, expressed it succinctly: "Revolutions are true as movements but false as regimes" ([1955] 1973, 207).

We are left with one last question: Will Cuba and Venezuela return to democracy? Using the image of a journey, Rojas (2019) identifies serious obstacles in the way of the various journeys Cubans want to make: the daily journey to work and home, the journey of people on the island to elsewhere in the world, and the journey of the diaspora back to their homeland. Some of the obstacles come from the outside, especially the US government sanctions; other obstacles come from the inside, especially the unresponsive leadership on the island, in particular its most orthodox wing, which opposed the normalization of relations with the United States and remains wedded to Maduro's Venezuela.

Rojas (2019) asserts that, with his sanctions, Trump succeeded in consolidating the immobile core of the Cuban political elite: those who felt threatened by the economic reforms that were taking place and joined the debates regarding the new Constitution rather late, reverting its most progressive demands in the final text. Even more, through various decrees (e.g., laws 349 and 373), the Cuban government has already reinterpreted the new 2019 Constitution, making sure that the civil liberties and due process that rendered the text flexible cannot be used to subject the system to the public's criticism. Thus, in May 2019, a march of the LGBTQ community ended with violence and arrests; in recent years, some universities expelled several university professors for political reasons. This constitutes a return to the old days, in the late 1960s and early 1970s, when such actions were justified with the slogan everyone imagined had disappeared: "The university is for revolutionaries." When a protest took place via a letter signed by over 3,000 academics both on the island and the diaspora, government functionaries insisted they had no right to give opinions regarding their country, calling the professors "mercenaries," "enemies," and *cubanólogos*. Thus, Rojas concludes, of the many difficult journeys full of obstacles in the way of Cubans, none is more arduous than the journey toward a free nation and a democracy: *un estado de derecho*. That journey has become a real odyssey, Rojas argues, an epic one, in a country where its leaders chose to go against the logic of diversity that defines the twenty-first century.

In their analysis, Flores and Nooruddin (2016) stress the importance of a nation's *democratic stock* as well as its capacity to develop a *loyal opposition*. Elections are more likely to succeed, to bring about future democracy, in countries with a longer experience of democracy. Venezuela's democratic stock runs far deeper than Cuba's: 40 years of democracy prior to Chávez's arrival, as well as the continuation of elections under both Chávez and Maduro. While elections are not synonymous with democracy, neither can democracy be achieved without them (Schmitter and Karl 1991). Thus, we may expect that in due time Venezuela will find its way back to the electoral solution of its social problems, perhaps improving on its past performance, having developed a stronger loyal opposition and less corrupt government. That remains to be seen.

By contrast, Cuba's democratic stock is very shallow. Electoral democracy has not been practiced for over two-thirds of a century under communism. Even more, long before the revolution, the periods of electoral democracy were few and brief. Cuba's historical lack of acquaintance with democratic electoral processes does not augur well for the arrival of a democratic future. It is, thus, entirely possible that if the present economic crisis were to continue and a new political crisis were to develop, a situation of conflict and violence might unfold that could call for the assistance of international actors, such as the United Nations and the Red Cross. That, too, remains to be seen.

Cuba and Venezuela are cases of two revolutions and two models of unsuccessful social processes. They began their journey with enormous expectations and enormous hope; in the end, their results are questionable. Their present is dismal, and their future is grim. This is not an optimistic ending, but a realistic one. Yet hope and faith lie always in the heart of those who love their nations, as we do, as did Simón Bolívar and José Martí. Perhaps our intellectual exercise will assist the return of complete electoral democracy to both nations. Electoral democracy, hand in hand with a true social democracy, and an educated population, could be a path to a better future. As Goldstone (2001) highlights, the twin principles of effectiveness and justice are the two pillars of stable societies; while the absence of one may be tolerated, the absence of both leads to revolution. When a future built on effectiveness and justice arrives, the exodus out of their nations will become small, as young people will want to share it. Everywhere in the world, whatever the name of their political system, people want to feel that they belong, that they have a voice, and that they can make a difference. Cuba and Venezuela are no exceptions.

References

Abadi M., Anabella. 2017. "4 años de recesión económica en cifras." *Prodavinci*, December 28, 2017. https://prodavinci.com/4-anos-de-recesion-economica-en-cifras/.

Agrupación Católica Universitaria. 1957. "¿Por Qué Reforma Agraria?" Report by Melchor W. Gastón, Oscar A. Echevarría, and René F. de la Huerta. Serie B-Apologética Folleto 23. La Habana: Buró de Información y Propaganda.

Aguirre, Benigno E. 1976. "The Differential Migration of Cuban Social Races." *Latin American Research Review* 11: 103–24.

Aguilar-León, Luis E. [1959] 1972. *Cuba: Conciencia y Revolución*. Miami: Ediciones Universal.

Alfonso, Pablo. 1985. *Cuba, Castro y los católicos*. Miami, FL: Ediciones Hispanamerican.

Alandete, David. 2008. "Condoleezza Rice: Rusia es cada vez más agresiva que en el exterior y autoritaria." *El País*, September 19.

Alonso, José Antonio, and Pavel Vidal. 2013. *¿Quo Vadis, Cuba? La Incierta Senda de la Reforma*. Madrid: Catarata.

Alzugaray-Treto, Carlos. 2012. "Las (inexistentes) relaciones Cuba-Estados Unidos en tiempo de cambio." *Nueva Sociedad* 242 (November–December): 139–48.

———. 2009. "Cuba cincuenta años después: continuidad y cambio." *Temas* 60 (October–December): 37–47.

Amaro, Nelson. 1981. "Mass and Class in the Origins of the Cuban Revolution." In *Cuban Communism*, edited by Irving Louis Horowitz. New Brunswick, NJ: Transaction, 221–51.

Amaro, Nelson, and Alejandro Portes. 1972. "Una sociología del exilio: situación de los grupos cubanos en los Estados Unidos." *Aportes* 23:6–24.

Ameringer, Charles D. 2000. *The Cuban Democratic Experience: The Auténtico Years, 1944–1952*. Gainesville: University of Florida Press.

Amnesty International. 1992. *Cuba: Silencing the Voices of Dissent*. New York: Amnesty International.

Aminzade, Ron, Jack A. Goldstone, Doug McAdam, E. J. Perry, and William Sewell Jr. 2001. *Voice and Silence in Contentious Politics*. New York: Cambridge University Press.

Anderson, John Lee. 2010. *Ché Guevara: A Revolutionary Life*. New York: Grove.

Aranguren, Emilio. 2003. "Memorias a mi Regreso." *Vitral* 9: 65–70.

Archivo Cuba (Cuba Archive). 2021. *Database on Deaths and Disappearances in Cuba, March 1952–December 2020.* https://CubaArchive.org/database/.
Associated Press. 2018. "Defying Pundits, GOP Share of Latino Vote Steady under Trump," December 27. https://www.nbcnews.com/politics/donald-trump/defying-pundits-gop-share-latino-vote-steady-under-trump-n952411.
Association of American Physicians and Surgeons. 2009. "Medical Journal Exposes Cuba's Failed Doctor Diplomacy." http://www.aapsonline.org.
Bach, Robert, Jennifer B. Bach, and Timothy Triplett. 1981/82. "The Flotilla 'Entrants': Latest and Most Controversial." *Cuban Studies* 11–12: 29–48.
Balmaseda, Liz. 1994. "Cuba Bleeds, and the Drops Are Called Rafts." *Miami Herald*, August 17.
Barkan, Elliott Robert. 2013. "Venezuelans." In *Immigrants in American History: Arrival, Adaptation, and Integration.* Santa Barbara, CA: ABC-CLIO.
Basch, Linda, Nina Glick Schiller, and Cristina Szanton Blanc. 1994. *Nations Unbound: Transnational Projects, Postcolonial Predicaments, and Deterritorialized Nation States.* Langhorne: Gordon & Breach.
Benemelis, Juan F. 1988. *Castro, Subversión y Terrorismo en África.* Madrid: San Martín.
Benford, Robert D., and David A. Snow. 2000. "Framing Processes and Social Movements: An Overview and Assessment." *Annual Review of Sociology* 26:611–39.
Berezin, Mabel. 1997. *Making the Fascist Self: The Political Culture of Interwar Italy.* Ithaca: Cornell University Press.
Berg, Ryan C. 2019. "Russia Is Gearing Up for a Conflict with the United States in the Caribbean." *Foreign Policy*, October 9, 2019. https://foreignpolicy.com/2019/10/09/russias-putin-venezuela-evade-oil-sanctions-preparing-conflict-united-states/.
Bermúdez, Ángel. 2009. "Memorando Opex N° 122: Relaciones Rusia–América Latina: perspectiva actual y desafíos para España." *La Fundación Alternativas*, April 21. https://www.fundacionalternativas.org/observatorio-de-politica-exterior-opex/documentos/memorandos/memorando-opex-no-122-2009-relaciones-rusia-america-latina-perspectiva-actual-y-desafios-para-espana.
Berry, John M. 2016. "Problems Everywhere: The Risk to the World Economy." *International Economy.* http://international-economy.com/TIE_W16_Berry.pdf.
Betancourt, Rómulo. 1967. *La Revolución Democrática en Venezuela, 1959–1964.* Vol. 1. Caracas: Imprenta Nacional.
Bikel, Ofra. 2001. "Saving Elián." PBS *Frontline*, February 6. https://pbs.org.
Blanco, Carlos. 2002. *Revolución y Desilusión: la Venezuela de Hugo Chávez.* Madrid: Catarata.
Blasier, Cole. 1983. *The USSR and Latin America.* Pittsburgh: University of Pittsburgh Press.
———. 1976. *The Hovering Giant: US Responses to Revolutionary Change in Latin America.* Pittsburgh: University of Pittsburgh Press.
Blasier, Cole, and Carmelo Mesa-Lago, eds. 1979. *Cuba in the World.* Pittsburgh: University of Pittsburgh Press.
Blue, Sarah A. 2007. "The Erosion of Racial Equality in the Context of Cuba's Dual Economy." *Latin American Politics and Society* 49, no. 3: 35–68.

Bolívar, Simón. 1819. Discurso de Angostura, 15 de febrero, Pronunciado en el Acto de Instalación del Segundo Congreso de Venezuela. Caracas: Archivo del Libertador, Volumen 100-B, Folios 1–32.

Bolton, Peter. 2016. "The Other Explanations for Venezuela's Economic Crisis." *Council of Hemispheric Affairs*, March 24.

Boyd, Gerald M. 1986. "Reagan Acts to Tighten Trade Embargo of Cuba." *New York Times*, August 23.

Boza-Masvidal, Eduardo, Monseñor. 1960. "¿Es cristiana la revolución social que se está verificando en Cuba?" *La Quincena*, 30 de Octubre. In *La Voz de la Iglesia en Cuba: 100 Documentos Episcopales. Conferencia de Obispos Católicos de Cuba*, 131–34. México, DF: Obra Nacional de la Buena Prensa, 1995.

Brenner, Philip, Marguerite Rose Jiménez, John M. Kirk, and William M. LeoGrande, eds. 2015. *The Revolution under Raúl Castro: A Contemporary Cuban Reader*. Lanham, MD: Rowman & Littlefield.

Brewer-Carías, Allan. 2012. *Práctica y Distorsión de la Justicia Constitucional de Venezuela*. Colección Justicia No. 3, Acceso a la Justicia. Caracas, Venezuela: Academia de Ciencias Políticas y Sociales, Universidad Metropolitana, Editorial Jurídica Venezolana.

Brinton, Crane. 1965. *The Anatomy of Revolution*. New York: Vintage.

Brocchetto, Marilia, Polo Sandoval, and Jaide Timm-García. 2017. "Venezuelans Flee to the U.S. in Search of Better Lives." *CNN*, June 11. https://www.cnn.com/2017/06/11/us/venezuela-asylum-seekers-us/index.html.

Bull, Benedict, and Antulio Rosales. 2020. "Into the Shadows: Sanctions, Rentierism, and Economic Informalization in Venezuela." *European Review of Latin American and Caribbean Studies* 109 (January–June): 107–33.

Burchardt, Hans Jürgen. 2017. "La crisis actual de América Latina: causas y soluciones." *Nueva Sociedad* 267 (January–February): 114–28.

Burggraff, Winfield J., and Richard L. Millet. 1995. "More than Failed Coups: The Crisis in Venezuelan Civil-Military Relations." In *Lessons of the Venezuelan Experience*, edited by Louis W. Goodman, Johanna Mendelson Forman, Moisés Naím, Joseph Tulchin, and Gary Bland, 54–78. Washington, DC: Woodrow Wilson Center.

Butto, Luis Alberto. 2012. "Marcos Pérez-Jiménez–Hugo Chávez: la élite militar al asalto del poder." In *Chavismo: Entre la Utopía y la Pesadilla*, Alejandro Cardozo-Uzcátegui, compiler, 224–63. Mérida: Editorial Venezolana.

Buzón, Leandro. 2020. "Todo lo que apunte a preserver la vida lo aplaudo y lo celebro." Interview in Hugo Prieto, *Prodavinci*, June 14. https://prodavinci.com.

Cannon, Barry. 2014. "As Clear as MUD: Characteristics, Objectives, and Strategies of the Opposition in Bolivarian Venezuela." *Latin American Politics and Society* 56, no. 4: 49–70.

———. 2010. *Hugo Chávez and the Bolivarian Revolution: Populism and Democracy in a Globalized Age*. Manchester: Manchester University Press.

Calvo-Ospina, Hernando. 2006. "Cuba Exports Health: Havana Medics Work around the World." *Le Monde Diplomatique*, English edition, August 11, 1–4.

Caraota Digital. 2018. "Presidente de Cuba–No habrá diálogo con EE UU mientras mantenga actitud aberrante." September 16.

Cardoso, Fernando Henrique, and Enzo Faletto. 1977. *Dependencia y Desarrollo en América Latina*. Buenos Aires: Siglo XXI.

Cardozo de Da Silva, Elsa. 2006. "La política exterior de Venezuela 1999–2002: Ni del estado, ni para la sociedad." *Revista de la Facultad de Ciencias Jurídicas y Políticas* 24 (May–August): 165–86.

———. 1998. "Cuarenta años después: la política exterior que tuvimos y la que necesitamos." *Revista Venezolana de Análisis de Coyuntura* 4, no. 1 (January–May): 43–63.

Carpenter, Colton. 2018. "The Cuban Paradox." *Harvard Political Review*, December 31, n.p.

Carr, Edward Hallett. 1954. *The Bolshevik Revolution: 1917–23*. London: Macmillan.

Carranza, Julio. 2021. "Living, Thinking, and Fighting at a Complex Conjuncture." Translated by Mariana Ortega-Breña. *Latin American Perspectives* 68, no. 6:44–47.

Carrère d'Encausse, Hélène. 2005. *Russie, La Transition Manquée*. Paris: Fayard.

Carrillo De Albornoz, Sara. 2006. "US Lifts Immigration Restriction for Cuban Doctors." *British Medical Journal*, August 24. https://doi.org/10.1136/bmj.333.7565.411.

Casal, Lourdes. 1987. "Images of Women in Pre- and Post-Revolutionary Cuban Novels." *Cuban Studies* 17: 25–50.

Casavantes-Bradford, Anita. 2014. *The Revolution Is for the Children: The Politics of Childhood in Havana and Miami, 1959–1962*. Chapel Hill: University of North Carolina Press.

Castellanos, Dimas. 2021. "Sin azúcar no hay país. ¿y entonces?" *Diario de Cuba*, May 14. https://diariodecuba.com/economia/1620990544_31131.html.

———. 2017. *La Revolución Fracasada*. Madrid: Editorial Hypermedia.

Castro, Fidel. 2013a. *Carta de Despedida a Hugo Chávez*. 18 de febrero. http.www://tachira.psuv.org.ve/

———. 2013b. *Segunda Carta de Despedida de Fidel al comandante Chávez*. 5 de marzo. http://www.elpatagonico.cl/?p:52454.

———. 2008. *Habla Fidel: 25 Discursos en la Revolución, 1959–2006*. Pedro Álvarez-Tabío, compiler. La Habana: Oficina de Publicaciones del Consejo de Estado.

———. 1989. "Una impostergable decisión consistente con nuestros principios." *Granma*, 13 de agosto.

———. 1980. "Informe del Primer Secretario Fidel Castro, en ocasión del Segundo Congreso del Partido Comunista de Cuba." *Granma*, 17 de diciembre.

———. 1980. Editorial del *Granma* sobre el éxodo por el Mariel, 22 de junio.

———. 1960. "This Is Democracy." In *Fidel Castro Speeches*, Vol. 2: *Our Power Is That of the Working People Building Socialism in Cuba*, edited by Michael Taber, 25–37. New York: Pathfinder, 1981.

———. 1959a. Television interview on Meet the Press, Washington, DC, April 19. Princeton University, Carlos Franqui Collection, Speeches, Press Conferences, and Declarations of Fidel Castro-Ruz from March 1959 to October 1970.

———. 1959b. Television interview on CMQ station's Before the Press, Havana, Cuba, May 21. Princeton University, Carlos Franqui Collection: Speeches, Press Conferences, and Declarations of Fidel Castro-Ruz from March 1959 to October 1970.

———. 1959c. Speech on "Neither Bread without Freedom nor Freedom without Bread."

In Nelson Amaro, "Mass and Class in the Origins of the Cuban Revolution." In *Cuban Communism*, edited by Irving Louis Horowitz. New Brunswick: Transaction: 237–38.
———. [1953] 1973. "La Historia me Absolverá." La Habana: Instituto Cubano del Libro.
Castro, Raúl. 2016. "Central Report for the 7th Congress of the Cuban Communist Party (PCC)." *CubaDebate*, August 30. https://CubaDebate.cu.
———. 2011. "Speech Delivered during the Closing Ceremony of the 6th Session of the 7th Legislature of the National Assembly of People's Power." *CubaDebate*, December 18. https://CubaDebate.cu.
———. 1979. "Discurso sobre el embargo de los EE UU." *Granma*, December 9.
Ceaser, Mike. 2007. "Cuban Doctors Abroad Helped to Defect by New U.S. Visa Policy." *World Politics Review*, August 1. https://www.worldpoliticsreview.com/articles/981/cuban-doctors-abroad-helped-to-defect-by-new-u-s-visa-policy.
Centeno, Miguel Angel, and Alejandro Portes. 2006. "The Informal Economy in the Shadow of the State." In *Out of the Shadows: Political Action and the Informal Economy in Latin America*, edited by Patricia Fernández-Kelly and Jon Shefner. University Park: University of Pennsylvania Press.
Chaliand, Gérard. 2008. *Les Guerres Irrégulières*. Paris: Gallimard.
Chávez, Hugo. 2014a. *El Abrazo de Dos Gigantes*. Caracas: Obsequio.
———. 2014b. *Agenda Alternativa Bolivariana*. Caracas: Obsequio.
———. 2011. *El Socialismo del Siglo XXI*. Caracas: Ediciones MinCI.
———. 2009. *Simón Bolívar: The Bolivarian Revolution,* edited by Matthew Brown. New York: Verso.
———. 2007a. "Discurso del presidente de la República Bolivariana de Venezuela, en el acto de firma de acuerdos entre Venezuela y Cuba." *Granma*, 15 de octubre.
———. 2007b. *Declaraciones sobre la posibilidad de una Confederación de Repúblicas Suramericanas*. El Universal, 14 de octubre.
———. 2006. *"Aquí Huele a Azufre": Discurso del presidente Hugo Chávez ante la Organización de las Naciones Unidas*. 20 de septiembre. Caracas: Ediciones MinCI.
———. 2005. *Discurso de clausura de la VI reunión de la comisión mixta del convenio integral de cooperación binacional entre Venezuela y Cuba*. Ministerio de Relaciones Exteriores de Cuba, 5 de octubre.
———. 2004. *Discurso de Hugo Chávez-Frías en el Aula Magna de la Universidad de la Habana, Cuba, 14 de diciembre, 1994*. (Reproducido en el Discurso pronunciado por Fidel Castro-Ruz en el acto de condecoración con la Orden "Carlos Manuel de Céspedes" al presidente de la República Bolivariana de Venezuela, Hugo Chávez, en el X Aniversario de su primera visita a Cuba, en el Teatro "Carlos Marx," 14 de diciembre, 2004). http://www.cuba.cu/gobierno/discursos720047esp/f141204e.html.
Chávez, Hugo, and Luis Bilbao. 2002. *Diez Años de la Revolución Bolivariana. Conversaciones con Luis Bilbao*. Buenos Aires: Capital Intelectual.
Chilcote, Ronald H. 1970. *Revolution and Structural Change in Latin America: A Bibliography on Ideology, Development and the Radical Left (1930–1965)*. 2 vols. Stanford: Stanford University Press.
Comisión Económica para América Latina y el Caribe (CEPAL). 2020a. *Estudio Económico*. Santiago de Chile: CEPAL.

———. 2020b. "Dimensionar efectos del COVID-19 para pensar en la reactivación." Santiago de Chile: CEPAL.

———. 2017. *Balance Preliminar de las Economías de América Latina y el Caribe 2016*. Santiago de Chile: CEPAL.

Conferencia de Obispos de la Iglesia Católica en Cuba. 2020. "Mensaje de Navidad de los Obispos de Cuba." December 12. https://iglesiacubana.org/cocc/pages/articles/1466.

Coppedge, Michael. 2005. "Venezuela: Soberanía Popular versus Democracia Liberal." In *Construcción de Gobernabilidad Democrática en América Latina*, edited by Jorge I. Domínguez and Michael Shifter, 183–212. México: Fondo de Cultura Económica.

Córdoba, Efrén. 1995. *Clase Trabajadora y Movimiento Sindical en Cuba, vol. 1: 1819–1959; vol. 2: 1959–1996*. Miami: Ediciones Universal and Center for Labor Research and Studies, Florida International University.

Coronil, Fernando. 1997. *The Magical State: Nature, Money, and Modernity in Venezuela*. Chicago: University of Chicago Press.

Corrales, Javier. 2015. "Autocratic Legalism in Venezuela." *Journal of Democracy* 26, no. 2: 37–51.

———. 2006. "Hugo Boss: How Chavez Is Refashioning Dictatorship for a Democratic Age." *Foreign Policy*, January–February, 32–40.

Corrales, Javier, and Michael Penfold. 2015. *Dragon in the Tropics: Venezuela and the Legacy of Hugo Chávez*. Washington: Brookings Institution.

Corrales, Javier, and Carlos A. Romero. 2013. *U.S.-Venezuela Relations since the 1990s: Coping with Mid-Level Security Threats*. New York: Routledge.

Corrales, Javier. 2012. "Cuba's 'Equity without Growth' Dilemma and the 2011 Lineamientos." *Latin American Politics and Society* 54, no. 3: 157–84.

Correo del Orinoco. 2018. "Venezuela celebra designación del presidente Miguel Díaz-Canel." 19 de junio. http://www.correodelorinoco.gob.ve/comunicado-andante-de-venezuela-celebra-talante-democratico-del-pueblo-cubano-y-designacion-del-president-miguel-diaz-canel/

Cuban American National Foundation. 2007. "FNCA y Solidaridad Sin Fronteras Recaudan Fondos para Médicos Cubanos que Desean Alcanzar la Libertad." Miami, Florida, July 16.

Cuban Economic Research Project. 1965. *A Study on Cuba: The Colonial and Republican Periods, the Socialist Experiment*. Coral Gables: University of Miami Press.

Daugherty, Alex. 2019. "Guaido's Representatives Reject Dialogue with Maduro and Call for Imminent Elections." *Miami Herald*, January 31.

Dávila, Luis. 2013. "La situación actual de la industria energética de Venezuela." Caracas, Venezuela. Manuscript.

De la Fuente, Alejandro. 2020. "Racism with Equality in Cuba: 1980–2010." Paper presented at the annual Meeting of the Association for the Study of the Cuban Economy (ASCE), August 14.

———. 2019. "Special Issue of the Journal Dedicated to the Issue of Race in Cuba and the Afro-Cuban Movement." *Cuban Studies* 48.

———. 2001. *A Nation for All: Race, Inequality, and Politics in Twentieth-Century Cuba*. Chapel Hill: University of North Carolina Press.

De la Torre, Carlos. 2020. "Populist Leadership and the Politics of the Extraordinary." Paper presented at the annual Meeting of the American Sociological Association, San Francisco, California, August 11.

———. 2019. "Populisms: Lessons from Latin America." Paper presented at the annual Meeting of the American Sociological Association, New York City, August 12.

De Tocqueville, Alexis. 1955. *The Old Regime and the French Revolution*. Translated by Stuart Gilbert. New York: Doubleday.

Del Pino, Rafael. 1991. *Proa a la Libertad*. México: Planeta.

Diamint, Rut. 2005. "Cuestiones Militares en América Latina." In *Construcción de Gobernabilidad Democrática en América Latina*, Jorge I. Domínguez and Michael Shifter, compilers, 47–81. México: Fondo de Cultura Económica.

Domínguez, Jorge I. 2013. "La Política Exterior de Cuba según un extraterrestre: ¿es conservadora?" *Foreign Affairs Latinoamérica* 13, no. 3 (julio–septiembre): 145–46.

———. 2006. *Cuba Hoy: Analizando su Pasado, Imaginando su Futuro*. Madrid: Editorial Colibrí.

———. 2004. "La Política Exterior de Cuba y el Sistema Internacional." In *América Latina en el Nuevo Sistema Internacional*, Joseph S. Tulchin and Ralph H. Espach, compilers, 255–86. Barcelona: Bellaterra.

———. 1997. "Comienza una Transición Hacia el Autoritarismo en Cuba." *Encuentro*, 6–7 (Fall–Winter): 7–23.

———. 1992. "Cooperating with the Enemy? U.S. Immigration Policies toward Cuba." In *Western Hemisphere Immigration and U.S. Foreign Policy*, edited by Christopher Mitchell, 31-88. University Park: Pennsylvania State University Press.

———. 1989. *To Make the World Safe for Revolution: Cuba's Foreign Policy*. Cambridge: Harvard University Press.

———. 1985. *Castro's Challenge*. PBS *Frontline*. Part of the film series on "Crisis in Latin America," series editor.

———. 1978a. *Cuba: Order and Revolution*. Cambridge, MA: Belknap Press of Harvard University Press.

———. 1978b. "Cuban Foreign Policy." *Foreign Affairs* 57, no. 1: 83–108.

Domínguez, Jorge I., and Rafael Fernández de Castro. 2010. *Contemporary US-Latin American Relations: Cooperation or Conflict in the 21st Century*. New York: Routledge.

Domínguez, Jorge I., Omar Everleny Pérez-Villanueva, and Lorena Barbería. 2004. *The Cuban Economy at the Start of the Twenty-First Century*. Cambridge: Harvard University Press, David Rockefeller Center for Latin American Studies.

Duany, Jorge. 2018. "Relaciones económicas de cubanos y venezolanos emigrados con sus países de origen." Paper presented at the annual Meeting of the Association for the Study of the Cuban Economy (ASCE), Miami, Florida, July 27.

———. 2015. "Cuba, Estados Unidos, y la Diáspora." *El Nuevo Día*, 14 de enero.

Dufoix, Stéphane. 2000. "The Coriolanus Complex: War, Politics, and Aliens." Paper presented at the Meeting of the Social Science History Association (SSHA) in Pittsburgh, Pennsylvania, October 27.

Dunning, Thad. 2010. "Endogenous Oil Rents." *Comparative Political Studies* 43: 379–410.

Echevarría, Oscar A. 1995. "Cuba and the International Sugar Market." *Cuba in Transi-*

tion 5. Proceedings of the Meeting of the Association for the Study of the Cuban Economy (ASCE), Miami, Florida, August 10.

Eckstein, Susan Eva. 2009. *The Immigrant Divide: How Cuban Americans Changed the U.S. and Their Homeland.* New York: Routledge.

Economist. 2012. "Indecision Time: Never Rapid, Raúl Castro's Reforms seem to Be Stalling." September 15. https://www.economist.com/the-americas/2012/09/15/indecision-time.

Eisenstadt, S. N. 1977. *Revolution and Transformation of Societies: A Study in Comparative Civilizations.* New York: Free Press.

Ellner, Steve. 1997. "Recent Venezuelan Political Studies: A Return to Third World Realities." *Latin American Research Review* 32:201–18.

El Nuevo Herald. 2019. "Maduro felicita a Cuba por el aniversario de su revolución," January 2.

Entous, Adam, and John Lee Anderson. 2018. "The Mystery of the Havana Syndrome." *New Yorker,* November 19. https://newyorker.com/magazine/2018/11/19.

Enzensberger, Hans Magnus. 1974. "Portrait of a Party: Prehistory, Structure, and Ideology of the PCC." In *Politics and Crime,* edited by Michael Roloff, 126–55. New York: Seabury.

Erisman, Michael H., and John M. Kirk. 2018. *Cuban Foreign Policy: Transformation under Raúl Castro.* Boulder: Rowman & Littlefield.

Espina-Prieto, Mayra. 2004. "Social Effects of Economic Adjustment: Equality, Inequality, and Trends toward Greater Complexity in Cuban Society." In *The Cuban Economy at the Start of the Twenty-First Century,* edited by Jorge I. Domínguez, Omar Everleny Pérez-Villanueva, and Lorena Barbería, 209–44. Cambridge: Harvard University Press.

Espinosa-Chepe, Oscar. 2011. *Cambios en Cuba: Pocos, Limitados y Tardíos.* Habana: Reconciliación Cubana. https://reconciliacioncubana.wordpress.com/publicaciones.

Etzioni, Amitai. 2007. *Security First: For a Muscular, Moral Foreign Policy.* New Haven: Yale University Press.

Ezrow, Natacha, and Erica Frantz. 2011. "State Institutions and the Survival of Dictatorships." *Journal of International Relations* 65 (Fall–Winter): 1–13.

Ewell, Judith. 1996. *Venezuela and the United States: From Monroe's Hemisphere to Petroleum's Empire.* Athens: University of Georgia Press.

Fagen, Richard R., Richard A. Brody, and Thomas J. O'Leary. 1968. *Cubans in Exile: Disaffection and the Revolution.* Stanford: Stanford University Press.

Falcoff, Mark. 2003. *Cuba, The Morning After: Confronting Castro's Legacy.* Washington: AEI.

Feinberg, Richard E. 2020. "The Cuban Economy." In *Handbook of Caribbean Economies,* edited by Robert E. Looney. New York: Routledge Handbooks Online. https://routledgehandbooks.com/doi/10.4324/9780429265105-18.

———. 2016. *Open for Business: Building the New Cuban Economy.* Washington: Brookings Institution.

Feinsilver, Julie M. 2010. "Fifty Years of Cuba's Medical Diplomacy: From Idealism to Pragmatism." *Cuban Studies* 41:85–104.

———. 1993. *Healing the Masses: Cuban Health Politics at Home and Abroad.* Berkeley: University of California Press.

Ferguson, James. 2015. *Give a Man a Fish: Reflections on the New Politics of Distribution.* Durham: Duke University Press.

Fernandes, Sujatha. 2010. *Who Can Stop the Drums? Urban Social Movements in Chávez's Venezuela.* Durham: Duke University Press.

Fernández, Mirta, and Pablo Díaz-Espí. 2018. "23,000 médicos menos, un pésimo negocio para los cubanos." *Diario de Cuba*, 9 de noviembre. https://diariodecuba.com/cuba/1541762045_42885.html.

Fisher, Max, and Amanda Taub. 2017. "How Does Populism Turn Authoritarian? Venezuela Is a Case in Point." *New York Times*, April 1.

Fitzgerald, David Scott. 2019. *Refuge beyond Reach: How Rich Democracies Repel Asylum Seekers.* New York: Oxford University Press.

Flores, Thomas Edward, and Irfan Nooruddin. 2016. *Elections in Hard Times: Building Stronger Democracies in the 21st Century.* New York: Cambridge University Press.

Focus Economics. 2020. "Venezuela's Economy–GDP, Inflation, CPI, and Interest Rates." www.focus-economics.com/countries/venezuela.

Foran, John. 2005. *Taking Power: On the Origins of Third World Revolutions.* New York: Cambridge University Press.

———, ed. 1997. *Theorizing Revolutions.* New York: Routledge.

Forero, Juan. 2007. "Some Cuban Doctors Flee via Venezuela." *Washington Post*, February 21, 2007.

Franqui, Carlos. [1981] 1983. *Family Portrait with Fidel.* London: Jonathan Cape.

Fuentes, Norberto. 1999. *Dulces Guerreros Cubanos.* Barcelona: Editorial Seix Barral.

Gámez-Torres, Nora. 2019. "U.S. Restricts Travel, Remittances to Cuba as Part of a New Policy under Trump." *Miami Herald*, April 17.

García, María Cristina. 1996. *Havana USA: Cuban Exiles and Cuban Americans in South Florida, 1959–1994.* Berkeley: University of California Press.

García-Marco, Daniel. 2017. "Entrevista de Alberto Barrera Tyszka: 'La diáspora en Venezuela tiene un elemento afectivo brutal en un país que no había sido emigrante.'" *BBC New Mundo*, 9 de noviembre. http://BBC.com/mundo/noticias-america-latina-41910490.

Garrido, Alberto. 1999. *Guerrilla y Conspiración Militar en Venezuela.* Caracas: Fondo Editorial Nacional.

Goldstone, Jack A. 2009. "Rethinking Revolutions: Integrating Origins, Processes, and Outcomes." *Comparative Studies of South Asia, Africa, and the Middle East* 3, no. 1: 18–32.

———. 2001. "Toward a Fourth Generation of Revolutionary Theory." *Annual Review of Political Science* 4: 139–87.

———. 1993. "Predicting Revolutions: Why We Could (and Should) Have Foreseen the Revolutions of 1989–1991 in the USSR and Eastern Europe." *Contention* 2 (Winter): 127–52.

———. 1982. "The Comparative and Historical Study of Revolutions." *Annual Review of Sociology* 8: 187–207.

Gómez, Andy, Eugenio Rothe, Frank Mora, Héctor Castillo-Matos, and John Lewis. 2004. *Value Orientations and Opinions of Recently Arrived Cubans in Miami*. Miami: University of Miami, Institute for Cuban and Cuban-American Studies.

Goodwin, Jeff. 2001. *No Other Way Out: States and Revolutionary Movements, 1945–1991*. New York: Cambridge University Press.

González-Mederos, Lenier. 2013. "Las fuerzas armadas y el futuro de Cuba." *Espacio Laical*, March. http://espaciolaical.org/contens/esp/sd_224.pdf.

Granma. 2018. "Refuerza Cuba su abrazo médico a Venezuela." November 11.

———. 2012. "The Revolutionary Government of the Republic of Cuba Denounces the Escalation of Pressure and Actions of the United States Government." February 13.

———. 1968. "Microfaction Unmasked." February 4 and 11.

Gratius, Suzanne, and Carlos A. Romero. 2013. *La proyección internacional de la Venezuela post-chavista*. Madrid: Fundación para las Relaciones Internacionales y el Diálogo Exterior (FRIDE). http://www.fride.org/publicacion/1130/la-proyeccion-internacional-de-la.

Grenier, Guillermo, and Hugh Gladwin. 2018. "The FIU/Cuba Polls: 1991, 1993, 1995, 1997, 2000, 2002, 2004, 2007, 2008, 2011, 2014, 2018." Florida International University. https://cri.fiu.edu/cuban-america/cuba-poll/

Grenier, Guillermo, and Qian Lai. 2020. "FIU Cuba Poll: How Cuban Americans in Miami View U.S. Policies toward Cuba." Miami: Florida International University. https://cri.fiu.edu/research/cuba-poll.

Grenier, Yvon. 2019. "The Cuban Revolution: When Did It End? A Discussion with Jorge Domínguez, Julio César Guanche, Jennifer Lambe, Carmelo Mesa-Lago, Silvia Pedraza, and Rafael Rojas." *Cuban Studies* 47: 143–68.

Guerra, Lillian. 2012. *Visions of Power in Cuba: Revolution, Redemption, and Resistance, 1959–1971*. Chapel Hill: University of North Carolina Press.

Guevara, Ernesto Che. 1967. *El Diario del Che en Bolivia: noviembre 7, 1966–octubre 7, 1967*. La Habana: Instituto del Libro.

Hachemaoui, Mohammed. 2012. "La Rente Entrave-t-elle Vraiment la Démocratie? Réexamen Critique des Théories de 'l'État rentier' et de la malédiction des resources." *Revue Française de Science Politique* 62 (Avril): 207–30.

Hall, Stuart. 1986. "Cultural Studies: Two Paradigms." In *Media, Culture, and Society: A Critical Reader*, edited by Richard Collins, James Curran, Nicholas Garnham, Paddy Scannell, Philip Schlesinger, and Colin Sparks, 33–48. Beverly Hills: Sage.

Handlin, Samuel. 2016. "Mass Organizations and the Durability of Competitive Authoritarian Regimes: Evidence from Venezuela." *Comparative Political Studies* 49, no. 9: 1238–69.

Hansing, Katrin, and Bert Hoffman. 2020. "When Racial Inequalities Return: Assessing Cuban Society 60 Years after the Revolution." *Latin American Politics and Society* 62, no. 2: 29–52.

Havel, Vaclav. 1986. "Two Notes on Charter 77." In *Open Letters: Selected Writings, 1965–1990*, edited by Paul Wilson, 323–27. New York: Vintage.

———. 1978. "The Power of the Powerless." In *Open Letters: Selected Writings, 1965–1990*, edited by Paul Wilson 125–214. New York: Vintage.

Hernández, Tanya K. 2020. Discussant for Alejandro de la Fuente's presentation on "Racism with Equality? Measuring Racial Inequality in Cuba, 1980–2020," at the annual Meeting of the Association for the Study of the Cuban Economy (ASCE), August 14.

Hernández-Catá, Ernesto. 2008. "A Brief Comparative History of Gross Domestic Production in Revolutionary Cuba." *Cuba in Transition* 18. Proceedings of the Meeting of the Association for the Study of the Cuban Economy (ASCE), Miami, Florida, August 5.

Hirschman, Albert O. 1993. "Exit, Voice, and the Fate of the German Democratic Republic: an Essay in Conceptual History." *World Politics* 45: 173–202.

———. 1986. "Exit and Voice: an Expanding Sphere of Influence." In *Rival Views of Market Society and Other Recent Essays*, 77–101. New York: Viking.

———. 1970. *Exit, Voice, and Loyalty*. Cambridge: Harvard University Press.

Hirst, Mónica, Carlos Luján, Carlos A. Romero, and Juan Gabriel Toklatian. 2020. *La Internacionalización de la Crisis en Venezuela*. Berlin: Fundación Friedrich Ebert.

Hogenboom, Barbara. 2012. "Depoliticized and Repoliticized Minerals in Latin America. The New Politics of Mineral Extraction in Latin America." *Journal of Developing Societies* 28 (June): 133–58.

Inkeles, Alex, and Raymond Bauer. 1959. *The Soviet Citizen: Daily Life in a Totalitarian Society*. Cambridge: Harvard University Press.

Jácome, Francine. 2018. "Los militares en la política y la economía de Venezuela." *Nueva Sociedad* 274 (March–April): 119–28.

Jansen, Robert S. 2011. "Populist Mobilization: A New Theoretical Approach to Populism." *Sociological Theory* 29, no. 2 (June): 75–96.

Johnson, Haynes. 1964. *The Bay of Pigs*. New York: Norton.

Juventud Rebelde. 2018a. "Raúl Castro and Díaz-Canel Congratulate Nicolás Maduro on His Electoral Victory." May 21. http://www.juventudrebelde.cu/cuba/2018-05-21/Raul-Castro-y-Diaz-Canel-congratulates-Nicolas-Maduro-on-his-electoral-victory.

———. 2018b. "Despidió Raúl a Maduro." October 30. http:www.juventudsrebelde.cu/cub/2018-10-30/despidió-raul-a-maduro-1.

Kamorin, A. 1989. "The World and the U.S. Export Tropical Style, or Why Soviet and Cuban Partners are Ceasing to Understand one Another." *Izvestiya*, August 4.

Karl, Terry Lynn. 1997. *The Paradox of Plenty: Oil Booms and Petro-States*. Berkeley: University of California Press.

Karra, Sunayana. 2021. "Is Cuba's 'Army of White Coats' Medical Diplomacy or Contemporary Slavery?" Cornell SC Johnson College of Business, Emerging Markets Institute, May 19.

Kelly, Janet and Carlos A. Romero. 2005. *Venezuela y Estados Unidos: Coincidencias y Conflictos*. Caracas: Instituto de Estudios Superiores de Administración (IESA), Libros del Nacional, Colección Minerva.

Kirkpatrick, Jeane J. 1979. "Dictatorships and Double-Standards." *Commentary* 68, no. 5 (November): 34–45.

Kornblith, Miriam. 2007. *Venezuela: De la Democracia Representativa al Socialismo del Siglo XXI*. Caracas: Universidad Central de Venezuela.

———. 1997. "Crisis y Transformación del Sistema Político: Nuevas Reglas de Juego." In

El Sistema Político Venezolano: Crisis y Transformaciones, edited by Ángel Álvarez, 1–31. Caracas: Universidad Central de Venezuela, Instituto de Estudios Políticos.

Kornbluh, Peter, ed. 1998. *Bay of Pigs Declassified: The Secret CIA Report on the Invasion of Cuba*. New York: New Press.

Knoema. 2018. *World Data Atlas*. https://knoema.com.

Krogstad, Jens Manuel, and Antonio Flores. 2016. "Unlike Other Latinos, about Half of Cuban Voters in Florida Backed Trump." *Pew Research Center, Fact Tank*, November 15. https://pewresearch.org/fact-tankk/2016/11/15/.

Kunz, E. F. 1981. "Exile and Resettlement: Refugee Theory." *International Migration Review* 15: 42–51.

———. 1973. "The Refugee in Flight: Kinetic Models and Forms of Displacement." *International Migration Review* 7: 125–46.

Laclau, Ernesto. 2005. *On Populist Reason*. London: Verso.

Lainer-Vos, Dan. 2012. *Sinews of the Nation*. New York: Polity.

Laguerre, Michael S. 1998. *Diasporic Citizenship: Haitian Americans in Transnational America*. New York: St. Martin's.

Lander, Edgardo. 2018. "El estado mágico sigue ahí: Las continuidades y rupturas en la historia del petroestado venezolano." *Nueva Sociedad* 274 (March–April): 30–43.

Langue, Frédérique. 2002. *Hugo Chávez et le Venezuela: Un Action Politique au Pays de Bolívar*. Paris: L'Harmattan.

Lee, Everett S. 1966. "A Theory of Migration." *Demography* 3: 47–57.

Leiva, Miriam. 2019. *El Período Especial en Crescendo*. Habana: Reconciliación Cubana, Mayo. https://reconciliacioncubana.wordpress.com/publicaciones.

Lenin, Vladimir Ilyich. [1917] 1964. "The Dual Power." In *V. I. Lenin, Collected Works*, vol. 24, 38–41. Moscow: Progress.

LeoGrande, William M., and Peter Kornbluh. 2015. *Back Channel to Cuba: The Hidden History of Negotiations between Washington and Havana*. Chapel Hill: University of North Carolina Press.

LeoGrande, William M. 2015. "Normalizing US-Cuba Relations: Escaping the Shackles of the Past." *International Affairs* 91, no. 3: 473–88.

———. 1980. "Cuba's Policy in Africa, 1959–1980." Policy Papers in International Affairs. Berkeley: University of California Institute of International Studies.

Levine. Daniel H. 2017. "The Authoritarian Gambit." *Latin American Studies Association Forum* 48, no. 4: 1–2.

———. 1973. *Conflict and Political Change in Venezuela*. Princeton: Princeton University Press.

Levitsky, Steven, and Lucan A. Way. 2010. *Competitive Authoritarianism: Hybrid Regimes after the Cold War*. New York: Cambridge University Press.

Lewis, Gordon K. 1987. *Grenada: The Jewel Despoiled*. Baltimore: John Hopkins University Press.

Lewis, Flora. 1984. "The Roots of Revolution." *New York Times*, November 11.

Liebman, Robert C. 1992. "Revolutions." In *Encyclopedia of Sociology*, edited by Edgar F. Borgatta and Marie L. Borgatta, vol. 3, 672–76. New York: Macmillan.

Lindberg, Staffan, ed. 2009. *Democratization by Elections: A New Mode of Transition*. Baltimore: Johns Hopkins University Press.

Lipset, Seymour Martin. 1959. "Some Social Requisites of Democracy: Economic Development and Political Legitimacy." *American Political Science Review* 53 (March): 69–105.

López, Gustavo. 2015. "Hispanics of Venezuelan Origin in the United States, 2013." Pew Research Center, Hispanic Trends, Statistical Profile, September 15.

López-Segrera, Francisco. 1989. *Cuba, Política Exterior y Revolución, 1959–1988*. La Habana: ISRI.

Luis, Luis R. 2019. "Remittances to Cuba: Impact of New Measures." Association for the Study of the Cuban Economy (ASCE), November 12. https://ASCECuba.org/blog.

Maddison, Angus. 2001. *The World Economy: A Millennial Perspective*. Paris: Organization for Economic Cooperation and Development (OECD), Development Center Studies.

Maduro, Nicolás. 2018. "Comunicado felicitando a Cuba por los 59 años del triunfo de su revolución." http://mppre.gob.ve/wpcontent/uploads/sites/12/2018/01/Comunicado-Revolución-Cubana-.pdf.

———. 2013. "Discurso de juramentación como nuevo presidente de Venezuela." *El Universal*, 19 de abril.

Magdaleno, John. 2018. "Escenarios en la encrucijada venezolana." *Nueva Sociedad* 274 (March–April): 152–64.

Mahoney, James. 2000. "Strategies of Causal Inference in Small-N Analysis." *Sociological Methods of Research* 23: 3–32.

Mahoney, James, and Richard Snyder. 1999. "Rethinking Agency and Structure in the Study of Regime Change." *Studies in Comparative International Development* 34, no. 3. https://doi.org/10.1007/BF02687620.

Mainwaring, Scott, and Aníbal Pérez-Liñán. 2013. *Democracies and Dictatorships in Latin America: Emergence, Survival, and Fall*. New York: Cambridge University Press.

Mañach, Jorge. 1959. "El Drama de Cuba." *Bohemia*, January 11.

Mann, Thomas. 1940. *War and Democracy*. Address delivered to the Friends of the Colleges at Claremont, October 3.

Mannheim, Karl. 1952. *Essays in the Sociology of Knowledge*. New York: Oxford University Press.

Manrique, Miguel. 1996. *La Seguridad en las Fuerzas Armadas Venezolanas*. Caracas: Fondo Editorial Nacional.

Marsteintredet, Leiv. 2020. "With the Cards Stacked against You: Challenges to a Negotiated Transition to Democracy in Venezuela." *European Review of Latin American and Caribbean Studies* 109 (January–June):87–106.

Martí, José. [1891] 1963. *José Martí, 1853–1895, Obras Completas*. La Habana: Editorial Nacional de Cuba.

Martínez-Fernández, Luis. 2014. *Revolutionary Cuba: A History*. Gainesville: University Press of Florida.

Martínez, Eugenio. 2020. "¿El voto venezolano: decisivo en las elecciones de Florida?"

Encuesta realizada por el Laboratorio de Investigación de la Universidad del Norte de la Florida para *El Diario*, 28 de agosto, presentación virtual.
Martínez, Luis. 2010. *Violence de la Rente Pétroliére: Algérie-Irak-Lybie*. Paris: Presses de Sciences Politiques.
Matos, Huber. 2002. *Como Llegó la Noche*. Barcelona: Tusquets.
Matthews, Herbert L. 1961. *The Cuban Story*. New York: George Braziller.
Mazzuca, Sebastian. 2013. "The Rise of Rentier Populism." *Journal of Democracy* 24, no. 2: 108–22.
McAdam, Doug, John D. McCarthy, and Mayer N. Zald. 2008. "Social Movements." In *Handbook of Sociology*, edited by Neil J. Smelser, 695–737. Beverly Hills: Sage.
McAdam, Doug, Sydney Tarrow, and Charles Tilly. 2001. *Dynamics of Contention*. New York: Cambridge University Press.
McCoy, Jennifer and David J. Myers, eds. 2004. *The Unraveling of Representative Democracy in Venezuela*. Baltimore: John Hopkins University Press.
McCoy, Jennifer, Andrés Serbin, William C. Smith and Andrés Stambouli, eds. 1994. *Venezuelan Democracy under Stress*. New Brunswick: Transaction.
Merleau-Ponty, Maurice. [1955] 1973. *Adventures of the Dialectic*. Translated by Joseph Bien. Evanston: Northwestern University Press.
Méndez-Pupo, Yarimis. 2021. "Por qué se van los que se fueron? Un acercamiento a las motivaciones y expectativas de migrantes cubanos calificados de la oleada migratoria de los años 1995–2017." Paper presented at the annual Meeting of the Association for the Study of the Cuban Economy (ASCE), Miami, Florida, August 13.
Mesa-Lago, Carmelo. 2020. *Cuba: Crisis económica, sus causas y políticas de rescate*. Madrid: Real Instituto Elcano de Relaciones Internacionales.
———. 2019a. "The Cuban Economy after 60 Years of Revolution: Continuities and Changes." *Cuba in Transition* 29. Proceedings of the Meeting of the Association for the Study of the Cuban Economy (ASCE), Miami, Florida, July 24.
———. 2019b. "There's Only One Way Out for Cuba's Dismal Economy." *New York Times*, March 28.
———. 2018. *Voices of Change in Cuba from the Non-State Sector*. Pittsburgh: University of Pittsburgh Press.
———. 2012. *Cuba en la Era de Raúl Castro: Reformas Económicas-sociales y sus Efectos*. Madrid: Editorial Colibrí.
———. 2011. "Social Services in Cuba: Antecedents, Quality, Financial Sustainability, and Policies for the Future." In *The Cuban Economy: Recent Trends*, edited by José Raúl Perales, 51–81. Washington: Woodrow Wilson International Center for Scholars, Center Reports on the Americas.
———. 2000. *Market, Socialist, and Mixed Economies: Comparative Policy and Performance in Chile, Cuba, and Costa Rica*. Baltimore: Johns Hopkins University Press.
———. 1978. *Cuba in the 1970s: Pragmatism and Institutionalization*. Albuquerque: University of New Mexico Press.
Mesa-Lago, Carmelo, ed. 1971. *Revolutionary Change in Cuba*. Pittsburgh: University of Pittsburgh Press.

Mesa-Lago, Carmelo, and Jorge F. Pérez-López. 2013. *Cuba under Raúl Castro: Assessing the Reforms*. Boulder: Lynne Rienner.

———. 2005. *Cuba's Aborted Reforms: Socioeconomic Effects, International Comparisons, and Transition Policies*. Gainesville: University Press of Florida.

Mesa-Lago, Carmelo, and Pavel Vidal-Alejandro. 2019. "El impacto en la economía cubana de la crisis venezolana y de las políticas de Donald Trump." Manuscript. Real Instituto Elcano de Relaciones Internacionales, Madrid.

Miami Herald. 1980. "U.S. Opens Arms to Cuban Exodus," May 6.

Ministerio de Relaciones Exteriores de Colombia. 2020. "Evolución de la Crisis Migratoria con Venezuela: 5 Años de Historia." https://migracioncolombia.gov.com.

———. 2018. "Extranjeros en Colombia Aproximación Histórica a sus Trayectorias en Colombia, 2005–2016." Departamento Administrativo Nacional de Estadística.

Ministerio de Relaciones Exteriores de Cuba. 2000. Acuerdo de Cooperación Integral entre Cuba y Venezuela, 30 de octubre.

Miroff, Nick. 2015. "What the 'Pope Francis Effect' Hasn't Delivered in Cuba." *Washington Post*, October 7.

———. 2012. "Pope Meets Fidel Castro, Wraps Up Visit to Cuba." NPR *All Things Considered*, March 28.

Montaner, Carlos Alberto. 2005. "Slaves in White Coats." *Firmas Press*, September 12.

———. 2001. *Viaje al Corazón de Cuba*. Barcelona: Plaza & Janes Editores.

Montgomery, Paul. 1981. "For Cuban Refugees, Promise of U.S. Fades." *New York Times*, April 19.

Moore, Barrington, Jr. 1966. *Social Origins of Dictatorship and Democracy*. Boston: Beacon.

Moore, Carlos. 1988. *Castro, the Blacks, and Africa*. Los Angeles: Center for Afro-American Studies, University of California.

Morales, Emilio. 2022. "Cuba: GAESA se apodera de ETECSA e 'inventa' ORBIT S.A." *Diario de Cuba*, 8 de Febrero. https://diariodecuba.com/economia/1644355058_37358.html.

Morales-Domínguez, Esteban. 2018. "El tema racial en Cuba y el informe a Naciones Unidas del 2018. Un balance crítico." http://estebanmoralesdominguez.blogspot.com/2018/08-el-tema-racial-en-cuba-y-el-informe.html.

Morello, Carol. 1998. "A Family Divided." *USA Today*, January 12.

Morán-Arce, Lucas. 1980. *La Revolución Cubana (1953–1959): Una Versión Rebelde*. Ponce: Imprenta Universitaria, Universidad Católica.

Morse, Yonatan L. 2012. "The Era of Electoral Authoritarianism." *World Politics* 64 (January): 161–98.

Müller, Alberto. 2014. *Che Guevara: Valgo Más Vivo que Muerto*. Madrid: Editorial Biblioteca Nueva de España.

Müller, Jan-Werner. 2015. "Parsing Populism: Who Is and Is Not a Populist These Days?" *Juncture* 22, no. 2: 80–89.

Murillo, María Victoria. 2016. "Latin American Democracies Breaking the Left-Wing Tide or Electoral Alternation with a Plebiscitarian Flavor?" *Columbia University Journal of Politics & Society* 26, no. 2 (Spring): 2–6.

Myers, David J. 2017. "The Struggle to Legitimate Political Regimes in Venezuela: From Pérez Jiménez to Maduro." *Latin American Research Review* 52, no. 4: 1–9.

———. 1994. "Perceptions of a Stressed Democracy: Inevitable Decay or Foundation for Rebirth?" In *Venezuelan Democracy under Stress*, edited by Jennifer McCoy, Andrés Serbin, William C. Smith, and Andrés Stambouli, 107–38. New Brunswick: Transaction.

Naím, Moisés. 2005. "Prólogo: La internacionalización de Hugo Chávez." In *Venezuela y Estados Unidos: Coincidencias y Conflictos*, Janet Kelly and Carlos A. Romero, 201–12. Caracas: Instituto de Estudios Superiores de Administración (IESA), Libros del Nacional, Colección Minerva.

Naím, Moisés, and Ramón Piñango, compilers. 1984. *El Caso Venezuela: Una Ilusión de Armonía*. Caracas: Ediciones IESA, Instituto de Estudios Superiores de Administración.

Nationmaster. 2019. "Top Countries in Practicing Physicians Density, 2017–2019." *Data from the World Bank*. www.nationmaster.com/country-info/stats/health.

Navas, Francisco. 2018. "In Miami, Cuban Americans Have the Power to Push the State to the Left." *Guardian*, November 4.

Nebehay, Stephanie. 2019. "U.N. Rights Boss Decries Venezuela Crackdown; Says Sanctions may Worsen Crisis." *Reuters*, March 20.

New York Times. 1961. "Cuba Restricts Refugee Airlift," July 23.

Noe-Bustamante, Luis, Antonio Flores, and Sono Shah. 2019a. "Facts on Hispanics of Venezuelan Origin in the United States, 2017." *Pew Research Center, Hispanic Trends*, September 16.

———. 2019b. "Facts on Hispanics of Cuban Origin in the United States, 2017." *Pew Research Center, Hispanic Trends*, September 16.

O'Connor, John J. 1977. "TV: Visit with Castro." *New York Times*, June 9.

O'Donnell, Guillermo. 2004. "Quality of Democracy: Why the Rule of Law Matters." *Journal of Democracy* 15, no. 4: 32–46.

O'Donnell, Guillermo, and Philippe Schmitter. 1986. *Conclusiones Tentativas sobre las Democracias Inciertas. Colección: Transiciones desde un Gobierno Autoritario*, vol. 4. Buenos Aires: Paidos.

Oficina Nacional de Estadística e Información (ONEI). 2018. *Encuesta Nacional de Migraciones (ENMIG)*. La Habana: Centro de Estudios de Población y Desarrollo.

———. *Various years*. *Anuario Nacional de Estadística e Información*. La Habana: Centro de Estudios de Población y Desarrollo.

Ojito, Mirta. 2008. "Number of Defections by Cuban Doctors Increases." *Miami Herald*, August 17.

Olivares, Francisco. 2014. "Best and Brightest for Export." *El Universal*, September 24.

Oppenheimer, Andrés. 2003. "Best Anti-Castro Tool is Exile Moderation." *Miami Herald*, February 16.

———. 1993. *Castro's Final Hour*. New York: Simon & Schuster.

Organization for Economic Cooperation and Development (OECD). 2017. *Health Statistics*. http://www.oecd-ilibrary.com.

Orro, Roberto. 2009. "Petrolism in Cuba and Implications of US Investment in the Cuban Oil Sector." *Cuba in Transition* 19. Proceedings of the Meeting of the Association for the Study of the Cuban Economy (ASCE), Miami, Florida, July 31.

Ortega, Roberto. 2007. Panel on "Transition and the Cuban Military." University of Miami, Institute for Cuban and Cuban American Studies, February 27.

Padura, Leonardo. 2015a. "Cuba, a Country with a Broken Heart." In *A Contemporary Cuba Reader: The Revolution under Raúl Castro*, edited by Philip Brenner, Marguerite Rose Jiménez, John M. Kirk, and William LeoGrande, 307–16. Lanham: Rowman & Littlefield.

———. 2015b. "Living and Creating in Cuba: Risks and Challenges." In *A Contemporary Cuba Reader: The Revolution under Raúl Castro*, edited by Philip Brenner, Marguerite Rose Jiménez, John M. Kirk, and William LeoGrande, 317–22. Lanham: Rowman & Littlefield.

———. 2012. "Eppur si muove en Cuba." *Nueva Sociedad* 242 (November–December): 26–35.

Palacios, C. 2019. "Análisis de la restricción externa de la economía cubana en el actual contexto de incertidumbre." *Revista de la CEPAL* 127: 125–93.

Paige, Jeffrey M. 1975. *Agrarian Revolution: Social Movements and Export Agriculture in the Underdeveloped World*. New York: Free Press.

Panamerican Union. 1960. *América en Cifras, 1960–61*. Washington: Instituto Interamericano de Estadísticas.

Payá, Osvaldo. 2018. *La Noche no Será Eterna: Peligros y Esperanzas para Cuba*. Madrid: Editorial Hypermedia.

———. 2001. *Proyecto Varela*. La Habana: Movimiento Cristiano Liberación.

Pedraza, Silvia. 2023. "Transnationalism and Gender: Economic, Political, and Social Challenges." In *Beyond Economic Migration: Social, Historical, and Political Factors in Immigration to the United States*, edited by Min Zhou and Hasan Mahmud, 301–36. New York: New York University Press.

———. 2022. "Transnationalism among Cuban Immigrants: Economic, Political, and Social." Paper presented at the 13th Conference on Cuban and Cuban American Studies at Florida International University's Cuban Research Institute, Miami, Florida, February 3.

———. 2021. "Protests in Cuba: The Beginning of a New Revolution?" *University of Michigan News*, July 24. https://michigantoday.umich.edu/2021/07/20.

———. 2020. "El éxodo cubano: Cinco olas en sesenta años." Special issue on Indicadores [social indexes], *Foro Cubano* 3, no. 21 (June): 40–45.

———. 2019. "The Cuban Government Built and Rebuilt Itself Three Times." *Cuban Studies* 47: 154–56.

———. 2016a. "Fidel Castro: Was He David or Goliath?" CNN *Opinion*, December 4. https://www.cnn.com/2016/12/04/opinions/david-or-goliath-castro-pedraza/index.html.

———. 2016b. "Cuba and Its Exile: Political Generations." Paper presented at the University of South Carolina, Columbia, Sociology Department, October 17.

———. 2014. "Social Protest and Migration." In *The Encyclopedia of Global Human Migration*, edited by Immanuel Ness, 1–8. Malden: Blackwell.

———. 2013. "Cuban Revolution." In *The Wiley-Blackwell Encyclopedia of Social and Political Movements*, vol. 2, edited by David A. Snow, Donatella della Porta, Bert Klandermans, and Doug McAdam, 1–7. Hoboken: Wiley-Blackwell.

———. 2007. *Political Disaffection in Cuba's Revolution and Exodus*. New York: Cambridge University Press.

———. 2006. "Assimilation or Transnationalism? Conceptual Models of the Immigrant Experience." In *Cultural Psychology of Immigrants*, edited by Ram Mahalingam, 33–54. Boston: Lawrence Erlbaum.

———. 2000. "La perspectiva desde la isla." *El Nuevo Herald*, March 16.

Pedraza-Bailey, Silvia. 1985. *Political and Economic Migrants in America: Cubans and Mexicans*. Austin: University of Texas Press.

Pentón, Mario J. 2018. "Cuban Physicians Still Abandoning Missions despite End to US Parole Program." *Miami Herald*, March 12.

Pérez, Louis A., Jr. 2015. *Cuba: Between Reform and Revolution*. New York: Oxford University Press.

———. 2003. "Cuban Revolution." In *Encyclopedia of Cuba: People, History, Culture*, edited by Luis Martínez-Fernández, D. H. Figueredo, Louis A. Pérez, Jr., and Luis González, 242–46. Westport, CT: Greenwood.

Pérez, Lisandro. 1992. "Cuban Miami." In *Miami Now! Immigration, Ethnicity, and Social Change*, edited by Guillermo Grenier and Alex Stepich III, 83–108. Gainesville: University Press of Florida.

Pérez-Díaz, Victor M. 1993. *The Return of Civil Society: the Emergence of a Democratic Spain*. Cambridge, MA: Harvard University Press.

Pérez-López, Jorge F. 2017. "Cuba's Never-ending External Sector Crisis." *Cuba in Transition* 27. Proceedings of the Meeting of the Association for the Study of the Cuban Economy (ASCE), Miami, Florida, July 27.

Pérez-Serantes, Enrique. [1960] 1995. "Por Dios y por Cuba." In *La Voz de la Iglesia en Cuba: 100 Documentos Episcopales*, edited by the Conferencia de Obispos Católicos de Cuba, 107–114. México: Obra Nacional de la Buena Prensa.

Pérez-Stable, Marifeli. 2006. *Cuba en el siglo XXI: ensayos sobre la transición*. Madrid: Editorial Colibrí.

———. 1999. *The Cuban Revolution: Origins, Course, and Legacy*. New York: Oxford University Press.

Pérez-Villanueva, Omar Everleny, and Ricardo Torres-Pérez. 2015. *Miradas a la Economía Cubana: Análisis del Sector no Estatal*. La Habana: Editorial Caminos.

———. 2013. *Miradas a la Economía Cubana: Entre la Eficiencia Económica y la Equidad Social*. La Habana: Editorial Caminos.

Pérez-Villanueva, Omar Everleny. 2009. "La Economía en Cuba: un Balance Necesario y Algunas Propuestas de Cambio." *Nueva Sociedad* 216 (July–August): 49–64.

Petrásh, Vilma. 2000. *Venezuela y los Estados Unidos: Orígenes y Evolución de una "Relación."* Caracas: Ediciones Comala.

Petróleos de Venezuela, S.A. Various years. *Annual Report*. https://PDVSA.com.

Polanco, A. Tomás, Simón Alberto Consalvi, and Edgardo Mondolfi-Gudat. 2000. *Venezuela y Estados Unidos a Través de Dos Siglos*. Caracas: Venancham.

Portes, Alejandro, and Ruben G. Rumbaut. 1991. *Immigrant America: A Portrait*. Berkeley: University of California Press.

Portes, Alejandro, and Robert L. Bach. 1985. *Latin Journey: Cuban and Mexican Immigrants in the United States*. Berkeley: University of California Press.

Portes, Alejandro, Juan M. Clark, and Robert L. Bach. 1977. "The New Wave: A Statistical Profile of Recent Cuban Exiles to the United States." *Cuban Studies* 7: 1–32.

Prieto, Yolanda. 1987. "Cuban Women in the U.S. Labor Force: Perspectives on the Nature of the Change." *Cuban Studies* 17: 73–94.

Przeworski, Adam. 1986. "Some Problems in the Study of the Transition to Democracy." In *Transitions from Authoritarian Rule: Prospects for Democracy*, edited by Guillermo O'Donnell, Philippe C. Schmitter, and Laurence Whitehead, 47–63. Baltimore: Johns Hopkins University Press.

Puente, José Manuel. 2021. "Venezuela in the Stage of Macroeconomic Collapse: A Historical and Comparative Analysis." Paper presented at the Meeting of the Association for the Study of the Cuban Economy (ASCE) Conference, January 6.

Puyosa, Iría. 2019. "Rusia, Venezuela, y el ALBA: Compartiendo malas prácticas para el control de la información y de la sociedad civil." In *La Izquierda como Autoritarismo en el Siglo XXI*, compilado por Gisela Kozak Rovero y Armando Chaguaceda, 149–72. Guanajuato, México: Fundación CADAL (Centro para la Apertura y el Desarrollo de América Latina).

Radelat, Ana. 2000. "Deal Struck to Ease Embargo: House Leaders Approve Cuba Food Sales but Prohibit Financing by U.S." *Miami Herald*, June 28.

Ramírez, Gaspar. 2013. "Capriles y Maduro, frente a frente." *El Mercurio*, March 23.

Rasco, José Ignacio. 2012. *Acuerdos, Desacuerdos, y Recuerdos*. Miami: Ediciones Universal.

Rey, Juan Carlos. 2004. "La crisis de legitimidad en Venezuela y el enjuiciamiento y remoción de Carlos Andrés Pérez de la presidencia de la república." *Boletín Electoral Latinoamericano*: 67–112.

———. 1992. *La Democracia Venezolana y la Crisis del Sistema Populista de Conciliación*. Madrid: Centro de Estudios Constitucionales.

Ritter, Archibald R. M., and Ted A. Henken. 2014. *Entrepreneurial Cuba: The Changing Policy Landscape*. Boulder: Lynne Rienner.

Roca, Sergio. 1981. "Cuban Economic Policy in the 1970s: The Trodden Paths." In *Cuban Communism*, edited by Irving Louis Horowitz, 83–118. New Brunswick: Transaction.

Rodríguez, Andrea. 2014. "Cuban Doctors in Eye of Venezuelan Hurricane." *San Diego Union-Tribune*, April 15.

Rodríguez, José Conrado. 1995. "Cuando la patria peligra." *El Nuevo Herald*, March 25.

Rodríguez, Raúl. 2017. "Back to the Future: What Is New in Trump's New Cuba Policy?" Paper presented at the University of Michigan, School of Public Policy, October 19.

Rodríguez-Rosales, Dayron. 2018. "Nicolás Maduro: Aquí está el ALBA, con la bandera de Bolívar y Martí." *Granma*, 13 de Diciembre.

Rojas, Rafael. 2019. "La Odisea de los Derechos en Cuba." *Letras Libres* 249, no. 27 (septiembre): https://letraslibres.com/politica/la-odisea-de-los-derechos-en-cuba/.

———. 2012. *La Máquina del Olvido: Mito, Historia, y Poder en Cuba*. México: Taurus.

Romero, Carlos A. 2018. "Venezuela and Cuba." In *Cuban Foreign Policy Transformation under Raúl Castro*, edited by H. Michael Erisman and John M. Kirk, 209–24. Boulder: Rowman and Littlefield.

———. 2017. "Venezuela: ni paz ni pan." *Foreign Affairs Latinoamérica* 17, no. 3: 36–42.

———. 2016. "Fin de Fiesta." *El Universal*, 24 de enero.

———. 2011. "Cuba y Venezuela: La génesis y desarrollo de una utopía bilateral." In *Estados Unidos y América Latina Frente a los Desafíos Hemisféricos*, compiled by Luis Fernando Ayerbe. Barcelona: Icaria Editorial, 159–202.

———. 2009. "Venezuela y Cuba: una seguridad diferente." *Nuevo Mundo, Mundos Nuevos, Cuestiones del Tiempo Presente*. http://nuevomundo.revues.org/index55550.html.

———. 2006. *Jugando con el Globo: La Política Exterior de Hugo Chávez*. Caracas: Ediciones B.

———. 2004. "The United States and Venezuela: From a Special Relationship to Wary Neighbors." In *The Unraveling of Representative Democracy in Venezuela*, edited by Jennifer McCoy and David J. Myers, 130–51. Baltimore: John Hopkins University Press.

———. 1992. *Las Relaciones entre Venezuela y la Unión Soviética. Diplomacia o Revolución*. Caracas: Universidad Central de Venezuela, Consejo de Desarrollo Científico y Humanístico.

Romero, Carlos A., and Víctor Mijares. 2016. "From Chávez to Maduro: Continuity and Change in Venezuelan Foreign Policy." *Contexto Internacional* 38, no. 1: 191–227.

Romero, Carlos A., and Javier Corrales. 2010. "Relations between the United States and Venezuela, 2001–2009: A Bridge in Need of Repairs." In *Contemporary US-Latin American Relations: Cooperation or Conflict in the 21st Century*, edited by Jorge I. Domínguez and Rafael Férnandez de Castro, 218–46. New York: Routledge.

Romero, Carlos A., and Claudia Curiel. 2009. "Venezuela: Política Exterior y Rentismo." *Brazilian Journal of Latin American Studies* 8, no. 14: 39–61.

Ros, Enrique. 1995. *De Girón a la Crisis de los Cohetes: La Segunda Derrota*. Miami: Ediciones Universal.

———. 1994. *Girón: La Verdadera Historia*. Miami: Ediciones Universal.

Ross, Michael. 2011. "Does Oil Hinder Democracy?" *World Politics* 53, no. 3: 325–61.

Roy, Joaquín. 2000. *Cuba, the United States, and the Helms-Burton Doctrine: International Reactions*. Gainesville: University Press of Florida.

Sagás, Ernesto. 2003. "Cuba: U.S. Trade Embargo and Related Legislation." In *Encyclopedia of Cuba: People, History, Culture*, edited by Luis Martínez-Fernández, D. H. Figueredo, Louis A. Pérez Jr., and Luis González, 260–63. Westport: Greenwood.

Sanchez-R., Magaly. 2011. "Venezuelan Immigrants." In *Multicultural America: An Encyclopedia of the Newest Americans*, edited by Ronald H. Bayor, 2191–2227. Santa Barbara: ABC-CLIO.

Sanchez-R., Magaly, and Maria Aysa-Lastra. 2013. "Portrayals of Colombian and Venezuelan Immigrant Organizations in the United States." *Bulletin of Latin American Research* 32, no. 4: 451–67.

Schmitter, Philippe E., and Terry Lynn Karl. 1991. "What Democracy Is and Is Not." *Journal of Democracy* 2, no. 3: 75–88.

Schneider, William. 2001. "Elián González Defeated Al Gore." *Atlantic*, May 1. https://theatlantic.com/politics/archive/2001/05/elian-gonzalez-defeated-al-gore/377714/.
Schöllmann, Wilhelm. 2015. "Cuba's International Trade at a Glance." Brussels: European Parliamentary Research Service.
Schwirtz, Michael. 2009. "Chávez Throws in His Lot with Russia." *International Herald Tribune*, September 11.
Sen, Amartya. 2000. *Development as Freedom*. New York: Anchor.
Sewell, William H., Jr. 2010. "A Strange Career: The Historical Study of Economic Life." *History and Theory* 49 (December): 146–66.
———. 1985. "Ideologies and Social Revolutions: Reflections on the French Case." *Journal of Modern History* 57, no. 1: 57–85.
Shain, Yossi. 1989. *The Frontier of Loyalty: Political Exiles in the Age of the Nation State*. Middletown: Wesleyan University Press.
Shayne, Julie D. 2004. *The Revolution Question: Feminisms in El Salvador, Chile, and Cuba*. New Brunswick: Rutgers University Press.
Silva Michelena, José Agustín. 1967. *Exploraciones en Análisis y Síntesis*. Caracas: Universidad Central de Venezuela.
Skocpol, Theda. 1979. *States and Social Revolutions*. New York: Cambridge University Press.
Smilde, David. 2021. "From Populist to Socialist to Authoritarian Chavismo—Obstacles and Opportunities for Democratic Change." Venezuela Working Group, Latin American Program, Woodrow Wilson Center for Scholars, Washington, DC.
Smilde, David, and Daniel Hellinger. 2011. *Venezuela's Bolivarian Democracy: Participation, Politics, and Culture under Chávez*. Durham: Duke University Press.
Smith, Tony. 2000. *Foreign Attachments*. Cambridge: Harvard University Press.
Smith, Wayne. 1987. *The Closest of Enemies*. New York: W. W. Norton.
Solidaridad Sin Fronteras. 2019. *Comunicado Oficial–Barrio Afuera*, February 19.
Sonneland, Holly K. 2020. "Chart: How US Latinos Voted in the 2020 Presidential Election." *American Society/Council of the Americas* (AS/COA), November 5.
Spadoni, Paolo. 2019. "The Expansion of International Tourism in Cuba in the Post–Cold War Period." Paper presented at the 12th Conference on Cuban and Cuban American Studies, Cuban Research Institute, Florida International University, Miami, February 15.
Stinchcombe, Arthur L. 1999. "Ending Revolutions and Building New Governments." *Annual Review of Political Science* 2: 49–73.
Suárez-Salazar, Luis. 2009. *La cincuentenaria proyección externa de la revolución cubana: Nuestroamericanismo vs. Panamericanismo*. La Habana: Centro de Estudios sobre América. Manuscrito.
Sucre-Heredia, Ricardo. 2016. *Estructura Militar: Chávez-Maduro*. Caracas: Universidad Simón Bolívar. Manuscrito.
Taguieff, Pierre-André. 2007. *L'Illussion Populiste: Essai sur les Démagogies de l'Age Démocratique*. Paris: Editions Champs-Flammarion.
Tarrow, Sidney. 2018. "1968 as a 'Critical Juncture': Between Synoptic and Incremental

Change." In *Memory in Movements*, edited by Donatella della Porta, 3-18. Milan: Feltrinelli.

———. 2005. *The New Transnational Activism*. New York: Cambridge University Press.

———. 2001. "Transnational Politics: Contention and Institutions in International Politics." *Annual Review of Political Science* 4: 1-20.

Thomas, Hugh. 1971. *Cuba: The Pursuit of Freedom*. New York: Harper & Row.

Tilly, Charles, and Sidney Tarrow. 2015. *Contentious Politics*. New York: Oxford University Press.

Tilly, Charles. 1995. *European Revolutions, 1492-1992*. Malden: Blackwell.

———. 1981. *As Sociology Meets History*. New York: Academic Press.

———. 1978. *From Mobilization to Revolution*. Reading: Addison-Wellesley.

———. 1975. "Revolutions and Collective Action." In *Handbook of Political Science*, vol. 3, 483-555. Reading: Addison-Wesley.

Torres, María de los Ángeles. 2003. *The Lost Apple: Operation Pedro Pan, Cuban Children in the US, and the Promise of a Better Future*. Boston: Beacon.

Torres, Ricardo. 2020. *El rompecabezas económico cubano frente a la pandemia*. Nueva Sociedad, Mayo. http://nuso.org/edicion-digital?/page=7.

———. 2013. "Some Contradictions in Contemporary Cuban Economic Development." *Americas Quarterly* 7, no. 3: 32-37.

Torres-Cuevas, Eduardo. 2019. Personal communication.

Torres-Ramírez, Blanca. 1971. *Las Relaciones Cubano-Soviéticas: 1959-1968*. México: El Colegio de México.

Triay, Victor Andrés. 1998. *Fleeing Castro: Operation Pedro Pan and the Cuban Children's Program*. Gainesville: University of Florida Press.

Trimberger, E. Kay. 1978. *Revolution from Above: Military Bureaucrats and Development in Japan, Turkey, Egypt, and Peru*. New Brunswick: Transaction.

Trinkunas, Harold. 2004. "The Military: From Marginalization to Center Stage." In *The Unraveling of Representative Democracy in Venezuela*, edited by Jennifer McCoy and David J. Myers, 50-70. Baltimore: John Hopkins University Press.

Trotsky, Leon. 1992. *The History of the Russian Revolution*. Vol. 1. New York: Pathfinder.

United Nations Department of Social and Economic Affairs. 2019. *Global Migration Data Portal, Population Division*. https://www.un.org/en/development/desa/population/migration/data/index.asp.

United Nations High Commissioner for Refugees (UNHCR). 2020. "Venezuela Situation." https://www.unhcr.org/en-us/venezuela-emergency.html?query=Nuber%20of%20Venezuelan%20refugees.

United Press International. 2017. "Full Text of Trump's Speech to United Nations General Assembly," September 19.

US Census Bureau. 2020a. "US Trade in Goods with Cuba: 1992-2020." *US International Trade Data*. www.census.gov/foreign-trade/balance/c2390.html.

———. 2020b. "US Trade in Goods with Venezuela: 1992-2020." *US International Trade Data*. www.census.gov/foreign-trade/balance/c3070.html.

———. 2019. American Community Survey. "Hispanic or Latino Origin by Specific Origin." Table B03001. www.census.gov/bkmk/table/1.0/en/ACS/19_1YR/B03001.

———. 2000. "The Foreign-Born Population in the United States: March 1999." *Census 2000*, August 1. https://census.gov/library/publications/2000/demo/p20-519.html.

———. 1993. *Census 1990*. Public Use Microdata Samples, Public Data Queries, Ann Arbor, Michigan.

US Department of Agriculture, Foreign Agricultural Service. 2015. "U. S. Agricultural Exports to Cuba Have Substantial Room for Growth." *International Agricultural Trade Reports*, June 22.

US Embassy of Uruguay. 2015. "Secretary Kerry's Remarks at Flag Raising Ceremony," August 14. https://uy.usembassy.gov/secretary-kerrys-remarks-at-flag-raising-ceremony/.

Urreiztieta, María Teresa. 2013. "¿Emancipación o dominación? Subjetivación política y poder en la Venezuela del Siglo XXI." *Nuevo Mundo* 5, no. 11 (enero–abril): 124–54.

Valdés-Hernández, Dagoberto. 2014. *Ética y Cívica: Aprendiendo a Ser Persona y a Vivir en Sociedad*. Pinar del Río: Ediciones Convivencia.

———. 1997. *Reconstruir la Sociedad Civil: Un Proyecto de Educación Cívica, Pluralismo, y Participación para Cuba*. Caracas: Fundación Konrad Adenauer.

Valenta, Jiri, and Virginia Valenta. 1984. "Leninism in Grenada." *Problems of Communism* 33 (July–August): 1–23.

Valls, Jorge. 1991. *Filo, Contrafilo, y Punta*. Caracas: Saeta.

Van Rossem, Ronan, and Henk Roose. 2020. "The Victims Strike Back: Societal Transformations and Right-Wing Populist Attitudes in the EU." Paper presented at the Meeting of the American Sociological Association, August 11.

Veiga-González, Roberto. 2013. "Las FAR: Ante los retos de una nueva realidad nacional." *Espacio Laical* 224 (marzo). http://espaciolaical.org/contens/esp/sd_224.pdf.

Velasco, Alejandro. 2015. *Barrio Rising: Urban Popular Politics and the Making of Modern Venezuela*. Berkeley: University of California Press.

Velásquez, Efraín J. 2021. "Venezuela and Cuba's Crises: Political Control, Economics, and Social Welfare." Paper presented at the Meeting of the Association for the Study of the Cuban Economy (ASCE), January 6.

Vera, Leonardo. 2018. "¿Cómo explicar la catástrofe económica venezolana?" *Nueva Sociedad* 274 (marzo–abril): 83–96.

Vital, David. 1971. *The Inequality of States*. Oxford: Clarendon.

Volsky, George. 1971. "Cuba: Why Castro Put Up the 'No Exit' Sign." *New York Times*, September 5.

Walters, Barbara. 1977. "An Interview with Fidel Castro." *Foreign Policy*, September 15. https:// https://foreignpolicy.com/1977/09/15/an-interview-with-fidel-castro/.

Wassem, Ruth Ellen. 2007. "Cuban Migration to the United States: Policy and Trends." *Congressional Research Service*, Report 7–5700.

Weber, Max. 1978. *Economy and Society*. 2 vols. Edited by Guenther Roth and Claus Wittich. Berkeley: University of California Press.

Weyland, Kurt. 2013. "The Diffusion of Authoritarian Rule: An Analysis of Causal Mechanisms." Paper presented at the annual Meeting of the American Political Science Association (APSA), Chicago, Illinois, August 30.

———. 2003. "Economic Voting Reconsidered: Crisis and Charisma in the Election of Hugo Chávez." *Comparative Political Studies* 36, no. 7 (September): 822–48.

Wickham-Crowley, Timothy P. 2018. *Guerrillas and Revolution in Latin America: A Comparative Study of Insurgents and Regimes since 1956*. Princeton: Princeton University Press.

Wikipedia. 2017. "Revolution." https://en.wikipedia.org/wiki/Revolution.

Wilkinson, Tracy. 2019. "Trump Administration targets Cuba, Venezuela, and Nicaragua with new Sanctions." *Los Angeles Times*, April 19.

Winter, Bryan. 2018. "Luis Almagro: Venezuela Can't Become Another Rwanda." *Americas Quarterly*, September 20. https://www.americasquarterly.org/article/luis-almagro-venezuela-cant-become-another-rwanda.

Woldenberg, José. 2020. "México: la democracia a la defensiva." *Latin American Studies Association Forum* 51, no. 3: 37–44.

World Health Organization (WHO). 2021. *COVID-19 Data. Reported Cases and Deaths by Country*. https://covid19.who.int.

Wright, James D. 1976. *The Dissent of the Governed: Alienation and Democracy in America*. New York: Academic Press.

Wyden, Peter. 1979. *Bay of Pigs: The Untold Story*. New York: Simon & Schuster.

Zahler, Reuben. 2017. "Medium- and Short-Term Historical Causes of Venezuela's Crisis." *Latin American Studies Association Forum* 48, no. 4: 3–6.

Zeitlin, Maurice. 1966. "Political Generations in the Cuban Working Class." *American Journal of Sociology* 71: 493–508.

Zurbano, Roberto. 2013. "For Blacks in Cuba, the Revolution Hasn't Begun." *New York Times*, March 24.

Index

Page numbers in *italics* refer to illustrations

Acción Democrática (AD), Venezuela, 69–70; declining strength of, 81; US support of, 130
Afro-Cuban population, 31; Cuban Revolution support by, 38, 42; Cuba socialism impact on, 57; discrimination against, 38; in dissident movement, 224; Moore, Carlos, in exile, 54; "Patria y Vida" song of, 224–25; 2021 protests of, 221, 224; racial inequality movement, 222–23; remittances and racial inequality, 222, 223–24
Agrarian reform, Guevara, Ernesto Ché, and, 50, 52
Agrarian Reform Law, Castro, Fidel, 39
ALBA. *See* Bolivarian Alliance of the People
ALBA's People's Trade Treaty (ALBA-TCP), 158
Allende, Salvador, 119
Almagro, Luis, 241, 243
Amaro, Nelson, 34
Amaro, Nelson, and Alejandro Portes, 44, 47–48, 52, 56, 273
American Revolution, 3
ANC. *See* National Constituent Assembly
Angola: Cuba involvement with, 53–54, 107, 111, 119–20, 122; MPLA Cuba support, 107, 111, 119–20, 122; UNITA of, 53–54, 122
Angolan Civil War, 53–54, 122
Anti-Americanism, 4–5, 266; Cuban Revolution and, 42; of PSUV, 85
Arce, Luis, 243
Archivo Cuba (Cuba Archive), documentation of deaths and disappearances, 51
Asian-Cuban population, 31
los Auténticos. *See* Partido Revolucionario Cubano Auténtico
Authoritarianism: of Venezuelan regime from 2013 to present, 146; electoral oil, 81–82; in 1970s Latin America, 15; of Maduro, Nicolás, 97, 242; Venezuela gradual development of, 8

Baker Memorandum (1989), 112
Balseros, 1994 exodus from Cuba of, 56, 61–62, 185, *201*, 214, 225–26, 288. *See also* González, Elián
Barrio Adentro (Inside the Barrio) program, of Chávez, Hugo, *155*, 177, 179–81; COVID-19 and, 123; PDVSA payment for, 166; Cuban medical workers for Venezuela, 159
Barrio Afuera (Out of the Barrio), of Bush, George W., 165, 169, 178
Batista, Fulgencio, 19; Castro, Fidel, Castro, Raúl, and Guevara, Ernesto Ché, as rebels opposition to, 22; corruption of and repression by, 35, 39; 1952 coup d'état of, 22, 33–36; Cuban Revolution as political revolution against, 22, 33–34, 234, 273; Echeverría, José Antonio, opposition to, 22, 36; elite and middle class opposition to, 50–51; as PAU candidate, 35; 1940 presidential election of, 35; 1933 Revolt of the Sergeants and, 34; university students opposition to, 22, 36–37
Bay of Pigs invasion, 14, 19, 24, 27, 40–41; exile invasion of, 44, 46–47, 107, 200, 273; failure of, 46–47, 56, 264; Kennedy and, 46–47, 200
Benedict XVI (pope), 2012 visit to Cuba of, 227
Betancourt, Rómulo, 119, 129–30; confrontations with Cuba, 153; objection to Soviet Union relations, 135
Biden, Joe: Cuba humanitarian aid, 209; Cuban Americans vote, 192, 203; Cuba relations, 117, 229; Guaidó, Juan, recognition of, 19, 95, 132, 134, 245; Venezuela and, 97; Venezuela sanctions, 84–85, 94
Black Cubans. *See* Afro-Cuban population

Bolívar, Simón, 7, 91; Chávez, Hugo, on, 74, 77
Bolivarian Alliance of the People (ALBA), 83–84, 140, 155, 158, 243
Bolivarian Revolution (1999–present), 6–7; causes of, 68–73; conditions for, 26; Cuban Revolution as model for, 123; Cuban Revolution differences from, 19–20, 269–82; Cuban Revolution similarities to, 16–19, 262–69; Cuba support of, 154; economic crisis and, 87–89, 93–95; electoral politics means, 18; elite displacement, 19, 74, 79; exodus role in, 11, 12–13; first stage from 1999–2000 of, 74; future scenarios for, 253–55; geopolitical setting for, 11; multipolarity and, 20, 27; outcomes of, 84–87; populism in, 15; process of, 74–84; second stage from 2000–2004 of, 74–75; as socialist revolution, 10, 16–17, 68, 72; state bureaucracy control, 79; third stage from 2004 to present of, 75; US criticism of, 135; Venezuela present and future, 89–98
Bolivia: Guevara, Ernesto Ché, in, 53, 107–8; MAS and, 125, 252; Morales, Evo, in, 4
Bolivian Revolution (1952), 3
Bolsonaro, Jair, 4
Bonne-Carcasés, Félix, 235
Borges, Julio, 211
Boza-Masvidal, Eduardo (auxiliary bishop), 40; revolutionary state opposition, 45
Brazil: anti-Americanism of, 5; Bolsonaro, Jair, in, 4
Brezhnev, Leonid, 120
Bush, George H. W.: Cuba relations, 111–13; trade embargo retightening, 62, 111
Bush, George W., 84, 229; *Barrio Afuera* program, 165, 169, 178; Cuban Medical Parole Program of, 165; Cuban Americans vote, 189; Cuba trade and, 203
Buzón, Leandro, 80–81

Caldera, Rafael, 72
Camarioca exodus, Castro, Fidel, and, 55–56
Capriles, Henrique, 86
Caracas Mi Convive, Venezuela, 84; Buzón, Leandro, and Patiño, Roberto, founding of, 80–81
Caribbean: COVID-19 impact on, 96; Cuba interest in, 154; Cuba relations with, 272; political regimes studies, 15; Venezuela and US collaboration on, 130

CARICOM. *See* Community of Latin American and Caribbean States
Carter, Jimmy: Cuba Mariel exodus and, 59; Cuban Americans vote, 189; ban on Americans visiting Cuba lifted, 109
Castro, Cipriano, 128
Castro, Fidel, 4, 5, 6; proletarian internationalism for Africa, 53, 101; Agrarian Reform Law of, 39; anti-civil society totalitarianism, 37, 41; Batista opposition from, 22; Camarioca exodus and, 55–56; charisma and leadership abilities of, 15–16, 36, 264, 275–76; on Cuban economic crisis after Soviet Union collapse, 10, 18, 58, 162, 213–14, 218–19; Cuban Revolution as social revolution, 23; David or Goliath legacy, 233–35; death of, 25, 124, 233; Franqui, Carlos, on, 37; Guevara, Ernesto Ché, conflict with, 52; imprisonment of, 38; Mariel exodus and, 56; as Marxist-Leninist, 24, 46, 48, 121, 264; Mathews, Herbert L., meeting with, 36; Pazos, Felipe, and, 36; political help from trade embargo, 43; Rodríguez, José Conrado (priest), letter of criticism to, 225–26; Venezuela military coups support by, 153; Walters, Barbara, interview with, 110–11; on working class exodus, 28
Castro, Raúl, 4, 6, 7; totalitarianism, 37, 41; Batista opposition from, 22; Díaz-Canel, Miguel, choice of, 290–91; economic crisis recognition by, 245; economic reforms of, 25, 105, 124, 214–21, 268; Obama, Barack, relations with, 63–64, 105, 116, 229; trade embargo economic blame, 55
Catholic Church: Boza-Masvidal, Eduardo (auxiliary bishop), 40, 45; García-Rodríguez, Juan de la Caridad (cardinal), on Cuban suffering, 236–37; Castro, Raúl, meeting with, 219; Cuban Revolution opposition to, 40, 275; Cuban Revolution silencing of, 19, 41; Cuban Revolution support by, 38–39; Pérez-Serantes, Enrique, as archbishop of, 38–39, 45; Pope Benedict XVI's 2012 visit to Cuba, 227; Pope Francis I's 2016 visit to Cuba, 227–28; Pope John Paul II's 1998 visit to Cuba, 227, 228; revolutionary state division, 45; Rodríguez, José Conrado (priest), letter to Castro, Fidel, 225–26
CCD. *See* Committee for Cuban Democracy

CDR. *See* Committees for the Defense of the Revolution
Central America, Cuba exodus through, 63–67, 185, 226
Central Intelligence Agency (CIA), US, Cuban counterrevolution help from, 41, 46–47
CEPAL. *See* Comisión Económica para América Latina y el Caribe
de Céspedes-Quesada, Carlos Manuel, 34
Chávez, Hugo, 6, 7; anti-imperialism and, 84; authoritarian regime from 2013 to present of, 146; on Bolívar, Simón, 74, 77; brinksmanship use of, 132; charisma and leadership abilities of, 15–16, 72–73, 264; communal power plan of, 81; constitutional reform of, 18; on Cuba–Venezuela alliance, 17; death of, 25, 68, 84, 86, 239; development projects of, 12; 1998 election victory of, 68, 72, 73, 145; 2012 election victory of, 79; failed coup against, 75, 272; Fifth Republic Movement of, 72, 74; foreign policy, 125–26; on Fourth and Fifth Republic periods, 74; geopolitical commitments with China and Russia, 12; on indefinite presidential power, 75–76, 85; international activism of, 141; Left-wing populism of, 4; opposition to, 73–74, 80, 240–41; socialism program of, 75, 77–78; socialism reforms of, 239; socialism through electoral system of, 68, 72, 264; social missions of, 77, 81; Soviet Union agreements, 136; superpowers independence, 11; US confrontations by, 131–32; Venezuela petrostate under, 12
China: Chávez, Hugo, geopolitical commitments with, 12; Cuba trade with, 103
Chinese Revolution (1949), 23; Marxism-Leninism and, 3, 19, 24
CIA. *See* Central Intelligence Agency
el CID. *See* Cuba Independiente y Democrática
CITGO, Venezuela, 134, 140, 246, 248
Clinton, Bill, 106; Cuba relations, 112; remittances to Cuba, 206; on trade embargo, 62–63; "wet foot/dry foot" policy, 62, 63, 112, 226, 289
Clinton, Hillary, 192, 203
CMPP. *See* Cuban Medical Parole Program
Cold War: Cuban foreign policy and, 101; Cuban Revolution and, 20, 27, 40, 62, 264–65
Colombia: Guaidó, Juan, provisional government support for, 148; Venezuelan exodus to, 13, 148, 244, 269; Venezuelan opposition support, 148
COMECON. *See* Council for Mutual Economic Assistance
Comisión Económica para América Latina y el Caribe (CEPAL), 87, 256
Comité de Organización Política Independiente (COPEI), Venezuelan political party, 69–70; declining strength of, 81; US support of, 130
Committee for Cuban Democracy (CCD), 195
Committees for the Defense of the Revolution (CDR), Cuba, 172, 173
Comunas, communal power plan of Chávez, Hugo, 81
Communist Party of Venezuela (PCV), 129
Community of Latin American and Caribbean States (CARICOM), 105, 243, 255
Comparative historical method, 9; Moore, Barrington, Jr., on, 6
Constitution (1940), Cuban, 35, 37, 271
Constitution (1961), Venezuelan, 271
Constitution (1976), Cuban, 24, 49, 271
Constitution (1999), Venezuelan, 75–76, 85, 271
Constitution (2019), Cuban, 218, 271
Cooperation Agreement (2000), of Cuban health personnel for Venezuelan oil, 8, 9, 78, 123, *129*, *155*, 155–56, 158–59, 228, 255
COPEI. *See* Comité de Organización Política Independiente
Correa, Rafael, 4
Costa Rica, Cuba exodus to, 12
Council for Mutual Economic Assistance (COMECON), Cuba partner with, 54, 60
Counterrevolution, Cuba, 48, 56–57; CIA help to, 41, 46–47; Escambray Mountains, 8, 34, 49, 51; government crushing of, 58; MRP, MRR, MDC in, 41–42
Coups d'état: of Batista, Fulgencio, 22, 33–36; Castro, Fidel, support of Venezuelan military, 153; against Chávez, Hugo, failed, 75, 272; revolutions compared to, 23; Venezuelan military, 92–93, 153
COVID-19 pandemic: *Barrio Adentro* of Chávez, Hugo, and, 123; Cuban economic crisis and, 221; Cuba impacted by, 66, 127, 162, 189, 221, 237, *267*, 279, 291; Cuba vaccine manufacturing, 162; Latin America and Caribbean impacted by, 96; tourism in

COVID-19 pandemic—*continued*
  Cuba impacted by, 207, 216, 230–31; trade in Venezuela impacted by, 88; US impacted by, 291; Venezuelan economic crisis and, 238–39; Venezuelan exodus and, 210; Venezuela impacted by, 88, 127, 238, 239, 249
Cuba: agricultural sector in, 4; anti-Americanism of, 5; birth and death rate, 32; from capitalism to socialism, 29, 49; as Caribbean nation, 4; de Céspedes-Quesada, Carlos Manuel, provisional government of, 34; COMECON partner with, 54, 60; Constitution of 1940, 35, 37; Constitution of 1976, 24; COVID-19 impact on, 66, 127, 162–63, 189, 221, 237, 267, 279, 291; democratic system future for, 293–94; developing countries assistance, 122–23; Díaz-Canel, Miguel, as president of, 66; dissident movement in, 60–61, 219, 224, 235–36, 288–89; economic and political crises, 213; economic decline in, 20, 66; economy dependency in, 25; economy of, 277–80; equity and social inclusion in, 258–59; FAR armed forces in, 91; full state control by1968–69, 8; health care in, 160–63; history and culture collage, *30*; human and natural resources in, 258; industrial sector in, 4; Internet industry and, 260; massive protests of 2021, 208–9, 221, 224; OAS expulsion of, 54, 105; Obama, Barack, visit to, 195, 206, 207; Ochoa, Arnaldo, of, 122; ONEI on, 64–65; political crisis and political legitimacy, 232–37; political parties in, 35; pope visits to, 226–28; Prío-Socarrás, Carlos, as first president of independent, 22; proletarian internationalism, 53–54, 101, 120–22; social transformations in, 7–8; Spain colonization of, 29, 31; Spain migration to, 31; Spain's colonization of, 29, 31; statistics on, 29, 31–32; sugar production, 31–32, 54, 66, 103, 107, 117; Trump, Donald, relations with, 115, 229, 279
Cuba Independiente y Democrática (el CID), 166, 194
Cuban Adjustment Act (1966), US, 57, 124
Cuban Americans, *199*, 208–12; age and generations of, 197; Biden, Joe, vote, 192, 203; Bush, George W., vote, 189; Carter, Jimmy, vote, 189; Clinton, Hillary, vote, 192, 203; Cuban Adjustment Act, 57; cultural practices, *114*; demographic and cultural weight of recent immigrants, 64; demographic shift in, 188; elected and appointed officials, 184–85; exile political organizations, 193–97; exiles betrayal, 200–204; impossible triangle of, *198*, 198–99; impossible triangle war, 204–9; Kunz, E. F., on "vintages" of, 185–86; Mariel exodus, 56, 59–61, 110, 185; waves of migration, 185–86; naturalization rate, 192; "new" Cubans from 1989–2020 exodus, 187, 196; "new" Cubans low political organizations engagement, 196–97; Obama, Barack, vote, 189, 192; "old" Cubans from 1959–1973 exodus, 186–87, 196, 197; party identification, 189; polls on, 186, 187–88; presidential election vote, 191–92; Reagan, Ronald, vote, 189; remittances to Cuba, 64, 191, 197, 207; "special period" of Castro, Fidel, 187; on trade embargo, 188–89; transnationalism, 190–91; Trump, Donald, vote, 189, 192–93, 203–4; voting patterns of, 9, 191–93
Cuban Americans political organizations: *los intransigentes*, 194–95; *los moderados*, 194, 195
Cuban Democracy Act (1992) (Torricelli Act), US, 62, 112
Cuban Economic Research Project, 29
Cuban Medical Parole Program (CMPP), of Bush, George W., 165
Cuban Missile Crisis (October 1962), 11, 44, 48–49, 107, 118, 153, 265, 273
Cuban Refugee Program, US, 48, 55, 58–59
Cuban Revolution (1959), 6; Afro-Cuban population support of, 38, 42; Bolivarian Revolution differences from, 19–20, 269–82; Bolivarian Revolution similarities to, 16–19, 262–69; Catholic Church silenced, 19, 41; causes of, 26, 29–34; Cold War and, 20, 27, 40, 62, 264–65; democracy stage in, 34, 36–39; dissent externalized by, 27–28; electoral system and independent press vanquished, 19; elite displacement, 19, 39, 44; ending of, 23–24; Franqui, Carlos, on, 37; future scenarios for, 253–55; gender inequality challenged by, 42; geopolitical setting for, 11; health and education services expansion, 14, 161; humanism stage in, 34, 39–40; internal conflicts, 52–53; against internal

enemies, 48–49; international allies, 25, 32–33; Marxism-Leninism origin, 3, 19, 24; Marxism-Leninism stage in, 34, 47–48; media control, 41; military tribunals and executions, 39–40; nationalism stage in, 34, 40–43; old communists' organization in, 52; opposition from Catholic Church, 40, 275; ORI power, 52; outcomes in first 15 years, 48–51; political causes of, 36–37; Cuban Revolution as political revolution against Batista, 22, 33–34, 234, 273; population support for, 32–33; populism in, 15; private schools nationalized, 45; process of, 34–43; radical Cuban Americans support of, 194; social and economic causes of, 37–38; social changes from, 50; socialism stage in, 34; as socialist revolution, 10, 16–17; as social revolution, 23, 33–34; support of Catholic Church, 38–39

Cuban Spring protests (2003), 219, 289

Cuba-Soviet and Russian relations: after Brezhnev, Leonid, death, 120; communist integration, 118; Cuba Third World militant role, 120–21; Gorbachev, Mikhail, and, 120; ideological conflict from 1963–1969, 118; Khrushchev, Nikita, defense commitment, 117–18; remittances to Cuba, 102; Soviet international diplomatic relations, 118–19; Soviet Union alliance, 4–5, 40, 42, 54, 60, 101, 102–3, 264–65; Soviet Union collapse, 4, 10, 18, 58, 103, 121–22

Cuba-US relations, 8, *217*; Biden, Joe, and, 117, 229; Biden, Joe, humanitarian aid, 209; bilateral agreement of 1973, 109; Bush, George H. W., and, 62, 111–13; Bush, George W., and, 84, 165, 169, 178, 189, 203, 229; Clinton, Bill, and, 112, 200, 202–3; Cuba and US premises, 116; current standstill, 116–17; diplomatic relations in 2013, 123; *los intransigentes* opposition to normalization of, 194; *los moderados* normalization approval, 195; Obama, Barack, re-establishment of diplomatic relations, 113–15, 189, 228–31, 279; opening up from 1970 on, 109–10; Platt Amendment and, 117; Reagan, Ronald, anticommunism and, 110, 119; stages, 106–7; trade relations, 259–60; Trump, Donald, sanctions, 115, 117, 206, 216, 229–31, 279, 291; US diplomatic and economic war, 40; US economic dependence, 38; US presence in Cuban history, 117; US spy penetration program, 111. *See also* Bay of Pigs invasion; Cuban Missile Crisis; trade embargo

Cuba-Venezuela alliance, 104–5, *115*, 228, 255–61, 266–67; ALBA and, 83–84, 140, 155, 158, 243; anti-American foreign policy, 141, 156; Betancourt, Rómulo, confrontations with Cuba, 153; both economic immigrants and refugees interviews, 179–83; Castro, Fidel, military coups support, 153; Chávez, Hugo, and Castro, Fidel, relationship, 17, 153–54; collaboration projects, 157–58; contemporary, 121–27; COVID-19 help in Venezuela, 159; Cuban economic crisis and, 214, 216–17; Cuban health care, 160–63; Díaz-Canel, Miguel, support, 157; diplomatic and trade relations in 1970s, 153; economic support, 214, 216–17; Maduro, Nicolás, on, 17–18, 124, 158; Obama, Barack, and, 126; on socialism as positive model, 18; "special period" of Castro, Fidel, and, 267; stages of, 154–56; two nations relations, 153–58; Venezuela illicit trade, 101. *See also* Cooperation Agreement; *interviews of participants*

Las Damas de Blanco (The Ladies in White) dissidents, 219, 235–36, 289

Democracy: Castro, Fidel, on Cuban Revolution as, 41; Cuban Revolution stage of, 34, 36–39; Cuban university students and, 34; parliamentary democracy model, French Revolution, 49; delegative democracy, 15, 76; future for Cuba and Venezuela, 293–94; Latin America in 1980s and early 1990s, 15; Maduro, Nicolás, opposition to, 95–96; representative democracy, 15; electoral democracy, 25; in Venezuela 1959–1999, 11, 69, 128–29; in Venezuela 1999–2013, 146; participatory democracy, Venezuelan Revolution, 131

Díaz-Canel, Miguel, 66, 218; Castro, R., choice of, 290–91; protest against, *268*; protests harsh response from, 230, 290; Venezuela support of, 157

Directorio Revolucionario Estudiantil (DRE), 22, 48; Escambray mountains and, 36; Presidential Palace attack, 36

326 · Index

Dissident movement, Cuba, 60–61, 288; Afro-Cuban population in, 224. *See also* Tercera Opción; Las Damas de Blanco; UNPACU; La Patria es de Todos; Movimiento Cristiano Liberación; Proyecto Varela

DRE. *See* Directorio Revolucionario Estudiantil

Echeverría, José Antonio: Batista, Fulgencio, opposition to, 22, 36; death of, 22, 36; of FEU and DRE, 22

Economic crisis, Cuba: Castro, Raúl, economic reforms, 25, 105, 124, 214–21, 245, 268; COVID-19 impact on, 221; Cuba-Venezuela alliance and, 214, 216–17; recentralization of economy, 214; market socialism model for, 218; in 1991–1998, 14, 104; reform and, 213–21; self-employed sector support, 220; after Soviet Union collapse, 10, 18, 58, 162, 213–14, 218–19; "special period" of Castro, Fidel, and, 18, 20, 104, 154, 162, 213, 225; state-owned land distribution, 14, 216–21

Economic crisis, Venezuela: Bolivarian Revolution and, 87–89, 93–95; COVID-19 and, 238–39; economy collapse, 213; foreign trade decline, 88; government mismanagement, 88; hyperinflation, 238, 239; oil revenues decline, 70–71, 76, 79, 236, 238, 247–48, 278; reasons for, 239; Trump, Donald, economic sanctions and, 238–39

Economy, Cuba, 277–78; dependence on remittances, 65, 208, 216, 256, 268, 270, 279–80, 290; dependency of, 25; foreign trade dependence, 103; recentralization, 214

Economy, Venezuela, 277–78, 281–82; collapse of, 213; criminal, 253; international market and, 80

Ecuador: Correa, Rafael, in, 4; Cuban exodus through, 63–67, 185, 226

Eisenhower, Dwight D., 54

Elites: Batista opposition from, 50–51; Bolivarian Revolution displacement of, 19, 74, 79; Cuban first wave exodus of, 44–55, *108*, 185; Cuban Revolution displacement of, 19, 39, 44

Encuesta Nacional de Condiciones de Vida (ENCOVI) survey, Venezuela, 251

Escalante, Aníbal, 52

Escambray mountains: Cuba counterrevolution, 8, 34, 49, 51; DRE and, 36; Guevara and, 36

Escobar, Reinaldo, 236

Exile community, Cuba: Bay of Pigs invasion of, 44, 46–47, 107, 200, 273; communism rejection, 204–5; Cuba and US relationship with, 8, 110; Cuban Americans betrayal, 200–204; Cuban Americans political organizations, 193–97; of elite social class, 44; on human rights violations, 204; Obama, Barack close relations with, 8; trade embargo support by, 204; Trump, Donald, betrayal of, 8; US size and role of, 230

Exile community, Venezuela, 8–9; demographics of, 209–10; Guaidó, Juan, representative in, 210–11; politics, 211; Temporary Protected Status (TPS) protection of, 210; Trump, Donald, and, 211–12; US areas of concentration, 210–11; voting patterns, 212

Exit-Voice relationships, 282; Exit and Voice increase in tandem, 286–92; those who Exited becoming Voice, 284–286; massive Exit impeded use of Voice, 283–84

Exodus: importance in revolution, 12–13; UN Department of Economic and Social and Affairs on, 13

Exodus, Cuba, 11, 13, 43–44, 161, 269, 280–81; of *balseros* in 1994, 56, 61–62, 185, *201*, 214, 225–26, 288; Camarioca exodus, Castro, Fidel, and, 55–56; Castro, Fidel, on working-class, 28; continuation of, 225–26; Cuba massive, 14, 20, 27, 225, 230; through Ecuador and Central America, 63–67, 185, 226; embargo and continuation of, 58–59; first wave from 1960–1964 of elite and professionals, 44–55, *108*, 185; third wave from Mariel harbor, 56, 59–61, 110, 185; middle-class, 47, 57; "new" Cubans from 1989–2020, 187, 196–97; from 1976–1999, 58–59; "old" Cubans from 1959–1973, 186–87, 196, 197; population decline from, 256; "push" and "pull" in, 57, 257–58; racial inequality in, 221, 223; regulation of, 112; Reno, Janet (attorney general), on 1994 rafters as illegal aliens, 61–62; second wave from 1965–1974 of petite bourgeoisie, 55–58, 185; "special period" massive, 225, 230; UMAP camps and, 56; to US, Spain, Puerto

Rico and Costa Rica, 12; "wet foot/dry foot" policy of Clinton, Bill, 62, 63, 112, 226, 289
Exodus, Venezuela, 11, 281; to Colombia, 13, 148, 244, 269; COVID-19 pandemic and, 210; Cuban doctors leaving Venezuela interviews, 163–68; growth in, 12–13; as humanitarian crisis, 27, 213, 244; from Venezuela massive under Maduro, Nicolás, 12–14, 20, 27, 88–89, 96, 147–48, 240

FANB. *See* Fuerza Armada Nacional Bolivariana
FAR. *See* Fuerzas Armadas Revolucionarias
FARC. *See* Fuerzas Armadas Revolucionarias de Colombia
Fariñas, Guillermo, 236
Federación de Mujeres Cubanas (FMC), Espín, Vilma, as leader of, 42
Federación Estudiantil Universitaria (FEU), 22
Ferrer, José Daniel, 61, 205
FEU. *See* Federación Estudiantil Universitaria
Fifth Republic (1999 to present), Venezuela, 74
Fifth Republic Movement. *See* Movimiento Quinta República
First Congress of Cuba's Communist Party (1975), 49
First Provisional Government members, resignation of, 40
First stage (1999-2000), of Bolivarian Revolution: Chávez presidential term beginning, 74; Constitution of 1999 and, 74; presidential election of 2000, 74
FMC. *See* Federación de Mujeres Cubanas
Foreign policy, Cuba, 120–27, 156; China trade, 103; Cold War and, 101; economy and foreign trade dependence, 103; direct investment of foreign tourism, 103–4; foreign direct investment, 103–4, 214; formal objectives and goals of, 101–6; global Leftist movement, 101, 104–5; international relations through oil, 140–41; Latin American relations, 104, 107, 111, 118–19, 154, 272; oil role in, 142; proletarian internationalism for Africa, 101, 120–22; sugar production and, 31–32, 54, 66, 103, 107, 117. *See also* Cuba-Soviet and Russian relations; Cuba-US relations; Cuba-Venezuela alliance
Foreign policy, Venezuela, 71, 78, 84, 129–49; anti-American alliance, 141, 156; of Chávez, Hugo, 125–26; environment of, 140–49; of Maduro, Nicolás, 141–42; old and new goals of, 128–30. *See also* Venezuela-Soviet relations; Venezuela-US relations
14yMedio independent journalism of Sánchez, Yoani, and Escobar, Reinaldo, 236
Fourth Republic (1959-1999), Venezuela, 74
Francis I (pope), 2016 visit to Cuba, 227–28
Franqui, Carlos, 37, 47
French Revolution (1789), 16, 23; Enlightenment principles of, 3; ideological transformation in, 33, 45–46; nationalism and, 3, 41; parliamentary democracy model, 49; revolution defined by, 20–21; theology of, 21
Fuerza Armada Nacional Bolivariana (FANB), 251
Fuerzas Armadas Revolucionarias (FAR), Cuba, 91
Fuerzas Armadas Revolucionarias de Colombia (FARC), Cuba peace agreement help, 123

GAESA. *See* Grupo de Administración Empresarial, S.A.
García-Rodríguez, Juan de la Caridad (cardinal), 236–37
Generations, political, 232–33
Geopolitics: Bolivarian Revolution setting of, 11; of Chávez with China and Russia, 12; Cuban Revolution setting of, 11; revolutions and international setting of, 28; US and Soviet Union nuclear competition link to, 11
Gómez, Juan Vicente, 11, 91–92; Venezuela military leadership of, 128
Gómez-Manzano, René, 235
González, Elián: Bush, George W., election after, 203; Clinton, Bill, and, 112, 200, 202–3; Cuba-US trade after case of, 105–6; dramatic case of, 112, 201–2
Gorbachev, Mikhail, 120
Grupo de Administración Empresarial, S.A. (GAESA), 206, 229, 271
Guaidó, Juan, 146, *246*; provisional government recognition, 19, 95, 132, 134, 147–48, 247, 252; R2P call from, 96; Trump, Donald, and Biden, Joe, recognition of, 19, 95, 132, 134, 245; Venezuela exile community representative, 210–11

Guevara, Ernesto Ché, 118; agrarian reform of, 50, 52; totalitarianism, 37, 41; Batista, Fulgencio, opposition from, 22; in Bolivia, 53, 107–8; Castro, Fidel, conflict with, 52; death of, 53, 108; Escambray mountains and, 36; proletarian internationalism of, 53

Health: Cooperation Agreement between Cuba and Venezuela, 8, 9, 78, 123, *129*, *155*, 155–56, 158–59, 228, 255; Cuban health care, 160–63; Cuban Revolution expansion of services in, 14, 161; Venezuelan crisis in, 249–50
Helms-Burton Act (1996), US, 112–13, 154, 204; Clinton, Bill, and, 62–63; *los intransigentes* on continuation of, 195; Trump, Donald, and, 63
"History Will Absolve Me," Castro, Fidel, speech, 38
Humanism, Cuban Revolution stage of, Castro, Fidel, on, 34, 39–40
Humanitarian crisis, of Venezuelan exodus, 27, 213, 244
Human rights violations: Cuba exile community on, 204; Maduro, Nicolás, and, 26, 27, 241, 244
Hyperinflation, in Venezuela, 238, 239

ICC. *See* International Criminal Court
Ideology: of Cuban and Bolivarian Revolutions, 263; of Cuba and Soviet/Russian conflict 1963–1969, 118; French Revolution transformation, 33, 45–46; revolutions shaped by, 21–22; Venezuelan adoption of Cuba, 85
IMF. *See* International Monetary Fund
Immigration Law, 302; US and Cuban travel, 113
Impossible triangle, *198*, 198–99, 204–9
Inequality, Cuba: Afro-Cuban movement against, 222–23; in Afro-Cubans remittances, 222, 223–24; city and countryside, 32; social class and race, 221–25; exodus racial, 221, 223; extreme social, 37–38; in housing, 223; pre-Revolution social class, 4, 37–38; racial inequality in 1990s, 222; racial inequality in tourism, 222, 223–24; racial inequality in remittances, 221–22;

racial inequality in university system, 223; women challenge to Cuban Revolution, 42
Inequality, Venezuelan rise in, 239–43
INRA. *See* Instituto Nacional de Reforma Agraria
Inside the Barrio. *See* Barrio Adentro
Instituto Nacional de Reforma Agraria (INRA), Guevara, Ernesto Ché, and, 52
Integrated Revolutionary Organizations (ORI), Cuba; Escalante, Aníbal, as founding member of, 52
Inter-American Treaty of Reciprocal Assistance (TIAR), Venezuela and, 95
International Criminal Court (ICC), Maduro investigation by, 243
International Monetary Fund (IMF), 238
Interview of Castro, Fidel, by Walters, Barbara, 110–11
Interviews of Cuban doctors and health personnel who left Venezuela as economic immigrants and refugees, 163–69, 179–83
Interviews of participants: Franqui, Carlos, 37, 47; Rexach, Rosario, 38; Esteve, Himilce, 38; Pazos, Felipe, 38; Peláez, Rafael (pseudonym), 39, 50; Rasco, José Ignacio, 35, 40, 47, 195, 205; Valls, Jorge, 41, 45; Buzón, Leandro, 80–81; Enriquez, Odelaisys, 168–69; Rivery, Isaac, 169–71; Vargas, Frank, 171–74; Rojas-Elías, Elizabeth, 174–76; Sánchez, Otto, 177–78; Lubián, Julio César, 178–81; Jiménez, Miguel, 181–83; Vargas-Gómez, Andrés, 205; Marquez, Eliexer, "el Funky," 209; Cifuentes, René, 276
los intransigentes Cuban Americans political organizations: Cuba-US normalization relations opposition, 194; on Obama, Barack, visit to Cuba, 195, 206; political transnationalism, 205; Republican Party and, 194; on trade embargo continuation, 195; Trump, Donald, and, 206–7
Iranian Revolution (1979), 23

John Paul II (pope), 1998 visit to Cuba, 227, 228
Johnson, Lyndon B., 55, 61–62

Kennedy, John F.: Bay of Pigs and, 46–47, 200; Cuban Missile Crisis and, 11, 48–49, 118
Khrushchev, Nikita: Cuba defense

commitment, 117–18; Cuban Missile Crisis and, 11, 48, 118
Kunz, E. F., 185–86

The Ladies in White. *See* Las Damas de Blanco
Latin America: authoritarianism in 1970s, 15; COVID-19 impact on, 96; Cuban foreign relations, 104, 107, 111, 112, 118–19, 154, 272; democratic optimism in 1980s and early 1990s, 15; political regimes studies, 15; populism in politics of, 3; US response to nationalism in, 5; Venezuela and US collaboration on, 130
Legitimacy, political: contingent and performance, 73, 78; Cuban political crisis and political, 232–37; Venezuelan political crisis and, 246–53
Leoni, Raúl, 119, 129–30
Lepage, Octavio, 72
Lima Group, 95, 96, 144, 146; Maduro, Nicolás, criticism by, 243, 246
López, Leopoldo, 146
Lula da Silva, Luiz Inácio, 5
Lyceum, women founding of, 38

Maduro, Nicolás, 6, *240*; antidemocratic political reforms of, 26; authoritarianism of, 97, 242; brinksmanship use of, 132; claimed election victory of 2018, 242, 246; on Cuba-Venezuela alliance, 17–18; democratic opposition to, 95–96; election victory of 2013, 86; failed economic policies, 27, 239–40; foreign policy of, 141–42; government not recognized, 19; human rights violations, 27, 241, 244; ICC formal investigation of, 243; Lima Group criticism of, 243, 246; OAS criticism of, 241, 243; opposition to, 18, 96–97, 240; insurrection against, 146–47; socialism through electoral system of, 68; superpowers independence, 11; UN Human Rights Council criticism, 244; Venezuela massive exodus under, 12–14, 20, 27, 88–89, 96, 147–48, 240; violence and repression of, 126
M.A.R. *See* Mothers Against Repression
Mariel exodus, Cuba, 61, 185; Carter, Jimmy, and, 59; Castro, Fidel, and, 56; Cuban Americans return to Cuba allowed, 59, 110;
Cubans in prison and, 59–60, 110; political prisoners, 60
Marxism-Leninism: Castro, Fidel, following of, 24, 46, 48, 121, 264; Chinese, Cuban Revolution and, 3, 19, 24; Cuban Revolution stage of, 34, 47–48; Cuban society basis, 58; Russian and Cuban Revolution origins in, 3
MAS. *See* Movement for Socialism, Bolivia
Mathews, Herbert L., 36
Matos, Huber, 40
MCL. *See* Movimiento Cristiano Liberación
MDC. *See* Movimiento Demócrata Cristiano
Media: Cuban government control of, 41; Venezuela conflict with, 242–43; Venezuela politics reliance on, 78
Mesa de la Unidad Democrática (MUD), 19, 140, 240–41, 273
Mexican Revolution (1911), 3
Migration: Cuban Americans waves of, 185–86; lack of political and civil freedom influence on, 14; "push" and "pull" theory, 57, 257–58; Spain to Cuba, 31; unfreedoms driving migration, 13–14
Military, Cuba, 270–71. *See also* GAESA
Military, Venezuela: coups of, 92–93, 153; political role of, 89–93, 270–71
Ministry of Tourism (MINTUR), Cuba, 229
MIR. *See* Movimiento de Izquierda Revolucionaria
los moderados (Cuban Americans political organizations): Cuba-US relations normalization approval, 195; Democratic Party and, 195; on Obama, Barack, visit to Cuba support, 195, 207; political transnationalism, 205; on trade embargo end, 195
Moore, Barrington, Jr., 6
Moore, Carlos, 54
Morales, Evo, 4, 125
Mothers Against Repression (M.A.R.), 194, 202
Movement for Socialism (MAS), Bolivia, 125, 252
Movimiento Cristiano Liberación (MCL), Cuba, 61; Payá, Oswaldo, founder of, 205, 235
Movimiento de Izquierda Revolucionaria (MIR), Venezuela, 129
Movimiento Demócrata Cristiano (MDC), Cuba, 37; counterrevolution, 42; Rasco, José Ignacio founder of, 40

Movimiento Quinta República (MVR) (Fifth Republic Movement), of Chávez, Hugo, 72, 271; PSUV from, 85
Movimiento Revolucionario del Pueblo (MRP), Cuba, 37; counterrevolution, 42
Movimiento Revolucionario de Recuperación (MRR), Cuba counterrevolution, 42
Movimiento San Isidro, 2020 protest, Cuba, 236, 289
MPLA. *See* People's Movement for the Liberation of Angola
MRP. *See* Movimiento Revolucionario del Pueblo
MRR. *See* Movimiento Revolucionario de Recuperación
MUD. *See* Mesa de la Unidad Democrática
MVR. *See* Movimiento Quinta República

National Constituent Assembly (ANC), Venezuela, 143–44, 241–42, 272
Nationalism: in American Revolution, 3; Cuban Revolution stage of, 34, 40–43; Cuban elite impacted by, 41; in French Revolution, 3, 41; populism and, 4; US response to Latin America, 5
National Union for the Total Independence of Angola (UNITA), 53–54, 122
The Nation Belongs to All. *See* La Patria es de Todos
"New" Cubans (Cuban American immigrants from 1989–2020), 187, 196–97
NGOs. *See* nongovernmental organizations
Nicaraguan Revolution, 10
Nongovernmental organizations (NGOs), 12, 135, 141, 144, 190, 210, 273
Nuclear competition of US and Soviet Union, geopolitics link to, 11

OAS. *See* Organization of American States
Obama, Barack, 62; Castro, Raúl, relations with, 63–64, 105, 116, 229; Cuba re-establishment of diplomatic relations, 113–15, 189, 228–31, 279; Cuban Americans vote, 189, 192; Cuba trade and, 203; Cuba-Venezuela alliance and, 126; visit to Cuba, 195, 206, 207; remittances, 113; "wet foot/dry foot" policy removal, 62, 63, 226, 289
Ochoa, Arnaldo, 122

Oficina Nacional de Estadísticas e Información (ONEI), Cuba, 64–65
Oil production, Venezuela, 25; CITGO and, 134, 140, 246, 248; Cooperation Agreement and, 8, 9, 78, 123, *129*, *155*, 155–56, 158–59, 228, 255; economic prosperity from, 69–70; and electoral oil authoritarianism, 81–82; international presence from, 84–85; PDVSA and nationalization of, 70; revenues decline of, 70–71, 76, 79, 238, 247–48, 278; revenues increase from 2001–2012 of, 76; and trade with US, 8, 11, 20, 128, 134; and world crude oil prices, 76, *76*, *77*, 78, 80
OLAS. *See* Organization of Latin American Solidarity
"Old" Cubans (Cuban American immigrants from 1959–1973) exodus, 186–87, 196, 197
ONEI. *See* Oficina Nacional de Estadísticas e Información
OPEC. *See* Organization of the Petroleum Exporting Countries
Operation Pedro Pan, Cuba, 45
Organization of American States (OAS), 75; Cuba expulsion from, 54, 105, 107, 109; economic sanctions against Cuba lifted in 1975, 109; Maduro, Nicolás, criticism by, 241; trade embargo and, 55
Organization of Latin American Solidarity (OLAS), 107
Organization of the Petroleum Exporting Countries (OPEC), 83, 130
ORI. *See* Integrated Revolutionary Organizations
Orinoco Oil Belt, Venezuela, 84–85
Ortega, Daniel, 243
Ortega, Roberto, 122
Ortega-Alamino, Jaime (cardinal), 56, 219
los Ortodoxos. *See* Partido del Pueblo Cubano Ortodoxo
Out of the Barrio. *See* Barrio Afuera

Padrino-López, Vladimir, *240*, 251
País, Frank, 37
Partido Comunista de Cuba (PCC), Cuba, 24
Partido de Acción Unitaria (PAU), Cuba, 35
Partido del Pueblo Cubano Ortodoxo (*los Ortodoxos*), Cuba, 35
Partido Demócrata Cristiano (PDC), Cuba, Rasco, José Ignacio, as founder of, 205

Partido Liberal (PL), Cuba, 35
Partido Revolucionario Cubano Auténtico (*los Auténticos*), Cuba, 35
Partido Socialista Popular (PSP), Cuba, 48
Partido Socialista Unido de Venezuela (PSUV), Venezuela, 19, 72, 80, 242, 274; anti-American foreign policy of, 85; from MVR, 85
Partido Unido de la Revolución Socialista (PURS), Cuba, 48
Patiño, Roberto, 80–81
La Patria es de Todos (The Nation Belongs to All) (Roca Vladimiro; Gómez-Manzano, René; Bonne-Carcasés, Félix; Roque, Marta Beatriz), 235
"Patria y Vida" Cuban dissident song, 208–9, 289; Afro-Cubans and, 224–25
PAU. *See* Partido de Acción Unitaria
Payá, Oswaldo, 61, 205, 235, 289
Pazos, Felipe, 36, 38
PCC. *See* Partido Comunista de Cuba
PCV. *See* Communist Party of Venezuela
PDC. *See* Partido Demócrata Cristiano
PDVSA. *See* Petróleos de Venezuela, S.A.
People's Movement for the Liberation of Angola (MPLA), 53; Cuba support of, 107, 111, 119–20, 122
Pérez, Carlos Andrés, 71–72
Pérez-Jiménez, Marcos: US support of, 128; Venezuela dictatorship by, 11, 69, 92
Pérez-Serantes, Enrique (archbishop), 38–39; revolutionary state opposition by, 45
Petrocaribe Agreement for Energy Cooperation (PetroCaribe), 125, 255
Petróleos de Venezuela, S.A. (PDVSA), 70, 136–37, 139–40, 141; Barrio Adentro program paid by, 166
Petrostate: external debt rise in, 20; Venezuela as, 12, 20, 82–83
PL. *See* Partido Liberal
Platt Amendment, 117
Political dissidents in Cuban Revolution: *Las Damas de Blanco* dissidents, 219, 232, 235–36, 289; *14yMedio* independent journalism, 236; Movimiento San Isidro 2020 and July 11, 2021 protests, 235–36, 289; *La Patria es de Todos*, 235; UNPACU, 61, 205, 224, 236; Movimiento Cristiano Liberación, 60–61, 205, 235, 289. *See also* "Patria y Vida."

Political generations, in Cuban Revolution, 232–33
Political revolutions, 22, 23
Populism: in Cuban and Bolivarian Revolutions, 15; in Latin American politics, 3; Left-wing, 4, 16, 119; nationalism and, 4; Right-wing, 4, 16
Presidential Palace, DRE attack on, 36
Prío-Socarrás, Carlos, 22
Proletarian internationalism: Castro, Fidel, and Africa, 53, 101; of Castro, Fidel, and Castro, Raúl, 153; of Cuba, 53–54, 101, 120–22; Guevara, Ernesto Ché, and, 53
Protests: of Afro-Cuban population, 221, 224; in Cuba July 11, 2021 (massive), 208–9, 221, 224; of Cuban Spring 2003, 219, 289; against Díaz-Canel, Miguel, *268*; Díaz-Canel's harsh response to, 230, 290; Movimiento San Isidro 2020, 236, 289. *See also* Dissident movement
PSP. *See* Partido Socialista Popular
PSUV. *See* Partido Socialista Unido de Venezuela
Puerto Rico: Cuba exodus to, 12; Puerto Ricans in US vote, 193
Puntofijo Pact (1958), Venezuela, 69–71, 92; breakdown of, 82; Caldera, Rafael, on recovery of, 72
PURS. *See* Partido Unido de la Revolución Socialista
"Push" and "pull," theory of migration, 57, 257–58
Putin, Vladimir, 4; Venezuela agreements with, 139–40

R2P. *See* Responsibility to Protect
Rasco, José Ignacio, 40, 205
Reagan, Ronald: anticommunism and Cuba relations, 110, 119; Cuban Americans vote, 189; trade embargo retightening, 60
Remittances, to Cuba, 62, 124, 163, 177, 269; Clinton, Bill, lowering amount of, 206; Cuban Americans position on, 64, 191, 197, 207; economy dependence on, 65, 208, 216, 256, 268, 270, 279–80, 290; increase in size of, 112; Obama, Barack, lifting of restrictions on, 113; racial inequality and, 221–22; Soviet Union promotion of, 102; "special period" and, 112, 230; statistics on, 207; Trump,

Remittances, to Cuba—*continued*
　Donald, restrictions on, 206, 216, 230, 279;
　US ban for, 109
Remittances, to Venezuela, 210, 238, 253
Reno, Janet, 61
Responsibility to Protect (R2P) thesis, 242;
　Guaidó, Juan, call to, 96
Revolts or rebellions, revolutions compared to, 23
Revolutions: civil wars compared to, 23; collective action and, 7; comparative history of, 3–5, 6, 292–93; conditions for, 292–93; coups d'état compared to, 23; defined, 20–21; electoral democracy as unlikely outcome of, 25; fourth-generation theories of, 21; geopolitical international setting in, 28; ideology and culture shaping of, 21–22; new order imposed by, 3; peaceful regime transitions compared to, 23; political, 22, 23; populist leader in, 28; resistance to perceived tyranny in, 3; revolts or rebellions compared to, 23; social, 22, 23, 33–34; state as ineffective and unjust and, 26; theories of, 20–28; third generation structural theories of, 21; various governments from, 24–25
Roca, Vladimiro, 235
Rodríguez, José Conrado (priest), 225–26, 288, 289–90
Roosevelt, Theodore, 128
Roque, Marta Beatriz, 205, 235
Rousseff, Dilma, 5
Rusk, Dean, 48
Russia. *See* Soviet Union collapse
Russian Revolution (1917), 23;
　Marxism-Leninism origin, 3; political and social revolution steps in, 34

Sánchez, Yoani, 236
Sanctions: Biden, Joe, and Trump, Donald, Venezuela, 84–85, 94; OAS lifting of Cuban sanctions, 109; Trump and Venezuela economic crisis, 238–39; Trump Cuba, 115, 117, 206, 216, 229–31, 279, 291; US and Venezuela economic and financial, 84–85, 94, 132–33, 142–44, 245–46, 249
Second stage (2000–2004), of Bolivarian Revolution: failed coup against Chávez, Hugo, 75, 272; instability and uncertainty in, 74–75; referendum in, 75

Socialism: Afro-Cuban population impacted by, 57; Chávez, Hugo, on electoral system and, 68, 72, 264; Chávez, Hugo, program of, 75, 77–78; Chávez, Hugo, reforms, 239; Cuba, from capitalism to socialism, 29, 49; Cuba, market socialism model, 218; Cuban Revolution stage of, 34; Cuba-Venezuela alliance positive model of, 18; Maduro, Nicolás, on electoral system and, 68
Social Origins of Dictatorship and Democracy (Moore, Jr., Barrington), 6
Social revolutions, 22, 23, 33–34
Solidaridad Sin Fronteras (SSF), 165–66
Soviet Union collapse, 4, 103, 121–22; Cuba influence reduced from, 122; economic crisis after, 10, 18, 58, 162, 213–14; special period of Castro, Fidel, and, 10, 24, 58, 60, 104, 112, 159, 257. *See also* Cuba-Soviet and Russian relations; Venezuela-Soviet relations
Spain: Cuba colonization by, 29, 31; Cuba exodus to, 12; migration to Cuba, 31; political prisoners release, 219
"Special period," of Castro, Fidel, 167, 169; Bush, George H. W., trade embargo retightening, 62; Cuba-Venezuela alliance and, 267; economic crisis of, 18, 20, 104, 154, 162, 213; economic reforms from 1993 to 1996, 214, 218; *Exit* and *Voice* options during, 288; Generation of Disbelief from, 233; massive exodus from, 225, 230; "new" Cuban immigrants and, 187; political crisis developed from, 225; remittances to Cuba and, 112, 230; after Soviet Union collapse, 10, 24, 58, 60, 104, 112, 159, 257
SSF. *See* Solidaridad Sin Fronteras
Sugar production, Cuba, 31–32, 66, 103; US interest in, 117; US sugar quota cancellation, 54, 107

Tercera Opción, 120
Temporary Protected Status (TPS), of Venezuelan exile community, 210
Third stage (2004 to present) of Bolivarian Revolution, Chávez, Hugo, socialism program, 75, 77–78
Third World, Cuba militant role in, 120–21
TIAR. *See* Inter-American Treaty of Reciprocal Assistance
Torricelli Act. *See* Cuban Democracy Act

Totalitarianism, of Castro, Fidel, Castro, Raúl, and Guevara, Ernesto Ché, 37, 41
Tourism, Cuba: Castro, Rául, economic reforms and, 215–16; COVID-19 impact on, 207, 216, 230–31; foreign direct investment for, 103–4; racial inequality in, 222, 223–24; Trump, Donald, restrictions on, 66, 216; from US increased in 1990–2018, 229
TPS. *See* Temporary Protected Status
Trade, Cuba: Bush, George W., and, 203; with China, 103; Cuba-Venezuela alliance relations in 1970s, 153; economy and foreign dependence, 103; González, Elián, case and US, 105–6; Obama, Barack, and, 203; US relations with, 259–60
Trade, Venezuela: COVID-19 impact on, 88; Cuba and illicit, 101; Cuba-Venezuela alliance relations in 1970s, 153; foreign trade decline, 88; oil trade with US, 8, 11, 20, 128, 134; Soviet Union oil and mine, 136–37; trade embargo of US, 249; US relations in, 245–46
Trade embargo, US and Cuba, 20, 27, 102, 104, 107, 259–60; Bush, George H. W., re-tightening of, 62, 111; Castro, Fidel, political help from, 43; Castro, Raúl, economic blame of, 55; Clinton, Bill, on, 62–63; Cuban Americans on, 188–89; Eisenhower, Dwight, imposing of, 54; exile community support of, 204; impact of, 54–55; *los intransigentes* on continuation of, 195; *los moderados* on end to, 195; OAS and, 55; Reagan, Ronald, retightening of, 60; US sugar quota cancellation, 54, 107
Trade Sanctions Reform and Export Enhancement Act (TSRA), US, 106, 203
Trump, Donald, 4, 125, 147; Cuban Americans vote, 189, 192–93, 203–4; Cuba relations, 115, 229, 279; Cuba sanctions, 115, 117, 206, 216, 229–31, 279, 291; economic sanctions and Venezuela economic crisis, 238–39; Helms-Burton Act and, 63; *los intransigentes* and, 206; remittances to Cuba restrictions, 206, 216, 230, 279; Right-wing populism of, 4; tourism restrictions by, 66, 216; Venezuela confrontations approach, 132–33; Venezuela exile community and, 211–12; Venezuela sanctions, 84–85, 94

TSRA. *See* Trade Sanctions Reform and Export Enhancement Act
26th of July Movement, 36, 37, 38, 48, 50–51

UJC. *See* Young Communists League
UMAP. *See* Unidades Militares de Ayuda a la Producción
UNDP. *See* United Nations Development Program
UNESCO. *See* United Nations Educational, Scientific, and Cultural Organization
Unfreedoms, migration driven by, 13–14
UNHCR. *See* United Nations High Commissioner for Refugees
UN Human Rights Council, on Maduro, Nicolás, 244
Unidades Militares de Ayuda a la Producción (UMAP): Cuban forced labor camps of, 56
Unión Patriótica de Cuba (UNPACU): Fariñas, Guillermo, of, 236; Ferrer, José Daniel, of, 61, 205, 236; growth of, 61
UNITA. *See* National Union for the Total Independence of Angola
United Nations Development Program (UNDP), 141, 257
United Nations Educational, Scientific, and Cultural Organization (UNESCO), 257
United Nations High Commissioner for Refugees (UNHCR), 9; on exodus numbers, 13
United States (US): COVID-19 impact on, 291; Cuba and exile community relationship with, 8, 110; Cuba diplomatic and economic war with, 40, 42; Cuban Refugee Program, 48; Cuba sugar production interest, 117; immigrant communities in, 9; Latin America nationalism response of, 5; Leftist government opposition, 119; Pérez-Jiménez, Marcos, support by, 128; remittances to Cuba ban, 109; trade embargo sugar quota cancellation, 54, 107. *See also* Cuban Americans; Cuba-US relations; Trade embargo; Venezuela-US relations; *specific acts*
University students, Cuba: Amaro, Nelson, as, 34; Batista, Fulgencio, opposition from, 22, 36–37; democracy and, 34; racial inequality for, 223
UNPACU. *See* Unión Patriótica de Cuba
US *See* United States

Valls, Jorge, 41
Vecchio, Carlos, 211
Velázquez, Ramón J., 72
Venezuela: agriculture neglect and food scarcity, 80; ANC in, 143–44; authoritarianism gradual development of, 8, 81–82; Biden, Joe, and, 97; birth and death rate, 32; social class response in, 252–53; comparative politics and, 144–46; COVID-19 impact on, 88, 127, 238, 239, 249; Cuba ideological package adoption by, 85; democratic system in 1959-1999 of, 11, 69, 128–29; democratic system in future of, 293–94; domestic and international criticism of, 127; dual power in, 246–54; economic and political crisis in, 142–43, 238–39; economic and political partners of, 124–25; 2020 elections of, 96–97; ENCOVI survey on, 251; globalization process crisis, 124–25; health crisis in, 249–50; history and culture collage, *90*; indefinite presidential power in, 75–76; inequality rise, 239–43; international alliances of, 83; international criticism of, 243; internationalization of crisis in, 96; media conflict, 242–43; military coups, 92–93, 153; military role in politics, 89–93; MUD opposition alliance in, 19; participatory democracy of, 131; PCV guerrillas sponsorship, 129; performance legitimacy in, 78; as petrostate under Chávez, Hugo, 12, 20, 82–83; political crisis and legitimacy in, 246–53; political polarization in, 79–80, 239–43; political stages, 146; political system problems, 70–71; politics reliance on media, 78; PSUV influence, 19, 72, 80, 85, 242, 274; regime change attempts, 96–97; remittances to, 210, 238, 253; representative democracy in 1999-2013 of, 146; social transformation in, 8; state mismanagement in, 20; transnational exchanges, 207–8; Trump, Donald, and Biden, Joe, sanctions, 84–85, 94. *See also* Bolivarian Revolution; Chávez, Hugo; Cuba-Venezuela alliance
Venezuelan presidents, 69; Betancourt, Rómulo, 119, 129–30, 135, 153; Caldera, Rafael, 72; Capriles, Henrique, and 2013 election attempt, 86; Guaidó, Juan, and provisional government recognition, 19, 95, 132, 134, 147–48, 247, 252; Gómez, Juan Vicente, and dictatorship, 11, 91–92, 128; Leoni, Raúl, 119, 129–30; Lepage, Octavio, 72; Maduro, Nicolás, and government not recognized, 19; Pérez, Carlos Andrés, 71–72; Pérez-Jiménez, Marcos, and dictatorship, 11, 69, 92; Velázquez, Ramón, 72
Venezuela-Soviet relations: Betancourt, Rómulo, objections to, 135; Chávez agreements, 136; late 1960s relations re-established, 135–36; military agreements, 138–39; oil and mine trade and investment relations, 136–37; Putin agreements with, 139–40; Russian weapon purchases, 138, 140; World War II diplomatic relations, 135
Venezuela-US relations, 130–35; AD and COPEI support by US, 130; Bolivarian Revolution criticism, 134; collaboration on Latin America and Caribbean, 130; confrontations, 131–32; economic and financial sanctions, 84–85, 94, 132–33, 142–44, 245–46, 249; oil trade, 8, 11, 20, 128, 134; oppositional stance to US, 130; severed diplomatic relations, 133, 245; trade embargo of, 249; trade relations, 245–46; Trump, Donald, and Biden, Joe, recognition of Guaidó, Juan, 19, 95, 132, 134, 245; Trump confrontations approach, 132–33; US skepticism of Chávez, 131
Voting: Cuban Americans vote, 9, 191–93; Puerto Ricans in US vote, 193; Venezuelan Americans vote, 212

Walters, Barbara, 110–11
"Wet foot/dry foot" policy, of Clinton, Bill, 112; Obama, Barack, removal of, 62, 63, 226, 289
Women: Cuban Revolution challenge to inequality for, 42; *Las Damas de Blanco* Cuban Revolution dissidents, 219, 235–36, 289; Lyceum founded by, 38; M.A.R. and, 194, 202
World crude oil prices, 76, *76*, *77*, 78, 80

Young Communists League (UJC), Cuba, 182

Silvia Pedraza is professor of sociology and American culture at the University of Michigan, Ann Arbor. Her work seeks to understand the causes and consequences of immigration as a historical process that forms and transforms persons and nations; as well as social revolutions' rupture with the past and attempt to create a different present. She holds a B.A. and M.A. from the University of Michigan and a Ph.D. in Sociology from the University of Chicago, where she specialized in Demography as well as Stratification, and in Latin American Studies. She is author of *Political Disaffection in Cuba's Revolution and Exodus*. She is a frequent contributor to *The New York Times, Los Angeles Times, CNN.com, BBC World News, The Miami Herald, El Nuevo Herald, Ann Arbor News,* among other newspapers, and has appeared on both radio and television.

Carlos Romero is a Venezuelan political scientist and professor emeritus of political science and international relations in the Institute of Political Studies at the Universidad Central de Venezuela. His research focuses on international relations and Venezuelan foreign policy. He has been visiting research scholar at the University of Pittsburgh (USA), Columbia University (USA), la Sorbonne V (France), Memorial de América Latina (Brazil), Universidad del Rosario (Colombia), AETI (Spain) and USP (Brazil). He is coauthor of *U.S-Venezuela Relations since the 1990s*. His work has appeared in scholarly journals throughout Latin America and in numerous book chapters.

www.ingramcontent.com/pod-product-compliance
Lightning Source LLC
Chambersburg PA
CBHW061251230426
43664CB00025B/2921